LIVING THE
NEW
TESTAMENT

DAILY READINGS FROM
MATTHEW TO REVELATION

LIVING THE
NEW
TESTAMENT

PAUL ENNS

Kregel
Publications

Living the New Testament: Daily Readings from Matthew to Revelation

© 2010 by Paul Enns

Published by Kregel Publications, a division of Kregel, Inc., P.O. Box 2607, Grand Rapids, MI 49501.

ISBN 978-0-8254-2536-3

Printed in the United States of America

10 11 12 13 14 / 5 4 3 2 1

Dedication

*Since the home going of my beloved Helen,
the people at Idlewild Baptist Church
have demonstrated enormous love,
encouragement, kindness, and help to me
in a profound and overwhelming way.
I am eternally grateful to them.*

CONTENTS

PREFACE

If you look at the coins in your pocket, you will notice they have a date on them: 2009, 1997, 2003—they are different dates but their dates all signify something very important. What is it? Legal documents and ordinary documents are dated when we sign them: August 27, 2010. The yearly dates are significant and some of them specify that by adding A.D., anno Domini, "in the year of our Lord." The point is we date our time, events, and business transactions in relation to the birth of Jesus Christ. When Christ came, a new era was ushered in: the New Testament era.

What is so special about the New Testament? When Jesus Christ came, He inaugurated a new covenant through His atoning death on the cross (Matt. 26:28). That changed everything—it brought the New Testament era. The Old Testament anticipated Christ, pointed to Christ—now He came to fulfill the promises about Himself and bring the age of the Law to its conclusion (Rom. 6:14). The twenty-seven books of the New Testament introduce this new era and describe the life of Christ (the Gospels), the history of the early church (Acts), and the teaching of the early church and for the church throughout the ages (the Epistles).

Living the New Testament is based on the premise of 2 Timothy 3:16, that all Scripture is "God-breathed" (NIV), and therefore inerrant in everything it says. And since the Scriptures are God-breathed, they are "profitable for teaching, for reproof, for correction, for training in righteousness." In *Living the New Testament,* you will get a clear picture of the meaning of biblical passages from Matthew to Revelation, as well as practical application and inspiration for living the truths of the New Testament. I encourage you to read the Scripture passage listed with the daily reading before you read the devotion, which provides a further explanation of the meaning of the passage and its application to life.

It is my prayer that *Living the New Testament* will stimulate your love of God's Word and encourage you to faithful, regular meditation in the Scriptures. The end result should be love for the Lord Jesus Christ and a daily trust and confidence in Him, giving you victory in life: "But in all these things we overwhelmingly conquer through Him who loved us" (Rom. 8:37).

THE ROYAL MESSIAH

MATTHEW 1:1–18; LUKE 3:23–38

The record of the genealogy of Jesus the Messiah,
the son of David. (Matthew 1:1)

Queen Elizabeth II rules on the throne of England. Since her lineage is of the House of Windsor she has the right and the qualification to rule as Britain's monarch. The one who succeeds her must similarly be of the House of Windsor.

The New Testament opens dramatically, immediately tracing Jesus to David, Israel's greatest king. In fact, both Matthew and Luke identify Jesus as a descendant from David and therefore a rightful claimant to David's throne. Luke additionally traces Jesus to Adam; thus, He is a representative of the entire human race. But the opening statement of the New Testament is important: as a descendant of David, Jesus came to rule—that is His right and His destiny. This is further reflected in the attention given to David; he is "David the king" (Matt. 1:6).

But why are there two genealogies? Matthew gives Jesus' lineage through Solomon, the son of David to Joseph, the adoptive father of Jesus. Joseph's lineage provides the *legal* right to the throne of David. Luke traces Jesus' lineage through Nathan, also a son of David, and gives the descent through Mary and gives the *physical* descent of Jesus. Matthew shows Jesus has the legal right to David's throne. Because Joseph was Jesus' adoptive father, Jesus had a rightful claim to the throne. If Jesus had been virgin born, but Mary had not been married to Joseph, Jesus could not have been a claimant to the throne of David. Jewish laws of inheritance came through the male (Gen. 49:1–27; Deut. 21:15–17).

Further, if Jesus had been the natural son of Joseph and Mary He could not have ruled because of the Coniah curse, which announced that no descendant of his would ever rule on the throne of David (Jer. 22:30). He would also then have had the sin nature which would have precluded Him from being the Messiah. Jesus *had to be* the adoptive son of Joseph to have a claim to the Davidic throne, but He had to be virgin born to be the Savior.

Matthew's genealogy reminds us that Jesus is the Savior of Israel; Luke's genealogy tells us that Jesus is the Savior of the world. In the incomprehensible wisdom of God, the Lord has provided a pure sinless Savior and King for both Israel and the world.

CONSIDER: *There is a great day coming when Jesus will rule on the throne of David and bring peace to a troubled world.*

THE VIRGIN BIRTH OF JESUS

LUKE 1:26–35; MATTHEW 1:18–25

When His mother Mary had been betrothed to Joseph,
before they came together she was found to be
with child by the Holy Spirit. (Matthew 1:18)

A well-known preacher in England preached a series of sermons entitled, "Things I Don't Believe." One of the sermons he preached was on the virgin birth—he rejected it. Is the virgin birth of Jesus important? Does the Bible teach it? How is it a vital doctrine?

The testimony of Scripture—both Old and New Testaments—are strong in teaching the virgin birth of Jesus. Matthew develops the genealogy from Abraham to Joseph with active verbs: "Abraham was the father of Isaac" (Matt. 1:2) means that Abraham produced, sired Isaac. The active verbs continue throughout the genealogy until verse 16 where the verbs change to the passive form: "by whom Jesus was born." This is purposeful, a clear statement reminding us that Joseph was not active in the birth of Jesus. Jesus had no earthly father.

Further, the pronoun "whom" is gender neutral in English but in the Greek text it is feminine (*hes*), again reminding the reader that Jesus was born only of Mary. Joseph had no relationship to Jesus' birth. The term "virgin" (*parthenos*) indisputably means sexually pure, one who has not known a man. This is also how the word should be understood in Isaiah 7:14 where Jesus' birth is foretold.

Matthew clarifies Mary's pregnancy by reminding the reader that she was pregnant before she and Joseph ever lived together as husband and wife. But Matthew also explains the nature of Mary's pregnancy: "she was found to be with child by the Holy Spirit" (v. 18). Luke provides a similar explanation (Luke 1:35). The Holy Spirit produced Mary's conception.

How is this significant? The virgin birth of Jesus was necessary if He would redeem the human race (Matt. 1:21). An ordinary man with a sin nature could not redeem anyone. The Redeemer had to be a sinless person (1 John 3:5). He had to be a man to represent man but He had to be God if His death was to have infinite value. At Bethlehem the eternal Christ took on humanity and became the God-Man: "Immanuel . . . God with us" (Matt. 1:23). Truly, this reveals both the manifold wisdom of God and the grace of God in having mercy on a fallen humanity.

CONSIDER: *Jesus came in sinless humanity joined with genuine deity that He might redeem all who call upon Him.*

January 3

THE CONFLICT OF GOOD AND EVIL

MATTHEW 2:1–12

When Herod the king heard this, he was troubled,
and all Jerusalem with him. (Matthew 2:3)

When our vacuum cleaner broke, we purchased a new one. As the salesman filled out the paperwork he recorded the date: December 1, 2004. For every business transaction, purchase, or contract, the paperwork records the year from the birth of Christ. Every coin in our pocket, every bill in our wallet states the date from the advent of Christ into this world.

Modern coinage, legal papers, and virtually all significant events have been dated from the birth of Christ. The dating system has been determined by B.C. ("before Christ") or A.D. ("anno Domini"—"In the year of Our Lord"). (It has now been established that Jesus was probably born in late 5 B.C. or early 4 B.C.)

When Jesus was born, magi from the east came to worship Him. Originally, the magi were a priestly class in Persia and later the term came to denote those involved in magical arts, sorcery, and astrology. In Jesus' day the magi were probably a mixture of scientist and astronomer.

But what was the star that led the magi? The astronomer Kepler suggested it was the conjunction of Jupiter and Saturn, but that occurred in 7 B.C.—too early for the birth of Christ. *Star (astera)* can be translated "light," "flame," or "fire." The star was likely the Shekinah glory of God through which God revealed Himself to the magi and supernaturally led them—not only to Israel, but to the very house where Jesus was. (The term *Shekinah* glory refers to the visible manifestation of God's presense, such as God's presense with the Israelites in the wilderness when He appeared as fire and cloud [Exod. 13:21].)

But when the magi came to Jerusalem, inquiring of the King who was born, Herod was upset. Herod was a ruthless murderer who had killed his wife Mariamne, her grandfather, and three of his sons—as well as numerous others. It is no wonder "all Jerusalem" was troubled too (Matt. 2:3).

After worshiping the Savior and bringing Him gifts, the Lord supernaturally led the magi away by a different route, avoiding contact with Herod. The serious conflict between good and evil had begun.

CONSIDER: *The birth of Christ intensified the conflict of good and evil—a conflict that persists to this day.*

THE CONTINUING CONFLICT

MATTHEW 2:13–23

"Get up! Take the Child and His mother and flee to Egypt,
and remain there until I tell you." (Matthew 2:13)

A Christian mission established a fledgling church in a north African country. The ministry was difficult and the response to the gospel was slow. But eventually a small church was established with about a dozen members that began to meet regularly for worship. But soon, one by one, the Christians began to disappear. Some were found, murdered. Eventually, the entire congregation was gone. The conflict of the ages, intensified at the birth of Christ, persists to the modern era.

After being warned by God in a dream, Joseph took his family and escaped to Egypt. It was the natural move. Egypt was close, but more important, it had a large Jewish population; Philo, writing in A.D. 40, says there were nearly a million Jews in Egypt.

Matthew immediately reminds us of the important personage: "the Child and His mother" is mentioned in that order four times (vv. 13, 14, 20, 21). The Child was the promised Messiah! But Herod wanted no rival king so he immediately had all the children in the region of Bethlehem killed. The death of the children is dramatically depicted in "Rachel weeping for her children" (v. 18), where Matthew is quoting from the book of Jeremiah. As the wife of Jacob, Rachel is the "mother" of all Jewish people. Rachel was buried in Bethlehem and is pictured weeping over the death of her children.

But God protected the Messiah Child. The family lived in safety in Egypt until the death of Herod and then returned to Israel. But upon arrival in Judea, Joseph discovered that Herod's evil son Archelaus was ruling. Archelaus began his career by killing 3,000 of the most influential people. God again directed Joseph and he took his family and settled in Nazareth—in further fulfillment of prophecy.

God has supernaturally led Joseph and his family, yet He didn't give them detailed information about the future. Joseph was called to walk by faith in the conflict between good and evil.

CONSIDER: *God watches over His people and directs their steps, and, ultimately, He will prevail in the conflict between good and evil.*

January 5

THE BAPTISM OF JESUS

MATTHEW 3:13–17; MARK 1:9–11; LUKE 3:21–23

In those days Jesus came from Nazareth in Galilee and was baptized by John in the Jordan. . . . And a voice came out of the heavens: "You are My beloved Son, in You I am well pleased." (Mark 1:9, 11)

Visiting the land of Israel stirs the emotions. To see the sites where our Savior walked and taught is a phenomenal experience. Our son Jeremy was baptized in the Jordan River just south of the Sea of Galilee. The baptism itself was a joyous event, but it was especially significant for Jeremy to be baptized where Jesus ministered.

Jesus Himself was baptized—but why? Baptism is a sign of repentance and faith in Christ. Jesus had nothing to repent of; why was He baptized? There are several reasons. First, Jesus was baptized "to fulfill all righteousness" (Matt. 3:15). Baptism was what the righteous people would do. Further, people were baptized to identify with the believing remnant in Israel. John was of Levitical descent but he wasn't ministering in the temple in Jerusalem; John taught in the desert regions east of the city. He was calling out a righteous people to separate themselves from the corruption of the Pharisees and Sadducees. Hence, those who were righteous responded and were baptized by John in the Jordan. Jesus identified Himself with that believing remnant.

But, most importantly, through His baptism Jesus was manifested to the nation as Israel's Messiah. At Jesus' baptism John the Baptist announced to the crowds who it was that had come for baptism: "Behold, the Lamb of God who takes away the sin of the world!" (John 1:29). John saw the Holy Spirit descending on Jesus, empowering His humanity for ministry (v. 32). And John pointed the people to Jesus—that was his ministry as forerunner. John was not the object of attention; he introduced people to the Messiah.

At His baptism Jesus also received divine authentication. A voice out of heaven announced, "This is My beloved Son, in whom I am well pleased" (Matt. 3:17). The Father's voice testified that Jesus—and no other—was the divine Messiah. Jesus is the unique, only, one-of-a-kind Son of God.

CONSIDER: *At His baptism Jesus identified with humanity—the sea of people that He came to rescue and redeem.*

January 6

THE TEMPTATION OF JESUS

MATTHEW 4:1–11; MARK 1:12–13; LUKE 4:1–13

Then Jesus was led up by the Spirit into the wilderness
to be tempted by the devil. (Matthew 4:1)

Suppose engineers build a bridge across an enormous chasm. When the bridge is finally completed, the engineers have trains from both sides slowly cross the bridge until they stop in the middle. What would be the purpose of such a test? To see if the bridge will collapse under the weight of the locomotives? Or to demonstrate the strength of the bridge, offering proof that it will not collapse? Obviously, the latter.

The purpose of the temptation of Christ is frequently misunderstood. It was not to see *whether* Christ could sin but to show the nation what a great Savior they have—He *cannot* sin! The temptation reveals that Jesus is the impeccable, sinless Son of God.

Jesus' temptation was in the same areas where all people are tempted: the lust of the flesh, lust of the eyes, and the pride of life (1 John 2:16; compare with the first sin recorded in Genesis 3:6). Jesus' first temptation involved the lust of the flesh and was directed toward His humanity. Since Jesus had not eaten for forty days, He became hungry, and so Satan tempted Him to turn the stones into bread. But Jesus was in the wilderness at the will of His Father—part of God's will for Him at this time was to hunger. To submit to Satan and food at this point would have been to abandon the will of God—and Jesus reminded Satan of this fact.

The second temptation was aimed at Jesus' messiahship and related to the pride of life. Satan took Jesus to the pinnacle of Herod's temple in Jerusalem. This location overhung the Kidron Valley, a sheer drop of 450 feet to the ground below. Satan tempted Jesus by enticing Him to do something spectacular by throwing Himself down from the temple. Jesus again answered Satan from Scripture, rebuking him. By throwing Himself down from the temple He would not be trusting the Father.

Jesus' third temptation, appealing to the lust of the eyes, was directed at His Kingship. Scholars have suggested that the temptation likely took place from the height of Quarantania, where the highways were visible leading away to Damascus, Egypt, Arabia, and Persia. Satan wanted to be worshiped so he offered Christ the kingdoms of the world if He would worship him. Christ rebuked him with a word of Scripture and summarily dismissed him. Jesus had triumphed over Satan!

CONSIDER: *We have an impeccable, strong, sinless Savior—One who is entirely trustworthy!*

CHRIST'S AUTHORITY OVER DISEASES

MATTHEW 8:1–4; MARK 1:40–45; LUKE 5:12–16

Jesus said to him, "See that you tell no one; but go, show yourself to the priest and present the offering that Moses commanded, as a testimony to them." (Matthew 8:4)

A IDS is a terrible disease, both physically and socially. Africa has seen the horrors of AIDS, with multiplied millions contracting the disease and untold numbers dying from it. But AIDS is not restricted to a continent. It is also in the Western world, in America. The disease has dreaded physical manifestations, and—because frequently the disease is spread because of immorality—social stigma.

Leprosy was a terrible disease, both physically and socially, rendering people unclean. Leprosy ostracized people from society and worship (Lev. 13:45–46). They sat is a separate compartment in the synagogue and in the street, when no wind was blowing they had to remain 100 feet distant from others. The man in today's Scripture readings, "full of leprosy," prostrated himself before Jesus, recognizing that Jesus had the power to heal him if He so desired. He knew Jesus had the authority; he did not know if Jesus was willing to heal him.

When Jesus touched him, the dreaded disease disappeared immediately. Jesus warned the man to tell no one, but "go, show yourself to the priest. . . ." What would the priest have said? The priest would have been astonished because he had never seen anyone healed of leprosy before. He would have asked: "How did you get well? Who healed you?" Jesus' command for the leper to show himself to the priest was designed to be a testimony to the religious leaders that the Messiah was in their midst. It would have stirred astonishment and vigorous discussion. But the evidence was apparent because Jesus of Nazareth healed lepers. It was a clear, strong testimony to His messiahship.

The unusual prohibition to "tell no one" was that Jesus did not want His acclaim to come from the masses. He wanted the religious leaders to recognize His messiahship; they in turn should point the masses to Jesus as their Messiah. But the man, overwhelmed by what had happened to him, told many people about his healing. He could not keep from telling others what Jesus had done for him.

CONSIDER: *Leprosy pictures the severity of sin, destroying life and soul, but Jesus, the Messiah, resolves our greatest dilemma.*

January 8

CHRIST'S AUTHORITY TO FORGIVE SIN

MATTHEW 9:1–8; MARK 2:1–12; LUKE 5:17–26

---

*"Take courage, son; your sins are forgiven . . . so that
you may know that the Son of Man has authority
on earth to forgive sins." (Matthew 9:2, 6)*

In Roman Catholicism the priest listens to the confession of the penitent person and then exclaims: "I absolve you from your sins, in the name of the Father, and of the Son, and of the Holy Ghost. Amen." The Council of Trent taught that priests "pardon sins, not only as ambassadors of Jesus Christ, but as judges, and by way of jurisdiction."

Of course, Jesus Christ, Himself entirely sinless, is the only One who can forgive sins. Since the leper had been healed, the religious leaders' curiosity was aroused and they came, from Galilee and Judea, to Capernaum to investigate Jesus. But they came with a critical, adversarial attitude.

Some friends brought a paralyzed man to Jesus, but were unable to get into the house because of the crowd. They demonstrated strong faith in Jesus by going up on the roof, removing some of the tiles, and lowering the man through the roof into the presence of Jesus!

Seeing their faith, Jesus made the strong statement, "son, your sins are forgiven." The Pharisees responded in indignation, charging Jesus with blasphemy. They were right in recognizing that only God can forgive sins, but they were wrong in saying Jesus had blasphemed. As God the Son, He can forgive sins.

In His omniscience Jesus was aware of their thoughts and challenged them: "Which is easier, to say, 'Your sins are forgiven,' or to say, 'Get up, and walk'?" (Matt. 9:5). The former was easier since it was not demonstrably verifiable. "Get up, and walk" was harder since it could be validated. Since Jesus did the harder—had the man rise and walk—why should they not acknowledge His ability to say the easier, "Your sins are forgiven"? The answer is that as Messiah He could do both. Man can do neither.

Jesus reminded them that the Son of Man has authority to forgive sins. "Son of Man" is a messianic title, anticipating Messiah consummating the ages with the establishment of the millennial kingdom (Dan. 7:13). Jesus Christ has the authority—the right within Himself—and the power to forgive sins.

CONSIDER: *Like the multitude, we should stand in awe at the wonder of forgiveness of sins through Christ.*

January 9

THE BIRTH ANNOUNCEMENT
LUKE 1:5–25

*"It is he who will go as a forerunner before Him in the spirit
and power of Elijah, TO TURN THE HEARTS OF THE FATHERS BACK TO THE
CHILDREN, and the disobedient to the attitude of the righteous,
so as to make ready a people prepared for the Lord." (Luke 1:17)*

Congratulations to Derwin & Jackie Anderson on the birth of their son Sebastian Miles on 11/20. It was in the church bulletin for everyone to read! It was an exciting time! Derwin is one of my seminary students and I had seen the excitement of Derwin and Jackie as they anticipated the day of their son's arrival in this world. And the birth of a newborn child should be exciting!

Zacharias, a priest, and Elizabeth, his wife, had waited a long time and yet they had no children. But, while serving in the temple, Zacharias received a revelation through an angel that his barren wife would give birth to a son whom they would name John. Zacharias must have been shocked and stunned—especially when the angel explained that this would be no ordinary boy. They—and many others—would rejoice and celebrate at his birth. Why? Because John would be the forerunner of the Messiah! What a phenomenal privilege!

John would be unique. He would be a Nazirite, not drinking wine or liquor; he would be supernaturally empowered by the Holy Spirit to turn people back to the Lord (Luke 1:16). Although John was not Elijah incarnate, he would minister in the spirit and power of Elijah (v. 17), fulfilling the prophecy given four hundred years earlier in Malachi 4:6.

What a great occasion this was! Since the time of Nehemiah and Malachi, for the past four hundred years, the Lord had been silent. No communication. Now a new day was dawning. The promised Messiah was coming and Zacharias's son would be the forerunner, heralding the way for the coming Messiah!

Zacharias found the revelation difficult to believe, and for his doubt the Lord struck Zacharias with silence. Unable to speak when he left the temple, Zacharias returned home. But the Lord was faithful to His promise and Elizabeth became pregnant. God had answered their petition and more—their son would be the forerunner of the Messiah.

CONSIDER: *God calls us to walk by faith and trust Him in unusual circumstances to experience His hand of blessing on our lives.*

THE REIGN OF THE FUTURE KING

LUKE 1:26–45

---

*"He will be great and will be called the Son of the Most High;
and the Lord God will give Him the throne of His father David;
and He will reign over the house of Jacob forever, and His
kingdom will have no end." (Luke 1:32–33)*

A church marquee reads: "Jesus is Lord and Mary is His Mother." The sign suggests that Mary is not only the mother of Jesus in His humanity but, as this denomination teaches, Mary is also the Mother of God. Of course God has no mother. He alone, in His triune being, is eternal.

Six months after Elizabeth became pregnant with John, the angel Gabriel appeared to Mary who was living in Nazareth, in Galilee. Significantly, Mary, like Joseph, descended from David, the kingly tribe. In his message to Mary, Gabriel pronounced the good news. The One who would be born to the virgin Mary would become great. Gabriel virtually quoted 2 Samuel 7:16, promising Mary that her Son would sit on the throne of David and "reign over the house of Jacob forever; and His kingdom will have no end." It was a promise of the glorious millennial reign of Christ (Matt. 25:31; Rev. 20:4).

Gabriel explained that Mary's conception would be supernatural, resulting in the virgin birth of the Messiah. The Holy Spirit would "overshadow" her, effecting the virgin birth. For that reason He would be called the Son of God. The second person of the Trinity, the eternal Son would, at Bethlehem, take an additional nature—humanity. Hereafter He would be the God-Man, two natures, humanity and deity in one person.

When Mary traveled to Judea to visit Elizabeth, the infant in Elizabeth's womb heard Mary's voice and, filled with the Holy Spirit, leaped in her womb. It was the forerunner's prenatal acknowledgment that Mary would give birth to the Messiah!

Filled with emotion, Elizabeth cried out, "Blessed are you among women . . ." (v. 42). Indeed, Mary was a humble, godly young woman. But she was a woman. Mary was blessed *among* women, not above women. Mary was privileged to birth the Messiah. She gave Jesus His humanity, but not His deity. Mary must have been a godly young woman, a clean vessel that God chose through whom the Messiah would come, but she too would need a Redeemer.

CONSIDER: *God can use the one who walks in humility and godliness in phenomenal and unusual ways.*

THE BIRTH OF JOHN THE BAPTIST

LUKE 1:46–80

"For you will go on BEFORE THE LORD TO PREPARE HIS WAYS;
To give to His people the knowledge of salvation
By the forgiveness of their sins." (Luke 1:76–77)

Jonathan Edwards was unquestionably one of America's greatest theologians and Christian leaders. His impact has been felt for centuries. Studying his posterity, it has been discovered that thirteen of his descendants became college presidents, sixty-five were college professors, one became vice-president of the United States, three were U.S. senators, thirty judges, one hundred lawyers, sixty physicians, seventy-five army and navy officers, one hundred missionaries and preachers, eighty public officials, and numerous others attained to prominence in their vocations.

Did Edwards's mother anticipate who her son would be and the legacy that he would leave? Undoubtedly, no. Consider Elizabeth giving birth to John the Baptist. Elizabeth and Zacharias had received divine communication. An angel had appeared to Zacharias, telling him that he would have a son and there would be enormous rejoicing at his birth. Moreover, he would be instrumental in leading the people of Israel back to their God. In fact, he would go "in the spirit and power of Elijah," fulfilling Malachi's prophecy (Luke 1:17: Mal. 4:6). But Zacharias doubted!

When Elizabeth gave birth to John, however, Zecharias recognized the uniqueness of his son. And Zecharias prophesied what his son would accomplish. He announced that John "will be called the prophet of the Most High; for you will go on before the Lord to prepare His ways; to give to His people the knowledge of salvation by the forgiveness of their sins" (Luke 1:76–77).

What a phenomenal position! What a transforming message! John would go as the forerunner, the introducer of Jesus Christ, the Messiah! What a privilege! God would use John the Baptist to reshape history as he was the herald who announced the coming of Christ, ushering in a new era.

CONSIDER: *While God has not called us to be a John the Baptist, He nonetheless calls us to serve Him uniquely. What has God called you to do? How has God called you to serve Him—in a unique way?*

THE DISCOVERY OF THE DESPISED

LUKE 2:1–20

"I bring you good news of great joy which will be for all the people;
for today in the city of David there has been born for you a
Savior, who is Christ the Lord." (Luke 2:10–11)

While driving in Budapest during a mission trip to Hungary, my wife and I noticed poor, ragged people—even young children—walking from car to car begging. Someone explained to us that these were gypsies. Through observation it became apparent that these were despised people. As I taught at a Bible school in the area I discovered that one of my students was a gypsy; moreover, there was a gypsy church where many had come to faith in Christ.

Luke's message was that the Savior came "to seek and to save that which was lost" (Luke 19:10). And to whom did this message of salvation come? To the lowly shepherds—those people who were outcasts from the temple because of their work with dead animals. But to these—the lowest on the social strata— the angels of heaven heralded the message of the Messiah. This was a reminder that Gentiles would also partake in Messiah's blessings through the Abrahamic covenant (found in Genesis 12:1–3).

God's glory shone forth from the angels (Luke 2:9), creating fear among the shepherds (see Exodus 33:20). But the shepherds need not have feared because this news was for "all people," not only the Jews, not only the aristocracy, but Gentiles and outcasts as well.

The angels explained the phenomenon of the newborn Child. He is a Savior, One who rescues someone—in this case, rescues from sin. He is also Christ, "the Anointed One"—He is anointed of God to be the Ruler, the King of the earth (Ps. 2:6–9). And He is Lord, not only Master and Ruler, but also deity (Ps. 110:1). What a phenomenal message! That is *good news!*

The sign of identification would be the Child lying in a manger. No royal garments, but wrapped in strips of cloth and lying in a cattle feeding trough (Luke 2:12).

The angels heralded their song of praise: "Glory to God in the highest, and on earth peace among men with whom He is pleased" (v. 14). Christ came to bring peace and that will ultimately occur in the millennial kingdom (Isa. 9:7). And who was it that first discovered the message of joy and peace? The lowly shepherds, the outcasts of society.

CONSIDER: *In a tumultuous world the stabilizing message of joy and peace is still there for those who seek it.*

THE RISE AND FALL OF MANY

LUKE 2:21–38

"Behold, this Child is appointed for the fall and rise of many in Israel, and for a sign to be opposed." (Luke 2:34)

A former Canadian Anglican priest abandoned the ministry and his faith in Christ, exclaiming that the idea of a god prepared to see his son murdered by the Romans to "assuage his own passion for righteousness" is "not only crude but immoral." He said he felt like Paul where he wrote, "when I became a man, I put away childish things." Of course, he quoted Paul entirely out of context, using the statement to indicate his abandonment of Christianity. In our reading today, Simeon prophesied an event like this.

Jesus was born under the Law (Gal. 4:4) and Mary and Joseph obeyed the Mosaic Law by having Jesus circumcised the eighth day (Gen. 17:12). Circumcision placed the person under the covenantal promises spoken to Abraham and the nation Israel concerning Christ. The promise would ultimately be fulfilled in Christ (Gal. 3:16).

According to the Law, childbirth ceremonially defiled a woman, so she had to remain absent from the temple for another thirty-three days after circumcision (Lev. 12:4). After the forty days had elapsed, Mary and Joseph came to present Jesus to the Lord in fulfillment of the Law (Exod. 13:2). The firstborn son belonged to the Lord, so the parents sanctified their firstborn son to the Lord by presenting a pair of turtledoves or two young pigeons for a sin offering (Luke 2:24).

When the aged Simeon saw Jesus, he prophesied that salvation had come to all people (a theme of Luke), "a light of revelation to the Gentiles, and the glory of Your people Israel" (v. 32). Simeon anticipated the blessings of the millennial kingdom when Messiah reigns from Jerusalem and blessings overflow to the Gentiles (Micah 4:1–5).

But Simeon also prophesied that the Messiah would be "appointed for the fall and rise of many." The unusual order "fall and rise" suggests that first the nation Israel will fall in unbelief and thereby rejection, but later, through repentance and faith in Jesus as the Messiah in the tribulation the nation will be restored (C. Marvin Pate, *Luke*). Israel's future glory will bring with it glory for Gentiles.

CONSIDER: *Jesus is the crucial issue: Those who acknowledge Jesus as Messiah will enter the millennial kingdom; those who reject Him will face eternal loss.*

THE BOYHOOD OF JESUS
LUKE 2:40–52

And Jesus kept increasing in wisdom and stature,
and in favor with God and men. (Luke 2:52)

As our group gathered at the base of Masada to begin our elevator ride up the mountain in southern Israel, Pitch, our Israeli tour guide explained how an Israeli boy became a man. When his own son turned 13, Pitch gave him a copy of the Torah and a rifle. The boy marched up Masada, the Torah in one hand and the rifle in the other. When he reached the top of the mountain, he was not a boy; he was a man.

Jesus is the God-Man: equal with the Father in every way, while simultaneously true man, but without the sin nature. In His humanity, Jesus developed, growing physically and mentally—at each stage perfect for the age He was (Luke 2:40).

This is the only record of Jesus' life between infancy and adulthood. At age twelve Jesus was preparing for manhood, which took place at age thirteen, when a Jewish boy became a man and "a son of the law" (*bar mitzvah*), obligated to keep the Law. In preparation, Jesus went up to Jerusalem for the Passover, a pilgrimage feast (as instructed in Exodus 23:14–17).

When Mary and Joseph were on their way home, they discovered Jesus was missing. Returning to Jerusalem they found Him in the temple, questioning the teachers, amazing them not only by His questions but in His answers! When Mary questioned Jesus, He revealed His Messianic self-knowledge. Although Mary referred to Joseph with "Your father and I . . ." (Luke 2:48), Jesus responded with "My Father's house" (v. 49). He recognized His messiahship—that He stood in a unique relationship to the Father—at that early age. He was the eternal Son, the second person of the Trinity. He never *became* the Son; He *is* the eternal Son of God. If there was a time when He became the Son, then there would have been a time when the Son was not the Son and the Father was not the Father. It would be a denial of both the eternality of the Son and the eternality of the Trinity.

Jesus' answer was too much for Mary and Joseph; they didn't understand Him (v. 50), and Mary reflected on His words in the following days (v. 51). Yet Jesus submitted to their authority, and in His humanity, Jesus matured mentally, physically, spiritually, and socially (v. 52)—the perfect God-Man at every age.

CONSIDER: *We have as our capable and effective Mediator, One who is God of very God but also true, sinless, and perfect Man.*

January 15

THE MAN FROM THE DESERT
MATTHEW 3:1–12; MARK 1:1–8; LUKE 3:1–14

"Repent, for the kingdom of heaven is at hand." (Matthew 3:2)

Daily, even hourly, news feeds bombard us with world events: wars in Afghanistan and Iraq, terrorism in countries around the world, political strife in our own country. The world is not a peaceful place! Truly the kingdom of God has not arrived.

John the Baptist was a puzzling person, appearing in the desert with a message for Israel. God had been silent for four hundred years. There had been no divine message. Then, finally, John the Baptist came on the scene, preaching in the barren desert. Although he was of Levitical lineage and could have been a priest, he separated himself from apostate Judaism by living in the desert.

John's message was terse: "Repent, for the kingdom of heaven is at hand" (Matt. 3:2). John was calling for the Hebrew people to prepare for Messiah's coming. They were to change their mind about God, the Messiah, and themselves. It was a call to return to the Lord in humility (2 Chron. 7:14). Repentance would result in God regathering Israel from the nations and restoring them to the land (Deut. 30).

John's announcement, "the kingdom of heaven is at hand," was a bold declaration that Messiah had come and was offering the kingdom to Israel. "Kingdom" involves both a physical, material realm and a spiritual dimension. It anticipates Messiah's earthly, physical rule over the Hebrew people from Jerusalem (Isa. 9:7; Dan. 2:44). But the inauguration of the kingdom required repentance, and that was John's message. (Israel will finally repent during the tribulation, as Zechariah 12:10–14 depicts.)

John came as a rugged individual, dressed like Elijah. And the people responded to John, being baptized as a sign of their repentance. So many people responded that the Pharisees and Sadducees came out of curiosity. But in stern words, John warned them to flee the impending wrath—God's judgment was about to fall on an unrepentant nation—the axe (judgment) was ready to cut down the tree (the nation Israel).

John warned that the nation would be baptized by fire—that judgment was imminent—which came about when the Romans destroyed Jerusalem in A.D. 70. But John also promised the coming ministry of the Holy Spirit, who was to be given at Pentecost (Acts 2:2–4). The Holy Spirit would regenerate the repentant Israelites who would one day usher in the glorious millennial kingdom (Ezek. 36:26–27).

CONSIDER: *Messiah will inaugurate a glorious, peaceful future kingdom that will bring an end to the wars and strife in this world.*

January 16

REJECTION IN NAZARETH

LUKE 4:16–30

"THE SPIRIT OF THE LORD IS UPON ME, BECAUSE HE ANOINTED ME TO PREACH THE GOSPEL TO THE POOR." (Luke 4:18)

In 1888 G. Campbell Morgan sought entrance into the Wesleyan ministry. Although he passed his written exam, after he gave his trial sermon, his name was among the rejected. He wired his father, "Rejected," then wrote in his diary: "Very dark. Everything seems still. He knoweth best." His father replied, "Rejected on earth, accepted in heaven. Dad" (Michael Green, *Illustrations for Biblical Preaching*).

Jesus' rejection in Nazareth by His own people anticipates the ultimate rejection of Him as Messiah. In Nazareth Jesus entered the synagogue on the Sabbath and read from Isaiah 61:1–2. The form of a synagogue service was as follows: (1) An opening prayer by the leader: "Bless ye the Lord who is to be blessed." The congregation followed similarly, then the reading of Deuteronomy 6:4–9. (2) A single individual prayer and the congregation responded "Amen." (3) A reading lesson from the Pentateuch with at least seven men taking part, reading through the Pentateuch in three years. The reading was in Hebrew; an interpreter translated it into Aramaic. (4) A reading from the Prophets. (5) If a competent person was present, he was asked to give an exposition of both passages. (6) A priest concluded with the Aaronic benediction (Num. 6:24–26) (Bruce Metzger, *The New Testament: Its Background, Growth, and Content*).

Jesus both read the section from the Prophets and gave the exposition. He startled the congregation by applying the reading from Isaiah 61:1–2 to Himself, stating, "Today this Scripture has been fulfilled in your hearing" (Luke 4:21). Luke's theme of emphasizing the outcasts of society is evident as Jesus mentioned the poor . . . captives . . . blind . . . oppressed. The sermon itself is not recorded; Luke simply mentions the "gracious words which were falling from His lips" (v. 22). The audience was startled and amazed at the attractive, gracious words that Jesus spoke. They couldn't understand it because they only knew Him as Joseph's son.

Jesus confronted them with their unwillingness to acknowledge Him. He reminded them that "no prophet is welcome in his hometown" (v. 24) and angered them with a reminder that in previous generations God blessed the Gentiles. He sent Elijah to the Gentile Sidonian widow and it was a Gentile, Naaman, that Elisha healed.

The reaction was hostile! In their anger they rushed at Jesus, attempting to kill Him by throwing Him over a cliff. But Jesus passed through their midst and left. The Messiah had come to them but they refused to hear His words and they rejected Him. Tragedy of tragedies.

CONSIDER: *Today, the depraved human heart continues to reject the Righteous One, Jesus, even as people have done historically.*

THE AUTHORITY OF CHRIST

MATTHEW 8:14–17, 23–27; MARK 1:21–39; LUKE 4:31–44

Jesus was going throughout all Galilee, teaching in their synagogues and proclaiming the gospel of the kingdom, and healing every kind of disease and every kind of sickness among the people. (Matthew 4:23)

Jesus demonstrated His messiahship through His words—His teaching—and His works—His miracles. When Jesus taught, His listeners recognized He was no ordinary man: "His message was with authority" (Luke 4:32). The scribes always taught by quoting the rabbis: "rabbi so-and-so says . . ." They did not speak on their own authority. Rabbi Eliezer "piously disavowed novelty: 'nor have I ever in my life said a thing which I did not hear from my teachers'" (Leon Morris, *Luke*). But Jesus had authority within Himself. He spoke with authority. He demonstrated He was the Messiah.

Jesus also demonstrated His authority by His miracles, revealing His authority over every realm. He demonstrated His authority over Satan and demons by casting out the unclean demon. Even the demons recognized Jesus as the Messiah and were subject to Him. With a spoken word Jesus cast the demons out of the man, causing amazement among the people as they saw the authority and power of Christ. This event was a harbinger of Jesus' conquest of Satan at His second coming (Rev. 20:1–3).

Leaving the synagogue in the beautiful city of Capernaum, Jesus walked to Peter's nearby home on the northwest shore of the Sea of Galilee. Peter's mother-in-law was sick with a "high fever." Jesus rebuked the fever, took her by the hand, and raised her up. The miracle was twofold: (1) She was cured of the fever, and (2) she immediately received strength to serve them. The latter would have been unusual even though she was cured. It showed the completeness of the miracle. The miracle itself demonstrates Messiah's authority over sickness and is a reminder that there will be no sickness in Messiah's kingdom (Rev. 21:4).

Later, Jesus departed to a solitary place to pray and when the disciples came looking for Him, He reminded them that He came to preach the kingdom of God to other cities also. This was the proclamation of the kingdom of God—offering the nation Israel the promised Messianic kingdom foretold by the Old Testament prophets. Jesus authenticated His messiahship through His preaching (His words) and His miracles (His works). He was indeed the promised Messiah!

CONSIDER: *There is a glorious day coming when, in the Messiah's kingdom, all illness and suffering will end.*

January 18

CHRIST'S AUTHORITY OVER MEN

MATTHEW 4:18–22; MARK 1:16–20; LUKE 5:1–11

---

*And He said to them, "Follow Me, and I will
make you fishers of men." (Matthew 4:19)*

It was still dark when I slipped out of the hotel, climbed a high stone fence, and walked to the seashore. It was Tiberias on the Sea of Galilee. And I was struck with awe as I contemplated this historic, biblical place. The sun was just beginning to come up, casting its golden rays across the sea where my Lord taught, worked miracles, and called His disciples. Emotion welled up in me as I reflected on the biblical events.

Peter and Andrew were fishermen who made their living fishing on the Sea of Galilee. Jesus approached the men and commanded them, "Follow Me!" Without hesitation, they left their fishing business and followed Christ as His disciples. This was more than a call to salvation. It was a call to identify with Him in His message and His ultimate rejection. It meant to follow Him physically—to hear His preaching, to see Him perform miracles. And they did.

Farther along the shore of the sea, Jesus encountered James and John, the sons of Zebedee, mending their nets. Jesus called them to follow Him, and they left both their fishing boats and their father to follow Jesus.

Some time passed. They had followed Jesus but had also continued fishing. Jesus again came and taught at the Sea of Galilee. Using Simon Peter's boat as a pulpit, Jesus sat down and taught according to the rabbinic custom. Afterward, Jesus instructed Simon to launch out into the sea and cast his nets for fish. Simon Peter protested, reminding the Lord that they had fished all night and caught nothing. Now, in the heat of the day, the fish would descend to lower, cooler levels in the lake, making it impossible to catch any fish. Reluctantly, Simon Peter obeyed the Lord and let down the nets, enclosing an enormous catch of fish. Peter recognized what had happened; he was growing in his awareness of Jesus of Nazareth. He knew the supernatural nature of the event and now he saw his own sinfulness in the light of the righteous Lord. But there was also a lesson to learn. Peter was no longer to focus on fish; Jesus commissioned him to catch men.

CONSIDER: *As a follower of Jesus, you have also been commissioned and you must be about the business of bringing people to faith in Him.*

THE ETERNALITY OF CHRIST

JOHN 1:1–18

In the beginning was the Word, and the Word was
with God, and the Word was God. (John 1:1)

With our finite minds we think in terms of beginnings and endings. A person is born, lives, and dies. We read birth announcements and we read obituaries—beginnings and endings. But Jesus Christ does not fit that category. He is eternal. In His deity Christ never had a beginning. This is a cardinal doctrine that we hold because the Bible teaches it.

These initial words to John's gospel form the prologue: John explains why he is writing the gospel and provides a brief summary. The Son was in eternal fellowship with the Father (v. 1); moreover, Christ is the creator of all things—meaning He was uncreated and eternal (v. 3). Christ came to give life and spiritual light to humanity (vv. 4–5). The apostle John uses the terms "light" and "darkness" to reveal the conflict between good and evil. John the Baptist, the forerunner, heralded the message concerning the Messiah. Jesus came as the true light, bearing witness to eternal life; yet the world that was made by Him rejected Him. He came to His very own—His own people and environment—yet He was rejected by them. They did not welcome Him. But those who did welcome Him became His children through faith: "as many as received Him, to them He gave the right to become children of God, even to those who believe in His name" (v. 12). This is a supernatural birth, a divine birth—not a manufactured human event (v. 13).

Yet this One who was eternally with the Father and also Creator of the world "became flesh"—He took on humanity (v. 14). He never subtracted His divine nature but He took upon Himself an additional human nature and became the *theanthropic person*, the God-Man. At the incarnation Jesus was fully God and fully man but without the sin nature. Like the presence of God in the Old Testament tabernacle, Jesus tabernacled—lived—among people. They saw Him, heard Him, and recognized His glory from the Father.

At the incarnation Christ ushered in the unique age of grace: "of His fullness we have all received, and grace upon grace" (v. 16). Grace existed in every age but when the Messiah came, grace profoundly entered the human arena (v. 17). It is the privilege of every believer in this age to drink deeply of the abundant grace of God in Christ.

CONSIDER: *The greatest demonstration of God's grace is through the coming of Christ, offering eternal life to those who receive Him.*

THE TESTIMONY OF JOHN

JOHN 1:19–34

*"Behold, the Lamb of God who takes
away the sin of the world!" (John 1:29)*

In a court of law, a witness is critical. A witness can save a person or indict and destroy a person. Further, the credibility of the witness is critical to the issue. Is the witness reliable? Is he credible?

John the Baptist and his family were well known. His parents, Zacharias and Elizabeth, were both of priestly descent, and honorable, respectable people. John himself was bold and straightforward, jealous for truth and righteousness. He ministered in the desert, preparing the people for the Messiah. As a result, the Pharisees sent a delegation to question John in an attempt to trap him. "Who are you?" they challenged. Perhaps they thought he would claim to be the Messiah.

But John was totally loyal. He readily admitted he was not the Messiah. Was he Elijah? "The Prophet"? "No," John exclaimed. In frustration they demanded that John give them an answer. John responded by quoting Isaiah 40:3, "I am a voice of one crying in the wilderness, 'Make straight the way of the Lord.'" John acknowledged he was the forerunner of Messiah, calling the people to repentance. People who acknowledged John's role and ministry came in repentance and were baptized by John, but John reminded the religious leaders that they did not know the Messiah. John saw himself as unworthy even to perform the duties of a slave for the Messiah in untying His sandals.

When John saw Jesus coming to him the following day, John boldly proclaimed: "Behold, the Lamb of God who takes away the sin of the world!" John probably thought of the Passover lamb and the required daily sacrifices (Exod. 29:38–39) that were meant to point forward to the ultimate sacrifice of Christ who would once for all remove sin through His one offering. The singular word "sin" indicates John recognized Jesus would deal with the sin problem of the whole world. And, indeed, Jesus would soon become the sacrifice for the world's sin. Having recognized Jesus as the Messiah, John acclaimed Him the "Son of God" (John 1:34). This expression has the fullest force; it means nothing less than deity.

CONSIDER: *Jesus, the Messiah, has once for all atoned for the entirety of sin, enabling us to enter into a relationship with Christ through faith in Him.*

BELIEF IN THE MESSIAH

JOHN 1:35–51

He found first his own brother Simon and said to him, "We have found the Messiah" (which translated means Christ). (John 1:41)

In the back of a Boston shoe store, D. L. Moody was wrapping shoes when Edward Kimball put a hand on his shoulder and told him of Christ's love. The light broke through to Moody and he gave his life to Christ. Thereafter Mr. Moody could not keep silent; he pointed people to Christ.

John the Baptist's ministry was not to build disciples around himself. He was a "way-shower," the forerunner of the Messiah. He pointed people to Christ. When John met Peter and Andrew, he informed them that Jesus was the Lamb of God. As a result, Peter and Andrew followed Christ.

The disciples soon began to recognize Jesus' greatness, addressing Him as "Rabbi," literally meaning "My Great One" (or "my master" from which we infer "my teacher"). When Jesus invited them with "Come, and you will see" (v. 39), He was using a rabbinic formula, inviting them to visit Him and, more particularly, acquire "special and important information" (Alfred Edersheim, *Life and Times of Jesus the Messiah*). Since it was the tenth hour (about 4:00 P.M.), Jesus was inviting them to spend the night. He was beginning to select a small band of men to whom He would reveal Himself, teaching them and entrusting His mission to them.

Recognizing he had discovered the Messiah, Andrew immediately found his brother Simon and informed him, "We have found the Messiah." "Messiah" (*Christos*) means "The Anointed One." Jesus was the One whom God had specially anointed as King, Savior, and Deliverer. In the Old Testament, priests and kings were anointed, set apart for a special ministry. But they all previewed, pointed to the ultimate One who would be anointed, the Great Deliverer; He would be *The* Anointed One, *The Messiah*.

When Simon Peter was brought to Jesus, Jesus renamed the vacillating fisherman; he would be Cephas, a stone. Giving Simon Peter a new name reflected the authority of Christ, exhibiting His authority over the person.

The next day Jesus found Philip and challenged him, "Follow Me!" (v. 43). To follow Christ as a disciple meant not only following Christ physically, but also identifying with Christ in His rejection and accepting His salvation. Nathanael, an innocent Israelite, also responded with a strong affirmation of faith: "You are the Son of God; You are the King of Israel" (v. 49). Indeed, Jesus had come as heaven's communication to earth, the link between heaven and earth.

CONSIDER: *Jesus is the only true communication between God and mankind, between heaven and earth.*

THE FIRST MIRACLE

JOHN 2:1–11

This beginning of His signs Jesus did in Cana of Galilee, and manifested His glory, and His disciples believed in Him. (John 2:11)

There are spurious writings, describing Jesus as a boy making birds out of mud and throwing them in the air. They fly away as Jesus created a real bird out of mud. Of course, the stories are fictitious. John makes it clear that the first miracle Jesus performed was in Cana.

A wedding was taking place in Cana, a town about nine miles north of Nazareth. It was a serious time but also a joyous time of celebration. The wedding followed a twelve-month engagement period where the couple had been carefully chaperoned. On the evening of the wedding, the wedding party escorted the bride from her home to the groom's home, amid a procession of torches and lamps, myrtle branches and flowers—all led by the friend of the groom. There was music with anointing oil and wine for the guests. At the groom's home a marriage formula was pronounced and, as the bride and groom were crowned with garlands, a contract was signed (Alfred Edersheim, *Life and Times of Jesus the Messiah*).

The wedding feast followed, lasting either a day or a week, depending on the family finances. The wine shortage created a problem; it was possible to take legal action when the groom and his family failed to provide a proper wedding gift. Mary saw the dilemma and reminded Jesus of the problem. She recognized His power to resolve the dilemma, in effect, saying, "Why don't you show Yourself openly as Messiah to the nation?"

Jesus' answer to Mary was not harsh. He, however, reminded her this was not the time to openly display His messiahship. His "hour" had not yet come (compare this with John 12:23; 13:1). Jesus answered Mary's request, but quietly. Six stone waterpots, each containing twenty gallons, were filled to the brim with water. When the headwaiter, who superintended the feast, sampled the water, he recognized the unique quality of the wine. The wine was a symbol of joy in Messiah's kingdom.

This was the first sign Jesus performed. A sign was the fingerpost of God, pointing to the One performing the miracle. As the people saw the quality of wine, it caused them to look at Jesus and recognize His messiahship. The sign revealed the glory of Jesus with the result that His disciples believed in Him. *Believing* involves believing the facts about Christ, having personal conviction, and trusting Him for salvation. Jesus performed the sign that people might recognize Him as the Son of God and receive eternal life through faith in Him (John 20:30–31).

CONSIDER: *The evidence reveals that Jesus is all that He claimed to be, that He is the Messiah. Have you believed in Him as your Savior?*

January 23

CLEANSING THE TEMPLE

JOHN 2:12–25

And He found in the temple those who were selling oxen and sheep and doves, and the money changers seated at their tables. And He made a scourge of cords, and drove them all out of the temple. (John 2:14–15)

Pictures of Jesus are rarely satisfying. Sometimes they portray Him as an anemic man, hardly fit for the life He led. In fact, Jesus was probably more than a carpenter; He was likely a builder who traveled with Joseph in Galilee, constructing buildings. As such, Jesus would have been a strong, vigorous man. And He portrayed Himself as such at the Passover.

The Passover Feast, one of the three pilgrimage feasts (Exod. 23:14, 17), was at hand and tens of thousands of pilgrims descended on Jerusalem, swelling the population from 20,000 to 125,000 (Joachim Jeremias, *Jerusalem in the Time of Jesus*). Many pilgrims would bring their own animals, intending to offer them as a sacrifice. However, the animals had to be inspected by the priests and the worshiper was confronted with the following: First, he had to pay the priest for inspecting the animal. Then, when his animal was rejected (and it usually was), he had to pay for another animal—and the price was considerably higher than normal. Finally, he would have to pay 20 to 33 percent for exchanging the money into local currency (Alfred Edersheim, *Life and Times of Jesus the Messiah*).

By this time his heart for worship was gone. It was a nauseating experience for the worshiper; he was being deceived and cheated. His worship experience was destroyed by the greed of the religious leaders.

When Jesus saw the deception and dishonesty, He took a scourge and chased the money changers from the temple. But this action aroused trouble with the high priest since Annas controlled the money-changing business, and ultimately incited the religious leaders to seek Jesus' death.

But Jesus' action had Messianic significance. One thousand years earlier, David had foretold this event (Ps. 69:9; John 2:17). Yet the religious leaders failed to recognize the sign. Instead, they challenged Jesus for a sign. Jesus promised them the ultimate sign—His resurrection (v. 19). Yet, they didn't understand it, thinking He was referring to Herod's temple. But the disciples remembered His words and when He was raised from the dead, they believed the Scripture and Jesus' own words concerning His resurrection.

This was a further messianic sign that Jesus displayed and many in Jerusalem believed in Him, although some superficially (vv. 23–25).

CONSIDER: *The life and testimony of Jesus should incite simple and sincere faith in Him.*

THE NEW BIRTH

JOHN 3:1–21

Jesus answered and said to him, "Truly, truly, I say to you, unless one is born again he cannot see the kingdom of God." (John 3:3)

At the age of twelve I was visiting my older cousin, Ernie, when he explained John 3:16 to me. I remember kneeling at the couch and praying, telling the Lord I was trusting in Jesus for salvation. And a new birth occurred!

Nicodemus, a leader and member of the Sanhedrin, the ruling supreme court of Israel, recognized the uniqueness of Jesus through the signs Jesus performed. He came to Jesus at night, probably for undistracted conversation. But Jesus confronted him with startling words: "Truly, truly, I say to you, unless one is born again he cannot see the kingdom of God." Entrance into eternal life and God's kingdom necessitates the new birth.

What is the new birth? Nicodemus immediately thought of human birth. How could a person be physically born a second time? Jesus explained that the new birth is a birth from above. "Again" (*anothen*) can be translated "from above." In contrast to the human birth in the natural realm, the new birth is a supernatural birth, a divine birth (John 1:13).

Jesus further explained that the new birth is "of water and the Spirit" (John 3:5). Some suggest this means water baptism, but it cannot be water baptism, since that would constitute a "work"—something that must be done to earn salvation. Salvation is by grace through faith, not works (Eph. 2:8–9). The words "water and Spirit" should be linked together in cleansing. In that sense Jesus' words refer back to Ezekiel 36:25–27—which Nicodemus knew and should have understood. The water indicates cleansing and repentance. And the effect of the new birth, like wind, is seen (John 3:8).

But Jesus further explains how the new birth takes effect. He draws a parallel with the bronze serpent found in Numbers 21:9. An Israelite who was bitten by a serpent could look up at the bronze serpent and be saved; so also those who look up at the crucified Christ will be saved. The new birth comes about through faith in Christ.

Jesus concluded His words to Nicodemus with some of the most profound words of Scripture: "For God so loved the world, that He gave His only begotten Son, that whoever believes in Him shall not perish, but have eternal life" (John 3:16). No works are necessary for salvation; it is by faith alone—accessing God's enormous grace.

CONSIDER: *Have you availed yourself of the enormity of God's love that gives you eternal life?*

January 25

THE TESTIMONY OF JOHN

JOHN 3:22–4:4

"He must increase, but I must decrease." (John 3:30)

The Christian Weight Loss Society should use this verse as their motto! It is a good incentive—with double meaning—for losing weight. The words reflect how every believer should view himself or herself. There is no room for pride, arrogance, and self-exaltation for the believer in Christ.

John was baptizing near Aenon, in the Decapolis province southeast of the Sea of Galilee. His disciples tried to stir up jealousy against Jesus because Jesus' disciples were baptizing and seemingly taking popularity away from John. But John would soon be thrown into prison (chronologically, after 3:36). John's rejection would be a reminder that the Messiah, whom John introduced, would Himself also be rejected.

But John reminded his disciples of his relationship to Jesus. John candidly explained that everyone has an assigned place. No one can claim something that has not been given to him. John was not the Messiah; he had been sent as the forerunner, to introduce the Messiah. He was the "friend" of the bridegroom. Although he was the "best man" at the wedding and the one who led the bride in the procession to the bridegroom, the focus was not on the friend. The attention was on the bridegroom—Christ. John's joy was in seeing others come to Christ, not to himself (v. 29).

John tersely emphasized that the focus must remain on Christ. He acknowledged and bore witness of Jesus' heavenly origin. By contrast, John was from the earth; hence, Jesus is greater than John since Jesus is eternal. Jesus testified to this truth, yet He was rejected, but some received His witness. John taught that Jesus is the revelation of God on whom God has fully placed His Spirit. The one who believes in Christ, the revelation of God, has eternal life, but the unbeliever faces the wrath of God in judgment (v. 36).

John's arrest precipitated Jesus' departure from Judea into Galilee and signaled Israel's ultimate rejection of Jesus as the Messiah. But Jesus departed for Galilee in an unusual way—"He had to pass through Samaria" (John 4:4). Jesus departed from conventional custom by walking through Samaria—the hated mixed race of people whose religion was an apostate form of Judaism. Here the Savior would reveal that even the socially despised and humbled can belong to the wedding party.

CONSIDER: *Pride is a faulty partner in a believer's union with Christ.*

January 26

RECEPTION IN SAMARIA
JOHN 4:5–42

"Whoever drinks of the water that I will give him shall never thirst;
but the water that I will give him will become in him a
well of water springing up to eternal life." (John 4:14)

As my wife and I were traveling by car in Austria, we were stopped on the autobahn by the *polizei*. As I tried to explain why I didn't have the necessary decal, I addressed the officer by the informal *du*. I got the ticket. When I explained this incident to my Austrian friend, he chuckled. "You lost it there," he said. "You should have used the formal *sie* in addressing the officer!"

There were cultural conformities in biblical times just as there are today. According to Pharisaic tradition it was unlawful for a rabbi to publicly talk with a woman. To speak to a Samaritan was entirely unheard of. Jesus broke the tradition (but never the Law) when He addressed the Samaritan woman. Jesus was resting at Jacob's well near Sychar, one and a half miles north of Shechem between Mount Ebal and Mount Gerazim. As He rested, Jesus revealed His true (but sinless) humanity. In the heat of the noonday sun He was thirsty and asked the Samaritan woman for a drink of water. It was an unusual time for her to be there but because of her reputation, she came in the heat of the day—when other women were not at the well.

When the woman questioned why Jesus, as a Jew, would ask her for a drink, He reminded her that if she knew His identity, she would ask Him for living water. Confused, the woman couldn't get past the concept of ordinary water. Surely He wasn't greater than Jacob! Jesus explained that He would quench the spiritual thirst of anyone who comes to Him. She would never have to thirst again! She would be satiated!

When Jesus confronted her, asking her to call her husband, she evaded the issue, saying she had no husband. Jesus revealed His deity, reminding her that she had five husbands and her current man was not her husband. Stunned, the woman recognized Jesus as a prophet and ran into the city and told the men of her meeting Jesus. As a result, many Samaritans came to faith in Jesus through the testimony of the woman, and then more when they heard Jesus speak. Those who were despised and scorned in society had received a reserved seat in the kingdom of heaven!

CONSIDER: *There is no "wrong side of the tracks" for those who desire to come to Jesus.*

CHRIST'S AUTHORITY OVER DISEASE

JOHN 4:46–54

"Go; your son lives." (John 4:50)

When I was a seminary student, a young man from a foreign country had come to study. But this young man had a serious, crippling disease. He tried every conceivable source of help but nothing resolved his illness. Medication did not help. Finally, he sought help from a so-called healer, only to be disillusioned. He wasn't healed. In his anxiety, he took an overdose of pills and died. Many people have been duped by false promises of healing.

The signs that Jesus performed are important in pointing to Him as the Messiah. John reminds us that the healing seen in today's reading is the "second sign" that Jesus performed. The sign points back to Jesus, the One performing the miracle. The Old Testament prophets indicated that Messiah would open the eyes of the blind, give hearing to the deaf, make the lame to walk and the dumb to speak (Isa. 35:5–6). The miracles were first of all a visible reminder that Jesus was the long-awaited Messiah.

In Cana, a royal official, one who was in the king's service, an officer of King Herod Antipas the tetrarch of Galilee, came to Jesus. His son was at the point of death at home in Capernaum. The official begged Jesus to come to Capernaum to heal his son. Although he had faith in Jesus' ability to heal his son, he thought it required the physical presence of Jesus.

Jesus merely spoke the words, "your son lives" and it was so (v. 50). "Lives" (*ze*) is a present indicative and means, "Your son is living!" (*Note*: The translation "your son will live" is incorrect. The son was living in full health the very moment Jesus spoke the words.)

The statement, "The man believed the word that Jesus spoke to him" is emphatic. He *believed*. This is evident because he delayed returning home that day. The distance from Cana to Capernaum is approximately twenty miles and Jesus healed the boy at 1:00 P.M. There was sufficient time to return home that afternoon but his delay until the next day is a strong indicator of his implicit faith in Jesus' words.

When the official returned home his servants explained that the boy was healed at the seventh hour (1:00 P.M.) on the previous day—precisely the time Jesus had spoken to the man! The event caused the man and his household of people to believe in Jesus as the Messiah. His words were trustworthy and true.

CONSIDER: *Do you trust Jesus' words and take them by faith?*

CHRIST'S AUTHORITY OVER MEN AND TRADITION

MATTHEW 9:9–17; MARK 2:13–22; LUKE 5:27–39

"But go and learn what this means: 'I DESIRE COMPASSION, AND NOT SACRIFICE,' for I did not come to call the righteous, but sinners." (Matthew 9:13)

As Jesus walked along the northern shore of the Sea of Galilee, He met Matthew, a tax collector. Tax collectors were among the most hated people; they were seen as traitors to Israel since they worked on behalf of Rome to collect exorbitant taxes, creating hardship for the people. Tax collectors purchased the privilege to collect taxes, then agreed to a designated amount for Rome. Whatever additional money they collected was their own profit. Tax collectors could establish the profit margin at whatever level they desired.

When Jesus called Matthew, the tax collector abandoned his business and followed Jesus. It says a great deal about Matthew since he left a very lucrative business to follow Jesus in hardship. His conversion was genuine.

Matthew immediately called his friends to dine with Jesus. These "tax collectors and sinners" were the despised of society. "Sinners" is a broad term, referring to those who refused to submit to the Pharisaic customs. The Pharisees viewed them with disdain. The Pharisees were separatists who would never eat with those who were ceremonially impure. Since Jesus ate with these people He revealed that He accepted them. This was unheard of among the religious people—the Pharisees taught that God hates sinners and delights in their death.

Jesus explained why He dined with these social outcasts. He came to provide spiritual health for those who were unhealthy—He came to call sinners to repentance. But the self-righteous would not respond to Jesus' call to repentance; they saw no need in themselves.

What Jesus was doing was radical. And He illustrated it by His two parables. No one sews a patch of unshrunk cloth on an old garment, because the patch will pull away and tear the garment. Nor does someone pour new wine into an old wineskin that has lost its elasticity, because the wineskin would burst. Jesus reminded His audience that He had not come to simply reform Judaism. He came to inaugurate an entirely new age. And He offered this glorious future to all—including social outcasts.

CONSIDER: *The Lord calls us to share the good news with all—including social outcasts—to ultimately share in the glory of the Bridegroom's kingdom.*

January 29

CHRIST'S AUTHORITY OVER THE SABBATH

JOHN 5:1–18

He . . . was calling God His own Father,
making Himself equal with God. (John 5:18)

A t 2:00 P.M. Friday the shops begin to close in Israel, to allow the employees to go home and prepare for sunset when all work ceases. The chief rabbi instructed the Hilton management that no Hebrew employee could write out bills or work on the Sabbath. Elevators are set on automatic so that no one will work by having to press an elevator button. At the Wailing Wall an announcer reminds the people that no more pictures may be taken at the precise moment the Sabbath begins.

The controversy with Jesus began at the pool of Bethesda. When the waters moved, the first person into the pool was healed of his disease. An invalid had been at the pool for thirty-eight years but had not been healed. Although the man exhibited no faith, Jesus simply told him, "Get up, pick up your pallet and walk" (John 5:8). Immediately the man was made well, his atrophied muscles became strong. And he picked up his bedroll and walked. John adds the crucial statement: "Now it was the Sabbath on that day" (v. 9).

The rabbis had constructed an elaborate system of thirty-nine works, which if done on the Sabbath, rendered the offender subject to death by stoning. These were "father works." There were additional laws called "descendant works." Wearing false teeth on the Sabbath was a descendant work of carrying a burden. A mother could pick up a child on the Sabbath but if the child was holding a stone, she had violated the Sabbath law. A woman was prohibited from looking in a mirror on the Sabbath—she might see a gray hair and pull it out, violating the Sabbath.

Ironically, the man who was healed did not know who it was that had healed him. When Jesus later confronted the man in the temple, he turned and told the Jews it was Jesus who had made him well.

The Jews persecuted Jesus for supposedly violating the Sabbath. But Jesus reminded them that He was working in concert with the Father. With that, the Jews sought His death, because He "was calling God His own Father, making Himself equal with God" (v. 18). The point is clear. By identifying Himself as the Son of God, Jesus claimed equality with the Father. Jesus' statement strongly argues for His deity—and the unbelieving Jews understood it as such.

CONSIDER: *As God the Son, Jesus is Lord of the Sabbath.*

EQUALITY OF FATHER AND SON
JOHN 5:19–47

". . . so that all will honor the Son, even as they honor
the Father. He who does not honor the Son does not
honor the Father who sent Him." (John 5:23)

It is Saturday late morning when the doorbell rings. I open the door to see two men carrying briefcases and holding *The Watchtower.* "Just a moment," I tell them as I get my Bible to talk to them outside. The critical issue with Jehovah's Witnesses is their denial of Jesus' deity. I usually turn them to John 5:23 and ask them, "Do you give Jesus the very same worship that you give to Jehovah?" When pressed, they answer "no."

When the Jews confronted Jesus about His claims He issued a discourse on the equality of the Son and the Father. He reminded them that the Son works in concert with the Father. The epitome of the equality is giving life by raising the dead. Just as the Father has the power to raise people from the dead so also the Son raises the dead to life. Further, the Son has the prerogative to judge. Just as the Father judges (Ps. 9:8), so also the Son judges (John 5:22). Central to Hebrew thinking was worship of the Lord; it was unique and singular. The Lord alone was to be worshiped; He shared His glory with no one (Deut. 6:13; Matt. 4:10), yet Jesus asserted that people were to honor the Son *even as* they honor the Father. The very same worship that was accorded the Father was to be given to the Son! It was a clear claim of equality.

Then Jesus reverted to the subject of judgment. Jesus came that people might, through faith in Him, avert the judgment of God. But at the end of the age, all humanity will be resurrected to face the Son's judgment.

But Jesus' audience was hostile so He reminded them of the witness to His authenticity: (1) The Father Himself testified to the Sonship of Jesus (vv. 32, 37–38). (2) They had inquired of John the Baptist and he bore witness to Jesus—and they had recognized John (vv. 33–35). (3) The works that Jesus did were a clear testimony to His messiahship (v. 36). He healed the sick, He gave sight to the blind, He raised the dead, He cleansed the lepers. (4) The Scriptures themselves bore testimony to Jesus (vv. 39–44) as did Moses (vv. 45–47). Their problem was not intellectual; it was spiritual. They were unwilling to respond, to volitionally come to Jesus. That clarion call of the authenticity of Jesus Christ remains for us today in the twenty-first century.

CONSIDER: *Jesus has all the prerogatives of deity and therefore, as the second person of the Godhead, He receives our worship.*

Controversy over Grain

MATTHEW 12:1–8; MARK 2:23–28; LUKE 6:1–5

"The Son of Man is Lord of the Sabbath." (Matthew 12:8)

Israel's chief rabbis have sought to resolve the dilemma of observing the Sabbath while also protecting against enemy missile attacks. Jewish law prohibits listening to the radio on the Sabbath. Regulations, however, may be overruled to save lives. The rabbis said it's permissible to leave the radio running on low volume during the Sabbath. "If there is a real alarm, you can turn up the volume, but in a nonconventional manner, with a stick or with your elbow," explained the Religious Affairs Minister Avner Shaki. "Controlling the volume in a different manner still marks the Sabbath as different from the rest of the week" (*St. Petersburg Times*, Jan. 19, 1991).

An earlier Sabbath controversy erupted between Jesus and the Pharisees when the Lord's disciples walked through a grain field and picked the heads of grain and ate them. According to the Talmud, two acts of sin were involved: "that of plucking the ears of corn, ranged under the sin of reaping, and that of rubbing them, which might be ranged under sifting in a sieve, threshing . . ." (Alfred Edersheim, *Life and Times of Jesus the Messiah*).

When the Pharisees reminded Jesus that the disciples' action was unlawful, Jesus countered by reminding them that David and his followers entered the tabernacle and ate the consecrated bread—yet they were innocent. Further, the priests worked on the Sabbath, therefore breaking the Sabbath—yet they were considered innocent. Jesus culminated His comments by reminding them "something greater than the temple is here" (Matt. 12:6). Messiah had come. And as the Son of Man, the Messiah was Lord of the Sabbath. Jesus is Lord over the Sabbath; the Sabbath does not dictate to the Messiah. And the disciples had not violated the Sabbath.

The problem of the Pharisees was a problem of the heart. The Pharisees used the Law to enslave people in a rigorous, legalistic manner. But God's desire, even the Old Testament Law, was compassion and mercy. The Pharisees, who pretended to keep the Law, exhibited no compassion, no mercy. They missed the heart of God.

CONSIDER: *It is possible to be rigorously religious and yet miss the heart of the matter.*

February 1

CONTROVERSY OVER HEALING

MATTHEW 12:9–21; MARK 3:1–12; LUKE 6:6–11

"BEHOLD, MY SERVANT WHOM I HAVE CHOSEN;
MY BELOVED IN WHOM MY SOUL is WELL-PLEASED;
I WILL PUT MY SPIRIT UPON HIM." (Matthew 12:18)

Walking along the beach on the east coast of Florida, my wife and I noticed a sign, warning people that if they damaged the turtles' eggs (which were buried in the sand) they would be liable to six months in prison. While I value animal life and believe they should have normal protection, I couldn't help but see the incongruity. Animals are protected but unborn children are not. Over thirty million unborn children in America have been killed.

When Jesus entered a synagogue He encountered a man with a paralyzed hand. The scribes and Pharisees were watching Him to see if He would heal the man so they could accuse Him. It is entirely possible that the religious leaders had planted the man there so they could trap Jesus. Phenomenal! They could accept His healing powers yet they failed to recognize the Messiah was in their midst!

Jesus commanded the man to come forward. As he did so, Jesus rebuked the hypocritical leaders, reminding them they could rescue a sheep on the Sabbath—but wasn't a man of more value than a sheep? Jesus concluded, it is lawful to do good on the Sabbath. With His challenging remarks Jesus had the man stretch out his hand and He healed it.

The conclusion is important. The Pharisees now planned how they might destroy Jesus. Their blindness is astonishing! They should have seen the works of Jesus—they pointed to His messiahship. Instead, they only saw that He violated their man-made traditions. He did not fit the Pharisaic mold and for that reason they sought to kill Him.

Because of the controversy, Jesus withdrew to the Sea of Galilee with large crowds following Him. Yet Jesus warned the people not to make Him known because His recognition as Messiah was to come from the religious leaders who were to point the people to Messiah. Although the Pharisees failed to recognize Him, the Father did recognize the Son. Messiah was the Servant, the Beloved upon whom God had put His Spirit. He would bring a message of hope to the Gentiles and they would trust in Him. The hope of the Gentiles anticipates Israel's ultimate rejection of Messiah. Their distorted, man-made traditions blinded them to Messiah's glory.

CONSIDER: *If we have a distorted value system, we will fail to recognize what is truly important.*

February 2

THE CHARACTER OF KINGDOM CITIZENS
MATTHEW 5:1–16; LUKE 6:17–26

---

*"You are the salt of the earth. . . . You are
the light of the world." (Matthew 5:13–14)*

When Giuseppe Garibaldi sought to free Italy from an enemy, he invited young men to join his crusade. "What do you have to offer us?" they demanded. "Offer you? I offer you neither pay, nor quarters, nor provisions. I offer only hunger, thirst, forced marches, battle, death. Let him who loves his country in his heart, not with lips only, follow me."

Crowds followed Jesus up a mountain northwest of the Sea of Galilee. As they came to a level place, He sat down and began to teach them. While the miracles of Jesus had demonstrated His authority through His *works*, the Sermon on the Mount, with its authoritative teaching, revealed the authority of Jesus through His *words*.

Disciples gathered around Jesus. Disciple simply means learner—without designating the depth of commitment. One can simply be a curious disciple, and in fact, an unbeliever (John 6:66). Or he can be convinced, yet uncommitted (Luke 18:18–27). Or he can be a committed disciple. Convinced of the claims of Christ, he commits himself to Christ (John 6:68; Luke 9:23–26).

In contrast to the false teaching of the Pharisees, Jesus taught the meaning of true righteousness in the Sermon on the Mount (Matt. 5:20). The character of a kingdom citizen is detailed in the opening verses (vv. 3–12). The kingdom citizen sees himself as God sees him: he is poor in spirit, broken and crushed under the recognition of his sin. For this reason he mourns over his sin, aware of his unworthiness. He cannot be proud any longer; he is gentle, submitted to God. He is God-controlled. Recognizing his sin, he hungers for righteousness in conduct—thoughts, words, and deeds. And now having experienced the mercy of God, he can only show mercy to others, flowing from a pure heart—not ceremonially pure but inwardly pure. Enjoying peace with God, he seeks peace with others—even to the extent of accepting persecution. His change is evident. Like salt on food, his life is attractive, reflecting his committed discipleship. Like the giant seventy-five-foot candelabra that shone from the temple on the hill in Judea, he pierces the darkness. He is a kingdom citizen—and people in the world see it.

CONSIDER: *Are you a curious, convinced, or committed disciple of Christ?*

THE STANDARD OF KINGDOM CITIZENS

MATTHEW 5:17–48; LUKE 6:27–36

*"For I say to you that unless your righteousness surpasses
that of the scribes and Pharisees, you will not enter the
kingdom of heaven." (Matthew 5:20)*

The Pharisees were meticulous in their outward activities, slavishly legalistic even in the minutiae—but it was all outward. And Jesus warned the people that unless their righteousness exceeded that of the Pharisees they would not enter the kingdom of heaven. Jesus then proceeded to correct the corrupted Pharisaic teachings. In doing so, Jesus had come to "fulfill" the Law—and fill it with meaning.

The Pharisees had restricted the command concerning murder to simply the outward act, but Jesus taught that the angry person, the one who called someone "blockhead" or "fool," had broken the Law and was guilty of murder! What was the resolution? Reconciliation. Sacrifices were of no significance without reconciliation. And while the Pharisees limited adultery to the physical act, Jesus taught that adultery could take place in the mind. The resolution? Removing things from the eyegate that would create lust. Through the "eye" temptation comes into the body and through the "hand" sin is carried out.

Pharisees misused the oath and would swear by the temple, the altar—even the dishes in the temple! But they didn't feel obligated to keep an oath if it wasn't tied to a sacrifice. It was deceitful and hypocritical. Jesus warned that the kingdom citizen's speech should be simple and honest—and without oaths.

While the Law taught "an eye for an eye," it was meant for civil justice. But the Pharisees took the law into their own hands, seeking revenge. It was wrong. Jesus warned his followers not to seek revenge when insulted, and even to refuse litigation against an opponent. There was to be submission to government and authority. Of course, Jesus was not prohibiting defense for one's life. He distinguished between revenge (coming from a malicious heart) and defense (which is necessary protection).

The consummating criterion for the disciple is love. Even the persecutors were to feel the effects of Christ's love through His disciples. The kingdom citizen is obligated to go beyond love of friends—he is to love the unlovely. In this we are called to be "perfect"—mature in love.

CONSIDER: *Are you reflecting the standards of a kingdom citizen? What are your thoughts? Attitudes? Are your words entirely truthful?*

February 4

ATTITUDES OF KINGDOM CITIZENS: IN PRAYER
MATTHEW 6:1–15

*"But if you do not forgive others, then your Father
will not forgive your transgressions." (Matthew 6:15)*

In the town where I grew up there was a bachelor who lived alone with his widowed mother. One day, as he came into the house, his mother was washing the floor. When John said something that annoyed her, she picked up the floor rag and threw it at him—and it hit him in the face. "Mother," he exclaimed, "I will never talk to you again." And he didn't. They lived together in the same house for a number of years, ate at the same table, but he never spoke to her again.

Forgiveness. It's a central subject in Christ's teaching about prayer. In the Court of Women were thirteen trumpet-shaped offering receptacles. They were narrow at the top (to prevent thieving) and wide at the bottom. When a coin was inserted it made a loud trumpet-like noise as it descended to the bottom of the chest. The Pharisees waited until a crowd gathered, then they would throw their coins into the chest for all to see and hear. It was a theatrical performance, like a stage actor in a role that is foreign to his nature. The Pharisees had their reward—the acclaim of people.

Synagogues were normally built at the highest location or busiest intersection in town. So when the Pharisees stood to pray outside the synagogue, many people were there to watch. And they had their reward.

By contrast, Jesus instructed his followers to pray in a place and in a way where they weren't looking for the acclaim of people. Jesus warned them against babbling meaningless words—saying the same words over and over. Jesus outlined the model prayer for them which included six petitions: three related to God and three related to human need. Prayer begins with worship, focusing on the Father and longing for the day when His earthly kingdom will be inaugurated and righteousness will reign. In the human arena, basic needs should be prayed for—food and shelter. But basic to prayer is forgiveness. Jesus repeated the warning: I cannot expect God to forgive me if I harbor malice and an unforgiving spirit toward others. Forgiveness is vital in kingdom life. Without forgiveness the spiritual life is a sham.

CONSIDER: *Are you harboring an unforgiving spirit against someone while expecting God to hear your prayer?*

ATTITUDES OF KINGDOM CITIZENS: IN WEALTH AND WORRY

MATTHEW 6:16–34

"So do not worry about tomorrow; for tomorrow will care for itself.
Each day has enough trouble of its own." (Matthew 6:34)

Donald Grey Barnhouse tells the story of his worrying wife. To help her resolve her problem of worry he instructed her to keep a "Worry Book" where she could record all her worries. At the end of the year they consulted her Worry Book and made an interesting discovery: the things she had worried about didn't happen but other calamities had come into her life that she hadn't previously been aware of and had not worried about. "So," exclaimed Barnhouse, "you worried about things that never came to pass but you didn't have the sense to worry about things that came to pass so you see it's pointless to worry!"

Jesus instructed His followers concerning the problem of worry. The Pharisees, who thought God blessed the wealthy, were guilty of accumulating wealth. Jesus warned his followers: "Do not store up for yourselves treasures on earth" (Matt. 6:19). Treasures are temporary. They don't last; they will ultimately undergo decay and destruction. Jesus told His followers to lay up treasures in heaven—that was lasting. Moreover, what a person treasures and values is what he will focus on with his heart. He tersely reminded them: "You cannot serve God and wealth" (v. 24).

But that created another problem for Jesus' disciples. If they didn't accumulate wealth then they would tend to worry because they lacked material things. But Jesus reminded them of the uselessness of worry: (1) Worry distracts from the important things (vv. 25–26). Life if more important than food and clothing. Besides, God even cares for the birds—and people are more important than birds. (2) Worry doesn't change anything (v. 27). Worry won't add to the length of life—but it may subtract years of life. (3) God will provide for our needs (vv. 28–30). If God creates the beautiful grassy fields we should be reminded that we are worth much more to God. Pagan unbelievers worry but believers have a heavenly Father who cares for them and He knows what we need. (4) It is useless to worry about that which may never happen (v. 34). Tomorrow has its own concerns and when it comes, God will provide for our needs. Therefore, "do not worry. . . ."

CONSIDER: *What are you worrying about that you need to trust the Lord for?*

ATTITUDES OF KINGDOM CITIZENS: IN JUDGING

MATTHEW 7:1–12

"Do not judge so that you will not be judged." (Matthew 7:1)

Surely, this command must be one of the most confusing and misunderstood statements of Jesus. Frequently, unbelievers chide Christians, "Oh, you're so judgmental!" But there are numerous examples in Scripture where believers judged. What can we conclude about judging?

It is necessary to judge doctrine and moral actions. John the Baptist judged the hypocrisy of the Pharisees and Sadducees (Matt. 3:7). He also judged the immorality of Herod (Matt. 14:3–4). Peter judged the deceitfulness and dishonesty of Ananias and Sapphira (Acts 5:1–11). Paul judged incest in the Corinthian church and warned the church to judge immorality within the church (1 Cor. 5:1–13). Since the doctrine of the true humanity and deity of Christ is vital to Christianity, John taught the necessity of judging people concerning the true doctrine of Christ (1 John 4) and avoiding fellowship with people who hold false doctrine (2 John 10). The ultimate example is Christ Himself. He judged. In the strongest language Christ denounced the false religious leaders (Matt. 23:13–37) and said they were from the devil (John 8:44). That's strong language!

It is wrong, however, to judge attitudes or pass sentence on motives. We cannot see the heart, the motives of people; we must wait until the Lord reveals the motives of men's hearts (1 Cor. 4:5). The one who judges another's motives is like a person with a beam in his eye attempting to remove the speck from another's eye.

In Matthew 7:6, Jesus warned against the failure to judge with the analogies of giving what is holy to dogs and throwing pearls to the swine. Who are the swine and the dogs? Unquestionably they are unbelievers. Shouldn't we give the gospel to unbelievers? Yes, but not in a haphazard, thoughtless way. "It means we must recognize the different types and persons . . . we must also become expert in knowing what to give to each type. You do not handle a Pilate and a Herod in exactly the same way; you answer the questions of a Pilate, but you say nothing to a Herod. . . . We must learn to know which particular aspect of the truth is appropriate in particular cases" (D. Martyn Lloyd-Jones, *Studies in the Sermon on the Mount*).

Surely that calls for wisdom and prayer! Hence, Jesus instructed His followers to pray for wisdom regarding judging—and all other matters (Matt. 7:7–11). Jesus told them to keep on asking . . . keep on seeking . . . keep on knocking. Jesus concluded His instruction to the kingdom citizens with the summation of the Old Testament Law: "treat people the same way you want them to treat you" (v. 12). The heart and resolution of spiritual life lies not in judging, but in love—love for God and love for your neighbor.

CONSIDER: *We need the wisdom of God in judging truth while refraining from judging motives.*

TESTS OF KINGDOM CITIZENS

MATTHEW 7:13–27

"You will know them by their fruits." (Matthew 7:20)

Tom and Carol were having marital problems so Tom began getting counseling at Atlanta's Dianetics Center, affiliated with the Church of Scientology. Soon Carol joined the counseling sessions and both became Scientologists. Their new organization, rather than their family, consumed their lives. In two years they spent $60,000 on Church of Scientology—in addition to all their time. Their daughter acknowledged, "They took our lives away."

Jesus warned against false prophets who offer a false way of salvation. They make the way attractive to people; it is wide and spacious, easy to access and easy to travel. They lure people with a false message. But Jesus reminded His followers that His way is small and narrow and, as a result, few will find it. Few find the right road because false prophets deceive people into taking the wrong road.

The false prophets who appear as innocent sheep are really ravenous wolves who devour their prey. How can they be recognized? By their fruits. One televangelist promised his viewers he "gave everything" to the ministry. But afterward he bought a Rolls Royce and a $400,000 home in Palm Springs.

Jesus provided a simple illustration in identifying false prophets. When a tree doesn't bear good fruit, it is apparent that it is rotten and it is cut down. A good tree bears good fruit and a rotten tree bears rotten fruit. The teacher's life and effect reveal his nature. When he lives for himself, accumulating wealth through taking it from innocent people, it is apparent he is a false teacher.

But these people will one day stand before the Lord and attempt to confess their allegiance to Him, only to hear the condemnatory words, "I never knew you." They never belonged to Him. They were imposters.

People that build their lives on false teachers have a foundation of sand—their spiritual house is bent for destruction. But those who build their lives on Jesus Christ will stand the ultimate test and they are eternally secure.

CONSIDER: *Are you building your life on the truth of Christ or on shifting sand?*

February 8

THE FAITH OF A GENTILE

MATTHEW 8:5–13; LUKE 7:1–10

*"Truly I say to you, I have not found such great
faith with anyone in Israel." (Matthew 8:10)*

In 1966 Northwestern Schools in Minneapolis closed their doors. But they
elected William B. Berntsen to serve as president of the college even though
its doors of operation were closed! Dr. Berntsen accepted the challenge. For six
years Dr. Berntsen maintained an office but there were no students, no faculty,
no classes. But Dr. Berntsen had faith. In 1972 Northwestern College reopened
and today has a bustling campus of well over 1,000 students. Dr. Berntsen had
a strong faith in Christ even though he could not foresee the resolution.

Jesus came to Capernaum where He was met by a centurion's delegation,
pleading on behalf of the centurion's servant who was paralyzed. Centuri-
ons were the backbone of the Roman army, commanding a hundred soldiers.
Wherever they are seen in the New Testament, they are viewed favorably. This
centurion was also a Gentile, but was loved by the Jewish people because he
had built them a synagogue.

When Jesus started on His way, He was met by the centurion himself who
said, "Lord, I am not worthy for You to come under my roof, but just say the
word, and my servant will be healed" (Matt. 8:8). The statement is remarkable,
exhibiting unusual faith—especially by a Gentile. He believed Jesus had the
power to heal over a distance, that Jesus did not have to be present to heal.
Particularly remarkable is his comment, "just say the word. . . ." He recognized
the authority of Jesus' words.

Then the centurion drew an analogy. As a centurion, he had the authority
of Rome. His simple command would draw an obedient response. By analogy, he recognized Jesus' authority in a greater realm. Jesus could speak with
heaven's authority and the servant would be healed.

Jesus marveled when He heard the centurion's words. Only twice does the
Scripture indicate Jesus marveled—here at a Gentile's faith and in Mark 6:6
at the unbelief of His own people. Jesus promised a future day when Gentiles
would come from around the world to enjoy the blessings of Messiah's kingdom. And faith is the ultimate issue.

CONSIDER: *Would Jesus marvel at your faith or your unbelief?*

February 9

CHRIST'S AUTHORITY OVER DEATH

LUKE 7:11–17

And when the Lord saw [the widow], He felt compassion for her. . . .
And He said, "Young man, I say to you, arise!" (Luke 7:13–14)

Who has not stood at a casket and wept? Every family experiences the heartache, the soul-wrenching sorrow when a loved one dies. Particularly sad is the death of a child. I clearly recall the hearse sitting in our neighbor's driveway. Their lovely, seventeen-year-old, Christian daughter, who was also our babysitter, had died of leukemia. Although she had a strong testimony of faith in Christ, tears and sorrow were still a part of the scene.

The incident in today's reading took place in Nain, a town about ten miles southeast of Nazareth in Galilee. As Jesus and His disciples approached the city, a large funeral procession was following the bier carrying a dead man. The tragic picture of grief is reflected in the narrative: "a dead man . . . the only son . . . she was a widow." It was an intensely tragic picture. She was alone. In that patriarchal culture it was essential for a woman to have a man caring for her. But her husband was dead and now her only son was also dead. She was alone in the world, left to fend for herself.

The grieving mother was walking at the head of the procession which included musicians and also mourners—with professional wailing women. The dead man was being carried on a stretcher, wrapped in a shroud. When Jesus saw her He felt compassion for her. He spoke to her a seemingly impossible command, "Do not weep" (Luke 7:13). It is noteworthy that He spoke these words *before* He did anything. Then He spoke another seemingly impossible command: "Young man . . . arise!" (v. 14). And the man got up. And Jesus presented the young man to his mother. What a joy that would have been!

The response was electrifying. Shock . . . fear . . . gripped all of them. A prophet was in their midst! It was a visitation of God! And they began glorifying and praising God. Jesus' authority was demonstrated in His power over man's greatest enemy: death. Jesus has broken the bondage of death and given eternal hope to His people (John 11:25–26; Heb. 2:14). Yes, we will still weep at a casket, but that is no longer the end of the story.

CONSIDER: *Jesus has broken the grief and power of death for you and me.*

WITNESS OF THE TWELVE

MATTHEW 9:35–10:15; MARK 6:7–11; LUKE 9:1–5

"Do not go in the way of the Gentiles, . . . go to the lost sheep of the house of Israel. And as you go, preach, saying, 'The kingdom of heaven is at hand.'" (Matthew 10:5–7)

Jesus came as Israel's king, offering Messiah's kingdom to the nation. But how would they know whether He was the promised Messiah? Jesus went throughout the cities, "teaching in their synagogues, and proclaiming the gospel of the kingdom, and healing every kind of disease . . ." (Matt. 9:35). Jesus' messiahship was authenticated through His *words* and His *works.*

To expand the proclamation of Jesus' messiahship, He sent out the Twelve. He chose twelve disciples and named them apostles ("sent ones"), giving them a unique authority to heal the sick, raise the dead, and cleanse lepers. This authority was restricted to the Twelve (Matt. 10:1–2; Luke 9:1) and Paul (2 Cor. 12:12). The apostles were special messengers, appointed by Christ and given a special authority to preach and perform miracles to *authenticate them as messengers and to authenticate their message that Jesus is the Messiah.* Their message was to announce to the Jewish people that their Messiah, in fulfillment of many Old Testament prophecies, had come.

The qualifications of an apostle are set forth in Acts 1:21–22—the apostle was one who followed Christ from the baptism of John until Christ's ascension. The office and gift of apostle was given for the foundation of the church (Eph. 2:20). The foundation is laid but once; it is not being laid today. No one today qualifies to be an apostle.

At that time, the message of the Twelve was restricted to the Jewish people, Israel (Matt. 10:5–7), and would be authenticated by the miracles that Christ had given them the authority to perform (Matt. 10:8). Their message would be either accepted or rejected (Matt. 10:9–15). The "worthy" person would be hospitable and welcome both the messengers and their message. The unworthy ones would not provide hospitality, indicating their rejection of the message.

Because the Jews had the advantage of the Old Testament prophecies, and then the eyewitness testimony of the apostles along with the miracles they performed, the Jews would have no excuse for rejecting Jesus. "In the day of judgment" they will suffer for their rejection of the Messiah—the King of heaven and earth.

CONSIDER: *Greater knowledge demands greater response.*

February 11

RESPONSE TO THE GOOD NEWS
MATTHEW 10:16–42

"And he who does not take his cross and follow
after Me is not worthy of Me." (Matthew 10:38)

Persecution of Christians whose only "sin" was that they spread the good news of the gospel of Christ fills the pages of books. Chinese communist persecution of Christians is well known. Islamic regimes have long prohibited the gospel of Christ from being proclaimed—and many Christians have gone to their death for telling others about Christ.

Jesus foretold that this would happen. He anticipated His rejection and warned His followers that they too would be rejected and suffer persecution. Jesus warned the Twelve of the vicious rejection of them and their message. This Scripture characterizes the response to the good news not only for the period of the apostles, but to the end of the age—"until the Son of Man comes" (v. 23).

But believers are exhorted not to fear. Yes, their identification with Christ will result in persecution; it is to be expected that if men persecuted the Teacher, they will persecute the disciple. Yet the disciples are not to fear men. Ultimately the truth will be revealed. Besides, all the enemy can do is kill the body; it makes more sense to fear God, who can destroy soul and body in hell. But God is sovereign and knows his disciples; He knows the very hairs on their head. He knows the sparrow that falls to the ground—and they are worth more to Him than a sparrow. So there is no need to fear.

Belief in Jesus brings opposition. His very name brings a sword—division. Within a household, one will believe, the other will not. Yet, the follower of Jesus takes up his cross—the stigma of being identified with Christ. It is the symbol of being despised. Yet this is truly "finding life." A life lost in Christ is finding it.

CONSIDER: *Will you boldly be identified with Christ in His rejection and repudiation by the world?*

February 12

REJECTION OF JOHN

MATTHEW 11:2–19; LUKE 7:18–35

"The BLIND RECEIVE SIGHT and the lame walk, the lepers are cleansed and the deaf hear, the dead are raised up, and the POOR HAVE THE GOSPEL PREACHED TO THEM." (Matthew 11:5)

John Bunyan, the well-known author of *The Pilgrim's Progress*, was a Baptist preacher in Bedford, England. He boldly proclaimed the gospel of Christ and because of it the authorities imprisoned him. Bunyan was in and out of prison for twelve years, from 1660 to 1672. But Bunyan persisted in evangelism, preaching the good news of Christ.

When Jesus began His public ministry, John the Baptist, the Messiah's forerunner, had been on the scene for many months, preaching the message of the kingdom of God. But John was imprisoned for his preaching. And John was puzzled. He knew Messiah had come to rule; why was he in prison? John sent messengers to Jesus, asking Him, "Are You the Expected [Coming] One?" The term "Expected One" was a technical designation for the Messiah, probably derived from Psalm 118:26 and Daniel 7:13.

In answering John, Jesus verified His messiahship by reminding John of the miracles He performed. The prophets had foretold Messiah's great works (Isa. 35:5–6). John was reminded that Jesus healed the blind, caused the lame to walk, cleansed the lepers, gave hearing to the deaf, raised the dead to life, and proclaimed good news to the poor. What did this mean? These were Messianic signs! There could only be one conclusion: Jesus of Nazareth is the Messiah!

But then Jesus spoke to the people about John. Did they think he was fickle? Did they think he vacillated like a reed in the wind? John was not unfaithful. If John had ministered to curry favor, he would have been dressed in royal clothing. But John was singularly significant. He was the forerunner of Messiah, prophesied by Malachi who would go before the Messiah (Mal. 3:1). Yet John was at a disadvantage. His imminent death meant he would not enjoy the privileges of Messiah's presence. But the people of that generation had rejected John—and they would also reject Jesus. They reflected the characteristics of this world where today it is culturally improper to speak the name of Jesus. But we, like John, are called to faithfulness in proclaiming Christ—amid opposition and cultural rejection.

CONSIDER: *Do adversity and opposition make you doubt or do they strengthen your faith?*

February 13

THE UNPARDONABLE SIN

MATTHEW 12:22–37; MARK 3:20–30

"Whoever speaks a word against the Son of Man, it shall be forgiven him; but whoever speaks against the Holy Spirit, it shall not be forgiven him, either in this age or in the age to come." (Matthew 12:32)

A distraught man came to me, unburdening himself. His pastor had admonished the people, warning them not to commit "the unpardonable sin." The man's wife was upset because she thought she had committed the unpardonable sin. Had she? What is the unpardonable sin? Is it possible to commit the unpardonable sin today?

Jesus' warning concerning the unpardonable sin must be understood in the context of Matthew. In Matthew 4, Jesus came to the nation Israel, offering them the kingdom. But what were His credentials? He demonstrated who He was through His teaching and His miracles. In Matthew 5–7, the Sermon on the Mount records Jesus' authority through His words. The people were amazed at His teaching, recognizing that He taught with authority, not as the scribes (7:28–29). In Matthew 8–10, Jesus demonstrated His authority through His works—His miracles. He healed the sick, He stilled the storm, He cast out demons, He healed a paralytic and "every kind of disease and every kind of sickness" (9:35). Who was this? The Messiah! Christ, the Promised One had come!

But what was the nation's response? Perhaps the most tragic verse in all of Scripture records their blasphemous words when the Pharisees exclaimed: "This man casts out demons only by Beelzebul the ruler of the demons" (12:24). They acknowledged that a miracle had occurred but they credited the work to Satan. Jesus pointed out that it would be contradictory for Satan to cast out Satan.

What was the blasphemy, the unpardonable sin? It was seeing Christ perform miracles in the power of the Holy Spirit and attributing it to Satan. God said the Messiah was His Servant, the One on whom He put His Spirit (12:18), but the Jewish leaders said it was through the power of Satan. That was the unforgivable sin.

The blasphemy against the Holy Spirit cannot be committed today because it would demand the physical presence of Christ performing miracles and attributing it to Satan.

CONSIDER: *There is no sin that cannot be forgiven today. We maintain fellowship with Him by confessing our sins and He readily cleanses and forgives us (1 John 1:9).*

February 14

CHANGED RELATIONSHIPS

MATTHEW 12:38–50; MARK 3:31–35; LUKE 8:19–21

"For whoever does the will of My Father who is in heaven, he is My brother and sister and mother." (Matthew 12:50)

A harsh word spoken in anger has destroyed many relationships. A son has disparaged a parent and the relationship is broken—sometimes destroyed so that there is no more fellowship or even communication. What a tragedy!

When the Jewish leaders assigned Jesus' miracles done in the power of God's Spirit to Beelzebul, they committed the unpardonable sin and led the nation into judgment and suffering.

Following their rejection of Jesus, the scribes and Pharisees came to Jesus, taunting Him by demanding a sign. Jesus knew their sinful hearts and warned them that He would not give them the sign that they were looking for but He would give them the ultimate sign: the sign of Jonah. What was that? Jonah's episode in the belly of the huge fish for three days and nights was a harbinger of Christ being in the grave three days and nights. The nation of Israel would get the sublime sign: the atoning death and the bodily resurrection of Christ!

The nation of Israel had been privileged: they had heard the unparalleled teaching of Christ; they had seen His miracles. Yet they had rejected Him. Privilege demands responsibility. The people of Nineveh, the Queen of the South, would one day judge the nation Israel because they had responded to a lesser revelation.

Now Jesus addressed those disciples who had responded to His words and His works—"Behold My mother and My brothers!" (Matt. 12:49). What a phenomenal acclaim! What a remarkable relationship! Believers in Christ go beyond a blood relationship with Him; they are joined to Him as a brother, a sister, a mother, indicating the closest fellowship possible.

CONSIDER: *Have you reflected on your unique relationship with Christ? How does that affect your daily life? Do you enjoy your unique relationship with Him?*

February 15

Speaking in Parables

Matthew 13:1–17

*Jesus answered them, "To you it has been granted to
know the mysteries of the kingdom of heaven, but to
them it has not been granted." (Matthew 13:11)*

Why did Jesus speak in parables? There is a dramatic shift, a turning point
in the Gospels at this point—and there is a reason. Jesus came to the
nation of Israel, proclaiming the kingdom of God (Matt. 4:17). But the kingdom
was conditioned on Israel's repentance. If the people repented, the glorious
kingdom promised by the Old Testament prophets (see Isaiah 11, for example)
would be inaugurated.

Jesus demonstrated His messiahship through His words and His works. In
Matthew 5–7 Jesus taught the Sermon on the Mount, authenticating His messiahship through His teaching. In Matthew 8–10 Jesus revealed His authority
over every domain through His miracles.

Despite the clear evidence of Jesus' messiahship, the nation's leaders and
the people rejected Jesus as the Messiah and His offer of the kingdom. The
rejection resulted in that generation being put under judgment and the kingdom postponed. In Matthew 13 Jesus taught what the interadvent age—the
period between His rejection and His future reception—would be. This intervening age would be the "mysteries of the kingdom."

What does this mean? The mystery form of the kingdom is not Christen-
dom, it is not the church, nor is it the millennial kingdom—that will be inaugurated at Christ's second coming. The mystery form of the kingdom is the
hidden form the kingdom takes from the time the nation Israel rejected Christ
as Messiah until that future day when Israel receives Him as Messiah and King.

The continuing lesson in this dramatic event is that privilege demands
responsibility. The nation Israel was highly privileged in seeing the Messiah,
in hearing Him teach. Yet her people failed to respond.

CONSIDER: *Are you sensitive to the Word of God? Are you quick to respond when
you read the Word of God or hear it proclaimed?*

THE PARABLE OF THE SOILS

MARK 4:3–25; LUKE 8:5–18

"The sower went out to sow; as he was sowing, some seed fell beside the road. . . . Other seed fell on the rocky ground. . . . Other seed fell among the thorns. . . . Other seeds fell into the good soil." (Mark 4:3–8)

When I was a seminary student I worked part-time in an architect's office and had the opportunity to share the gospel with the architects. Over the four years I was able to talk extensively with them. George listened but had only scornful comments to make so I stopped talking to him about spiritual things. But one day I leaned over my drafting table and shared the gospel with Frank. When I concluded, he exclaimed, "That sounds so simple." I realized I had communicated. When Billy Graham came to the city I invited Frank and his wife to accompany Helen and me. When Graham gave the invitation for salvation, Frank immediately went forward. I followed him and had the privilege of leading him to Christ. The seed of the Word of God had fallen on good soil.

When Jesus told the parable of the soils He was teaching the disciples the kind of response they could expect as they sowed the Word of God in this present age. It is the same Word sown but there are differing responses.

The seed sown beside the road (Mark 4:4, 15) is along the narrow pathway separating the grain fields. People walked along these paths and the seed that fell there did not germinate because the birds came and quickly ate the seed. This represents the people who hear the Word but Satan quickly snatches the Word away. How? Probably through false teachers who pervert God's Word.

The seed that fell on the rocky places (vv. 5, 16–17) displays the initial excitement of the hearer but it is short-lived. Trials reveal the absence of a genuine faith.

The seed that fell amid the thorns (vv. 7, 18–19) reflects the person who is obsessed by the world—materialism and financial pressures choke the Word and faith is nullified.

The seed that fell on the good soil (vv. 8, 20) reveals the one who hears the Word, understands it, and responds—and yields a bumper crop.

All four soils received the same Word from the same messenger but the result was different. Response is the issue.

CONSIDER: *How do you respond to God's Word when you read it or hear it? Do you actively engage the Word so that it bears an abundant crop, reflected in a new life?*

THE PARABLE OF THE WHEAT AND THE TARES

MATTHEW 13:24–30, 36–43

"The kingdom of heaven may be compared to a man who sowed good seed in his field. But while his men were sleeping, his enemy came and sowed tares among the wheat, and went away." (Matthew 13:24–25)

When the Berlin wall, dividing communism and the free world, came down in 1989, enormous advancements of the gospel took place. Christian organizations and schools moved in and began to evangelize and teach the believers in the former communist countries. But parallel to the Christian advances were the advances of the cults. While evangelicals were sowing the good news, the cultists were spreading their false doctrines. And that parallels the parable of the wheat and the tares (common weeds that resemble wheat).

Jesus Himself began the sowing when He taught (Matt. 13:37). This sowing would continue throughout this interim age until the harvest and judgment at the return of Christ (vv. 30, 40–42).

The good seed represents believers (v. 38), while the bad seed is the enemy, the devil (vv. 25, 39). The harvest is the end of the age (v. 39) and the furnace of fire represents hell (v. 42). The barn represents the millennial kingdom (v. 43).

The sowing continues throughout this entire age, with Christ sowing the seed through believers. But there is also a counterfeit sowing; Satan sows tares. The false teaching of the cultists may seem true but upon examination it is found deficient. Sometimes the false is indistinguishable and won't become evident until the harvest.

At the return of Christ, His emissaries, the angels, will gather the false teachers and thrust them into eternal punishment but His people will radiate the splendor of God's glory in Messiah's kingdom. Believer, stay focused!

CONSIDER: *Looking at the progress of cults and false teachings may result in discouragement; believers must resolutely look to the return of Christ when the true will be separated from the false.*

February 18

PARABLE OF THE MUSTARD SEED AND LEAVEN

MATTHEW 13:31–33

*"The kingdom of heaven is like a mustard seed, which a man
took and sowed in his field; and this is smaller than all other seeds,
but when it is full grown, it is larger than the garden plants
and becomes a tree." (Matthew 13:31–32)*

Some years ago the *Dallas Morning News* carried a story of a Methodist minister in Oak Cliff who brought a mustard seed from Israel and planted it in front of the Methodist Church. In one year it grew to a height of thirty-two feet! When my wife and I visited Israel, our Israeli guide stopped by a mustard tree and put some of the seeds in the palm of his hand. The seed was a tiny speck—about the size of a dot made by a sharp pencil on a piece of paper. Yet this tiny seed grows into an enormously large plant.

The phenomenal growth of the mustard seed illustrates the humble beginning of the kingdom in this interim age. It began with eleven disciples but ultimately has grown to multiplied millions around the world. In its inception, it quickly grew from eleven to three thousand (Acts 2:41) and then five thousand men (4:4).

Remember, a parable teaches *one central truth.* The details within the parable should not be interpreted—in this case, the birds should not be interpreted. The fact that the birds of the air nest in the branches suggests the enormous growth of the mustard seed, teaching the great growth of believers in Christ, from the inception of the church until Christ returns.

The parable of the leaven forms a couplet with the parable of the mustard seed, illustrating the same truth. (While leaven often represents evil in Scripture, here is an instance where it does not.) Just as yeast permeates the entire lump of dough, so the kingdom grows throughout the world. Jesus reveals that in this interim age, the kingdom will not be established with outward means, but will, through the Holy Spirit, spread throughout the world (John 15:26; 16:7–11).

CONSIDER: *What is your part—what are you doing—in seeing the mystery form of the kingdom being spread throughout the world? Are you involved in spreading the Word in your neighborhood? In missions around the world?*

February 19

THE PARABLE OF THE HIDDEN TREASURE AND THE PEARL

MATTHEW 13:44–46

"The kingdom of heaven is like a treasure hidden in the field, which a man found and hid again; and from joy over it he goes and sells all that he has and buys that field." (Matthew 13:44)

Off the coast of Florida and in the Caribbean lie many sunken ships; some are the result of pirates like Captain Morgan who attacked, marauded, and sank numerous ships. Adventurers have sought these sunken ships, hoping to find some treasure. The concept of a treasure hunt has fascinated many a person. But the greatest treasure is not found in a chest filled with gold coins and pearls.

Like parables one and two, and three and four, these two parables also form a couplet, teaching the same truth. The parable of the hidden treasure relates to Israel, while the second parable has reference to Gentiles. In the first parable, the field refers to the land of Israel in which the treasure is found. Israel is God's treasured possession (see Deuteronomy 14:2). The man is Christ and the treasure is believers. The imagery is taken from common life in the Middle East where it was normal for people to bury valuables for safekeeping. To obtain the treasure, the man "sells all that he has and buys that field." This pictures Christ redeeming believers through His atoning death on the cross.

The second parable is similar. The merchant is Christ, the fine pearls are believers, and the sea represents Gentile nations. Christ sold all that He had—left heaven's glory and took on humanity—and He bought the pearl. Christ made atonement for Gentiles as well as Jews. He has provided redemption for both.

But isn't the man who sells all that he has to buy the field a picture of the believer who gives up everything to trust Christ? No, that would be a salvation by works. Rather, the parable pictures the great value of the people Christ has redeemed and the great lengths to which Christ has gone to provide redemption.

CONSIDER: *Have you considered how valuable believers are to Christ? You are a treasure, a priceless pearl.*

THE PARABLE OF THE DRAGNET

MATTHEW 13:47–50

"The kingdom of heaven is like a dragnet cast into the sea,
and gathering fish of every kind." (Matthew 13:47)

When we were living in Jacksonville, my wife and I frequently walked along the beach at the Atlantic Ocean. We sometimes saw people seining, dragging a net about twenty feet long and three or four feet wide into the ocean. Then they closed the net, capturing fish, and brought the net to shore. On the shore they separated the edible fish from the inedible.

The parable of the dragnet carries this present age to its conclusion. The first parable began with Christ sowing the word at His first coming and the seventh parable concludes with the judgment at the end of this present age. The parables cover the entire era from the ministry of Christ at His first coming to His judgment of the world at His second coming.

This parable illustrates God's judgment at the end of this age. Just as the bad fish are thrown away, so unbelievers will be cast into the lake of fire at the judgment when Christ returns. Jesus warned, "these will go away into eternal punishment, but the righteous into eternal life" (Matt. 25:46). Angels are Christ's emissaries in gathering the unbelievers together for judgment.

The righteous are gathered into "containers" (Matt. 13:48), illustrating believers entering Christ's kingdom on the new earth. Unbelievers, on the other hand, are cast into the lake of fire where there is "weeping and gnashing of teeth" (v. 49). This is a solemn reminder of the continuous anguish and anger by those in the lake of fire; their punishment will be unabated.

CONSIDER: *It is a solemn thought to recognize that this present age will conclude with Christ's judgment and there will only be two options—heaven or the lake of fire.*

February 21

CHRIST'S POWER OVER NATURE

MATTHEW 8:18, 23–27; MARK 4:35–41; LUKE 8:22–25

*The men were amazed, and said, "What kind of a man is this,
that even the winds and the sea obey Him?" (Matthew 8:27)*

After Jesus taught the disciples through parables, He left the eastern side of the Sea of Galilee and sailed with the disciples to the other side. The Sea of Galilee, which is some 700 feet below sea level, lies in the Jordan Rift Valley, an elongated, north-south depression in the land, that begins in the north at the Sea of Galilee. Because of this depression, the wind coming down from Mount Hermon (9,100 feet above the Mediterranean Sea) flows south along the Jordan Rift Valley, which acts as a funnel for the wind. As a result, storms are often sudden, the Sea of Galilee quickly becoming a cauldron of fury. It was a fisherman's nightmare.

The storm is described as a *seismos*, an "earthquake in water." The waves crashed over the boat so that the disciples feared for their lives. But the Savior was asleep in the boat. "Save us, Lord; we are perishing!" they cried (Matt. 8:25).

With the storm still raging, Jesus rebuked the disciples for their weak faith. He was the Master; He was in control. He knew what He was going to do. The Creator of all things (John 1:3) simply spoke to the winds and the sea: "Hush, be still" (Mark 4:39). "Be still" means "to muzzle." Immediately, the waves and the sea became calm. The Creator has authority over His creation. Jesus merely spoke and creation obeyed Him.

"Who then is this, that even the wind and the sea obey Him?" the disciples asked (Mark 4:41). It was an important question. Jesus was authenticated through His spoken word and His work of stilling the storm. He revealed He is the Messiah when He merely spoke and the storm obeyed Him. It was a work of deity. Only God can still the storm (Ps. 107:29). Jesus is the Master who stills not only the storm on the sea but He can still the storms of life. He has the authority and power over *every aspect* of life and He is waiting for us to demonstrate faith in Him so He can demonstrate His power in our lives.

CONSIDER: *What storms do you have raging in your life? Do you recognize the absolute sovereignty of Christ who has absolute authority over your life?*

February 22

CHRIST'S POWER OVER DEMONS

MATTHEW 8:28–34; MARK 5:1–20; LUKE 8:26–39

They came to Jesus and observed the man who had been demon-possessed sitting down, clothed and in his right mind. (Mark 5:15)

The Gadarenes (also called Gerasenes) was the territory on the eastern shore of the Sea of Galilee around the city of Gadara. It was Gentile territory, observable because of the swine the people kept. Pigs were unclean according to the Law (Lev. 11:7).

Two men who were demon possessed approached Jesus (Matt. 8:28); one was particularly well known (Mark 5:2; Luke 8:27). The man was wild and violent; even chains couldn't hold him. He went around naked, living in tombs. Symptomatic of demon possession, the man would cut himself. At a distance he called out to Jesus, "What business do we have with each other, Son of God? Have You come here to torment us before the time?" (Matt. 8:29). The demons recognized Jesus as the Messiah—and they realized their ultimate destiny!

"Come out of the man, you unclean spirit!" Jesus commanded (Mark 5:8). When Jesus asked the demon his name, he replied, "Legion; for we are many" (v. 9). The man was inhabited not by one demon, but by many. Since demons seek to inhabit a body, they begged Jesus not to send them into the abyss (as seen in Revelation 20:3), but to allow them to indwell the pigs feeding nearby. "Go!" Jesus commanded (Matt. 8:32). Immediately as the demons entered the pigs, the herd rushed headlong down the bank into the sea and were drowned.

When the herdsmen widely reported the event, the people came to Gadara and found the formerly demon-possessed man "sitting down, clothed and in his right mind" (Mark 5:15). Jesus had transformed the man by casting out the demons. Jesus has authority over every realm—including the realm and domain of Satan and He is able to transform lives that have been destroyed by Satan's emissaries. No person, no situation is beyond the power of Christ to redeem and set free.

CONSIDER: *Nothing is too hard for Christ. He has the power to change lives and give new life to those who have been ravaged to the extreme. What a great Savior!*

CHRIST'S POWER OVER DISEASE AND DEATH

MATTHEW 9:18–26; MARK 5:21–43; LUKE 8:40–56

"Little girl, I say to you, get up!" . . . Immediately the girl
got up and began to walk. . . . And immediately they
were completely astounded." (Mark 5:41–42)

Unquestionably, the greatest grief we experience on this earth is standing beside the casket of a loved one, bidding a final farewell. My heart was broken on that February day when my beloved wife, with whom I had shared forty-five honeymoon years, was laid to rest. But the story of life's greatest heartache does not end at the cemetery.

Crossing the Sea of Galilee, Jesus and His disciples came to the region of Capernaum where they were met by Jairus, who held an important position in the synagogue, having oversight of it. He approached Jesus, apparently in two sessions. First, he pleaded with Jesus because his twelve-year-old daughter was near death (Mark 5:23; Luke 8:42). Soon afterward, his attendants came, informing him that his daughter had died (Matt. 9:18; Luke 8:49).

As Jesus set out for Jairus's home, He was accosted by a woman with a hemorrhage that she had endured for twelve years. She came secretly, touching the fringe of His cloak. Immediately, her hemorrhage stopped—she was healed! Recognizing power had gone out of Him, Jesus called the woman out from the crowd. When she came, acknowledging that she had been healed, Jesus said, "Daughter, your faith has made you well; go in peace and be healed of your affliction" (Mark 5:34). She came to Jesus in faith and Jesus rewarded her faith.

When Jesus continued to Jairus's home, people from his household told him his daughter had died. Hope was gone. There was no need to trouble Jesus any further. But the Savior exclaimed, "Do not be afraid any longer, only believe" (v. 36). Faith in Jesus is the essence of life in a fallen world. Trust Jesus. When Jesus arrived at Jairus's home, the noisy professional wailing women were already lamenting the girl's death. Taking the inner three and the girl's parents, Jesus entered the room. Taking the girl by the hand, Jesus said, "Little girl, I say to you, get up!" (v. 41). What a dramatic moment! Immediately, the girl got up and began to walk. We can only speculate concerning the overwhelming joy of the parents!

As the second person of the Trinity, Jesus has authority over sickness and death. And in that role Jesus will ultimately and finally eradicate all sickness and death.

CONSIDER: *A great and glorious day is coming on the new earth when Christ will forever remove all sickness and death. No more death! No more tears or sorrow!*

CHRIST'S POWER OVER BLINDNESS

MATTHEW 9:27-34

---

*Then He touched their eyes, saying, "It shall be done
to you according to your faith." (Matthew 9:29)*

I visited an older friend recently. He lives by himself in a large house. He is a peaceful man, quiet and contented through a strong faith in Christ. But he is blind. He has sections of his home cordoned off with chairs so he won't wander too far and become disoriented. Because of his blindness, he is entirely restricted in what he can and cannot do. It is a tragic personal dilemma.

But Jesus has authority over the greatest dilemmas that afflict us in this life. As Jesus continued His ministry in Galilee, two blind men, aware of Jesus' presence, began to follow Him, crying out, "Have mercy on us, Son of David!" (Matt. 9:27). Unquestionably, these men had heard Jesus preach or had heard others talk about Him. They revealed their insight concerning Jesus when they called him "Son of David." This was a messianic title reflecting the Promised One who would come to restore the nation in righteousness and rule as king over the Jewish people (Ezek. 37:24). And it was for that purpose that Jesus had come (Matt. 1:1).

When the blind men confessed their faith in Jesus, He healed them of their blindness. This miracle was particularly noteworthy since there is no record of any blind person being healed in the Old Testament, nor is there any record of any blind person being healed in the New Testament by anyone except Jesus. Yet, there are more recorded miracles of Jesus healing the blind than any other miracle He performed. What is the significance? It was a messianic sign (Isa. 35:5). The physical blindness pointed to Israel's spiritual blindness and it was a reminder that only Jesus the Messiah could heal the nation's spiritual blindness.

CONSIDER: *Only Jesus heals the blind. As Messiah, He will one day terminate all physical blindness; as Savior, He lifts the veil of spiritual darkness from the eyes of those who believe in Him.*

REJECTION OF CHRIST IN NAZARETH

MATTHEW 13:54–58; MARK 6:1–6

*And they took offense at Him. But Jesus said to them,
"A prophet is not without honor except in his hometown
and in his own household." (Matthew 13:57)*

A few days ago I chatted with a lady down the street. "Why can't people be tolerant of others and just love each other?" she exclaimed. "There is a problem," I suggested. "It is sin. But that's why Jesus came to resolve the sin problem so we could in fact be capable of loving each other and one day going to heaven." She didn't like my answer; she was offended when I said Christ was the exclusive way of salvation. She reminded me of her good Hindu neighbors. She complained that Christians are too narrow in their views.

But this is nothing new. When Jesus came to His hometown of Nazareth and began to teach in the synagogue, the people were astonished at His wisdom and His miraculous powers. His words and His works revealed that He was the promised Messiah, yet the people of His hometown rejected Him. They heard His wisdom, they saw His miracles, yet they could not get past their thesis of His identity: "Is not this the carpenter's son?" (Matt. 13:55). They knew Him only as the one who grew up in their village and worked with Joseph in his trade. They knew His mother, Mary, and His half-brothers and half-sisters. How could He be someone unusual? How could He possibly be the Messiah?

Interestingly, the people referred to Jesus as the "carpenter's son." It is generally assumed that Jesus worked in a carpenter's shop, building ordinary household things like tables and chairs. However, the word "carpenter" (*tekton*) has a wide range of meanings, from a shipbuilder to a sculptor—it is even used of a physician. Generally, it indicates a craftsman of considerable skill. Jesus would not have built ordinary items like tables and chairs since men did that themselves. Jesus probably traveled around the country with Joseph in the building trade, perhaps constructing buildings of stone. Because of this, He would have been a strong man. (Imagine Him removing the moneychangers from the temple, as seen in Matthew 21:12 and John 2:15.)

What was the effect of Jesus' ministry in Nazareth? "They took offense at Him." "Took offense" (*skandalizonto*) means "to be repelled by someone, take offense at someone, of Jesus; by refusing to believe in him" (F. W. Gingrich and F. W. Danker, *A Greek-English Lexicon of the New Testament*). Tragically, the very people Jesus came to redeem rejected Him. They stumbled over Him because He was "one of their own." (Romans 9:31–33 shows Christ as the "stumbling stone" who people "trip over" in their attempt to gain salvation in their own way.)

CONSIDER: *The message of Jesus Christ is both narrow and exclusive—and people still stumble over it.*

DEATH OF THE FORERUNNER

MATTHEW 14:1–12; MARK 6:14–29; LUKE 9:7–9

He sent and had John beheaded in the prison. . . .
His disciples came and took away the body and buried it;
and they went and reported to Jesus. (Matthew 14:10, 12)

On April 18, 2007, five Muslim extremists entered a Christian publishing office in Malatya province in Turkey and brutally killed three young Christians. The militants tied the Christians to chairs, slit their throats, and stabbed their bodies multiple times. These devout Christians paid the extreme price for spreading the good news about Jesus Christ.

This rejection of Christ and the gospel is not new. Jesus' own forerunner who proclaimed the good news of the King's coming was rejected and killed. And it was a significant event—the rejection of John anticipated the rejection of Jesus.

Herod Antipas, son of Herod the Great, had a personal purpose in getting rid of John. The forerunner had denounced Herod Antipas for his incestuous life—he had unjustly divorced his wife and married Herodias, the wife of his half-brother, Philip, violating Jewish law (Lev. 18:16). John was fearless in defending the truth and is a reminder that God's people must stand for truth no matter what the consequences.

The low morality of the Herodian family was evident in the shameless dancing of Salome, Herodias's daughter. This may well have been prearranged by Herodias to achieve her vengeance against John for his indictment of their sin. Her hatred and malice becomes evident when she asks for the death of John the Baptist. Salome had pleased the guests through her dancing and Herod, in perhaps thoughtless comment, offered her any request she might make in order to please his guests. When her mother asked for the head of John the Baptist, Herod complied—because it would have pleased his guests. His morality was governed by political expediency.

John paid the ultimate price for his preaching but John's death was a harbinger of Jesus' rejection and death. This was—and still is—a reminder that society does not want the good news that Jesus Christ brought—and society will go to extreme lengths to reject the life-transforming message of Christ.

CONSIDER: *To what extent would you go to stand for and defend biblical truth?*

February 27

CHRIST FEEDS THE FIVE THOUSAND

MATTHEW 14:13–21; MARK 6:30–44; LUKE 9:10–17; JOHN 6:1–13

---

*And they all ate and were satisfied. They picked up what was
left over of the broken pieces, twelve full baskets. (Matthew 14:20)*

Jesus came as Israel's king; He was—and is—the Jewish Messiah. What does
that mean for Gentiles? Is He also the Messiah of the Gentiles? Yes, He is the
Messiah of both Jews and Gentiles as this miracle demonstrates.

This miracle took place on the eastern side of the Sea of Galilee, in Gentile
territory. Because of Israel's rejection of the kingdom offer, this event reflects
the movement of the gospel from the Jews to the Gentiles in God's outworking
of His program.

The crowds followed Jesus from Bethsaida to the eastern side of the Sea of
Galilee. When Jesus saw them, He had compassion on them because they were
like sheep without a shepherd; the religious leaders were leading the people
astray. But Jesus had mercy on them and healed their sick.

When it was evening, the disciples urged Jesus to send the people to the
city to buy food. But Jesus tested Philip's faith—where could they buy enough
food for all these people? Had Philip learned who Jesus was? Did he recognize
His authority and messiahship?

Jesus commanded the disciples to have the five thousand recline on the
grass. He then took the five loaves and two fish, blessed the food, and "kept
giving them to the disciples" (Mark 6:41). The verb "kept giving" sees the continuous action of Jesus giving the bread and fish to the disciples, revealing
that the miracle took place in Jesus' hands.

The miracle is a magnificent picture of Christ's work as king when His
kingdom is inaugurated at His second coming. The Old Testament prophets
anticipated Messiah's reign when there would be abundance on the renewed
earth. The trees, the pastures, the vineyards would be lush with produce (Joel
2:22–24; 3:18; Amos 9:13–15). In feeding the five thousand, Jesus was pointing
the people to the kingdom where He would reign supreme and His people
would have abundance—as they were reminded by the twelve full baskets.

CONSIDER: *As the king on the new earth, Jesus will provide abundantly for His
subjects, Jews and Gentiles, and everyone will have sufficient provision.*

CHRIST STILLS THE STORM

MATTHEW 14:24–33; MARK 6:47–52; JOHN 6:16–21

When they got into the boat, the wind stopped. And those
who were in the boat worshiped Him, saying, "You are
certainly God's Son!" (Matthew 14:32–33)

When Hurricane Katrina struck the Louisiana coast, the devastation to New Orleans and the coastal communities was enormous. Businesses were destroyed, homes were shattered, and lives were lost. Despite our technological advances, there is nothing we can do to avert a hurricane or any other natural calamity in this fallen world.

However, there is a future day coming when this fallen world will be renovated to pristine conditions when Christ establishes His glorious kingdom and reigns supreme on this earth. The miracles of Christ revealed the nature of Christ's future kingdom.

Jesus had sent the Twelve across the lake to the other side—knowing full well what He was going to do. A fierce wind, roaring down from Mount Hermon into the Jordan Rift Valley, suddenly created a turbulent storm as the Sea of Galilee erupted with tumultuous waves. The disciples had been rowing for hours—it was now the fourth watch of the night—between 3:00 A.M. and 6:00 A.M. They were physically and emotionally spent. And Jesus came to them, walking on the waves!

They were terrified, crying out, "It is a ghost!" (Matt. 14:26). But Jesus comforted them, announcing His presence, "Take courage, it is I; do not be afraid" (v. 27). "It is I" (*ego eime*) is literally "I AM" and is a strong claim of deity. (See God's words to Moses in Exodus 3:14.) Jesus identifies Himself with Yahweh of the Old Testament. He is God, the second person of the Trinity and there is no other! The disciples were overawed when the storm suddenly stopped. Who is this who can still the turbulent storm on the sea? The disciples drew a correct conclusion when they worshiped Him and exclaimed, "You are certainly God's Son!" (Matt. 14:33).

The stilling of the storm is a reminder, a harbinger of the great day when Christ returns and will bring peace and order to all of nature. Meanwhile, we live with turbulence outwardly and inwardly but the anticipation of Christ's future kingdom should bring peace to our hearts amid the turbulence (John 14:27; 16:33).

CONSIDER: *Jesus, as the second person of the Trinity, walks with us through the storms of life and therefore we can take comfort and have courage in life's difficulties.*

CHRIST, THE BREAD OF LIFE

JOHN 6:22–51

Jesus said to them, "I am the bread of life; he who comes to Me will not hunger, and he who believes in Me will never thirst." (John 6:35)

There are starving people on every continent of this world. From the street people in America to orphans in Africa, our world is filled with hungry people. And while it is a good thing to feed the starving, they also need the kind of food that is more important and more valuable than physical food. We eat food today but tomorrow we are hungry again. There is a food that assuages our hunger once and for all.

When the multitudes followed Jesus, He rebuked them because, being omniscient, He knew their motives. They followed Him for the physical benefits they derived from Him—and they failed to see the messianic signs in His words and works. He reminded them that the physical satisfaction they sought would ultimately perish (John 6:27). They should have sought the greater, the more important.

While the people linked themselves to Moses, Jesus reminded them it was not Moses but the Father who had given them the bread in the wilderness. But significantly, that pointed forward to Jesus who is the bread of life. The Israelites ate the bread in the wilderness but they perished. Jesus offered the bread by which they would never perish.

The words "I AM" again reference Jesus' deity and they stand in the emphatic position. Moreover, the one who partakes of Christ—believing, trusting in Him—shall "not never" hunger and "not never" thirst. The double negative doesn't negate itself; instead, it is meant as a double emphasis: Jesus thoroughly satisfies the soul. The longing, the yearning that is never fulfilled in materialism finds its rest and fulfillment in Christ alone. He satisfies. He completely satisfies the hunger of our soul. He nourishes us spiritually. Jesus has the words of eternal life; there is no other source of eternal life. Many stumbled at His words, especially when He used metaphorical language (like that found in John 6:54) and they continue to stumble at His words in our society. But the message remains the same. We can come to the well of water that Christ provides and drink deeply. Jesus satisfies.

CONSIDER: *In our materialistic society we can make the horrific error of striving after that which is temporary—and lose the eternal. Only Christ satisfies our deepest longing.*

March 1

CHRIST: WORDS OF ETERNAL LIFE

JOHN 6:52–71

[Jesus said,] "The words that I have spoken to you are spirit and are life." . . . Simon Peter answered Him, "Lord, to whom shall we go? You have words of eternal life." (John 6:63, 68)

After sharing the gospel with a Jewish maintenance man in my home recently, he exclaimed, "I don't believe in Moses and I don't believe in Jesus." I was disappointed and saddened. The name of Jesus is the line of demarcation. His is the most important name in the history of humanity. Belief in Jesus is critical—and eternally impactful. With Him we await an eternity of joy and fulfillment; without Him, people await an eternity of torment and darkness.

Having confronted the Jewish people with His dramatic words, "I am the Bread of Life" (John 6:35), the people immediately began to grumble and complain. How could a person make an exclusive statement like that? But Jesus continued to voice His claims: "Everyone who has heard and learned from the Father, comes to Me" (v. 45). He had given evidence that He was the Messiah, through His words (His teaching) and His works (His miracles). Now they were obligated to respond.

In dramatic language, Jesus continued to reinforce His claims, "He who eats My flesh and drinks My blood has eternal life" (v. 54). What did Jesus mean? Eating His flesh and drinking His blood is synonymous with beholding the Son and believing in Him (v. 40).

When Jesus continued His claims, "many of His disciples withdrew and were not walking with Him anymore" (v. 66). The people could not accept His exclusive, narrow statements. (*Note*: Disciple simply means "learner," it does not necessarily mean they were true believers.)

And that attitude prevails today as well. In the age of tolerance, people cannot accept Jesus' statements that He alone is the way to God. But that doesn't change the truth. Jesus, and Jesus alone, has the words of eternal life.

CONSIDER: *Have you responded to the unique claims of Christ? Do you recognize Jesus, and Jesus alone, as having the words of eternal life?*

CHRIST IS REJECTED BECAUSE OF TRADITION
MATTHEW 15:1–20; MARK 7:1–23; JOHN 7:1

"It is not what enters into the mouth that defiles the man, but what proceeds out of the mouth, this defiles the man." (Matthew 15:11)

Many of us have seen (and participated in) some form of Christian legalism. When my wife and I were first married, it was considered wrong for a woman to use makeup or wear slacks. Some thought men should only wear white shirts to church. Movies were taboo (perhaps that's one to rethink for today). The list was endless.

The Pharisees had their own brand of legalism: hand washing. They prescribed in detail how they should be washed: hands had to be lifted up so the water would run down to the wrist, then each had to be rubbed in a prescribed way. If the hands were "defiled" then two washings were necessary, the first with the hands elevated, the second with the hands depressed (Alfred Edersheim, *Life and Times of Jesus the Messiah*).

Jesus was blunt with these hypocrites. They had substituted their manmade traditions for the Scriptures, teaching them as doctrines. The commandment to honor father and mother, for instance, was judiciously sidestepped. When a Pharisee saw his aged parents coming to him for help, he quickly pronounced "Corban" on all his belongings. When they approached him he told them everything he had was "devoted to God" and could not be employed for secular use. And he turned his parents away. He had substituted the Word of God with his man-made tradition.

Gathering the multitudes together, Jesus explained the source of the problem: the heart. He reminded them it was not what entered into the mouth that defiled them. The heart—the center and source of thought, feeling, and decision—was the problem. From the evil heart comes evil thoughts, murders, adulteries . . . that is the problem. Unwashed hands are not the problem.

Thankfully, Jesus Christ can give us a new heart when we trust Him as our sin-bearer on the cross and volitionally, consciously trust Him. At that point Christ gives us a new heart, transforming our thought life now to please Him, no longer seeking justification through legalism.

CONSIDER: *Do you have any belief or practice that supplants biblical truth and teaching?*

CHRIST ACCEPTED BY GENTILES

MATTHEW 15:21–28; MARK 7:24–30

Then Jesus said to her, "O woman, your faith is great;
it shall be done for you as you wish." And her
daughter was healed at once. (Matthew 15:28)

Reflecting Israel's rejection of Messiah, Jesus performed three miracles in Gentile territory, revealing the transition from Israel to the Gentiles. Jesus departed for the region of Tyre and Sidon, major Canaanite cities lying on the Mediterranean coast, some thirty to fifty miles northwest of the Sea of Galilee.

The news of Jesus' ministry had obviously spread to this Gentile region, as we see from the Canaanite woman's dramatic approach. The very name "Canaanite" is a reminder that the one now seeking help from Jesus descended from the very people the Israelites had displaced. The Canaanites were heathen *to the core, reflected in every aspect of their lives lived in uncleanness and immorality.*

As she approached Jesus, she called Him, "Son of David," a distinct messianic title. She demonstrated remarkable faith since she was a pagan Gentile, from the heart of Gentile territory. It is unlikely that she had ever heard Jesus in person but she had certainly heard of Him and now came to believe in Him as the Messiah.

Jesus' response, "I was sent only to the lost sheep of the house of Israel" (Matt. 15:24) is a reminder that Jesus came as Israel's Messiah. National blessings for the Gentile people cannot come until Israel first recognizes her Messiah (as prophesied in Zechariah 12:10–14), then Gentile nations will also partake of the messianic blessings (Zech. 14:16–19).

But the Gentile woman had faith. She recognized that she was a Gentile but reminded Jesus that even household pet dogs receive a benefit from the master's house.

Although Jesus' language sounds harsh, "the distinction between 'dogs' . . . and 'children' of 'masters' emphasizes precedence only: the children get their food first, the household dogs afterward" (David Hill, *The Gospel of Matthew*). The children were to eat before the household dogs; in other words, Israel was to first believe in Jesus as Messiah before blessings would be poured out on the Gentiles. The word used here for dogs (*kunaria*) is not derogatory; it refers to household pets, not street scavengers.

The Lord commended the woman for her faith and He healed her daughter. The incident is a stark reminder of the contrast between the unbelief of Israel—though having seen and heard the Messiah—and the faith of this pagan Canaanite woman.

CONSIDER: *Those who are privileged in society and have heard the good news but have scorned it are overshadowed by the lowly, humble, and destitute who have been receptive to the good news and have eagerly responded to the call of Christ.*

March 4

JESUS MINISTERS TO THE GENTILES

MATTHEW 15:29–38; MARK 7:31–8:9

The crowd marveled as they saw the mute speaking, the
crippled restored, and the lame walking, and the blind seeing;
and they glorified the God of Israel. (Matthew 15:31)

Leaving the Mediterranean coastal cities of Tyre and Sidon, Jesus embarked on a circuitous journey to the Decapolis region, the cities southeast of the Sea of Galilee. This was Gentile territory. It appears also that Jesus avoided the northern shore of the Sea of Galilee to abstain from further contact with the multitudes who had a false motive in attempting to make Him king and also to avoid further encounter with the religious leaders (Louis Barbieri, *Mark*).

When Jesus was met by a deaf man with unclear speech, Jesus put His fingers in the man's ears and then spit and touched the man's tongue. The Gospels evidence that there was no uniform method that Jesus used to heal. But there were reasons why He healed the way He did. It was necessary that the Gentiles would understand He was indeed the Messiah. "The use of the Lord's fingers and saliva emphasized the truth that the healing power proceeded from His own person" (Barclay Swete, *Gospel According to St. Mark*). Immediately, the man began to speak with clarity. It was evident to the Gentiles what Jesus had done. He had healed the man. They were shocked beyond measure.

At the same time, people brought the lame, crippled, blind, and mute to Jesus and He healed them. The Gentiles recognized the uniqueness of Jesus and they praised the God of Israel. Acclaim was coming to Messiah from the Gentiles—but it should have first come from Israel. Jesus had come as the Messiah from the Jewish people.

When Jesus saw the multitudes He had compassion on them because they had nothing to eat. The disciples were with Jesus and had seen Him work in the past—had they learned anything? Astonishingly, they exhibited unbelief. Why? Couldn't Jesus work in a Gentile territory? Although this was the second time Jesus had miraculously fed a crowd, perhaps they still thought that as Israel's Messiah He could only work for the Hebrew people. Jesus took seven loaves and a few small fish and fed the multitudes and they all ate their fill. Seven large baskets of leftovers remained as a reminder of the event. Jesus' ministry was a reminder that in the kingdom there will be blessings for both Jews and Gentiles. Everyone will enjoy both health and an abundant provision from Jesus Christ the Messiah. And everyone—Jew and Gentile alike—will give praise to God.

CONSIDER: *Jesus' ministry is not restricted by nationality or ethnicity—but He is restricted when people exhibit a lack of faith.*

JESUS CONFRONTS THE RELIGIOUS LEADERS

MATTHEW 15:39–16:12; MARK 8:10–21

"Watch out and beware of the leaven of the
Pharisees and Sadducees." (Matthew 16:6)

A pastor in England preached a series of messages on "Things I Don't Believe." Then he proceeded to preach—denying the virgin birth of Jesus Christ, His deity, His substitutionary atonement, His bodily resurrection, and other major doctrines. Of course, the tragedy of His doctrinally erroneous sermons was that he was leading people astray. Probably unsuspecting people.

Crossing the Sea of Galilee, Jesus came to Magadan, in the district of Dalmanutha, on the western side of the Sea of Galilee. When He arrived, He was confronted by the Pharisees and Sadducees—ironic indeed, since these two religious groups hated each other. But through their common rejection of Jesus, they united against Him. Their motive is immediately evident, since they came to Jesus, "testing Him" and demanding a "sign from heaven" (Matt. 16:1). Perhaps they were asking Him to duplicate Elijah's calling down fire from heaven.

Where had they been? Jesus had performed many signs. Since they had rejected the many obvious messianic signs Jesus had performed (notice the fulfillment of Isaiah 35:5–6 in passages such as Matthew 11:5; 12:22; and Luke 7:21), He refused to give them any further signs. But He would give them the ultimate sign: the sign of Jonah—the sign of Jesus' death and resurrection (Matt. 16:21; 17:23). In being in the belly of the fish, Jonah served as a type of Christ, prefiguring Jesus' death and resurrection three days later.

Crossing the sea to Bethsaida on the northwestern shore, the disciples realized they had forgotten to take bread with them. Jesus warned them, "Watch out and beware of the leaven of the Pharisees and Sadducees" (Matt. 16:6). The disciples were slow to understand; they thought Jesus rebuked them because they had not taken bread with them. When Jesus explained that He meant the teaching of the Pharisees and Sadducees, then the disciples understood. It was the Pharisees and Sadducees that led the nation away from following Jesus and accepting Him as their Messiah. Their leaven—their false teaching—captivated the hearts of many and ultimately led to the destruction of the nation of Israel.

CONSIDER: *Are you under faithful, biblical teaching that is in accord with Scripture, or are you being captivated and led astray by modern Pharisees and Sadducees?*

March 6

PETER'S CONFESSION OF CHRIST
MATTHEW 16:13–20; MARK 8:27–30; LUKE 9:18–21

*Simon Peter answered, "You are the Christ, the
Son of the living God." (Matthew 16:16)*

Who is Jesus? He made enormous claims yet the nation of Israel did not receive Him. What was going on in the minds of the disciples? Had they been wrong in following Him? Were the religious leaders and the masses right? After all, He had been rejected in Nazareth, by King Herod, and by the scribes, Pharisees, and Sadducees. What were the disciples to believe?

Jesus took the Twelve to Caesarea Philippi, in Gentile territory near the base of Mount Hermon. Jesus knew the hearts of the disciples, so He pointedly asked, "Who do people say that the Son of Man is?" (Matt. 16:13). Jesus wanted them to solidify the answer in their minds. "John the Baptist . . . Elijah . . . Jeremiah . . . one of the prophets," they responded (v. 14). But to provoke them personally, Jesus challenged them, "But who do *you* say that I am?" (v. 15, emphasis added).

Simon Peter rose to the occasion: "You are the Christ, the Son of the living God," he exclaimed. It was a bold confession, recognizing Jesus as the Anointed One of God, the Messiah. Through His miracles and His teaching, Peter recognized Jesus as the Messiah and boldly confessed Him as the King who was to come and establish God's kingdom and rule over the nations (Ps. 2).

The Lord acknowledged Peter's confession, saying, "You are Peter, and upon this rock I will build My church; and the gates of Hades will not overpower it" (Matt. 16:18). What was Jesus saying? There is a play on words: The name *Peter* is the Greek word *petros*, which means a building stone, and the word *rock* is the Greek *petra*, which means a large mass of rock, a quarry. Peter is (as the other apostles are) a building stone, laying the foundation of the church (Eph. 2:20) but Christ is the cornerstone, the rock base (1 Cor. 3:11; Matt. 7:24–27) upon which the church is built. This church (composed of all believers since Pentecost) will endure; the gates of Hades, signifying death, will not prevail against it. The resurrected Christ has triumphed—and Christ's church will prevail to the end.

CONSIDER: *In light of world events and the hostility against Christianity, it is a great comfort to know that death will never overtake the true church, even as it did not triumph against the One who was raised from the dead.*

PREDICTION OF CHRIST'S DEATH AND RESURRECTION

MATTHEW 16:21–28; MARK 8:31–9:1; LUKE 9:22–27

---

*From that time Jesus began to show His disciples that He
must go to Jerusalem, and suffer many things from the elders
and chief priests and scribes, and be killed, and be raised
up on the third day. (Matthew 16:21)*

None of us knows what tomorrow holds.

"From that time" infers a transition in the life of Christ. He has demonstrated through His words and works that He is the Messiah but He has been rejected. The kingdom will be held in abeyance; now, instead of reigning, He will go to the cross.

Jesus evidences His deity in that He knows the precise details concerning His own future. Think of it: Christ knew that the events would occur in Jerusalem, that He would first suffer intensely and then be killed. He knew the Sanhedrin would be responsible for it. He also knew that He would rise from the dead and that it would occur on the third day.

The same Peter who rose to testify to Jesus' preeminent position now regressed and admonished Jesus, "This shall never happen to You" (Matt. 16:22). With that Peter received the Lord's stern rebuke, "Get behind Me, Satan; for you are not setting your mind on God's interests, but man's" (Mark 8:33). Man's interest was to preserve life; God's interest was for the Son of God to make atonement for the sins of the world. Certainly, Satan would attempt to interfere with God's program and prevent God's salvation plan for humanity.

Jesus expanded His explanation: "If anyone wishes to come after Me, he must deny himself, and take up his cross and follow Me" (v. 34). What was the cross? It was the symbol of humiliation and rejection. To take up the cross meant to suffer ridicule in being identified with Christ.

Jesus' next statement was similar: "Whoever wishes to save his life will lose it, but whoever loses his life for My sake and the gospel's will save it" (v. 35). The love of this world will cause the loss of one's soul, but rejection of the world and its philosophy will be eternal gain through finding true life in Jesus Christ.

CONSIDER: *Are you willing to be identified, even humiliated, in identification with Christ? It is only as you lose your life in Christ and for Christ that you truly gain life and truly find it.*

March 8

TRANSFIGURATION OF JESUS

MATTHEW 17:1–13; MARK 9:2–13; LUKE 9:28–36

And He was transfigured before them; and His face shone like the sun, and His garments became as white as light. (Matthew 17:2)

Albert Schweitzer was confused about Jesus' statement in Matthew 16:28 that some of those standing with Him would not taste death until they saw the Son of Man coming in His kingdom. As a result, he concluded that Jesus had a messianic complex, falsely thinking He would inaugurate the kingdom. It was Schweitzer who was false.

The prediction of Matthew 16:28 is fulfilled in the transfiguration of Jesus. Peter had just confessed Christ as the Son of the living God; now Peter and the other two would see Christ transfigured before them—verifying Peter's testimony. It would reveal that Jesus is indeed the eternal God, the second person of the Trinity.

As Peter, James, and John went up the mountain with Jesus, He was transfigured (*metamorphothe*) before them. The word *metamorphosis* is derived from this Greek word and means a change of form that is outwardly visible. The glory of God shone forth—the eternal glory that Jesus always had with the Father (John 17:5)—as further evidence of Jesus' deity. Jesus' radiance and the Father speaking from the cloud are reminiscent of God's presence with Israel in the wilderness, both as a pillar of fire and a cloud (Exod. 13:22).

Moses and Elijah appeared, talking with Jesus. Moses is representative of the Old Testament Law while Elijah is representative of the Old Testament prophets; Moses symbolized those who went to heaven through death while Elijah represented those who would enter heaven without dying. Peter immediately recognized the significance of this event; he wanted to build three tabernacles to celebrate the Feast of Tabernacles (or Feast of Booths; see Leviticus 23:34–43), a festival which remembered God's protection of the Israelites in the wilderness while it anticipated the return and rule of Messiah in the kingdom.

The Father's voice from heaven validated Jesus as the Messiah, the Son of God, even though the religious leaders and masses had rejected Him. It also likely encouraged the disciples and further validated their trust in Jesus.

CONSIDER: *Though the majority of people may not acknowledge Jesus as the Son of God, His transfiguration and the Father's testimony are a reminder of the certitude of His claims.*

March 9

CHRIST HEALS THE DEMONIAC BOY

MATTHEW 17:14–23; MARK 9:14–32; LUKE 9:37–45

"Truly I say to you, if you have faith the size of a mustard seed, you will say to this mountain, 'Move from here to there,' and it will move; and nothing will be impossible to you." (Matthew 17:20)

Frequently, when we have had a spiritual high, we are confronted by an insurmountable difficulty—and our faith is challenged. So it was with Peter, James, and John. They had just experienced seeing the kingdom in miniature at the transfiguration of Jesus. Then, coming down from the mountain, they were confronted by a different scene. A large crowd had gathered and the scribes were arguing with the other disciples. A boy, who was demon possessed, was suffering intensely. The demons would cause convulsions in the boy, throwing the boy into the fire and water. When the disciples attempted to heal the boy, they were unable.

Jesus had strong words of rebuke, but for whom? He rebuked the "unbelieving and perverted generation"—the unbelieving people in general who saw the messianic signs but refused to believe. But Jesus also rebuked the nine disciples for their lack of faith. They had been given power and authority to heal (Matt. 10:7–8), but they failed to appropriate the power that Jesus had delegated to them. And this was not their first failure and exhibition of a lack of faith (Matt. 14:16–17, 26).

When they brought the boy to Jesus, He questioned the father. The father told Jesus that the boy had possessed the evil spirit from childhood. Jesus reminded the father that "All things are possible to him who believes" (Mark 9:23). The father exhibited humility amid faith, crying out, "I do believe; help my unbelief" (v. 24).

With simply a word, Jesus rebuked the demon, commanding him to come out of the boy. Jesus merely spoke and the demon had to obey. The demon came out immediately. Jesus demonstrated His messiahship and His authority over the realm of Satan. In the kingdom, Jesus will exercise authority over every realm, including Satan's realm.

It is a sobering realization that, like the disciples, we may fail our Savior by failing to trust Him after committing our problems and needs to Him. The Lord has called us to walk by faith.

CONSIDER: *What area of your life do you need to commit to Christ and walk by faith, entirely trusting Him to resolve the issue that you are hopeless to solve?*

JESUS TEACHES CONCERNING SONSHIP, HUMILITY, AND PRIDE

MATTHEW 17:24–18:14; MARK 9:33–50; LUKE 9:46–50

"Unless you are converted and become like children, you will not enter the kingdom of heaven. Whoever then humbles himself as this child, he is the greatest in the kingdom of heaven." (Matthew 18:3–4)

Every fisherman loves telling an unusual fishing story—and the Lord gave Peter the fishing story of all fishing stories. At Capernaum the tax collectors challenged Peter, assuming Jesus did not pay the two-drachma tax paid by all Jewish males. Jesus explained to Peter that kings taxed the people but not their own sons; since Jesus is the Son of God, He is exempt from the tax. Nonetheless, Jesus paid the tax in a most unique way. He told Peter to throw a hook into the sea, take the first fish he caught, open its mouth and take out a stater, a coin equivalent to four drachmas, the precise tax for both Jesus and Peter! What a fishing venture! It reflects the omniscience of Jesus—He knew there was a fish that had swallowed a stater; it also reflects the omnipotence of Jesus—He forced that particular fish to bite Peter's hook. What a Savior!

During this time Jesus had been showing them who He was—the unique Son of God. But He also had been reminding them of the sober truth that He would be betrayed, and killed, but then raised from the dead (Matt. 17:22–23). His words captured them for a moment but then they were back to their favorite subject: who would be greatest in the kingdom of heaven! In His omniscience, Jesus knew what they had been discussing so He placed a child in their midst and explained true greatness: it was becoming like this child; it was being "last of all and servant of all" (Mark 9:35). He was teaching them humility.

The lesson didn't stop there. When they saw others serving Christ, they adopted a sectarian, partisan spirit. Jesus rebuked them for their prideful spirit. They still had not learned the lessons of our Lord. Jesus used strong language in warning them not to offend others, especially new believers. Using metaphorical language of cutting off a hand or foot, Jesus was telling the Twelve to remove the offence that was hindering them spiritually—in this case, pride.

CONSIDER: *Unquestionably we are no different than the disciples, as readily capable of pride as they were. Is there any element of pride in your heart that you need to eliminate?*

March 11

JESUS TEACHES CONCERNING FORGIVENESS

MATTHEW 18:15–35

Jesus said to him, "I do not say to you, up to seven times, but up to seventy times seven." (Matthew 18:22)

A woman wrote "Dear Abby" after she had been married ten years and her fourth child was born. Her husband told her he didn't love her anymore and left her. She gained forty-seven pounds, got hooked on tranquilizers, and suffered a mental breakdown. Her husband put her in a mental institution and had an affair with her best friend. He later told his wife he planned to drive her to commit suicide. When she was released, her husband came back but then went back to his girlfriend. She lost her house, and her children despaired. One day her husband left his girlfriend and came home. His wife forgave him and took him back, and she also forgave her friend.

Forgiveness. It is a major issue in life. Jesus instructed His followers concerning forgiveness. First, the offended party is to confront the one who has sinned against him privately. He is to be made aware of his fault to produce conviction. It is good if it is resolved at this point, but if not, then the offended party is to take two or three witnesses in order to prevent a my-word-against-your-word scenario. If he still fails to listen, the matter is to be brought to the church. If the person remains unrepentant, refusing to respond when his sin is told to the church, he is to be excommunicated and treated like an unbeliever (Matt. 18:17).

When believers confront a sinner about his sin, seeking his restoration, they pray in unity about the issue (vv. 19–20). Agreeing in prayer, they are in unity in recognizing the unrepentant person's sin and the need to excommunicate him from the fellowship.

But, Peter asked, how often should a person forgive someone? Seven times? The rabbis taught that it was necessary to forgive someone only three times, based on Amos 1:3, 6. Jesus answered Peter, "I do not say to you, up to seven times, but up to seventy times seven." Peter went beyond the norm. But Jesus taught that forgiveness was to be innumerable. Limitless. We forgive others countless times because God has forgiven us far more than we will ever forgive others. To illustrate the importance of forgiveness, Jesus told a parable of a man who owed an insurmountable debt and was forgiven. But he then failed to forgive a fellow slave a small debt.

Forgiveness lies at the center of Christian living. God has forgiven us much—we *must* forgive others. Whom do you need to forgive today? Should you go to a person, make a phone call, or write a letter to someone? Resolve it *today*.

CONSIDER: *Forgiveness characterizes a kingdom citizen. Since God has forgiven you much, you are obligated to forgive others.*

March 12

CHRIST CREATES CONTROVERSY
JOHN 7:2–31

There was much grumbling among the crowds concerning
Him; some were saying, "He is a good man"; others were saying,
"No, on the contrary, He leads the people astray." (John 7:12)

A t a New York meeting in which Christopher Hitchens, author of *God Is Not Great*, moderated a panel discussion for the opening of *Chicago 10*. Discussing the Vietnam-era documentary film, *MTV News'* Suchin Pak noted that young people today are not as passionately antiwar as their counterparts were in the Vietnam era. Hitchens exclaimed, "I really hate to hear that the young are becoming more Christian. If that's true, that's the worst news of the night!" (*World*, Mar. 22/29, 2008). Jesus Christ creates controversy—He did so while ministering on this earth and His name continues to create controversy today.

With the approach of the Feast of Tabernacles, Jesus' half-brothers challenged Him to go to Jerusalem and openly display His messiahship to the people. But the request was not genuine; it was ridicule and rejection. John explains, "For not even His brothers were believing in Him" (John 7:5).

Jesus did go up to the feast but not in the way his brothers demanded. His presence immediately created controversy. The Jewish leaders were looking for Jesus but with ill intent. Others, likely pilgrims who had not been negatively affected by the residents of Jerusalem, recognized His goodness. Still others thought He was leading the people astray. What did Jesus do? He challenged them to a test. Did they really want to know the truth? If they really wanted to do God's will, they would discover whether Jesus was speaking from God or simply as a man. They would realize that He was seeking God's glory—that was the issue—in stark contrast to the religious leaders who sought glory for themselves.

As Jesus continued to teach, the controversy continued. Some concluded that they knew where Jesus came from; therefore He couldn't be the Christ. These, in fact, sought to kill Him. Yet others recognized the significance of the signs that Jesus performed—they were messianic—and many believed in Him. So response to Jesus' ministry resulted in some believing in Him while others vented their hatred and rejection. And the controversy continues—into the twenty-first century. Do not be surprised when atheists write books against Christ and Christians.

CONSIDER: *Do you sincerely want to know the truth? Come to Christ—read the biblical record of His teaching and discover the truth of who He is.*

March 13

The Invitation of Christ

John 7:32–52

"If anyone is thirsty, let him come to Me and drink. He who believes in Me, as the Scripture said, 'From his innermost being will flow rivers of living water.'" (John 7:37–38)

I once heard a story about the pitcher of a baseball team that had just won the World Series. After the thrill of winning, he supposedly went on a drinking binge in celebration. Riding home depressed in a cab he exclaimed to the taxi driver: "Is that all there is? I thought winning the World Series was God." He was disillusioned. And he was thirsty—only he didn't realize what, or rather *who*, he was thirsty for. Jesus is the only one who can slake the thirst of people.

Contention with the religious leaders continued as they sought to arrest Jesus; in fact, it united the Pharisees and Sadducees against Him. Recognizing His imminent death, Jesus told the people of His departure—but they misunderstood Him.

Multitudes of pilgrims and locals had gathered for "the great day of the feast" (John 7:37), the last day of the Feast of Tabernacles. Booths built of branches would have been seen throughout Jerusalem, typifying living in Messiah's kingdom. A priest would lead a procession to the pool of Siloam to fill a golden pitcher with water and, amid music and singing, he would return to the altar and pour the water into a silver funnel beside the altar. The people would begin chanting the Hallel (Pss. 113–118), concluding with Psalm 118:25–26: "O Lord, do save, we beseech You; O Lord, we beseech You, do send prosperity! Blessed is the one who comes in the name of the Lord" (Alfred Edersheim, *The Temple*).

The entire event signaled Messiah's blessings in the coming kingdom. At this climactic moment Jesus stood and shouted, "If anyone is thirsty, let him come to Me and drink. He who believes in Me, as the Scripture said, 'From his innermost being will flow rivers of living water'" (John 7:37–38). Jesus was declaring that the purpose of the Feast of Tabernacles—with the booths and the ritual of pouring out water—was all fulfilled in Him. He is the promised Messiah! Moreover, the thirsty pilgrims who would come to Jesus and drink— believing in Him—would have their thirst quenched.

The people were shaken. Some responded while others rejected Him. Yet the provision for slaking their thirst was available. Are you thirsty today? Are you attempting to quench your thirst in materialism, in the world? It will never happen. Come to Jesus and drink. He will *forever* quench your spiritual thirst.

CONSIDER: *Jesus alone can quench your thirst so you will never be thirsty again.*

THE LIGHT OF THE WORLD

JOHN 8:12–59

---

*"I am the Light of the world; he who follows Me will not walk
in the darkness, but will have the Light of life." (John 8:12)*

During the Feast of Tabernacles the candelabra, which stood seventy-five feet high, was lit in the Court of Women ("the treasury," John 8:20), illuminating the entire city and countryside. Since Jerusalem was located on the central hill country, some 2,500 feet above sea level, at night the light emanating from Jerusalem could be seen at a great distance. It reminded people that the light—the truth—came from Jerusalem. The Feast of Tabernacles with the brilliant candelabra was prophetic of Messiah's reign in the millennial kingdom, bringing light to all the nations.

When Jesus spoke the dramatic words, "I am the Light of the world," He proclaimed that He is the spiritual light-giver to the world. Isaiah foretold Messiah as the light to both Jews and Gentiles (Isa. 9:1–2). "The Light was a Jewish title of Messiah" (J. W. Shepard, *Christ of the Gospels*). Further, in continually emphasizing "I AM," Jesus was boldly announcing both His deity and His messiahship.

The people understood His claims and challenged Him, but He reminded them that His witness was not alone; the Father also bore witness to Him (John 8:18). But the burden lay with the Jews. If they refused to believe in Him, they would die in their sins. Jesus dramatically continued to reference His deity in "I AM" statements (vv. 24, 28, 58). The Jews were facing the Messiah! He had come as God incarnate and would make atonement for sin—and His was the only solution to the problem of sin. And that would be evidenced when He would be lifted up on the cross (v. 28). Some expressed a superficial belief in Him but Jesus reminded them that the genuineness of their belief and discipleship would be evidenced by their remaining in His word. They quickly revealed that their faith was not genuine. They based their hope on being Abraham's offspring and soon engaged Jesus in debate, finally threatening to kill Him (v. 40) and slurred His birth by inferring He was born of fornication (v. 41) and was a Samaritan and demon-posssessed (v. 48). Yet no one had ever identified sin in His life (v. 46)—He was sinless.

What a tragedy! These people had heard His words and seen His works. He was the promised Messiah! He was God incarnate. He offered them the light of truth through which they would never see death (v. 51); but, influenced by the religious leaders, they rejected the Light of the world. Could there be a greater tragedy?

CONSIDER: *Jesus takes us out of the darkness of sin and enables us to walk in the light of truth in fellowship with Him.*

March 15

CHRIST HEALS THE BLIND MAN

JOHN 9:1–41

And he said, "Lord, I believe." And he worshiped Him. (John 9:38)

Blindness is a tragic human condition—yet God can use even this serious ailment to His glory. Though blinded in infancy through a medical doctor's faulty procedure, Fanny Crosby went on to write some 8,000 hymns to the glory of God. When Jesus gave sight to the blind man in today's Scripture reading, the man went on to worship Jesus and to boldly confront the hypocritical Pharisees.

Giving sight to the blind also has spiritual overtones—it is more than physical healing. In John 8, the Jews who should have had spiritual insight rejected the Messiah who came as the light of the world. They had physical sight but they were spiritually blind. Now, a man, who was both physically and spiritually blind, received both physical and spiritual sight.

Why was he blind? The rabbis suggested he could have sinned in his mother's womb or he had sinned in a previous existence or his parents' sins were being passed on to him (Homer Kent Jr., *Light in the Darkness*). Jesus explained that neither he nor his parents caused the blindness by their sin; rather, it was an opportunity for God to work. So Jesus spat on the ground, made clay, and anointed the blind man's eyes with it, and then he told the blind man to go and wash in the pool of Siloam. And the man came back seeing!

Immediately a conflict arose. Jesus had healed on the Sabbath. Some recognized the miracle; others rejected it as not coming from God because it occurred on the Sabbath. The Pharisees approached the man's parents, but, in their cowardice, his parents refused to answer. When the Pharisees approached the healed man he challenged them: "You do not want to become His disciples too, do you?" (John 9:27). He recognized the uniqueness of receiving sight—it had never occurred in past history. The Pharisees were indignant—and they excommunicated him from the synagogue. Later, when Jesus met him, the man recognized who Jesus was and exclaimed, "Lord, I believe" (v. 38). And he worshiped Jesus. He had received *both* physical and spiritual sight.

CONSIDER: *Jesus came as the light of the world to give spiritual sight to the spiritually blind.*

March 16

CHRIST, THE GOOD SHEPHERD

JOHN 10:1–21

---

*"I am the good shepherd; the good shepherd lays
down His life for the sheep." (John 10:11)*

While in the countryside in Israel, we saw a shepherd with a flock of sheep. The shepherd was carrying a lamb in his arms. "What a tender shepherd!" someone exclaimed. But when the shepherd saw us, he immediately grasped the lamb by its hind legs and held it up in ridicule. He was not a good shepherd.

Throughout His ministry, Jesus had a conflict with the religious leaders of His day; they opposed Him and His ministry. In this stalwart speech Jesus made a dramatic statement: "I am the good shepherd." He was bringing a myriad of Old Testament prophecies to the forefront, identifying Himself as the fulfillment of the beautiful Twenty-third Psalm and other passages, such as Isaiah 40:11; Jeremiah 23:1; and Ezekiel 34:11. When Jesus described Himself as the True Shepherd, He set Himself against the Pharisees who pretended to be the shepherds of Israel—but they were impostors.

In this extended metaphor, the shepherd is Jesus, the fold is Israel, the doorkeeper is John the Baptist, the thief represents the Pharisees, the sheep are believers, the strangers are the Pharisees, the one flock is the church, and the door is Jesus.

Jesus, the Good Shepherd, came to the sheepfold by entering the door, probably a reference to the virgin birth of Jesus (Homer Kent Jr., *Light in the Darkness*). The shepherd knows the names of His sheep and calls them by their names. What a phenomenal comfort—He knows us by name! The sheep, the true followers of Christ, would not respond to the voice of the Pharisees, the false shepherds, but would only listen to the voice of the True Shepherd (John 10:5).

"I am the door," Jesus proclaimed (v. 7); He was referring to salvation. He is the entrance that leads to salvation. There is no other door. In each of these statements, Jesus exclaimed with the decisive "I AM" referencing His deity (as in Exodus 3:14). It was a dramatic and forceful claim.

But as the Good Shepherd, Jesus would lay down His life for the sheep (John 10:11); moreover, He did it willingly. No one could take His life from Him. He had the *authority* (*exousia*) both to lay his life down and to take it up again (v. 18). He had complete authority over His life—but as the Good Shepherd He willingly chose to go to the cross to resolve the dilemma of sin for the human race.

CONSIDER: *Jesus—and He alone—is the door that leads to salvation and the Good Shepherd who makes atonement for sin, providing eternal life for His people.*

March 17

Witness of the Seventy

LUKE 10:1–24

"The kingdom of God has come near to you." (Luke 10:9)

It was getting late. It was fall, A.D. 32—only six months before the crucifixion. Jesus had come as Israel's Messiah but, for Him to reign as King, the people had to respond and receive Him as their Messiah. The Twelve had faithfully proclaimed the message throughout the land but now Jesus sent out seventy others, in a short, swift mission proclaiming Jesus as the Messiah.

Would the people respond? The time was critical. The leaders had already rejected Christ (Matt. 12). Now the seventy announced, "The kingdom of God has come near to you." But how did the people know? The Lord gave the seventy authority to perform the messianic miracles, validating their message. Messiah had come! If the people responded, they would receive the messengers and Messiah's peace would come upon the house.

But what if they failed to respond? Greater judgment would come upon them because they had received greater revelation and greater knowledge. They would be rejected, symbolized by the seventy shaking the dust off their feet. It would remind them that since they had rejected the Messiah, Messiah would reject them.

It is a reminder that there is a greater judgment on those who have received a greater revelation. The cities of Chorazin, Bethsaida, and Capernaum—those privileged cities near the Sea of Galilee that had seen the Savior's miracles and heard His preaching—their judgment would be greater than the pagan cities of Tyre and Sidon. Had those Gentile cities seen the miracles the Galileans had seen, they would have responded in repentance and faith.

Yet many common people did respond to the proclamation of the seventy. In fact, when they returned and reported to Jesus, He told them He saw Satan fall from heaven (v. 18). This revelation anticipated Satan's defeat at the cross as well as His ultimate defeat when he will be cast out of heaven during the tribulation (Rev. 12:9) and thrown into the abyss (20:1–3).

Jesus reminded them of their blessed estate in seeing and hearing the Messiah. They were privileged. And so are we when we read the Scriptures and trust Jesus implicitly.

CONSIDER: *Greater revelation demands greater response. There is a greater judgment on those who have received greater information and knowledge of Christ.*

March 18

THE GOOD SAMARITAN

LUKE 10:25–37

---

*"YOU SHALL LOVE THE LORD YOUR GOD WITH ALL YOUR HEART,
AND WITH ALL YOUR SOUL, AND WITH ALL YOUR STRENGTH, AND WITH
ALL YOUR MIND; AND YOUR NEIGHBOR AS YOURSELF." (Luke 10:27)*

I asked a man, "How do you hope to get to heaven?" "I'm a good person," he replied. "I'm a faithful husband and I've never harmed anyone." He was basing his hope of heaven on good works.

The Pharisees developed their own interpretation of the Mosaic Law and they expected to gain eternal life by it. But the purpose of the Law was not for gaining eternal life; it was to show the redeemed of the Old Testament how to live. Justification is by grace through faith in every age, including the Old Testament (as seen in Genesis 15:6; Psalm 32:1–2; and Habakkuk 2:4). But the Law would reveal who was a redeemed believer—that person would want to live by the Law.

The lawyer who came to Jesus, testing Him, was one who had studied the Law and interpreted and expounded it for the people. The lawyers also taught the law in the schools and synagogues. This lawyer came to Jesus with a wrong motive; he thought he had to "do" something to gain eternal life. When Jesus quizzed the lawyer, he correctly stated the summation of the Law: love God and love your neighbor. It is the summation of the 613 Levitical laws.

When Jesus responded, "do this and you will live" (Luke 10:28), Jesus was not agreeing with a works salvation. Jesus knew the man had not kept the law; He knew the law would condemn the man. When the lawyer attempted to justify himself with the query, "who is my neighbor?" Jesus told him the story of the good Samaritan. In the parable, Jesus answered the man's question and showed him the futility of attempting to achieve salvation through the law. In the parable, the priest and the Levite did not respond to help their neighbor in need. They failed to love their neighbor. By their determination to avoid breaking the law by not defiling themselves, they broke the command to love one's neighbor (Lev. 19:18). Jesus showed them they could not attain eternal life by "doing." By contrast, the despised Samaritan—who was of a mixed race—demonstrated the reality of his salvation by helping the wounded man.

CONSIDER: *Salvation is always by grace through faith and when we love God and love our neighbor, we demonstrate the reality of our salvation.*

Conflict with the Pharisees

Luke 11:14–54

*"He who is not with Me is against Me; and he who
does not gather with Me, scatters." (Luke 11:23)*

O ur adversary, the devil, will always oppose the truth and he does that through people and false religious systems. Although they saw His miracles, the religious leaders of Jesus' day refused to acknowledge Jesus as the Messiah. They led the people in opposition to Him.

This incident is similar to Matthew 12 yet it is a different event, occurring a year later. Further, the event of Matthew 12 occurred in Galilee while this episode occurred in Judea. When Jesus cast the demon out of a mute man, he was able to speak. The people marveled, but some accused Him of casting out demons by Beelzebul, the ruler of demons. It was a blasphemous accusation. Jesus' rebuttal (Luke 11:17–23) was similar to His earlier words. He had stern words for the onlookers. If they had heard His words and seen His works and yet rejected Him, they were in danger of coming to a more devastating end than before (vv. 24–26).

Later, when a Pharisee invited Jesus to lunch with him and Jesus neglected to wash His hands in Pharisaic ceremonial fashion, it revealed the hypocrisy of Pharisaic ritualism. Jesus went on to expose their hypocrisy: they stressed the outward but neglected the inward. Jesus denounced both the Pharisees and the lawyers—the interpreters of Scripture. He introduced His denunciations with "woe," an interjection expressing pain and lament (Horst Balz and Gerhard Schneider, eds., *Exegetical Dictionary of the New Testament*). Jesus denounced the Pharisees because:

They failed in justice and love of God. They meticulously tithed their vegetables but neglected others, which exhibited their depraved heart.
They loved preeminence, enjoying the prominent seats in the synagogue.
They misled the people. Tombs were marked because they were considered a source of defilement. Like an unmarked tomb, the Pharisees misled the people, so that people were defiled without realizing it.
They burdened the people with their excessive and minute laws of tradition.
They were guilty in killing the prophets. In rejecting Christ, the Jewish leaders revealed the same attitude as those that had killed the prophets.
They hindered the people's knowledge of God, leading others to reject Christ.

What somber words of denunciation for these false teachers who led the people away from Jesus!

CONSIDER: *The heart is at the center of all that we do. To live right, our heart must be right. Is your heart right?*

March 20

Instruction on Hypocrisy and Coveting
Luke 12:1–34

"Where your treasure is, there your heart will be also." (Luke 12:34)

In movies and television programs actors perform a role of someone other than who they really are. They are actors. It is a performance. It is not reality. That is what the Pharisees did in their religious performances. It was an act, not reality.

Jesus warned the disciples concerning the hypocrisy of the Pharisees, referring to it as leaven—it had a permeating influence upon the masses—it spread. Yet Jesus reminded the disciples that the hidden motives, the hypocrisy, would one day be revealed. That is a serious, solemn thought for everyone.

Because of the Pharisees' influence, persecution against Jesus' followers would result. But Jesus encouraged the disciples not to fear the ones who could only kill the body; they should fear God because a greater tragedy could occur—God has the power to cast into hell. Despite persecution, Jesus' followers can live without worry because God cares for them. He knows the number of hairs on their head—they can rest in His sovereign care for them. Their only concern should be to openly confess Christ—then He will also confess them before the angels in heaven.

Since the Pharisees were lovers of money, Jesus warned the disciples concerning greed—life does not consist in one's possessions. In a parable, Jesus told of a rich man who built larger barns to store his grain and his goods. He had enough wealth for many years of enjoyment; he could eat, drink, and be merry. But that very night God took his soul. He was a fool because he left God out of the equation. He was rich toward himself but not toward God.

But there is an opposite of greed: worry. Perhaps the disciples didn't exhibit greed and therefore didn't possess many worldly goods. But their neglect of material things could cause them to worry because they lacked basic necessities. So Jesus instructed them not to worry. He reminded them of the ravens that didn't gather food into a barn yet the Lord took care of them. He reminded them of the lilies of the field that God clothed. If He would do so for mere birds and flowers, how much more would He do so for them.

The disciples' stringent concern—and ours—should be the kingdom of God—seeking the righteous standard that God has revealed through His Word. When we focus on heaven, with our heart—our will, our ambition, our desires—then we will have treasure in heaven.

CONSIDER: *When our heart is right, singularly focused on God and His kingdom, then—and only then—will we be laying up treasures in heaven.*

March 21

LOOK FOR HIS COMING!

LUKE 12:35–59

"You too, be ready; for the Son of Man is coming at an hour that you do not expect." (Luke 12:40)

As hurricane Elena approached the Gulf Coast of Florida, some people threw a "hurricane party" in a beachside motel. When the hurricane roared in, authorities ordered beachside residents to evacuate. The people partying in the motel refused to leave. When Elena struck the coast, a great wave smashed the motel and carried the revelers out to sea. Everyone drowned.

Christ had come as Israel's Messiah but they were unprepared for His coming. Jesus warned the disciples to be watching for His coming. He instructed them concerning His unexpected coming. He emphasized preparedness; they should be ready, waiting, and alert. Why? Because "the Son of Man is coming at an hour that you do not expect." Since the religious leaders were unprepared for His first coming, Jesus spoke these words with particular reference to the Jewish people who would ultimately be in the tribulation period. They were to anticipate His second advent.

When Peter questioned the Lord, Jesus spoke a second parable, adding an emphasis on faithfulness (vv. 42–48). A landowner who had authority over his slaves, entrusted his estate to the management of a slave. To mismanage an estate could have meant death in that culture. The slave who knew what the master expected but did not obey would be beaten with many lashes. The slave who did not know the master's will and disobeyed it would be beaten with few lashes. What is the point? Faithfulness. In what? In spreading and proclaiming God's Word. Those who know God's Word have a responsibility to disseminate the word. Rejection of the Word, like that of the religious leaders in Jesus' day, would ultimately result in greater judgment. They did not respond to the Word although it had been clearly presented by Christ Himself.

Christ's coming brought "fire upon the earth" (v. 49) which would bring division in families and judgment on the earth—the basis of which was the crucifixion of Christ. Some in a family would believe; others would not. They failed to "analyze this present time" (v. 56). Messiah had come and they failed to recognize Him! In the parable Jesus warned of those who failed to settle with their opponent, forcing them to appear before the judge who would throw them into prison (vv. 58–59)—a reference to appearing before the Lord at the great white throne judgment (Rev. 20:11–56). Are people today missing the message that Christ the Deliverer has come?

CONSIDER: *Christ is returning at an hour that we do not know; we must be faithfully serving Him while looking for His coming.*

March 22

REPENT!

LUKE 13:1–21

---

*"I tell you, no, but unless you repent, you
will all likewise perish." (Luke 13:3)*

The horrific destruction of the Twin Towers on September 11, 2001, in New York City with several thousand people dying was a great tragedy. Did that mean Americans are greater sinners than other people? Applying Jesus' teaching to the twenty-first century, the answer would be no.

Jesus told of two national calamities that had occurred. While pilgrims from Galilee were offering sacrifices in the temple, Pilate, the Roman procurator of Judea, killed these worshipers—right in the temple. Were these people greater sinners than other Galileans? No. When the tower of Siloam fell, it killed eighteen people. Were these people greater culprits than the people living in Jerusalem? No. But unless the people would recognize that God had sent His Son and repent and trust in Him, they would "all likewise perish."

In illustrating this somber truth, Jesus warned of coming judgment (vv. 6–9). Reflected through the parable, Jesus had revealed His messiahship to the nation of Israel for three years. Now He was looking for fruit—a response to His messiahship. If the nation would not bear fruit by believing in Him as their Messiah the nation would be "cut down"—a dramatic picture of the Roman destruction of Jerusalem coming in A.D. 70.

But the nation continued to reflect its unbelief and confrontation between Jesus and the religious leaders continued (vv. 10–17). The Pharisees had established elaborate laws, falsely interpreting and applying laws concerning the Sabbath. When Jesus healed a woman who had suffered from a sickness, being bent over double for eighteen years, the synagogue official became indignant. Jesus reminded him that even their rules allowed animals to be led out by a chain and water to be drawn and poured into a trough for them. If the Pharisees care for animals on the Sabbath, surely they should be considerate of a sick Hebrew woman! Jesus indicted them for their hypocrisy—they were stage actors, presuming to be something (religious) though they were not (v. 15).

Since the religious leaders rejected Jesus, did that mean that the kingdom program of Christ would fail? To encourage the disciples Jesus told them two parables. Both the parable of the mustard seed and the parable of the leaven emphasize the growth of the kingdom. In this interadvent age, between the first and second comings of Christ, the mystery of the kingdom is growing rapidly.

CONSIDER: *The coming of Christ calls for repentance—a complete change of mind about God and about self.*

March 23

CLAIMING DEITY

JOHN 10:22–39

*"My sheep hear My voice, and I know them, and they follow Me;
and I give eternal life to them, and they will never perish; and
no one will snatch them out of My hand." (John 10:27–28)*

The Feast of Dedication (Hanukkah) was an important event on the Hebrew calendar. It commemorated the cleansing and rededicating of the temple under Judas Maccabaeus in 164 B.C. following its defilement under Antiochus Epiphanes who had blasphemed Hebrew worship by offering a swine on the altar. The event was foretold in Daniel 8:9–14. At that time the Lord had delivered Israel from oppression; would He do it again—delivering them from oppression now by the Romans?

Since it was winter and rainy, the temple's covered colonnade known as "Solomon's portico" offered the people protection from the cold rain. It would later become a popular meeting place for Christians (Acts 3:11; 5:12).

At this festival, discussion concerning the identity of Jesus would have been intense, hence, the Jews confronted Christ again, challenging Him: "How long will You keep us in suspense? If You are the Christ, tell us plainly" (John 10:24). Jesus simply reiterated some of His earlier statements, pointing to His works as authenticating His messiahship. His works fulfilled the prediction of Isaiah 35:5–6 promising that the blind would see, the deaf would hear, and the lame would walk.

But they did not believe because they were not His sheep. If they were His sheep they would recognize the voice of the Shepherd and trust in Him. Moreover, Jesus would give eternal life to His sheep and they would never perish. "Never" (*ou me*) is a double negative: "they will *not never* perish!" He guaranteed the security of His sheep; they were safely in His hand and in the Father's hand (John 10:28–29). To intensify the conversation, Jesus announced His unity and equality with the Father: "I and the Father are one" (v. 30). It is a strong statement. The Jews understood the claim (v. 33) and would not have attempted to stone Him had He not claimed deity.

Jesus reminded them that the leaders and the judges of Israel were sometimes called *Elohim* ("gods"; as in Exodus 7:1). Jesus reminded them that if these leaders received the title, how much more could Jesus Himself be called *Elohim*—He whom the Father had sanctified and sent. Jesus' comments about being sent indicate He is claiming to be the fulfillment of the Messiah prophecy of Daniel 7:13. Jesus clearly claimed to be God (John 10:30, 33, 36). Understanding His claims, the people sought to seize Him but He eluded their grasp.

Jesus is always the crucial dividing line between belief and unbelief. There is no middle ground; there is no neutrality.

CONSIDER: *Jesus made strong claims of deity and He is unequivocally deity— God come in the flesh as the second person of the Godhead.*

March 24

ENTERING THE KINGDOM

JOHN 10:40–42; LUKE 13:22–35

"Strive to enter through the narrow door; for many, I tell you, will seek to enter and will not be able." (Luke 13:24)

Messianic Jews living in Arad, Israel, have been subjected to persecution, with ultraorthodox Jews torching the Bible shop and arresting the victims. An ultraorthodox organization placed ads in an Israeli newspaper, seeking information about Christian "missionaries" (*World*, April 5/12, 2008). They remain hostile to the Christian message.

The continued rejection of Jesus by the nation's leaders marked a significant turn of events in the life of Christ. Since the nation had rejected Him, He would devote Himself to training the Twelve for ministry following His departure.

Leaving Judea, the apex of religious turmoil, Jesus crossed the Jordan and departed for Perea. This was where John had been baptizing. Many of John's followers came to realize that what John had taught them about Jesus was indeed true and many believed in Jesus as the Messiah. Yet the destiny established for the Savior remained the same. He had been rejected; the cross was imminent.

As Jesus proceeded toward Jerusalem, someone asked Him, "Lord, are there just a few who are being saved?" (Luke 13:23). The question pointed to the nation—would there be a national turning to Him as Messiah? The Jews taught that virtually all Jews would ultimately be saved. On the contrary, Jesus solemnly answered that, in fact, very few would be saved. The door is narrow. Yet many Gentiles would come from distant nations and enter the millennial kingdom while the generation of Jews that saw the works of Christ and heard His teaching would be cast out where there would be "weeping and gnashing of teeth" (v. 28).

When some Pharisees warned Jesus that Herod wanted to kill Him, Jesus responded with an enigmatic statement, "today and tomorrow, and the third day" (v. 32). Jesus was on a mission, going to Jerusalem where, on the third day, He said He would "reach My goal." The statement reflects Jesus' omniscience; He knew the Father's program for Him—it was the cross.

Recognizing Israel's rejection of Messiah, Jesus lamented over the city and the people whom He sought to redeem and bless. He foretold the enormous destruction that would come upon Jerusalem in A.D. 70. And they would not see Him again until He returned in glory at the second coming.

CONSIDER: *Opportunity to respond to Christ comes only in this life; when this life is over, eternal destiny is established.*

THE COST OF DISCIPLESHIP

LUKE 14:1–35

*"If anyone comes to Me, and does not hate his own father
and mother and wife and children and brothers and sisters, yes,
and even his own life, he cannot be My disciple." (Luke 14:26)*

When Jesus was invited to the home of a Pharisee on the Sabbath, they watched Him closely—probably to trap Him. A man with dropsy was present (perhaps planted by the Pharisees so they could accuse Jesus). They were watching to see if Jesus would heal the man since it was the Sabbath. Jesus rebuked them, reminding them if they had a son or an ox fall into a pit, they would rescue him. The Law allowed for that. Jesus was not violating the Law when He healed on the Sabbath. And so He did.

In noticing how the people clamored for the important seats at the dinner table, Jesus told them a parable. In a marriage feast, the person invited should go to the last place and remain there until invited to recline in a more prominent place. It was a lesson in humility.

In a second parable, Jesus told of a man giving a big dinner, inviting many people. In a great banquet, there were two invitations, one well in advance of the event and the second just prior to the banquet. The second invitation went to those who had accepted the invitation the first time. Now, however, these same people refused to attend the banquet, offering excuses. As a result, the master invited the poor, crippled, lame, and blind. These and many more would fill the banquet hall but those who had first been invited would not enter the banquet hall.

Jesus' parable spoke of the Jewish people who had received the first invitation into God's kingdom through the Old Testament prophets. Now that Jesus had come and offered the kingdom (representative of the second invitation), the nation refused to respond to Him. As a result outcasts—Gentiles—would be invited; the generation that refused Christ would not enter Messiah's kingdom.

When large crowds followed Jesus, apparently many with false motives, Jesus challenged them. He warned them of true discipleship. It meant Jesus had priority over all else including family associations. A true disciple of Jesus would "hate his own father and mother and wife and children. . . ." What was Jesus saying? He was not referring to malice but to preference. Hate (*misei*) means "loving less" (Cleon Rogers Jr. and Cleon Rogers III, *The New Linguistic and Exegetical Key to the Greek New Testament*). A true disciple would still love father, mother, wife, and children—but he would put Jesus first. It was not a haphazard decision; a true disciple counted the cost. Many of Jesus' followers were not true disciples but were following Him for the material benefits.

CONSIDER: *Salvation is by grace through faith alone but the walk of discipleship involves a cost. Jesus must be first; He must be preeminent. Have you counted the cost?*

GOD'S ATTITUDE TOWARD THE LOST

LUKE 15:1–32

---

*"There is joy in the presence of the angels of God over one sinner
who repents. . . . His father saw him and felt compassion for
him, and ran and embraced him and kissed him." (Luke 15:10, 20)*

In contrast to Jesus' teaching, the Pharisees had a saying, "There is joy before God when those who provoke Him perish from the world" (Alfred Edersheim, *Life and Times of Jesus the Messiah*). When they saw Jesus talking and eating with tax collectors and sinners (those who were immoral or who practiced vocations that the religious leaders considered contrary to the Law) they were incensed. The Pharisees had a faulty understanding of God's attitude toward sinners—they incorrectly assumed that God hates sinners and delights in their death.

To explain why He associated with unbelievers, Jesus told three parables. The parables would also teach God's attitude toward sinners: He delights in their repentance.

In the first parable, Jesus told of a man who had one hundred sheep but he lost one. The man searched for the one lost sheep until he found it and when he returned home with the sheep on his shoulders, he called his friends to rejoice with him because the sheep that had been lost was found. The man reflected the Father's attitude in seeking the lost. He rejoices when a sinner repents.

In the second parable, a woman had ten silver coins and lost one of them. The coins may have been her life's savings or they may have been part of her wedding dowry that she wore around her neck. To lose a coin would have been a great tragedy, perhaps even reflecting infidelity. She diligently searched for the coin until she found it. Just as the woman rejoiced when the coin was found, so God rejoices when a sinner repents.

In the third parable, the older son represents the Pharisees while the younger son represents the tax collectors and sinners. After receiving his inheritance, the younger son departed and squandered all his money. He was forced to take a job herding swine—the lowest vocation for a Jew. When the young son came to his senses, he decided to go home, even as a slave. His intended confession indicates that he recognized that his sin was primarily against God (Luke 15:18). But the father is pictured as already looking for his son. This is God's attitude toward sinners—God is seeking them out. The father's kiss was a sign of acceptance. The father would not even permit the son to finish his words of repentance—he accepted him. The father gave him the best robe, normally reserved for an honored guest; a ring, a symbol of authority; and sandals, a reminder that he was a son, not a slave who would have been barefoot. The repentant son received full family privileges! The entire story reflects God's attitude toward repentant sinners.

CONSIDER: *The Father welcomes repentant sinners home.*

March 27

THE LOVE OF MONEY

LUKE 16:1–31

---

*"No servant can serve two masters; for either he will hate the
one and love the other, or else he will be devoted to one and
despise the other. You cannot serve God and wealth." (Luke 16:13)*

Someone is supposed to have asked Rockefeller, "How much is enough?"
"Just a little bit more," was his reply. That may well be the thinking of people
at all levels of income.

In this parable on the use of wealth, Jesus tells of an unfaithful steward
who was entrusted with his master's finances. He had considerable authority
and responsibility in superintending his master's household but he had squandered the master's possessions. When confronted by his master, the steward
sought to remedy his dilemma by eliminating his profit in the transactions and
by so doing, he obeyed the Law (Exod. 22:25; Lev. 25:36).

Jesus commended the steward for acting prudently and He exhorts believers to use their money wisely—to reap eternal benefits. Jesus warned that it
is impossible to serve both God and money—yet this is precisely what the
Pharisees sought to do (Luke 16:14).

To dramatize His point that it is impossible to serve God and money, Jesus
told the story (not a parable) of the rich man and Lazarus. The Pharisees
thought that wealth was a sign of God's blessing, and poverty was a sign of
God's judgment because of sin. Hence, the Pharisees thought the rich would
inherit heaven and the poor would go to hell. Jesus shows that they are wrong.

Jesus tells of a rich man who was a poor steward of his wealth; he didn't use
his money to make friends. By contrast, an extremely poor man, a beggar named
Lazarus, sat in the town square begging, with no one caring for him but dogs.
Then both men died. Lazarus "was carried away by the angels to Abraham's
bosom" (v. 22), a picture of the joy in reclining in fellowship at a banquet with
friends. Conversely, the rich man died and it is simply stated he "was buried."
But the rich man awoke in Hades, the New Testament designation for hell. The
final destination for both men was irreversible.

The story teaches that hell is a place of torment (vv. 23, 28); there is con-
sciousness and remembrance (vv. 27–28); it is permanent, there is no release
(v. 26); they see heaven but have no access (vv. 23–24); and it is too late for
repentance (vv. 27–30). And, in this case, the man arrived in hell because of
his love of money. People cannot trust their wealth to bring them to heaven.
The story is a strong warning that devotion to God is singular. Divided loyalties have disastrous results.

CONSIDER: *It is impossible to love God and love money.*

THE RAISING OF LAZARUS

JOHN 11:1–54

Jesus said to her, "I am the resurrection and the life; he who believes in Me will live even if he dies, and everyone who lives and believes in Me will never die. Do you believe this?" (John 11:25–26)

Unquestionably, the death of a loved one is the most difficult experience we will ever encounter. The agony, the grief, the sadness of standing at my wife's casket is indescribable. Yet, for believers in Jesus Christ, this is the watershed of faith. It distinguishes Christianity from religion. Jesus Christ alone has risen from the dead; there is no other. And He has promised eternal life to those who believe in Him!

Jesus had a special fellowship with Mary, Martha, and Lazarus in Bethany, just over the Mount of Olives from Jerusalem. But Lazarus had died. When Jesus heard of it, He said Lazarus's death was "for the glory of God" (John 11:4). Through the raising of Lazarus, Jesus would reveal His messiahship, and many would come to faith.

After Jesus heard of Lazarus's illness, He remained in Perea two more days, purposefully returning after Lazarus had been dead four days. Jews believed that the soul hovered around the body for three days after death; during that time there was still hope. After three days all hope was gone. Then Jesus arrived.

Mary and Martha are seen in their characteristic roles (see Luke 10:38–42): Martha, bustling with activity, ran out to meet Jesus; Mary, who earlier sat at Jesus' feet, was placid even now. The sisters had probably discussed Jesus' ability to heal since they both made the same remark: "Lord, if You had been here, my brother would not have died" (vv. 21, 32).

Martha exhibited enormous faith, believing that even after death, Jesus could raise Lazarus (v. 22). In response, Jesus made the most comforting statement of all time, "I am the resurrection and the life; he who believes in Me will live even if he dies, and everyone who lives and believes in Me will never die" (vv. 25–26). Jesus was saying that a believer may die physically, but he will experience physical resurrection and eternal life through faith in Him. Those who believe in Christ will never die spiritually, in the sense of being separated from the source of life.

When Jesus approached Lazarus's tomb, "He was deeply moved" (v. 33), an expression connoting anger, like the snorting of horses (Cleon Rogers Jr. and Cleon Rogers III, *The New Linguistic and Exegetical Key to the Greek New Testament*). Jesus was angry at what sin had done to the human race. Then He shouted, "Lazarus, come forth" (v. 43). With the wrappings still encircling his body, Lazarus came out of the tomb! Jesus demonstrated His messiahship and His authority over death. He revealed His authority over the most devastating enemy of the human race—and it is a reminder that in the coming kingdom there will be no death for believers in Christ.

CONSIDER: *Jesus has conquered death. Does that truth fill you with peace and comfort?*

March 29

THE COMING KINGDOM

LUKE 17:11–37

*"For just like the lightning, when it flashes out of one part
of the sky, shines to the other part of the sky, so will the
Son of Man be in His day." (Luke 17:24)*

Along the border of Galilee and Samaria, ten lepers met Jesus outside a village. This was unusual in itself since Jews did not travel south through Samaria; they avoided the Samaritans whom they despised. While Jesus was still outside the village, He was met by ten lepers who, by the Law, had to live by themselves outside the town (Lev. 13:46). They must have heard about Jesus since they cried to Him for help, "Jesus, Master, have mercy on us!" (Luke 17:13). Jesus simply said, "Go and show yourselves to the priests" (v. 14). It demanded faith on their part to begin walking to the priest. But they did it. And as they walked they were healed!

But only one, a Samaritan, turned back to give thanks to Jesus and glorify God. Perhaps it is a reminder that the nine were Jewish, and even while recognizing Jesus' power to heal, they nonetheless rejected Him as Messiah.

Jesus' rejection prompted Him to instruct the disciples concerning His return. The healing of the leper was clearly a sign of the kingdom—there will be no leprosy, no illness of any kind in the kingdom. It appears the Pharisees witnessed the event, prompting them to ask when the kingdom was coming. Jesus reminded them, "the kingdom of God is in your midst" (v. 21). Wherever the king is, there is the kingdom—although the kingdom was not yet inaugurated.

Jesus reminded them that when the kingdom would be inaugurated, then it would be observable, coming suddenly, like lightning. In that day, when He comes to establish His kingdom, Jesus' glory will envelope the earth (see Matt. 24:30). Yet Jesus, in His omniscience, knew that He would first be rejected by His own people in this very generation. The kingdom of God would be postponed until His second coming.

The people were blinded; they were consumed with the mundane, ordinary things of life—just as in the days of Noah and Lot, when the people were unprepared for God's judgment. They were eating, drinking, marrying, buying, selling, planting, building. There was nothing wrong with those things except that by concentrating on the ordinary they lost sight of the extraordinary. Messiah had come and they didn't recognize His coming. They were guilty of concentrating on this life, failing to see the life to come. Jesus warned, "Whoever seeks to keep his life will lose it, and whoever loses his life will preserve it" (Luke 17:33). The one seeking to preserve his life here would be taken away in judgment, but the one who would lose his life for Christ would preserve it by entering the kingdom.

CONSIDER: *Are you guilty of concentrating on the ordinary, the mundane, the temporal, while failing to see the eternal, the everlasting?*

March 30

PERSISTENCE IN PRAYER

LUKE 18:1–14

---

*Now He was telling them a parable to show that at all
times they ought to pray and not to lose heart. (Luke 18:1)*

A man, past eighty years old, stood in a prayer meeting and said, "Friends, sixty-five years ago my dying mother said to me, 'You are the only Christian in the family so I commend your brothers to you. Pray for them every day until they are saved.' This morning I received a letter from my remaining brother in which he said he had the best news—he was saved!" Persistence in prayer—that is the lesson Jesus taught.

When Jesus taught this lesson on prayer, He linked it with his previous teaching on prophecy. People were to be ready for His return and not "lose heart" while they waited.

He illustrated the truth with the parable of the unjust judge and the widow. The widow was poor. She was in no position to bribe the judge. She was the epitome of helplessness. Because of the widow's persistence in pleading, however, the judge responded to her request.

Persistence is the point of the parable. The unjust judge should not be compared to God. Rather, they are opposites. The judge was reluctant to answer the widow's petition, but God will quickly bring about justice for His own. "Quickly" stands in the emphatic position in the Greek text.

Rather than relying on God and persisting in prayer, there were some who trusted in themselves, in their own righteousness while viewing others with contempt. Jesus contrasted the Pharisee with the tax collector. The Pharisee's prayer was devoid of humility, which was not unusual. Rabbi Nehunia used to pray: "I give thanks to Thee, O Lord my God, that Thou has set my portion with those who sit in the Beth Ha-Midrash (House of Learning) and Thou has not set my portion with those who sit in (street) corners, for I rise early and they rise early, but I rise early for words of Torah and they rise early for frivolous talk, I labour and they labour, but I labour and receive a reward and they labour and do not receive a reward; I run and they run, but I run to the life of the future world and they run to the pit of destruction" (Talmud, *Berakhoth* quoted in Leon Morris, *Luke*).

The tax collector made certain he exceeded the Law, but he had a problem. He was consumed with self-righteousness. By contrast, the tax collector was so humble he didn't dare even lift his eyes toward heaven. He exhibited humility in sorrow for sin and genuine repentance. And the Lord responded and justified the tax collector. God wants both persistence and penitence in prayer.

CONSIDER: *God is not reluctant to answer our prayers and will, in fact, answer quickly—but He will see, through our persistence, whether we are serious in prayer.*

INSTRUCTION ON DIVORCE

MATTHEW 19:1–15; MARK 10:1–12

"Whoever divorces his wife and marries another woman commits adultery against her; and if she herself divorces her husband and marries another man, she is committing adultery." (Mark 10:11–12)

As Jesus came into Judea, the Pharisees approached Him, testing Him on the issue of divorce. They wanted Him to take sides on the interpretation of Deuteronomy 24:1. The school of Shammai taught it was valid to divorce one's wife only for adultery; the school of Hillel taught one could divorce his wife for virtually any reason: if she was found in public with her head uncovered, if she burned the bread, if she was quarrelsome, if she was disrespectful to her in-laws . . . the validity for divorce was limitless. What did Jesus say concerning divorce? Which view would He hold?

Jesus answered the Pharisees by emphasizing the permanence of marriage. No one is to break the inseparable, one-flesh union that God has joined together (Matt. 19:6; Mark 10:9). "The first human male and female were intended solely for each other; the principle involved in their creation was that their union was complete and indissoluble. And they were the norm for each succeeding pair. Each married couple is a reproduction of Adam and Eve, and their union is therefore no less indissoluble" (A. H. McNeile, *Gospel According to St. Matthew*).

Divorce was not God's original intent; the permission came "because of your hardness of heart" (Matt. 19:8). This was God's permissive will but it was not so designed from the beginning. The contrasting expressions are clear: the Pharisees said, "why then did Moses command . . ." (v. 7); Jesus answered, "Moses permitted . . ." (v. 8).

Jesus permitted divorce in only one case: immorality (*porneia*; v. 9). This exceptive clause does not occur outside of Matthew (see Mark 10:11–12; Luke 16:18; Rom. 7:1–3; 1 Cor. 7:39). The word *porneia* is a broad word, signifying immorality before marriage. While some infer the exceptive clause refers to adultery, that is *moicheia*, a different word that relates specifically to infidelity in marriage.

Why does Matthew alone use the exceptive clause? Matthew, in writing to a Jewish audience, is referring to the betrothal period (engagement) during which a Jewish couple was considered "husband" and "wife" and which could be terminated only by divorce. A Jewish couple was normally engaged for twelve months; if she was found to be pregnant during this time, the man could break the engagement, but only by divorce (see Matt. 1:18–19). Since this was a Jewish custom, the exceptive clause does not occur in Mark and Luke, which were written to Gentile audiences.

Marriage was designed to be permanent—and the disciples recognized this.

CONSIDER: *God intended marriage to be permanent: one man and one woman for life. What are you contributing to your marriage, either present or future, to make that happen?*

April 1

ENTERING THE KINGDOM

MATTHEW 19:16–20:16; MARK 10:17–31; LUKE 18:18–30

"So the last shall be first, and the first last." (Matthew 20:16)

In the town where I grew up there was a wealthy businessman, a manufacturer of farm machinery. The pastor talked to him about salvation and the businessman said he would think about it. When the businessman met with the pastor again, he exclaimed, "No, I don't believe I will take Jesus as my Savior." His wealth hindered his response to Christ.

With their belief falsely rooted in Deuteronomy 28, the Pharisees taught that whomever the Lord loved, He would bless materially. They could not understand Jesus' constant association with the poor. Surely they were poor because they had sinned and were being chastened by God!

A rich, young ruler came to Jesus calling Him, "Good Teacher." In Jewish literature "The Good One of the world" was a title of God (J. W. Shepard, *Christ of the Gospels*). When Jesus responded as He did, He gave the man an opportunity to recognize Him as Messiah and give a confession of his faith—just as Peter had in Matthew 16:16.

Then Jesus cited the fifth through ninth commandments. When the young man professed to have kept all these commandments, Jesus exposed the problem: "go and sell your possessions and give to the poor" (Matt. 19:21). The essence of the Law was love God (Deut. 6:5) and love your neighbor (Lev. 19:18). Jesus showed the man that he had failed to keep the Law. By not giving to the poor, he was violating both the first and second commandments: he was putting his riches ahead of God and he did not show love for his neighbor by helping the poor. The ruler went away sad because he was very wealthy.

Jesus reminded the disciples of the difficulty of a wealthy person entering the kingdom—as difficult as a camel going through the eye of a literal needle (not, as some suggest, the small gate in entering Jerusalem). Peter quickly reminded the Lord that the disciples had left everything in following Him. What would there be for them? Jesus responded by telling a parable about rewards (Matt. 20:1–16). In the parable, those that came later were ultimately paid the same as those that came early, to the consternation of those that came early. The Lord's lesson was that in the kingdom the world's measures of greatness are reversed (Matt. 19:30; 20:16). Many that are first in this world will be last in the kingdom—meaning they will not enter the kingdom.

CONSIDER: *Worldly wealth prevents many from entering heaven; yet, through God's grace, salvation is possible for both rich and poor.*

April 2

THE SON OF MAN WHO SERVES

MATTHEW 20:17–34; MARK 10:32–52; LUKE 18:31–43

"The Son of Man did not come to be served, but to serve, and to give His life a ransom for many." (Matthew 20:28)

As Jesus and the disciples were going up to Jerusalem He reminded them of His impending death. Jesus foretold that He would be betrayed and handed over to the religious leaders who would convict Him of a crime and sentence Him to death. They in turn would hand Him over to the Romans who would mock Him, spit on Him, and finally scourge Him and crucify Him. But on the third day He would rise from the dead. Jesus knew the minute details of His impending death and resurrection. It reflects His omniscience—Jesus is God as well as man!

But the disciples had other thoughts. *Then*—at the very time Jesus was explaining His horrific death to them—they were thinking of themselves, the exaltation of *themselves!* Who is the most important among the disciples? To assure their preeminence, James and John had their mother negotiate their status with Jesus! They were thinking of glory; Jesus was contemplating the cross. They did not have the spirit of the Son of Man, who came to serve. They had the attitude of the rulers of the Gentiles, who loved to exercise their authority. They wanted greatness, but true greatness, Jesus reminded them, was found in being a servant. That was what the Son of Man demonstrated.

Jesus reminded them, "whoever wishes to be first among you shall be your slave; just as the Son of Man did not come to be served, but to serve, and to give His life a ransom for many" (Matt. 20:27–28). Greatness would come in service. Jesus would demonstrate the ultimate service at the cross, giving His life a ransom for others, buying the release of slaves. We were bound as slaves to sin but through His death, Jesus sets us free from slavery to sin. Jesus died as our substitute, making atonement for sin and satisfying the holiness of the Father.

As Jesus and the disciples left old Jericho (Matt. 20:29) and approached new Jericho (Luke 18:35), they were met by two blind men, one being Bartimaeus. Moved with compassion, Jesus healed them of their blindness, demonstrating both His messiahship as well as the servant message He had just conveyed to the disciples. The world compels us to lord authority over others; Christ calls us to serve others.

CONSIDER: *If Jesus came not to be served but to serve, what should your role in life be? Will you find greatness in serving others?*

FAITHFUL KINGDOM BUSINESS
LUKE 19:1–27

"Well done, good slave, because you have been faithful in a very little thing, you are to be in authority over ten cities." (Luke 19:17)

Each gospel has a unique presentation of Christ. Luke emphasizes that Jesus came for all people, men and women, rich and poor, the elite and the outcasts of society. This is uniquely illustrated in this event in which a despised person will enter the kingdom. As Jesus was passing through Jericho, crowds had gathered to see and hear the Savior—and with them, a hated, despised man: Zaccheus, a chief tax collector. This is the only mention in Scripture of a chief tax collector. It meant he had other tax collectors working under him—for Rome. And for that he was hated by the Jews. And this was a prime area; Jericho was rich in balsam and was also on the trade route for the caravans—a marvelous opportunity for taxing people.

When Zaccheus attempted to see Jesus, the crowd had ample opportunity to vent their hatred against him, blocking his view. But when Zaccheus climbed a sycamore tree, Jesus saw him and announced that He would be a guest in his home. Surely, this unsettled the crowd of Jews! But Zaccheus was converted to faith in Jesus. His repentance was evidenced in his promise to repay the people he had defrauded. This was significant. Restitution called for the original amount plus twenty percent (Lev. 6:5; Num. 5:7) but Zaccheus was willing to go further. He wanted to repay four times as much—the penalty for stealing (Exod. 22:1). Zaccheus had become a kingdom citizen!

Jesus' teaching prompted people to think the "kingdom of God was going to appear immediately" (Luke 19:11). Jesus told them a parable to show that the kingdom would neither be established right then, nor would it be only spiritual, but it would be delayed. It would be a future kingdom. The parable describes the present, intervening age.

Jesus told of a nobleman who was going to a distant country to receive a kingdom for himself and then he was returning. Meanwhile, he entrusted his affairs to his slaves. In the parable, Jesus is the nobleman who has gone to heaven, to return later to inaugurate His kingdom. The slaves are the stewards of God's truth (the Israelites, as seen in Romans 9:4). The minas represent God's truth. The citizens are the Jews that rejected Messiah's reign over them (Luke 19:14). The ten and five mina slaves are those who faithfully proclaimed the truth about Jesus as the Messiah. They will be rewarded in the kingdom. The third slave refused to believe and proved unfaithful; he did nothing with the truth he had received. He portrayed a nation in unbelief that had rejected Messiah and would undergo horrific judgment at the destruction of Jerusalem in A.D. 70.

CONSIDER: *Jesus came to offer citizenship in His kingdom to all classes of society: "The Son of Man has come to seek and to save that which was lost" (v. 10).*

April 4

THE TRIUMPHAL ENTRY

JOHN 11:55–12:1, 12–19; MATTHEW 21:1–11, 14–17;
MARK 11:1–11; LUKE 19:29–44

---

*"Hosanna to the Son of David; BLESSED IS HE WHO COMES IN THE NAME OF THE
LORD; Hosanna in the highest!" (Matthew 21:9)*

When President George H. W. Bush came to McDill Air Force Base in Tampa, I, along with many others, gathered nearby to welcome the president. It was an exciting moment to stand within a few dozen yards of the president of the United States of America.

Far more significant was Jesus' entry to Jerusalem. It was a tense time; Jews were converging on Jerusalem for the Passover. Many were curious about Jesus since they had heard about the raising of Lazarus. The religious leaders had determined that if He were found, they would kill Him.

On that momentous day Jesus had sent two disciples to Bethphage, on the eastern slope of the Mount of Olives. Arrangements had been made for Jesus to ride an unbroken colt into the city of Jerusalem. What was the significance?

First, riding an unbroken colt was a fulfillment of the messianic prophecy found in Zechariah 9:9. It demonstrated that, as Messiah, Jesus has authority over nature; even the unbroken animal, "on which no one yet has ever sat" (Mark 11:2), became docile under Messiah's authority. And second, riding the colt into Jerusalem was a sign of Jesus' kingship. When Solomon succeeded David as king, he rode the king's mule (1 Kings 1:33).

Furthermore, by spreading the garments along the path for Jesus, the people were paying homage to His kingship—it was a carpet for royalty (as seen in 2 Kings 9:13). Cutting branches from trees and spreading them on the road pointed to the Feast of Tabernacles, a further recognition that Jesus had come to establish the messianic kingdom. The chanting of messianic psalms—the psalms that looked forward to the coming Messiah (Psalm 118:26, for example)—reflected recognition of Jesus' messiahship. "He who comes" was a messianic title: He is "the Coming One" (see Revelation 1:4, 8). And the people's cry of "Hosanna" (meaning "Save now! Help!") was a cry for salvation and deliverance which only the Messiah could bring.

Jesus rode down the western slope of the Mount of Olives, entering the eastern gate of Jerusalem, known in that day as "Messiah's Gate." People exited the gate but no one entered it because it was Messiah's Gate—only He could enter it. The city was "stirred" (*eseisthe;* compare with the English *seismo-,* meaning "earthquake") because they recognized His claim of messiahship.

Luke records that Jesus wept over the city because the people did not know "this day" (Luke 19:42)—although they recognized His claim to messiahship, they did not recognize Him as Messiah. It was precisely the day that fulfilled Daniel's prophecy of Messiah's entry into Jerusalem (Dan. 9:25)—March 30, A.D. 33. And the people missed it.

CONSIDER: *Jesus is the Messiah, the King who is destined to rule the world with all creation subject to Him.*

April 5

Judgment on the Nation

Matthew 21:12–13, 18–19; Mark 11:12–18; Luke 19:45–48; John 12:20–50

But though He had performed so many signs before them,
yet they were not believing in Him. (John 12:37)

As Jesus returned to Jerusalem on Monday following the triumphal entry, he was hungry. Seeing a lone fig tree He expected to find figs but there were none—only leaves. Fruit preceded the leaves and since there were leaves, the fig tree professed to have figs. The fig tree was making an empty profession. The fig tree frequently symbolized the nation Israel (as in Hosea 9:10 and Joel 1:7). When Jesus pronounced a curse on the fig tree, it symbolized the impending judgment on the unbelieving nation of Israel.

For a second time Jesus cleansed the temple by overturning the tables of the moneychangers. The disciples saw this as a clear messianic sign (John 2:17; Ps 69:9). Jesus entered the outer Court of the Gentiles, which was a marketplace. Here animals were sold and money was exchanged for the pilgrims and all who came to offer animals for sacrifice. Annas, the father-in-law of Caiaphas, the high priest, owned the bazaars which were called "the bazaars of Annas." It was an extremely lucrative business: they charged exorbitant fees to change the pilgrims' money into local currency; they charged an inspection fee; they rejected the animal as blemished; and then they sold the worshiper another animal at an exorbitant price. Jesus denounced the moneychangers, calling it a "robbers' den."

The Greeks coming to Jesus, recorded in John 12, was significant. Since the Jews rejected their Messiah, the Greeks, representing the Gentiles, anticipate the gospel going to the world. They are the "other sheep" Jesus spoke about (John 10:16).

But the die was cast—the cross was imminent. Israel had rejected their Messiah. Jesus answered the Greeks by saying, "The hour has come for the Son of Man to be glorified" (John 12:23). And yet, tragedy would turn to triumph. Just as a grain of wheat must be sown in the ground and die in order to bear fruit, so the Son of Man would bring salvation to many people, including Gentiles. The Father's voice from heaven authenticated Jesus as the Messiah. Through Christ's atonement, Satan would be judged and defeated.

Jesus has come into the world as the light of the world to bring people out of darkness into the light. Those who believe in Him have eternal life; the ones that refuse to believe will be judged because they have rejected Him despite the clear evidence.

CONSIDER: *Jesus turned tragedy into triumph when, through His crucifixion, Satan was defeated and salvation was brought to both Jews and Gentiles.*

April 6

THE KING'S AUTHORITY CHALLENGED

MATTHEW 21:23–22:14; MARK 11:27–12:12; LUKE 20:1–19

"THE STONE WHICH THE BUILDERS REJECTED, THIS BECAME THE CHIEF
CORNER stone; THIS CAME ABOUT FROM THE LORD, AND IT IS
MARVELOUS IS OUR EYES." (Matthew 21:42)

Jesus was teaching openly in the temple, to the consternation of the religious leaders. They came to Jesus, challenging His right to teach. Anyone teaching had to be authorized by other rabbis or the Sanhedrin. Authority was handed down from a teacher to a disciple; hence, appeal was always to a great teacher or the Sanhedrin.

Jesus responded by asking them a question about John: Was his authority from heaven or men? Christ's opponents recognized their dilemma and refused to answer His question. Amid their dilemma, Jesus told three parables.

In the parable of the two sons, one son refused to obey his father and go and work, but later, he repented and went. The other son said he would go but did not. The religious leaders acknowledged the one who repented and went to work did the father's will—without realizing they represented the disobedient son who refused to go. As a result, Jesus reminded them that the outcasts of society—the tax collectors and prostitutes—would enter the kingdom before them because they repented.

In the second parable, the landowner is God, the vineyard is Israel, the slaves are the prophets, the son is Christ, and the vine growers are the religious leaders. The parable reveals Israel's continued rejection of God's prophets and the ultimate rejection of God's Son. Jesus taught that Israel would be set aside because of her unfaithfulness, because her people rejected the Messiah. Yet, Jesus reminded them that the very one they rejected would become the cornerstone of the nation. Meanwhile, the kingdom that had been offered to them would be taken away from that generation (Matt. 21:43). They would not inherit the kingdom; a future generation of repentant Israelites would inherit the kingdom (as foretold in Zechariah 12:10–14).

In his third parable Jesus told of a wedding feast prepared by a king for his son. When the king's servants called those who had been invited, they made excuses and finally mistreated the messengers and even killed them. The enraged king sent his armies to destroy the rebels' city. Then the invitation was broadened to include everyone. Jesus' parable foretold the destruction of Jerusalem by the Romans in A.D. 70 and the terrible loss of that privileged generation. It would be set aside. It was also a reminder that the message would ultimately go out to both Jews and Gentiles. But only those clothed with the garments of righteousness would enter the banquet hall of the king—the kingdom of God.

CONSIDER: *Privilege demands responsibility. How have you responded to the truth that you have received?*

HERODIANS AND SADDUCEES CHALLENGE CHRIST

MATTHEW 22:15–33; MARK 12:13–27; LUKE 20:20–40

"Have you not read . . . 'I AM THE GOD OF ABRAHAM, AND THE GOD OF ISAAC, AND THE GOD OF JACOB'? He is not the God of the dead but of the living." (Matthew 22:31–32)

Hatred of a common enemy brings strange alliances. The Pharisees opposed Roman rule of Israel while the Herodians supported the family of Herod the Great which accepted Roman rule of their land. Because of this, "Herodians would certainly have supported the payment of taxes to Rome where the patriotic Pharisees emphatically would not" (W. F. Albright and C. S. Mann, *Matthew*).

Conspiring against Jesus, the Pharisees and Herodians challenged Jesus: "Is it lawful to give a poll-tax to Caesar, or not?" (Matt. 22:17). The poll-tax was exacted by Rome from males over the age of 14 and females over 12 and had to be paid annually. It was "considered by the Jews as a special badge of servitude to the Roman power; hence the disputes among the rabbis about paying especially this tax" (R. C. H. Lenski, *Interpretation of St. Mark's Gospel*).

In reminding them "render to Caesar the things that are Caesar's; and to God the things that are God's" (v. 21), Jesus taught that it is both possible and necessary to give proper allegiance to both civil and religious authorities—to the government and to God.

But the challenges continued. The Sadducees—who reject belief in the resurrection—attempted to create a dilemma for Jesus. The Sadducees believed the soul dies with the body. As a result, they also rejected rewards and punishment in Hades. The Sadducees postulated a hypothetical event: A man died after having married a woman; ultimately the woman married his six brothers who all died. Whose wife would she be in the resurrection?

Jesus answered their challenge by revealing their errors: They did not understand the Scriptures since the Scriptures indeed teach the resurrection. Since the Sadducees accepted only the Pentateuch, Jesus quoted Exodus 3:6: "I am . . . the God of Abraham, the God of Isaac, and the God of Jacob." Then Jesus reminded them that God is not the God of the dead, but of the living. Although Abraham, Isaac, and Jacob were dead when God spoke those words to Moses, God used the present tense, "I AM," inferring that the patriarchs were indeed alive in glory awaiting the resurrection. Further, the Sadducees did not understand the power of God. He is able to raise the dead (Matt. 22:29–30). Finally the Sadducees did not understand the relationship of God to His own people—they are living (vv. 31–32).

CONSIDER: *It is obligatory for the believer to obey both God and the government—which includes paying taxes. It is also the believer's ultimate joy in knowing the resurrection is a reality.*

April 8

CHRIST IS LORD!

MATTHEW 22:34–46; MARK 12:28–37; LUKE 20:41–44

"YOU SHALL LOVE THE LORD YOUR GOD WITH ALL YOUR HEART, AND WITH ALL YOUR SOUL, AND WITH ALL YOUR MIND. . . . YOU SHALL LOVE YOUR NEIGHBOR AS YOURSELF." (Matthew 22:37, 39)

The religious leaders of Israel had categorized the Mosaic Law into 613 commandments—248 positive and 365 negative commands. Since the law demanded differing retribution for failure to keep certain commands, they concluded some were more important than others. So which of the 613 commandments was the most important? A Pharisaic scribe, one skilled in the interpretation of the Law, tested Jesus with a question, "Teacher, which is the greatest commandment in the Law?" (Matt. 22:36). It was an attempt to trap Jesus.

Jesus responded with two statements. The first statement recognized their responsibility to God: "YOU SHALL LOVE THE LORD YOUR GOD WITH ALL YOUR HEART, AND WITH ALL YOUR SOUL, AND WITH ALL YOUR MIND." The second, their responsibility to man: "YOU SHALL LOVE YOUR NEIGHBOR AS YOURSELF." Jesus concluded, "on these two commandments depend the whole Law and the Prophets" (v. 40). It is picturesque. The word "depend" means "to hang"; the whole Old Testament (here called the "Law and the Prophets") *hangs* on these two commandments.

But now Jesus asked the Pharisees a question: "What do you think about the Christ, whose son is He?" (v. 42). They revealed their lack of understanding when they responded, "The son of David." They saw the Messiah only as a descendant of David. Nothing more.

Christ confused them when He challenged them with David's statement from Psalm 110:1, "The Lord said to My Lord . . ." David called his descendant "Lord." How could Messiah simply be a descendant of David? A man may call his descendant "son" but he assuredly would not call him "Lord"—unless he indeed was Lord!

The statement is a dramatic endorsement of the deity of Messiah—the deity of Jesus. David recognized that a descendant of his would come who would be greater than he was. That descendant would be the Messiah, and, as such, He was and is deity. The Lord had silenced His critics. No one dared challenge Him again.

CONSIDER: *Do you love God with all your heart, soul, and mind? Do you love your neighbor as yourself? Do you recognize the uniqueness of Christ, namely, His deity?*

Seven Woes

Matthew 23:1–39; Mark 12:38–44; Luke 20:45–21:4

---

*"But the greatest among you shall be your servant. Whoever
exalts himself shall be humbled; and whoever humbles
himself shall be exalted." (Matthew 23:11–12)*

One Saturday morning two Jehovah's Witnesses came to my house. I went outside and confronted them about the person of Christ. "Well, He's not God!" one of them shouted. At that point I told him to leave my property; I would not allow him to blaspheme the name of my Savior on my property. Sometimes, we are called on to speak forcefully on a biblical truth. Christ on many occasions spoke in a strong, straightforward way.

As the spiritual leaders in the community, the Pharisees ought to have led the people to faith in Jesus as their Messiah. But they rejected Him, and as a result Jesus issued severe denunciations against the Pharisees. He denounced their emphasis on externals—tying small leather cases of Scriptures to their arms and foreheads—to be seen by people (Matt. 23:5). They relished preeminent places and greetings that honored them. In contrast, Jesus warned His disciples to seek the place of servitude.

Jesus pronounced a series of serious warnings, or *woes*. He denounced the Pharisees for their deception, their hypocrisy in preventing people from entering the kingdom because of their false teaching—but neither would they enter. They zealously proselytized but their converts became twice as much a child of hell. They were blind leaders, leading people astray, emphasizing the minutia, tithing the tiniest seeds while ignoring the major matters like justice, mercy, and faithfulness.

The Pharisees emphasized the externals while neglecting the heart. Outwardly, they were as beautiful as a whitewashed tomb, but inside they were as filthy as dead men's bones. Ultimately, they were as guilty as their forefathers in killing the prophets that God sent to them.

Jesus lamented over Jerusalem: the prophets had prophesied Messiah's coming and they killed the prophets; now Messiah had come and they rejected Him. Tragedy would befall the nation. Their house—pointing to the temple—would be left desolate; Jesus once again foretold the horrific destruction of Jerusalem by the Romans in A.D. 70. They had scorned the Messiah and they would not see Him again until they, in repentance, would embrace Him at His second coming.

CONSIDER: *Do you serve Christ with an emphasis on externals or does your devotion to Him arise from your heart?*

April 10

THE IMPENDING TRIBULATION

MATTHEW 24:1–14; MARK 13:1–13; LUKE 21:5–19

"Then they will deliver you to tribulation, and will kill you, and you will be hated by all nations because of My name." (Matthew 24:9)

Self-styled prophets regularly report the end of the age: A booklet entitled, "88 Reasons Why the Rapture Will Be in 1988"; then, "The Final Shout: Rapture Report 1989"; later, the same man wrote, "The end will begin on Sept. 25, 1995, and on the 23rd day, World War III will explode. A nuclear bomb will hit us at 2 a.m. California time, and 204 million Americans will die instantly." These times have all come and gone. What's the point? God alone knows the future.

Since Israel had rejected Jesus as Messiah, Jesus forewarned the disciples of the unparalleled calamitous days that would descend upon the nation. As they left the city, the disciples were in awe of Herod's magnificent temple. But Jesus warned them that this magnificent structure would be decimated—not one stone would be left upon another. The disciples were stunned. When they arrived at the Mount of Olives they quizzed the Lord, "When will these things happen, and what will be the sign of Your coming, and of the end of the age?" (Matt. 24:3).

In Matthew 24:4–26, Jesus explained the future tribulation coming upon the earth. The purpose of the tribulation is twofold: to bring Israel to repentance and faith in Messiah, and to pour out His wrath in judgment upon unbelievers. The church has no relationship to the tribulation; it will be raptured prior to the tribulation (see Romans 5:9 and 1 Thessalonians 4:13–18).

Jesus spoke of the first half of the tribulation in Matthew 24:4–8. The emphasis on "you" is a warning to the Jewish people of the coming suffering (vv. 4, 9). The tribulation will begin with false christs, wars, famines, and earthquakes. Yet this will only be the beginning. The second half of the tribulation is the subject of verses 9–14. In the middle of the tribulation, severe persecution of the Jewish people will be initiated. They will be universally hated. Integrity will fail. False teachers will arise. And yet the gospel will be proclaimed and multitudes will be saved! The saved will be persecuted, but the ones who endure the persecution will remain alive to enter the glorious millennial kingdom of Christ.

Is the stage for these events set? How many friends does Israel have today?

CONSIDER: *Rejoice that Christ has delivered us from the wrath of God against rebellious unbelievers; we will be raptured before these horrific events.*

April 11

The Great Tribulation

MATTHEW 24:15–31; MARK 13:14–27; LUKE 21:20–27

"Then the sign of the Son of Man will appear in the sky, and then all the tribes of the earth will mourn, and they will see the SON OF MAN COMING ON THE CLOUDS OF THE SKY with power and great glory." (Matthew 24:30)

M r. Ahmadinejad, the president of Iran, "described Israel as 'a stain of shame that has sullied the purity of Islam' promising it would be 'cleansed very soon.' . . . He was inaugurating 'A World Without Zionism'—a week of special events in thousands of mosques, schools, factories, offices and public squares, dedicated to mobilizing popular energies against the Jewish state" (Amir Taheri, *New York Post*, October 28, 2005).

Jesus warned of a future day when fierce persecution of Israel and the Jewish people would take place. It would begin with "the ABOMINATION OF DESOLATION" (Matt. 24:15), popularly called "the Antichrist." The Antichrist will take his place in Jerusalem, usurping the place of deity, and will launch a furious persecution of the Jewish people. Jesus warned that they should flee to the Judean hills, south of Jerusalem, for hiding and protection. The people in Israel would need to hurry to escape. It would be a calamity for a pregnant mother—better to be childless in those days (see also Luke 23:28–29). Since the Jews were restricted to traveling two thousand feet on the Sabbath, better the persecution did not occur on the Sabbath. All because this would be *great tribulation*, a reference to the last three and a half years of the tribulation. Fortunately, these three and a half years will come to an end; otherwise, no people would be left alive (Matt. 24:22).

These calamitous days will come to an end with the second coming of Jesus Christ. Christ returns to a world where the majority of the population has died (see Revelation 6:7–8 and 9:13–21). He comes to judge a corrupted earth, illustrated by vultures feeding on a decaying carcass (Matt. 24:28; also see Rev. 19:17–18). There will be phenomena in the heavens—the sun will be darkened, the moon will not shine, stars will fall—but then the glory of Christ will encircle the earth and will be seen around the world. And God's people, Israel, will recognize their Messiah and they will repent and embrace Christ in faith (Matt. 24:30, where "all the tribes" indicates Israel). The Jewish people will be gathered from around the world, descending upon the land of Israel. They will be redeemed and restored to the land in anticipation of the millennial blessings.

CONSIDER: *When you see immorality and open sin and rebellion against God, remember Christ will one day judge this world. Everything will be laid open.*

April 12

SIGNS OF CHRIST'S SUDDEN COMING

MATTHEW 24:32–51; MARK 13:28–37; LUKE 21:28–36

*"Therefore be on the alert, for you do not know which
day your Lord is coming." (Matthew 24:42)*

When former President Eisenhower was vacationing in Colorado, he heard of a six-year-old boy that was dying of cancer and wanted to see the president. One Sunday morning the presidential limousine pulled up to the boy's home. The president stepped out, went to the door, and knocked. The boy's father—wearing blue jeans, an old shirt, and with an unshaven face—answered the door. The president entered the home, spoke with the boy, and left. The boy was overjoyed but the father would never forget: the president of the United States called on his home—and he was unprepared.

Jesus illustrated that when they would see the fig tree putting forth leaves, they knew summer was near. Similarly, when the people would see the events of the tribulation that Jesus had just described (Matt. 24:4–24), they would know His second coming was near (v. 33). But people will be unprepared, as in Noah's day, going on with normal issues of life—eating and drinking and marrying—but ignoring God and the warnings of His coming. In their unprepared state, Christ will return and they will be taken away in judgment. Two men will be working in a field; one will be taken and one will be left. Two women will be grinding at the mill; one will be taken, and one left. The one taken is the one taken away in judgment. The one left is the one who is prepared; that one will enter the millennial kingdom.

Christ will return "at an hour when you do not think He will" (v. 44). But the "faithful and sensible slave" (v. 45) will be prepared. He represents the believing Jew during the tribulation. He has trusted in Christ and has prepared for His return. He distributes his master's food; namely, he spreads the Word of God in evangelism during the tribulation. The evil slave is the unbelieving Jew that has not prepared. He has not trusted in Christ and does nothing with the Word of God with which he has been entrusted. His ending will be tragic as he is assigned "a place with the hypocrites; in that place there will be weeping and gnashing of teeth" (v. 51).

CONSIDER: *Christ's second coming will be unexpected. While church age believers will be raptured prior to the tribulation, we nonetheless should be anticipating the trumpet call at the rapture.*

April 13

Christ's Unexpected Return
Matthew 25:1–30

*"Well done, good and faithful slave. You were faithful with
a few things, I will put you in charge of many things; enter
into the joy of your master." (Matthew 25:21)*

Marguerite Higgins, a war correspondent, described the fifth company of Marines, originally eighteen thousand, in combat with one hundred thousand Chinese communists during the Korean War: "It was particularly cold, 42 degrees below zero. The weary soldiers, half frozen, stood by their dirty trucks eating from tin cans. A huge marine was eating cold beans with his trench knife. His clothes were stiff as a board; his face covered with a heavy beard crusted with mud. A correspondent asked, 'If I were God and could grant you anything you wished, what would you most like?' The man stood motionless, then raised his head and replied, 'Give me tomorrow.'"

There is a phenomenal tomorrow coming—but preparedness is the issue. Jesus told the parable of ten virgins who were awaiting the bridegroom, but five were foolish and five were prudent. In the Jewish wedding, the marriage is arranged through the betrothal, a year in advance. Then, on the day of the marriage, the bridegroom comes to get his bride from her parents' home. He then leads the jubilant bridal procession to his home for the wedding celebration and festivities—a picture of celebration in the kingdom of God. Meanwhile, people would wait along the roadside, not knowing when the bridegroom would come. The five foolish virgins represent unbelieving Israel. They failed to make preparations while waiting for the bridegroom. The prudent virgins represent believing Jewish people, converted during the tribulation. They will be prepared for Christ's return and will enter into the millennial kingdom, pictured by the celebration of the wedding feast.

Jesus told a second parable, illustrated by a man who entrusted his estate to slaves, giving one five talents, another two, and another one. The slaves represent Israel while the talents represent spiritual truth that has been uniquely entrusted to Israel (as detailed in Romans 9:4–5). Although the distribution was uneven, it was "each according to his own ability" (Matt. 25:15). The five- and two-talent men represent Jews that were converted during the tribulation and who spread the truth of Christ. The one-talent man was an unbeliever who did not believe in Christ and therefore did not spread the message of Christ.

The Lord will reward those slaves who have faithfully served Him, giving them authority and service in the millennial kingdom. The one who ignored God's truth will have a tragic end, where "there will be weeping and gnashing of teeth" (v. 30).

CONSIDER: *While the parables relate to Israel, there is nonetheless an application that in the church age we have been gifted and will be held responsible for what we did with our gifts.*

JUDGMENT AT THE SECOND COMING

MATTHEW 25:31–46

*"These will go away into eternal punishment, but the
righteous into eternal life." (Matthew 25:46)*

When Jesus returns at His second coming, He will establish His kingdom and He will reign as King of the earth, with authority over all the Gentile nations. He is the Son of Man (prophesied in Daniel 7:13–14). When He initiates His eternal reign, He will fulfill the Davidic covenant found in 2 Samuel 7:16.

The nations (*ethne*, which implies Gentiles) will be gathered in judgment before Christ. But He will not judge *nations*; He will judge *individual* Gentiles, separating them into two groups—the sheep, representing believing Gentiles, and the goats, representing unbelieving Gentiles. The picture is taken from Hebrew culture. In Israel the sheep and goats would graze together during the day, but in the evening the shepherd would put the sheep and goats into separate folds. The shepherd would stand at the gate, directing the sheep into one fold, the goats into another.

In the parable, those that enter the kingdom are the ones who fed Christ when He was hungry, gave Him water to drink, invited Him in, clothed Him, and visited Him. Those that will not enter the kingdom are the ones who failed to do these things. What does the parable teach? Does it teach salvation by good works?

The key to understanding the parable is the phrase, "to the extent that you did it to one of these brothers of Mine, even the least of them, you did it to Me" (Matt. 25:40). The context is the tribulation. The "brothers" are Jesus' Jewish brethren. During the tribulation 144,000 Jewish evangelists spread the gospel (Isa. 66:19; Rev. 7), but there will be severe persecution of the Jews and so it will be essential for the 144,000 to receive help from the Gentiles. Who would provide food and lodging for them? Those who respond to their gospel message. The ones who respond will invite the messengers into their homes, feed them, and give them lodging and clothing.

Those on His left (Matt. 25:41) are condemned because these Gentiles refused to respond to the gospel proclaimed by the Jewish believers and, because they rejected the gospel, they did not offer hospitality to the Jewish evangelists. These Gentiles will go into "eternal punishment" and the Gentiles who responded will go into "eternal life" (v. 46). The final statement is also a denial of annihilation. The same adjective "eternal" modifies "punishment" and "life." Once established, one's eternal destiny is sealed.

CONSIDER: *The Jewish people are God's specially ordained people and should be the objects of special love and respect by Gentiles.*

A PLANNED BETRAYAL!

MATTHEW 26:1–16; MARK 14:1–11; LUKE 21:37–22:6

"You know that after two days the Passover is coming, and the Son of Man is to be handed over for crucifixion." (Matthew 26:2)

On Tuesday of the Passover week Jesus reminded the disciples that in two days, when the Passover would begin at sunset, Christ would be betrayed and handed over to the Romans for crucifixion. On a number of other occasions Jesus had precisely detailed His future betrayal, crucifixion, and resurrection. This is noteworthy. It displayed the omniscience of Jesus—an attribute of God in which He knows the details of the future. But Jesus was also genuine humanity, though sinless. He would go to the cross, bearing our sins as the God-Man.

This would come about through the betrayal of a disciple. A man who had heard the teaching of Jesus and seen His miraculous works would betray Him! Through cunning deceit and treachery, the religious leaders (!) planned to kill Jesus. But not during the festival—that would disturb the people! Their religiosity was only an outward show; as Jesus had earlier declared, inwardly they were dead men's bones (see April 9 Scripture reading and devotional).

While Judas would display his deception, Mary, the sister of Martha and Lazarus, would display her love for Jesus by anointing Him. Taking an alabaster flask, Mary poured the very expensive perfume (worth a year's wages) on Jesus' head. What was the significance? It was a present for a king. In the Old Testament, on God's command, Samuel anointed first Saul (1 Sam. 10:1) and then David (1 Sam. 16:12–13) as king of Israel. Mary had heard Jesus' teaching; she understood His claims. She was lovingly and devotedly anointing Him as king.

The disciples were infuriated. But who initiated the indignation? While Matthew tells us "the disciples were indignant" (Matt. 26:8), only John reports that Judas Iscariot was upset (12:4–5). It is a reminder that Judas must have been a smooth operator; the Eleven never suspected him. Jesus reminded the disciples that Mary's act was prophetic: it was in anticipation of His burial (Matt. 26:12).

Stung by the rebuke, Judas determined to betray Jesus. In that mind-set, Satan took control of Judas as he hurried to the chief priests and bargained to betray Christ. They agreed on thirty pieces of silver, the price of a male slave in the Old Testament (Exod. 21:32). While Judas was responsible for his dastardly deed, it had been prophesied five hundred years earlier (Zech. 11:12). From that moment Judas "began looking for a good opportunity to betray Jesus" (Matt. 26:16). All the words of Jesus that Judas had heard for three years were set aside; he was now controlled by Satan.

CONSIDER: *We are responsible for our decisions and actions; we can betray Jesus Christ or we can exhibit our love and devotion to Him.*

April 16

A LESSON IN SERVITUDE

MATTHEW 26:17–20; MARK 14:12–17; LUKE 22:7–16; JOHN 13:1–20

---

*"If I then, the Lord and the Teacher, washed your feet, you also
ought to wash one another's feet. For I gave you an example
that you also should do as I did to you." (John 13:14–15)*

When I was a college student, I worked as an architectural draftsman for a Christian businessman who tended to be rather straightforward with his employees. One day he approached me and said, "You know how Jesus taught His disciples that the greatest among them would be their servant? Well here, sweep the floor!" And he handed me a broom.

The Lord was about to teach the disciples a significant lesson in servitude. It was Thursday afternoon, the "day of preparation" for the Passover feast. Technically, the Passover was the fourteenth day of Nisan and the Feast of Unleavened Bread was Nisan 15–22, but the two feasts were taken together and the entire event was called the Passover.

The lamb was slain in the afternoon of Nisan 14, and eaten that evening. Jesus sent two disciples into the city to make preparations to eat the Passover with His disciples. The arrangement reflects the omniscience of Christ—the disciples would meet a man carrying a pitcher of water and they would follow him to the house.

Peter and John purchased a lamb and took it to the temple where the lamb was killed. The priest caught up the blood in a bowl and poured it out at the base of the altar of burnt offering. Parts of the lamb were removed and burned on the altar; then the lamb, on staves, was carried by Peter and John to the home where it was roasted and eaten. The feast was instituted both to commemorate Israel's release from Egyptian captivity and to foreshadow Christ, "our Passover Lamb" (1 Cor. 5:7).

In the evening Jesus came to celebrate the Passover with the disciples. Jesus knew that His hour had come—the crucifixion was imminent. It would be the ultimate demonstration of His love. Yet the entire event had been planned by the Father. History was on schedule (John 13:1, 3). Jesus had taken on humanity for this very purpose and He would again return to the Father. Amid Jesus' humiliation in going to the cross, the disciples were far from that mind-set. Upon entering a home, it was characteristic for a servant to wash the guests' feet. Yet no one had taken the place of a servant. Jesus got up, laid aside His outer garments, and, taking a towel, assumed the servant's position as He washed the disciples' feet. Peter was horrified. Notice the emphasis in the Greek text: "Lord, *You my* feet are washing?" Peter exclaimed. He saw the incongruity.

Jesus was not inaugurating a new ordinance but He was demonstrating the place of servitude that disciples of His should assume.

CONSIDER: *In the crucifixion, Jesus assumed the ultimate place of servitude for fallen humanity. How can you demonstrate a servant's heart to the Lord?*

The Last Supper and the Betrayer

MATTHEW 26:21–35; MARK 14:18–31; LUKE 22:21–40; JOHN 13:21–38; 18:1

---

*Jesus took some bread, and after a blessing, He broke it and gave
it to the disciples, and said, "Take, eat; this is My body." And when
He had taken a cup and given thanks, He gave it to them, saying,
"Drink from it, all of you; for this is My blood of the covenant, which
is poured out for many for forgiveness of sins." (Matthew 26:26–28)*

The apostles reclined on couches around a U-shaped table. Judas, Jesus, and John were at one end, with Judas in the place of honor, while Jesus was the host. Peter was across the table from the three (Alfred Edersheim, *Life and Times of Jesus the Messiah*).

Jesus certainly stirred the Twelve when He announced a betrayer in their midst. Immediately, there was grieving and turmoil as they questioned the identity of the betrayer. Across the table, Peter beckoned to John, who was leaning against Jesus, asking him to discover the betrayer's identity. Jesus identified the betrayer as the recipient of the morsel that He would give him. Then Jesus dipped the flat pancake type of bread into the common bowl filled with a sauce of mashed fruit—dates, raisins, and figs, with water, vinegar, and bitter herbs—and handed it to Judas.

Why didn't the disciples realize it was Judas? He was in the place of honor and they likely thought that Jesus gave the morsel to Judas for that reason. Further, amid the noisy conversation following Jesus' announcement, they may not have heard Jesus' remark identifying the betrayer. Even when Jesus told Judas, "What you do, do quickly" (John 13:27), the disciples didn't understand it. They thought Jesus was sending Judas on an errand. But Satan was controlling Judas and the betrayer left immediately. John adds, "and it was night" (v. 30), indicating the betrayer was entering the domain of spiritual darkness.

But Judas did not participate in the Lord's Supper. After the betrayer left, Jesus inaugurated a new event. This event was the last Passover and the first Lord's Supper. The Lord inaugurated the Lord's Supper as a memorial to His substitutionary death—a memorial that the church is commanded to keep perpetually. Although Jesus broke the bread, His body was not broken because He had to provide an unblemished sacrifice (John 19:36; Ps. 34:20). The common cup from which they all drank represented the blood of Christ, which poured forth from His body on the cross. Jesus' death was a *penal substitution*—Jesus died as our substitute, paying the price for the penalty of sins that all humanity incurred. With that Jesus inaugurated a "new covenant" (foretold in Jeremiah 31:31–34), which was given to Israel and will ultimately be fulfilled with regenerated Israel at the end of the age. Believers in the church age participate *individually* in the new covenant; Israel will fulfill it *nationally*. The new covenant provides the final resolution to the sin problem—forgiveness. Shedding blood—death—was necessary to provide forgiveness of sins.

CONSIDER: *The Lord's Supper is a significant memorial when we remember the enormous price that Jesus paid as our substitute to pay the penalty for our sins.*

April 18

JESUS COMFORTS THE DISCIPLES
JOHN 14:1–31

Jesus said to him, "I am the way, and the truth, and the life;
no one comes to the Father but through Me." (John 14:6)

The disciples were sorrowing. Jesus had just told them He was leaving them and they could not follow Him now. But Jesus responded with some of the most comforting words in all of Scripture, "Do not let your heart be troubled" (John 14:1). The disciples were in turmoil. They had walked with the Lord for three years and had come to love Him. Now He was leaving! But the Lord provided a wonderful promise. He was going to the Father's house to prepare a place for them. The picture is that of a wealthy landowner with a beautiful estate. When his children get married he simply adds to his estate, that all together they may live in "the Father's house." In a future day there would be no more separation—like a family, they would all be together in "the Father's house." What a premium promise! What wonderful comfort! Could they believe it? Yes, Jesus promised them, "if it were not so, I would have told you" (v. 2). *Jesus' words are reliable.*

And how would they get to the Father's house? By believing in Jesus. He uniquely is the way—and He alone is the way—there is no one else. And He provides life, *eternal, unending life.*

But how did the disciples know Jesus was the way? In His life and ministry Jesus had shown them the Father. The words that Jesus spoke—the discourses—they spoke of the union of the Father and the Son (v. 10). They had seen the Father in Jesus! But they had also seen the Father in Jesus' works (v. 11). When He healed the sick, gave sight to the blind, raised the dead—Jesus was revealing the Father. The Father and Jesus were operating in union.

But to assuage their sorrow Jesus reminded them that in their new relationship they could pray in His name and He would respond and answer their requests. And Jesus gave them another unique promise. Although He was leaving them, He and the Father would send them "another Comforter," another Helper of the same kind as Jesus who would come alongside to help them in their need. Moreover, the Helper, the Holy Spirit, would have a unique relationship with them—He would remain with them permanently. The Holy Spirit would uniquely minister to them, helping them to remember all the things Jesus taught them so when they would later writer the canonical Scriptures. The Spirit would supernaturally give them accurate recall of the events.

But there was more. In His legacy to His disciples Jesus promised them peace. It would be a unique peace, not found in the world. It was the very peace of Christ Himself that would bring tranquility to their hearts so they would not longer be in turmoil.

CONSIDER: *Jesus has provided for our present and our future. He Himself is the way to our future home, the Father's house. And in the present He gives us His peace.*

ABIDE IN ME

JOHN 15:1–16:4

---

*"If you abide in Me, and My words abide in you, ask whatever
you wish, and it will be done for you." (John 15:7)*

As we traveled through the countryside of Israel, vineyards were evident. In Scripture, the vineyard is often symbolic of Israel (Isa. 5:1–7). God had planted Israel as a vineyard and cultivated it to produce fruit. But Israel failed, only producing wild fruit. In contrast to Israel's failure, Jesus declared, "I am the true vine" (John 15:1). He was the true Israel, the true Son of God. He produced fruit—and His disciples would follow suit.

Jesus encouraged the disciples by explaining the new relationship they could enjoy with Him: "Abide in Me, and I in you" (v. 4). "Abide" (*meinate*) simply means "to remain, to stay, to live with." It means to believe in and remain with.

What a phenomenal truth! We can live in a union of fellowship with Christ and be productive, living fruitful lives. In this unique union, we can approach Christ with confidence that He hears our petitions (John 15:7). The outcome of this unique relationship is joy—the very joy that Jesus had would also be the joy of His disciples. The joy of Jesus was fulfilling the Father's will; the joy of His disciples is living in union with Jesus and doing His will. And this is a fulfilled joy, a complete joy (v. 11).

Entering into this joy means loving one another, laying down one's life for another. And by abiding in Christ, we enter a new relationship with Him: He calls us "friends" (v. 15). What is a friend? "The friends of Jesus are those who habitually obey Him" (Leon Morris, *Gospel According to John*). It is someone that we take into our confidence and trust. Hence, Jesus shared these profound truths (ch. 14–16) with His friends.

But Jesus also had some stark words for the disciples. As His friends, they could expect the world to hate them. The world hated Him; could they expect less? But the reason the world hates Jesus and His followers is that their origin is not of this world. The world loves its own but His followers have their origin with Christ—and that is why believers in Christ are hated. In the event that they would falter, the Helper, the Holy Spirit, would confirm the truth of Christ to them (v. 26). And when these hostilities from the world would come, the disciples could remind themselves of Jesus' words.

Do not be dismayed at the opposition you receive in the world. Jesus promised us the hatred of the world. Instead, enter into the joy of living in an abiding fellowship with Jesus!

CONSIDER: *Are you living in fellowship with the world or are you living in genuine, devoted fellowship with Christ, abiding in Him?*

THE HELPER

JOHN 16:5–33

"But when He, the Spirit of truth, comes, He will guide you into all the truth; for He will not speak on His own initiative, but whatever He hears, He will speak; and He will disclose to you what is to come." (John 16:13)

The disciples were filled with sorrow at the thought of Jesus leaving them, yet Jesus had promised them joy (John 15:11; 16:24). But now Jesus would explain the necessity of His departure. It was imperative that He leave them, because in so doing He would send the *Paraclete*, the Helper, who would not only be the "one called alongside to help" them, but He would have a distinct ministry in the world. The Holy Spirit would act as a legal prosecuting attorney in the world. He would convict—prosecute—the world for not believing in Jesus; He would convict—convince—the world concerning the righteousness of Christ, confirming His death, resurrection, and ascension. He would also judge the world through judgment of Satan, the prince of this fallen world.

But the Holy Spirit would also have a unique ministry for His followers. Just as a guide leads people through uncharted territory, so the Holy Spirit would guide the Lord's people "into all the truth" (v. 13). Whatever the Spirit would hear from the Lord, He would speak to them, and He would unveil the coming world events. His purpose would be to exalt and glorify Christ. The Holy Spirit would point them to Christ.

The disciples were puzzled: Jesus said, "A little while, and you will no longer see Me; and again a little while, and you will see Me" (v. 16). What did He mean? Jesus was referring to the cross and the resurrection. They would weep in sorrow at the crucifixion and would not see Him when He was buried but then, when He was resurrected they would see Him—and their sorrow would be turned to joy!

That would result in a new relationship and a new joy. He would ascend to heaven, and, as their Advocate, He invited them: "Until now you have asked for nothing in My name; ask and you will receive, so that your joy may be made full" (v. 24). Their temporary sorrow would be turned to great joy! In this new relationship, they could come boldly to the Father in Jesus' name, and the Father who loves them would grant their request.

Meanwhile, still living in a hateful world, they would be scattered because of persecution, yet the ultimate legacy Jesus would leave them was His peace. Although living amid tribulation in the world, they would at the same moment enjoy His peace.

CONSIDER: *The Holy Spirit is our Divine Helper, guiding us into God's truth while also judging the world for not having believed in Christ.*

April 21

Praying to the Father

JOHN 17:1–26

"They are not of the world, even as I am not of the world. Sanctify them in the truth; Your word is truth. As You sent Me into the world, I also have sent them into the world." (John 17:16–18)

Jesus and the disciples left the "upper room" (Luke 22:12), where they had celebrated Passover and Jesus had instituted the Lord's Supper, and walked through Jerusalem on the way to the garden of Gethsemane. Jesus now anticipates the cross—but the cross will reflect the victory Jesus has just announced (John 16:33). At the cross, Jesus overcomes the world. Now Jesus prays to the Father concerning Himself (17:1–5), the disciples (vv. 6–19), and the church (vv. 20–26). Jesus prays out loud, so the disciples can learn from His communication with the Father.

Recognizing that His hour had come, Jesus committed Himself to the will of the Father. He prayed for the Father to glorify Him, referring to the crucifixion. "Glorify" (*doxason*) means "divine honor," "divine splendor," "divine power," and "divine visible radiance" (Gerhard Kittel, *Theological Dictionary of the New Testament*). Jesus prayed that divine honor would be given Him so that, in return, His death on the cross would bring divine honor to the Father. That divine honor would be displayed in Jesus' provision of eternal life through the cross.

Jesus prayed for the disciples—to whom Jesus had revealed the Father and who have kept His word. They received the words from the Father through Christ and they believed them. They realized that Jesus had come from the Father and revealed the Father to them. Jesus now intercedes for them.

But Jesus' concern for the disciples is because they will still be in the world. He prayed that the Father would "keep them" and "that they may be one" (v. 11). Jesus is not praying for organizational unity; He prays "that they may 'continually be' one" (Leon Morris, *Gospel According to John*). And now, since Jesus was leaving, He prayed for their protection and that, despite His departure, they might have His joy. This was essential because they were being left in a world that hates them. Nonetheless, Jesus' disciples must remain in the world although they do not have their origin and character from this world's system.

Finally, Jesus prays for all who will believe in Him that they labor in unity in evangelizing the world—that the world may believe. "The unity for which Christ prays is to lead to a fuller experience of the Father and the Son" (Leon Morris, *Gospel According to John*). This will effect the propagation of the gospel, resulting in people believing in Christ. The ultimate desire of Jesus is that His followers "be with Me where I am" (v. 24). That day will be ushered in on the new earth when His people will bask in His glory.

CONSIDER: *What a phenomenal privilege to know that Jesus Himself prays for you and me! Reflect on that sublime truth.*

April 22

Agonizing in Gethsemane

Matthew 26:36–46; Mark 14:32–42; Luke 22:40–46

Then Jesus came with them to a place called Gethsemane. . . .
Then He said to them, "My soul is deeply grieved, to the
point of death. . . ." (Matthew 26:36, 38)

Gethsemane, meaning "oil press," was an enclosed garden less than a mile from the eastern wall of Jerusalem. It lay on the western slope of the Mount of Olives. It was a quiet place where Jesus frequently came to pray, rest, and sleep.

Leaving the other nine, Jesus took Peter, James, and John—the inner three—and went a little farther to pray. As the One who would bear the penalty of the sins of all humanity, Jesus began to grieve and be distressed in facing horrific suffering. His soul was overwhelmed with sorrow and distress. Leaving the three, Jesus went a little farther, and, falling on His face, prayed, "My Father, if it is possible, let this cup pass from Me" (Matt. 26:39). Was Jesus asking that the Father provide a resolution apart from the cross? No. Jesus was not praying to avoid the cross. He knew the Old Testament Scriptures, such as Isaiah 57, that He would atone for sin, and He had come to do the Father's will (Heb. 10:7).

Jesus knew that in death He would be separated from the Father as our sin-bearer (as we see in Matthew 27:46). He also knew that in the crucifixion He would be made sin for all humanity (2 Cor. 5:21). Since Jesus was bearing physical and spiritual death for the human race, taking it upon Himself, He prayed that the Father might accept His death as full payment for sin and bring Him out of death and restore Him to life again. Psalm 16:10 confirms this.

Returning to the disciples and finding them sleeping, Jesus admonished them, "Keep watching and praying that you may not enter into temptation" (Matt. 26:41). Three times Jesus agonized in prayer to the Father. Returning to the disciples a final time and seeing them sleeping again, He alerted them concerning the occasion: "Behold, the hour is at hand and the Son of Man is being betrayed into the hands of sinners" (v. 45). Jesus, in His omniscience, knew precisely what was about to transpire; yet, in His humanity He experienced the normal agonizing emotion at the prospect of the suffering that awaited Him. Yet Jesus was resolute: He had come to do the Father's will. And that culminated in the cross, serving as a substitute for all humanity, bearing the penalty of the sins of the world upon Himself. He did not shrink from this horrific suffering. His devotion to the Father's will and His love for humanity took Him to the cross. Jesus woke the disciples, "Get up, let us be going; behold, the one who betrays Me is at hand!" (v. 46).

CONSIDER: *Who can fathom the mental and emotional anguish our Savior suffered in becoming the sin-bearer for all humanity?*

CHRIST IS BETRAYED AND ARRESTED

MATTHEW 26:47–56; MARK 14:43–52; LUKE 22:47–53; JOHN 18:2–12

---

*Now he who was betraying Him gave them a sign, saying, "Whomever
I kiss, He is the one; seize Him." Immediately Judas went to Jesus
and said, "Hail, Rabbi!" and kissed Him. (Matthew 26:48–49)*

A prominent evangelist shared the platform with Billy Graham in the early
days of his ministry. This man was a superb preacher and many people
responded to his gospel invitations. Yet one day he turned his back on Christ
and the ministry, declaring, "I could no longer continue in something I didn't
believe in."

Far more phenomenal is the case of Judas. For three and a half years he
heard the profound teaching of Jesus and saw His astonishing miracles, yet
now Judas turned away. And he betrayed Christ. Leading a Roman cohort
(two hundred or six hundred soldiers) as well as temple officers from the chief
priests, along with Pharisees, Judas and these men came with lanterns and
weapons. They thought Jesus would run and they would have to look for Him
and fight to apprehend Him.

As they approached Jesus, He stepped out to meet them. When they
announced they were looking for Jesus the Nazarene, He responded, "I am
He" three times (John 18:5, 6, 8). These words draw attention to the deity of
Jesus Christ. To Jewish ears "I AM" was equivalent to Jehovah (Yahweh) the
covenant name of God. The power and majesty of Jesus' words "I AM" sent
the soldiers falling backward.

Leading the military contingent was Judas, who came to Jesus and kissed
Him. The kiss, a common eastern greeting, now became a tool of Satan. The term
"kissed" is intensive in form and means "to kiss repeatedly or fervently" (as is
also seen in Luke 15:20). Hypocrisy was added to betrayal.

Jesus recognized the hypocrisy, addressing Judas as "friend" (*etairos*),
better translated "fellow," an impersonal term normally used when the other
person's name was unknown. Jesus never addressed the other apostles that
way. Jesus knew entirely that Judas was betraying Him.

When Peter drew his sword and cut off the ear of Malchus, the slave of
the high priest, Jesus rebuked Peter, reminding him that He could summon
His Father and have twelve legions of angels (72,000) at His disposal. Why did
Jesus submit to the Romans? Jesus explained that "all this has taken place to
fulfill the Scriptures of the prophets" (Matt. 26:56). Jesus was destined for the
cross—yet this did not absolve Judas—he was responsible for his dastardly
deed. But at the arrest of Jesus, fear gripped the Eleven and they "left Him and
fled" (v. 56). Jesus went to the cross alone.

CONSIDER: *It is a solemn, provocative thought that a person can listen to the
words of Jesus, see His astonishing miracles—and yet walk away from Him.*

April 24

THE TRIAL OF JESUS

MATTHEW 26:57–75; MARK 14:53–72; LUKE 22:54–65; JOHN 18:13–27

*Again the high priest was questioning Him, and saying to Him,
"Are You the Christ, the Son of the Blessed One?" And Jesus said, "I am;
and you shall see THE SON OF MAN SITTING AT THE RIGHT HAND OF POWER,
and COMING WITH THE CLOUDS OF HEAVEN." (Mark 14:61–62)*

There is no parallel in human history to what transpired here. The only sinless and entirely righteous person that ever lived stood trial for nonexistent crimes before prosecutors and judges whose own hands were stained with sin and guilt.

There were three phases to the religious trial of Jesus. First, He was led to Annas, the father-in-law of Caiaphas. Although Annas had been deposed as high priest, in the minds of the people he was still recognized as the authoritative leader. Eventually, five sons of Annas ruled as high priest. It was a corrupt priesthood.

Annas questioned Jesus about the movement. How many disciples did He have? How widespread was the movement? What was Jesus teaching? Was it contrary to the Law? Jesus did not answer Annas directly because the procedure was wrong. Jewish law did not require a man to implicate himself by testifying against himself. The proper procedure was to bring witnesses to testify against the accused. Annas failed to do this; instead, he attempted to get Jesus to testify against Himself.

The trial was entirely illegal: (1) They questioned Jesus (John 18:19). (2) They struck Him (John 18:22; Matt. 26:67). (3) The trial was at night. (4) They called false witnesses.

In the second phase of the trial, Jesus was brought before Caiaphas. They continued in their illegality by attempting to obtain false witnesses. Finally, two came forward, saying Jesus said He could destroy the temple and rebuild it in three days. But Jesus kept silent. Finally, the high priest demanded to know whether He was the Christ, the Son of God. Jesus responded by quoting Daniel 7:13, reminding them they would see the Son of Man sitting at the right hand of power, coming on the clouds of heaven.

The religious leaders drew their conclusion: blasphemy! They spat in His face, beat Him with their fists, and slapped Him. And they condemned Him—death!

Where were the disciples? Far away. They had run. Peter stood at a distance and ultimately denied three times that he knew Jesus.

CONSIDER: *The utter sinfulness of humanity is evidenced as religious people implicate the only Righteous One who ever walked this earth. Even His disciples denied Him by running away. What would we have done?*

April 25

MANIPULATION, DECEPTION, AND SUICIDE

MATTHEW 27:1–14; LUKE 22:66–23:5; JOHN 18:28–38; ACTS 1:18–19

Therefore Pilate said to Him, "So You are a king?" Jesus answered,
"You say correctly that I am a king. For this I have been born, and
for this I have come into the world, to testify to the truth." . . .
Pilate said, . . . "I find no guilt in Him." (John 18:37–38)

The illegalities of the Jewish leaders continued through the night and into the morning. Recognizing they had no legitimate accusation to bring against Jesus to the Roman authorities they constructed an accusation to deceive the Romans. The Romans were entirely disinterested in the Sanhedrin charge of blasphemy against Jesus.

When Jesus was brought before the Sanhedrin, they questioned Him about His claim to be the Messiah. Jesus answered with clarity: "But from now on the Son of Man will be seated at the right hand of the power of God" (Luke 22:69). They continued their questioning: "'Are You the Son of God, then?' And He said to them, 'Yes, I am'" (v. 70). It was all they wanted to hear. They considered Jesus' claim of messiahship and Sonship as blasphemy. But now they would have to manipulate the Roman authorities.

In the meantime, Judas had had time to reflect on his horrific betrayal of Jesus. Likely he remembered the teachings of Jesus and visualized His miracles. Judas recognized he had betrayed innocent blood—he was guilty of delivering Jesus over to death. When he attempted to resolve the issue by returning the money, the Sanhedrin scorned him. They had benefited from Judas; now they rejected him. In frustration Judas threw the money into the sanctuary and went out and hanged himself.

Although the Sanhedrin had pronounced the death penalty on Jesus, they did not have the authority to implement the death penalty, so the religious leaders delivered Jesus to Pilate, the Roman governor, for crucifixion. This was now the civil phase of the trial and would result in fulfillment of Jesus' prediction about the kind of death He would die (John 3:14; 8:28; 12:32–33).

When Pilate questioned Jesus, the Lord acknowledged that He is a king, but His kingdom did not have its origin in this corrupt world's system. The messianic kingdom will be a kingdom of righteousness, when Christ will indeed rule on this earth (Isa. 11). Having questioned Jesus, Pilate concluded, "I find no guilt in Him." The most heinous, sinful act in human history was about to take place: the crucifixion of Christ.

CONSIDER: *Remorse may come too late—and in the wrong way. There is a sorrow of the world that leads to death (2 Cor. 7:10).*

THE ROMAN TRIAL

MATTHEW 27:15–26; MARK 15:6–15; LUKE 23:6–25; JOHN 18:39–19:16

Then he released Barabbas for them; but after having Jesus scourged, he handed Him over to be crucified. (Matthew 27:26)

J esus had been arrested and placed under Roman jurisdiction, under Pontius Pilate. When Pilate heard that Jesus was a Galilean, he sent Jesus to Herod, who had jurisdiction over Galilee. Apparently there had been a conflict between Herod and Pilate over authority. By sending Jesus to Herod, Pilate secured a better relationship with Herod. Herod had been visiting Jerusalem because of the feast of Passover. Herod had long wanted to see Jesus perform a miracle and so he questioned Him but Jesus refused to answer Herod. When Herod realized Jesus would not accommodate his curiosity, Herod had his soldiers dress Jesus in a robe—mocking and ridiculing Jesus' claim of kingship. Then they sent Jesus back to Pilate.

At the time, a notorious prisoner named Barabbas was being held on a charge of insurrection against Rome. He was guilty of the very crime with which they tried to charge Jesus. In that, Jesus became Barabbas's substitute.

When Pilate volunteered to release Jesus, the people, influenced by the religious leaders, kept shouting their vehement resistance. "Crucify Him!" "Crucify Him!" they screamed with intense emotion. When Pilate was unable to placate the Jews, in frustration he ceremonially washed his hands, proclaiming his innocence. Undeterred the Jews cried out, "His blood shall be on us and on our children!" (Matt. 27:25).

Acknowledging the wishes of the people—and to prevent an unfavorable report being sent to Caesar— Pilate released Barabbas and delivered Jesus over for scourging and crucifixion. Scourging was a most brutal form of punishment. "The sufferer was stripped and bound to a pillar or post, bending forward so as to expose his back completely; the heavy whip or strap often containing bits of bone or metal, and tore the quivering flesh into one bloody mass" (John Broadus, *Commentary on the Gospel of Matthew*). Scourging frequently left the prisoner half dead—with bowels gushing out of their torn bodies. The scourging sometimes flayed the prisoner to the bone, exposing and tearing the veins and body organs. Some died from the scourging. It was the most severe form of torture. And Jesus, the innocent One, underwent this horrific torture and suffering for you and me—the guilty ones.

CONSIDER: *Jesus suffered the most intense torture, suffering, and pain that He might make atonement for the sins of you and me—and the entire world.*

April 27

THE ROAD TO GOLGOTHA

MATTHEW 27:27–34; MARK 15:16–23; LUKE 23:26–33; JOHN 19:17

After they had mocked Him, they took the scarlet robe off Him
and put His own garments back on Him, and led Him away
to crucify Him. (Matthew 27:31)

A friend of mine ministers to students in public schools. Recently he asked a principal if he was permitted to use the name of Jesus in a public assembly. "Absolutely not," exclaimed the principal. The name of Jesus provoked ridicule and rejection in the first century and it continues in the twenty-first century.

After having scourged Jesus, the Roman soldiers took Jesus to the Praetorium, the palace where the Roman governor lived, probably Herod's old palace. The scourging would have caused unparalleled pain, yet Jesus had to walk to the Praetorium. Then, ridiculing His claim to be King of Israel, they mockingly provided Him with a kingly robe, crown, and sceptor—a coat worn by soldiers, a garland of poterium spinosum with its slender spikes, and a grass cane. They spit on Him and beat Him on the head. Little did they realize the One before them was indeed the King of Kings. Someday they would all bow before Him (Phil. 2:8–11).

Since Jesus had been weakened by the scourging, the Romans apprehended Simon the Cyrenian to carry Christ's cross. Multitudes of men and women followed the procession, hitting their chests in anguish while wailing and lamenting over what was happening to their Lord. The Romans brought Jesus to Golgotha, the "Place of a Skull," outside the northern wall of Jerusalem. But Jesus warned the women to weep for themselves because of the horror that would come upon the nation as a result of their rejection of Messiah. This would have both a near and distant fulfillment—untold numbers of Jewish people would soon die at the destruction of Jerusalem by Rome in A.D. 70, but also during the yet-future Tribulation, the majority of Jews will die through the seal, trumpet, and bowl judgments.

In fulfillment of prophecy found in Psalm 69:21, they gave Jesus wine to drink mingled with gall, but He refused it. The wine was a narcotic used to deaden the pain. Jesus refused the drink so that He might bear the full effects of the crucifixion. For us, for you, for me.

CONSIDER: *One day all humanity—including those who have rejected and ridiculed Christ—will bow in submission to His lordship.*

THE CRUCIFIXION

MATTHEW 27:35–50; MARK 15:24–37; LUKE 23:34–46; JOHN 19:18–30

About the ninth hour Jesus cried out with a loud voice, saying,
"ELI, ELI, LAMA SABACHTHANI?" that is, "MY GOD, MY GOD, WHY HAVE
YOU FORSAKEN ME? . . . It is finished!" (Matthew 27:46; John 19:30)

From the cross Jesus spoke seven paramount statements—words that have impacted all humanity and forever will.

"Father, forgive them; for they do not know what they are doing" (Luke 23:34). Jesus spoke these words repeatedly (the present tense signifying this). As the Romans nailed His hands and feet to the cross—"Father, forgive them. . . ." As the unbelieving crowd howled in ridicule—"Father, forgive them . . . ."

To the repentant thief Jesus spoke the promising words, "Truly I say to you, today you shall be with Me in Paradise" (v. 43). Today! Paradise! Because of grace!

But amid His suffering, Jesus still had concern for His mother. To Mary, Jesus said, "Woman, behold your son!" To John, He said, "Behold, your mother!" (John 19:26–27). Jesus was entrusting Mary to the care of the disciple John.

Darkness covered the earth from the sixth hour (noon) until the ninth hour (3:00 P.M.). The darkness was supernatural; nature itself was suffering in sympathy with the Savior. The darkness symbolized Jesus' suffering as the sin-bearer in making atonement for the sins of the world. The darkness was also a sign of judgment by God. At the end of the three hours Jesus cried aloud, "My God, My God, why have You forsaken Me?" The first and last words of Jesus began with "Father," but now the fellowship was interrupted as the Father turned His face away from Jesus and our Savior bore the penalty of our sins on the cross alone. We cannot fathom the depth of Christ's pain, suffering for all the sins that ever have been committed and ever will be committed.

Knowing atonement for sin had now been made, Jesus exclaimed, "I am thirsty" (John 19:28). Attendants put a sponge full of sour wine upon a branch of hyssop and gave it to Jesus. Then Jesus made the dramatic statement: "It is finished!" (v. 30). Redemption's work was complete! Jesus had accomplished salvation's work!

Now, in the trusting words of a childlike prayer, Jesus spoke His last saying from the cross: "Father, into Your hands I commit My spirit" (Luke 23:46). Then He bowed His head and dismissed His spirit. His death shows that He willingly gave up His life on behalf of others; no one took it from Him (John 10:18). This was not the death of an ordinary man.

CONSIDER: *Amid incomprehensible pain and abuse, Jesus voluntarily gave His life as a substitutionary atonement for sin—available to all who trust in Him.*

April 29

WITNESSES OF JESUS' DEATH

MATTHEW 27:51–58; MARK 15:38–45; LUKE 23:45–52; JOHN 19:31–38

Now the centurion, and those who were with him keeping guard over Jesus, when they saw the earthquake and the things that were happening, became very frightened and said, "Truly this was the Son of God!" (Matthew 27:54)

The temple veil—sixty feet long, thirty feet wide, and six inches thick separating the Holy Place from the Holy of Holies—was torn from top to bottom, indicating it was a divine act. God had torn the veil, opening the way into His presence for all believers (see Hebrews 4:14, 16). The death of Christ now provided direct access to God.

As an earthquake shook the world, God was reminding the world that He was speaking. Believers were resurrected and entered the city after Christ was raised. The Roman centurion bore witness to Jesus' claims saying, "Truly, this was the Son of God!" The women who had faithfully followed Jesus stood at a distance, witnessing the historic event, among them Mary Magdalene. Many others beat their chests in lamentation over Christ's suffering.

In crucifixion death came through asphyxiation. The body hung, slumping down, making breathing difficult and eventually impossible. When the person tried to raise his body to breath by pushing up with his legs, the pain became excruciating, causing him to slump again, once more hindering his breathing and, eventually, leading to his death. Since the Law required the removal of all bodies from the cross on the day of death (Deut. 21:22–23), the soldiers sought to speed the death process by breaking the legs of the criminals. However when the soldier came to Jesus, he discovered Jesus had already died, so he avoided breaking His legs, in fulfillment of prophecy (Ps. 34:20).

A soldier thrust his spear into Jesus' side, causing blood and water to flow forth. Why was this significant? It was a reminder of the genuine humanity of Jesus, but also a reminder that we are saved through the blood of Christ (John 6:53–56) and that Jesus is the living water (John 7:38). "John is reminding us that life, real life, comes through Christ's death" (Leon Morris, *Gospel According to John*). It is difficult to grasp the magnitude of the atonement, the Righteous One dying for the unrighteous, that we may be forgiven and have genuine life.

CONSIDER: *Although Jesus was deity, He was also humanity, as evidenced by His death, which multitudes witnessed.*

THE BURIAL OF JESUS

MATTHEW 27:59–66; MARK 15:46–47; LUKE 23:53–56; JOHN 19:39–42

*And Joseph took the body and wrapped it in a clean linen cloth,
and laid it in his own new tomb, which he had hewn out in the rock;
and he rolled a large stone against the entrance of the tomb
and went away. (Matthew 27:59–60)*

To avoid having the body thrown into the Valley of Hinnom, as was done to unclaimed bodies, a wealthy man, Joseph of Arimathea, came to claim the body of Jesus. When Pilate was assured of Jesus' death, he granted Joseph the body. Nicodemus, a member of the ruling Sanhedrin, also came to anoint the body of Jesus for burial. He brought seventy pounds of myrrh and aloes, placing the spices in the sheets around the body. This was a lavish provision, indicating that Nicodemus was wealthy, but perhaps it was also an indication that he desired to do for Jesus in death what he failed to do in life (Leon Morris, *Gospel According to John*). The entire body would have been wrapped in strips of cloth, with the head, arms, and legs wrapped separately.

The men placed Jesus in a new tomb in a garden. Although Joseph would be defiled by touching a dead body, his devotion to Jesus is evident as he took the body and wrapped it in a clean linen cloth and placed it in his own new tomb. "This was an action of some generosity, for a rock tomb was expensive and it was not permitted to bury a criminal in a family grave; the tomb could probably not be used afterward for anyone else" (Leon Morris, *Gospel According to Matthew*).

Mary Magdalene and other women who had loyally followed the Lord watched and followed to see where they laid the body of Jesus. Then, showing their devotion, they came to anoint His body with spices.

Meanwhile, the Jews, fearing that Jesus' prediction of His resurrection would lead to the disciples stealing His body, requested that the Romans station guards at the tomb. Humanly speaking, the adversaries did everything they could to prevent Jesus' body being removed from the tomb: they secured the grave with a stone; they placed guards in front of the tomb; they placed a Roman seal on the tomb. But . . .

CONSIDER: *The authenticity of Jesus' death is demonstrated by His burial, which also revealed the devotion of several aristocrats and women.*

THE EMPTY TOMB!

MATTHEW 28:1–8; MARK 16:1–8; LUKE 24:1–8; JOHN 20:1

*"He is not here, for He has risen, just as He said. Come, see
the place where He was lying. Go quickly and tell His disciples
that He has risen from the dead." (Matthew 28:6–7)*

The story is told that after the communist revolution in Russia in 1917, a communist leader came to a village and, in the public square, harangued the people about the virtues of communism and the folly of religion. At the end of his lecture he contemptuously told a Christian pastor he had five minutes to respond. The pastor replied, "I don't need five minutes; only five seconds." The pastor rose to the platform and shouted, "The Lord is risen!" As one man, the villagers thundered back, "The Lord is risen indeed!"

The bodily resurrection of Jesus Christ is the foundation of the Christian faith. Without His resurrection, there is no faith, but because the bodily resurrection of Jesus Christ is a historical fact, it is also the hallmark of history, the foundation of faith.

Matthew 28:1 begins "Now," literally "but." Despite the efforts of the unbelieving Jewish leaders and the ridiculing Romans, Jesus Christ would not remain in the grave. The guards . . . the stone . . . the seal . . . would all be to no avail. Christ will rise! Late on the Sabbath (the Sabbath having ended), the women came to the tomb to embalm the body of Jesus. They would be rewarded for their devotion to Christ.

In a divine visitation, the Lord shook the earth with an earthquake, announcing the resurrection of His Son to the world. Christ had twelve legions of angels (72,000) at His disposal, but only one was needed to remove the stone from the entrance! Cornelius à Lapide said, "The earth, which trembled with sorrow at the Death of Christ as it were leaped for joy at His Resurrection." The stone was removed, not to let the Lord *out*, but to let the women and the world *in* to see what had happened.

The angel made the dramatic announcement to the women: "He is not here, for He has risen, just as He said. . . . Go quickly and tell His disciples that He has risen from the dead." That is the message! That is the resolution to every sorrow, every pain, all suffering, all crying. Yes, we weep at the graveside of a loved one but the separation for believers is temporary. We now have a living hope (1 Peter 1:3)!

CONSIDER: *The bodily resurrection of Jesus Christ is a historical fact and the foundation of our faith. Because He lives, we shall live also!*

WITNESSES TO THE RESURRECTION (1)

MATTHEW 28:8–10; LUKE 24:9–12; JOHN 20:2–10

Simon Peter also came . . . and he saw the linen wrappings lying there, and the face-cloth which had been on His head, not lying with the linen wrappings, but rolled up in a place by itself. (John 20:6–7)

Shortly after World War II, Konrad Adenauer, the new Chancellor of Germany, invited Billy Graham to visit him in Germany. Mr. Adenauer asked Billy Graham, "Do you believe in the resurrection of Jesus Christ?" Billy Graham replied, "Mr. Adenauer, I would have no gospel to preach if I didn't believe in the resurrection of Christ." Mr. Adenauer was silent, walked to the window which looked out at the rubble of the devastation of World War II and replied, "There is no hope for mankind apart from the resurrection of Christ."

Instructed by the angel, Mary Magdalene ran and reported the good news of the resurrection to Peter and John. Immediately the two disciples ran to the tomb. Arriving first, John stooped down and "saw the linen wrappings" (John 20:5). The Greek word used for "saw," *blepei*, means "to look"; John simply scanned the scene—he didn't yet see what had occurred.

When Peter arrived at the tomb, he rushed past John into the tomb and "saw the linen wrappings lying there, and the face-cloth . . . rolled up in a place by itself" (vv. 6–7). The Greek word used for "saw" in this instance, *theorei*, means "to theorize." Peter saw more than John; Peter theorized what had happened. The head, which was wrapped separately from the body, was still circular in shape, lying by itself. The linen wrappings retained their form as they had been wrapped around a body, but now slightly collapsed from the weight of the spices. But the body was not there! There was only one explanation. The body had risen right through the linen wrappings!

When John finally entered the tomb, "he saw and believed" (v. 8). In this verse, the Greek word used for "saw," *eiden*, means "spiritual and mental vision." Now John understood what had happened! John believed when he saw the linen wrappings without the body because he realized it was impossible to wrap the headpiece in a circular form; it was impossible to wrap the collapsed bandages in the shape of a body—without the body. The fact that the wrappings retained the shape of a body meant only one thing: the body that had been there had passed right through the wrappings, leaving them lying there with the appearance of a body—but without the body! Jesus Christ had risen from the dead! And they believed.

CONSIDER: *Peter and John saw and validated the resurrection of Christ—and it changed them forever. And knowledge of the resurrection will change us forever.*

WITNESSES TO THE RESURRECTION (2)

MATTHEW 28:11–15; MARK 16:9–13; LUKE 24:13–35; JOHN 20:11–18

"O foolish men and slow of heart to believe in all that the prophets have spoken! Was it not necessary for the Christ to suffer these things and to enter into His glory?" (Luke 24:25–26)

Filled with grief because Jesus had been crucified, Mary Magdalene arrived at the tomb. Her grief intensified, thinking the body of the Lord had been stolen. When Mary turned she saw what she thought was the gardener. Smitten with grief, she didn't recognize the Lord, even when He asked her why she was weeping. Suddenly, she heard her name, "Mary!" She recognized the voice! Rabboni! It was Jesus! Jesus was raised in the same material body in which He died, but His body was now glorified.

But Jesus told Mary, "Stop clinging to Me, for I have not yet ascended to the Father" (John 20:17). Jesus was not telling Mary she couldn't touch Him; He was informing her that she could not continue to cling to the old relationship that they had previously enjoyed. But He would ascend to the Father, then she could cling to Him, but in a new way. It would be through the Holy Spirit whom He would send.

Along the way Jesus met the women and said hello (Matt. 28:9). When they recognized Him, they worshiped Him. Jesus instructed them to tell the disciples to go to Galilee where He would meet them.

Meanwhile, the chief priests bribed the guards by giving them a large sum of money to say that the body of Jesus had been stolen while they slept. Tragically, the nation destined for blessing through the Messiah rejected Him, and even sought to deceive others in their unbelief.

On the very day of the resurrection two disciples were walking to Emmaus when suddenly Jesus was walking with them—but they did not recognize Him. They were sad, talking about the crucifixion of Christ. As they approached Emmaus, the disciples invited Jesus to stay with them. Later, as they broke bread, their eyes were opened. They recognized the risen Savior! Immediately Jesus disappeared. Although Jesus had a material body, in its glorified state He could disappear and reappear.

CONSIDER: *The resurrection of Christ is a historical fact: (1) The empty tomb; (2) the wrappings in the tomb which still retained the shape of Jesus' body; (3) the appearances of Christ to Peter, Mary and other women, the apostles, James, Paul, plus five hundred others (as found in 1 Corinthians 15:5–8); (4) the change in the apostles following the resurrection; and (5) the subsequent growth of the church, which is built on the resurrection of Christ.*

THE SAME JESUS!

MARK 16:14; LUKE 24:36–43; JOHN 20:19–31

---

*These [signs] have been written so that you may believe
that Jesus is the Christ, the Son of God; and that believing
you may have life in His name. (John 20:31)*

While our faith in Jesus Christ is rooted in the historical fact of His incarnation, life, death, and bodily resurrection, yet we come to Him in faith. That is the issue. Faith. Without faith it is impossible to please God (Heb. 11:6).

The disciples were in turmoil and fear. They had witnessed the death of Christ on the cross but later had also seen the empty tomb and the grave clothes without the body. The high priest had inquired about them (John 18:19); they would be marked men, guilty by association. We can only imagine the turmoil in their minds.

In their fear, the disciples had gathered behind locked doors on that first resurrection Sunday. Suddenly, Jesus stood in their midst! "Peace be with you," he enjoined them (John 20:19). While this was a normal Hebrew greeting, on this occasion it had more significance. Jesus had earlier taught them of His peace (John 14:27; 16:33). Then Jesus showed them His hands and His side. His wounds were a reminder to the disciples that He was the same Jesus with whom they had walked for over three years. The same Jesus! It was a genuine body of flesh and bones. He reminded them, "See My hands and My feet, that it is I Myself; touch Me and see, for a spirit does not have flesh and bones as you see that I have" (Luke 24:39).

This is also a reminder that the resurrection of Christ was a *bodily* resurrection. Jesus rose again in the same corporeal body that He walked in prior to His crucifixion. Although He now had a glorified body, He was still *the same Jesus.*

A week later, when the disciples again met on the first day of the week, He came and stood in their midst. Previously, Thomas had been absent. Jesus invited Thomas to touch His hands and His side—showing the doubting Thomas that it was really Jesus. The enjoiner to Thomas is relevant for us all: "do not be unbelieving, but believing" (John 20:27). Thomas believed and acknowledged the deity of the risen Christ: "My Lord and my God" (v. 28). Thomas believed—he had seen the risen Christ! We are called to believe in Christ even though we have not seen Him. This is singularly the most important issue we will ever consider. *Have you believed in Christ?*

CONSIDER: *The same Jesus, the risen Lord, now glorified, He is the Son of God who gives life to all who believe in His name.*

May 5

RESTORED AND COMMISSIONED

JOHN 21:1–25; MATTHEW 28:16–20; LUKE 24:44–49; ACTS 1:3–8

"All authority has been given to Me in heaven and on earth.
Go therefore and make disciples of all the nations, baptizing them
in the name of the Father and the Son and the Holy Spirit, teaching
them to observe all that I commanded you; and lo, I am with you
always, even to the end of the age." (Matthew 28:18–20)

The disciples were confused and in turmoil. The kingdom Jesus had spoken about had not come. Their Lord had died but now they had seen Him. He had risen from the dead. What did all this mean? What should they do? Jesus had asked for them to meet Him in Galilee. But what were they to do there? They knew nothing better than to do what they knew best: fishing. So the disciples returned to Galilee.

But the disciples were about to encounter the Lord in a new, dramatic fashion. Peter led the fishing expedition but although they fished all night, they caught nothing. At daybreak, Jesus stood on the shore, although they didn't recognize Him. He told them to cast the net on the right-hand side of the boat. When they did, they caught a great number of fish. Peter's eyes were opened: "It is the Lord" (John 21:7).

When they reached the shore, Jesus had prepared breakfast; He had built a fire with fish and bread on it. They added fish to the charcoal fire and they all ate together. Then Jesus focused on Peter, "Do you love Me?" Three times Jesus asked the question and three times Peter answered in the affirmative. But the third time, Peter was grieved. The first two times Jesus questioned Peter He used the word *agapao* for love. *Agapao* reflects a rational, reasoned love that loves the object as a decision of the will. Each time Peter responded with *phileo*, a word for love that reflects fondness for a friend. But the third time Jesus questioned Peter He used *phileo*, questioning whether Peter even loved Him with the affection of a friend. This was why Peter was grieved. But this was important for Peter's restoration. How many times had Peter denied the Lord? Three times. Now the Lord challenged Peter: "Tend My lambs . . . Shepherd My sheep . . . Tend My sheep" (vv. 15–17). Not only was Peter restored by the Lord, but He was also commissioned to minister on behalf of the Savior.

Later, Jesus met the disciples at a mountain where He commissioned them to go not only to Israel but to the Gentile nations, making disciples and baptizing them in the name of the triune God. Later, in Jerusalem, Jesus instructed His disciples that "repentance for forgiveness of sins should be proclaimed in His name to all the nations" (Luke 24:47). This was a significant challenge for those who isolated themselves from the Gentiles. And the challenge remains.

CONSIDER: *The commission of our Lord goes out to every believer to make disciples of Christ. How are you fulfilling this command?*

May 6

JESUS ASCENDS TO HEAVEN

MARK 16:19–20; LUKE 24:50–53; ACTS 1:9–12

And after He had said these things, He was lifted up while they were looking on, and a cloud received Him out of their sight. (Acts 1:9)

The life of Christ is a historical event. Jesus was born in Bethlehem to Mary his mother; He ministered in Judea and Galilee for three and a half years. At the end of that time He was crucified, buried, and He rose bodily from the grave. That is history. Now the climactic event in the life of Christ is about to take place.

Jesus led the eleven disciples out toward Bethany, a familiar village on the east side of the Mount of Olives. As they came to the fork in the road, Jesus lifted up His hands and blessed them. Then, as He was blessing them, Jesus was separated from them and carried into heaven. Luke is very graphic in Acts 1:10: "as they were gazing intently into the sky while He was going." Both verbs "were gazing" and "was going" are present tense, emphasizing the continuous activity—the disciples were continuously gazing with fixation as Jesus was departing from them—not in a split second, but they were watching Him as He was moving upward toward heaven. What a dramatic moment! Finally, a cloud—indicative of the Shekinah glory, the visible presense of God—received Him out of their sight. Christ ascended into heaven from the Mount of Olives—precisely the place where the Shekinah glory of God departed from the temple (Ezek. 11:23) and where Christ will return in glory (as prophesied in Zechariah 14:4).

The disciples returned to Jerusalem with great joy, worshiping in the temple, and praising God (Luke 24:52–53). "Their fear was gone; they no longer hid behind locked doors. They had a Lord and Savior in heaven, who ruled all things with his omnipotent and omnipresent power and would make good all his promises" (R. C. H. Lenski, *Interpretation of St. Luke's Gospel 12–24*).

Was this the end? No. There is more! As the disciples were looking at Jesus ascending into heaven, two men (angelic messengers) reminded them, "This Jesus, who has been taken up from you into heaven, will come in just the same way as you have watched Him go into heaven" (Acts 1:11). How did He go? Physically. In full view. And that is how He will return. What a promise! What a magnificent hope! Dear reader, keep focused. Our resolution does not come from the world. Our resolution, our rescue, our ultimate blessing will come at the return of Jesus Christ for His own when He establishes His righteous kingdom on the new earth. Keep looking up!

CONSIDER: *Jesus ascended into heaven from the Mount of Olives in full view of the disciples.*

May 7

Jesus' Work Continues

Acts 1:1–11

---

*"But you will receive power when the Holy Spirit has come upon you;
and you shall be My witnesses both in Jerusalem, and in all Judea and
Samaria, and even to the remotest part of the earth." (Acts 1:8)*

We treasure letters from loved ones. When the mailman has passed our
house, we eagerly go to the mailbox and see if a letter from a family
member or friend has arrived.

Luke wrote his good friend Theophilus (meaning "Lover of God") but
because the letter was so lengthy, Luke had to write him twice. The papyrus
scrolls of the New Testament were usually not longer than thirty-five feet, so
Luke wrote Theophilus a second time, dedicating the book of Acts to him.

Luke reminds us that he previously wrote of the work that Jesus *began to
do* (the gospel of Luke). Jesus' work on earth continues—through the ministry
of the Holy Spirit. Before His ascension, Jesus commanded the apostles to take
the gospel to the ends of the earth (Matt. 28:19–20). But what was the basis of
His command? The resurrection! That was the remarkable truth they were to
take to the nations. Jesus had won the victory over sin and death and resolved
humanity's most distressing dilemma.

The apostles were confused. They thought Jesus would inaugurate the millennial kingdom in their day. Indeed, Jesus had offered the kingdom to Israel
but it had been rejected, and so the kingdom would now be held in abeyance.
The glorious reign of Christ would await His second coming (Rev. 19–20). In the
interim, Jesus commissioned them to spread the gospel.

But the apostles—and all who would follow after them—would need supernatural enablement to spread the good news of Jesus' resurrection. They were
to wait in Jerusalem for that divine appointment when the Holy Spirit would
indwell and empower them to carry the gospel not only to their neighbor-
hoods, but to the vast regions of the entire world. They would be "witnesses"
(*martures*). The English word "martyr" is derived from the same Greek word,
and some indeed did—and continue to—give their lives as witnesses for
Christ. Normally, *witness* means to testify to a truth in a legal sense. They had
seen the resurrected Christ with their own eyes and were legitimate witnesses
that Jesus was alive. Following the commission, Jesus ascended to the Father,
with the angels' promise that He will return in just the same way. The reality
of the resurrection would buoy the apostles to aggressively carry the gospel
to a needy world. The work of Jesus continues. . . .

CONSIDER: *You and I have been commissioned to continue the work of Jesus by
testifying to the risen Christ through the Holy Spirit's enabling power.*

THE ONE WHOM GOD USES

ACTS 1:12–14, 23–26

*These all with one mind were continually devoting themselves
to prayer, along with the women, and Mary the mother of
Jesus, and with His brothers. (Acts 1:14)*

Sometimes we hear people say—and maybe we have said it ourselves—
"God can't use me. I'm just an ordinary person." We think the apostles
were extraordinary and different from us. But as we study these men, we find
they were normal people—and God used them. Just who were these men?
Simon Peter, a braggart whose emotions fluctuated and sometimes rendered
him unstable. John and James, "sons of thunder," who, with their explosive
tempers, wanted to destroy the Samaritans. Andrew, the quiet and unobtru-
sive apostle, who worked "behind the scenes." Philip, who looked at the circumstances and lacked faith (John 6:7). Thomas, skeptic and pessimist (John
20:25). Nathanael (also known as Bartholomew), another skeptic, who won-
dered if any good thing could come out of Nazareth (John 1:46). Matthew, the
tax collector who had cheated people through his work for Rome. James the
son of Alphaeus, who was also known as James the Less or Little, probably
because he was younger or smaller in stature. Simon the Zealot, who exhibited
militant loyalty to the state. And the other Judas (son of James), who was curious, quizzing the Lord about His disclosure to them (John 14:22).

In obedience to Jesus' instruction the apostles returned to Jerusalem for
the divine appointment. They went to the "upper room," perhaps the home
of John Mark. It may even have been the same room where Jesus ate the Last
Supper with the disciples (Luke 22:12). The Eleven, all with differing tempera-
ments and abilities, were nonetheless supremely united in mind and in the
fellowship of prayer. Persistent prayer was important in seeking God's direction and ministry. The text emphasizes that they were "continually devoting
themselves to prayer" (Acts 1:14). And God answered.

In seeking a successor to Judas, Barsabbas and Matthias were put forward. Again the disciples prayed, seeking God's disclosure of the successor
by divine appointment. Matthias was named. Like the other apostles, Matthias
had been a witness of the resurrection. He would assume the office of apostleship and the ministry of spreading the good news of the risen Lord.

CONSIDER: *God uses ordinary men and women, with differing personalities, to
serve Him and spread the good news of the resurrected Christ.*

ARE THERE CONTRADICTIONS IN THE BIBLE?

ACTS 1:15–22

The Scripture had to be fulfilled. (Acts 1:16)

It is always a tragedy when people fail in the ministry.

At the gathering of believers following the resurrection of Christ, Peter explained what happened to Judas. He had been numbered with the apostles, having received authority from Christ for the ministry (Matt. 10). But he became a betrayer, a guide to those who arrested Jesus. Judas was paid thirty shekels of silver for betraying Jesus but in his remorse Judas flung the money back in the temple (Matt. 27:3–5). Apparently the priests considered the money to be legally Judas's so they bought a field in Judas's name. So the field was legally Judas's property (F. F. Bruce, *Book of Acts*) and became known as the "Field of Blood."

Finding no resolution to his enormous dilemma, Judas committed suicide. Matthew says, "he went away and hanged himself" (Matt. 27:5). But Peter provides additional information about Judas saying he fell headlong and "burst open in the middle and all his intestines gushed out" (Acts 1:18). Is this a contradiction? Not at all. Since the Scriptures are God-breathed, they are inerrant because God is incapable of error. When all the information is available, a resolution can be found to every difficult passage we encounter.

When Judas hung himself, the rope broke so that he fell "flat on his face" (translates "headlong"), and he burst open and his bowels gushed out (A. T. Robertson, *Word Pictures of the New Testament*). Judas apparently went to the valley west of where the Hinnom and Kidron valleys merge and hung himself, throwing himself forward and falling to the jagged rocks below. His body was torn apart as Peter described it (Alfred Edersheim, *Life and Times of Jesus the Messiah*). Judas's life was a tragedy, ending in bitter and total failure because of jealousy and covetousness (John 12:4–6).

CONSIDER: *The Scriptures are entirely reliable and trustworthy in everything they say about every issue.*

THE BIRTH OF THE CHURCH

ACTS 2:1–21

"I WILL POUR FORTH OF MY SPIRIT UPON ALL MANKIND." (Acts 2:17)

The Jews had assembled in Jerusalem for the Feast of Pentecost, a pilgrimage feast, having come from many nations of the world. They were unaware that they were also gathering for a birth. The birth of an age. The birth of a union. The birth of the church.

As the apostles assembled—likely listening to a discourse—suddenly a noise like a violent wind occurred. The descent of the Holy Spirit was audible. Tongues of fire settled on the apostles revealing the presence of the glory of God. When Solomon built his temple to the Lord, the Shekinah glory of God similarly filled the temple (1 Kings 8:10–11).

The Jewish pilgrims witnessed an unusual and unparalleled phenomenon. The apostles began to speak in other tongues. What are tongues? The ensuing biblical comments explain: the pilgrims were hearing the apostles speak in their own languages (Acts 2:6, 8, 11) from the numerous countries that the pilgrims had come from (vv. 9–11).

Peter explained the phenomenon to the stunned Jews. The Holy Spirit's descent was in fulfillment of prophecy (vv. 17–21; Joel 2:28–32). God had poured forth His Holy Spirit—and this marked the beginning of the church. The church is uniquely made up of believing Jews and Gentiles whom the Holy Spirit baptizes (places) into the body of Christ the moment they believe (1 Cor. 12:13). This is not water baptism nor is it experiential; the moment a person believes, the Holy Spirit baptizes them into the body of Christ and into union with one another (Rom. 6:3).

This is the uniqueness of the church. Through faith, people from all strata of life and differing ethnic backgrounds are brought into union with one another. Rich and poor, educated and uneducated, easterners and westerners—we are all brought into a marvelous union with Christ and with one another through the baptizing work of the Holy Spirit.

CONSIDER: *On the day of Pentecost, the church age was born, when all believers of differing races are united as one body in the church.*

THE MESSIAH: RESURRECTED AND LIVING!

ACTS 2:22–40

"God has made Him both Lord and Christ." (Acts 2:36)

Excitement filled the city of Jerusalem following the resurrection of Jesus. Thousands had gathered for the Feast of Pentecost. Now Peter stood to address both natives and visitors to Jerusalem. In stunning words he declared that Jesus' death was foreordained by God—yet the nation and the Romans were guilty of crucifying Christ. (This is an *antinomy*—something that has the appearance of contradiction yet both statements are equally true.) Peter then unfolded the Old Testament prediction 1,000 years earlier that the Messiah would be raised from the dead (Ps. 16:8–11). Peter clarifies that the prophecy did not refer to David himself, since he was dead and entombed (Acts 2:29). Rather, David's words anticipated the resurrection of Christ. Moreover, the proof of Jesus' resurrection was the outpouring of the Holy Spirit whom Christ sent following His ascension into heaven (v. 33).

The climax of Peter's message pointed to the majestic truth: Jesus was Lord, seated at the right hand of the Father awaiting the day when He would return to subdue the nations (v. 34–35).

Dismay swept the listeners. They were guilty of having crucified the Messiah! How could they possibly resolve their dilemma? Peter provided hope amid the tragedy. "Repent, and each of you be baptized in the name of Jesus Christ for the forgiveness of your sins" (v. 38). In the Greek text "repent" and "your sins" are plural while "be baptized" is singular. This means forgiveness of sins is related to repentance. It can be paraphrased: "All of you repent and you will all receive forgiveness of sins; then let each of you individually be baptized."

This baptism is also unique. It was an outward sign by the believing Jews that they were separating themselves from a nation under the judgment of God for having crucified the Messiah. That judgment came in A.D. 70 when the Romans destroyed Jerusalem.

Truly, the grace of God extends to the highest heights and lowest valleys. No matter how dark the past has been there is forgiveness of sins through Christ. Have you received the grace of God? Regardless of your past, it is sufficient to include you, to forgive you, and to promise you eternal life.

CONSIDER: *The resurrection of Christ has vindicated Him as Lord and Messiah since He has ascended and is seated at the right hand of the Father.*

THE NEW FAMILY FELLOWSHIP

ACTS 2:41–47

They were continually devoting themselves to the apostles' teaching and
to fellowship, to the breaking of bread and to prayer. (Acts 2:42)

During a time of praise and sharing in the evening service in a church on
the west coast a man stood up and said, "Today is the anniversary of the
time you all showed concern for me. I had lost my job as an engineer and was
out of work for six months. During that time you made my house payments
and paid all my bills. You brought me groceries and supplied for my family for
six months. I praise and thank God for all of you."

Born on Pentecost, the church grew quickly, both numerically and in its
concern and care for one another. In response to Peter's preaching, 3,000 were
immediately saved and baptized, welcoming the word (Acts 2:41)—synonymous with welcoming Jesus.

The new believers' joy was also combined with commitment. They "were
continually devoting themselves" (v. 42)—they persisted in the apostles' teaching and in fellowship with one another. The apostles had received authority
from Christ, and their teaching—in other words, *doctrine*—was foundational to
the fledgling church. Basic to the functioning of a church is doctrine; without it
a church cannot and will not survive. Foundational doctrines are the deity of
Christ, His substitutionary atonement, and His bodily resurrection. These are
cardinal doctrines that can never be compromised. Despite persecution and
imprisonment, the apostles continually taught these truths (Acts 5:42).

The church was also united in fellowship on that historic day. "Fellowship" (*koinonia*) means "association" and "sharing." That fellowship is defined
by "breaking of bread" and "prayer." In the early church the believers came
together for a fellowship meal, concluding it with the breaking of bread, the
fellowship of the Lord's Supper. Prayer was also a vital part of their fellowship—driven by persecution.

Their fellowship was significant, impacting the unbelieving community
that was awestruck by the courageous, loving fellowship of the Christians.
Persecuted by the religious leaders, the early church was driven to share their
possessions with one another. This is not a call to communism; rather, the
persecution forced the sharing of belongings. But the love, joy, and sincerity
of the believers greatly impacted the unbelieving community, so much so that
many became believers in Christ.

CONSIDER: *How is your fellowship in the church helping others and also impact-*
ing your unbelieving neighbors?

THE CONTINUING MINISTRY OF JESUS

ACTS 3:1–26

"The God of our fathers, has glorified His Servant Jesus. . . .
And on the basis of faith in His name, it is the name of Jesus
which has strengthened this man." (Acts 3:13, 16)

A s the apostles continued to witness about Jesus, God uniquely gave the apostles authority to heal, in order to corroborate their message that Jesus was the Messiah. At the 9:00 A.M. hour of prayer, Peter and John were on their way to the temple. As they neared the temple, they met a man who had been lame for over forty years, being carried on a litter. In a daily routine, he was deposited at the seventy-five-foot-high Corinthian brass Gate, called Beautiful, to beg from the worshipers at this strategic location. Seeing Peter and John, the beggar called out to them, hoping to receive some money. Unquestionably Peter startled the man with his words: "In the name of Jesus Christ the Nazarene—walk!" (v. 6). There is no indication the man exhibited faith before Peter grasped him by the hand and yanked him up! Immediately the former cripple began not only to walk but he entered the temple with Peter and John, "walking and leaping and praising God" (v. 8).

The miracle was significant—more so for the people than the man. In the Portico of Solomon, Peter immediately addressed the people, explaining how the man was healed. Although they were guilty of having rejected and disowned Jesus, God had glorified His servant Jesus by raising Him from the dead. It was through faith in His name (probably Peter's and John's faith) that the man was healed. The message Peter preached—that Jesus is the Righteous One, the Messiah—was authenticated by the healing of the crippled man.

Once more the audience was in a dilemma. They had crucified the Lord of glory. The resolution was to "repent and return, so that your sins may be wiped away" (v. 19). They were to "change their mind" about Jesus. They were to realize that the One they had repudiated was the "Holy and Righteous One." "To return" was Peter's call to conversion. They were to respond to Jesus as their sin-bearer and be converted.

Peter reminded them that when the nation of Israel repents, the "times of refreshing" will come, the time when Messiah will restore all things, inaugurating the kingdom (vv. 19–20; see Isaiah 11). Jesus came to bless first Israel and then all the families of the earth (Acts 3:25–26).

CONSIDER: *Every illness, every sickness, every malady is a reminder there is a future glorious day coming when Christ will restore all things.*

PERSECUTING GOD'S PEOPLE

ACTS 4:1–37

---

*"And there is salvation in no one else; for there is no
other name under heaven that has been given among
men by which we must be saved." (Acts 4:12)*

Persecution of Christians has been vigorous throughout the New Testament era. Communists have been particularly aggressive in persecuting Christians. Untold Christians have died in the Soviet Union, in China, in North Korea, and in other countries. But persecution can also take unusual forms. When Bill Foster became a mayoral candidate for St. Petersburg, Florida, critics questioned his ability to serve as mayor because of his belief in the biblical account of creation (*St. Petersburg Times*, September 19, 2009).

Peter and John fearlessly proclaimed the good news about Jesus Christ amid intense opposition. The Jewish leadership became enormously upset when the Christians preached about the resurrection of Christ. Finally, the Sanhedrin (the "Supreme Court of Israel") apprehended the two apostles. But Peter was undaunted. He accused them of having killed Christ, but affirmed that God's program would not be defeated: God raised Christ from the dead (Acts 4:10). Then Peter gave the singularly defining statement: "There is salvation in no one else; for there is no other name under heaven that has been given among men by which we must be saved" (v. 12).

This is not a popular statement today. The Christian belief is narrow. Christ is the only way to heaven. There is no other way. The Jewish leaders recognized the courage of Peter and John, marveling at them, particularly since a lame man had been healed. They had nothing with which to charge Peter and John, so they just warned them not to speak about Jesus and then released them. But Peter and John bravely responded, "we cannot stop speaking about what we have seen and heard" (v. 20).

But Peter and John knew where to go—to the fellowship of believers. They told them what had happened and they united in prayer to God, praying, "O Lord . . ." The Greek word used for Lord, *despota*, means "sovereign lord, one who holds complete power or authority over another" (Cleon Rogers Jr. and Cleon Rogers III, *The New Linguistic and Exegetical Key to the Greek New Testament*). They recognized the sovereignty of God and that gave them courage and made them fearless. And what was the result? The place where they were "was shaken, and they were all filled with the Holy Spirit and began to speak the word of God with boldness" (v. 31).

CONSIDER: *We, like Peter and John, should faithfully and fearlessly tell the good news of salvation in Christ alone—even amid opposition and persecution.*

CLEANSING, PERSECUTION, AND WITNESSING

ACTS 5:1–42

---

*And every day, in the temple and from house to house, they kept
right on teaching and preaching Jesus as the Christ. (Acts 5:42)*

Because of persecution, the early church combined their assets to help
each other in a communal form of living. It was voluntary, not obligatory.
Ananias and Sapphira sold a piece of property and, conspiring together, they
withheld some of the money—while giving the impression they gave everything to the believers' fellowship. It was a sin of hypocrisy. Peter knew of their
deception. When he confronted them individually, God judged them in death.
They had sinned against the Holy Spirit (Acts 5:3).

Donald Grey Barnhouse has said that if God dealt that way with Christians
today, every church would have to open a morgue in the basement! This was a
unique situation. The church was in its infancy; if it would be immediately corrupted, it could not be sustained. God judged the church to ensure its purity.

The judgment of Ananias and Sapphira had a purifying effect on the
church—and the people outside the church (v. 11). Furthermore, the church
was held in high esteem by outsiders. And the church enjoyed constant
growth. Meanwhile, the apostles used their unique giftedness in healing people and casting out demons. But the signs and wonders were restricted to the
apostles (recall Matthew 10:1). Their healing ministry validated their message
to Israel: Jesus is the promised Messiah.

But the ministry brought opposition. The Sadducees had them arrested
and jailed; however, an angel immediately opened the gates and released them!
Did the apostles run and hide? No, they went to the public square and continued to proclaim the good news—amid severe opposition. When they were
again apprehended and brought before the Sanhedrin, they received a great
compliment: "You have filled Jerusalem with your teaching" (v. 28). Indeed!
The apostles were fearless. It was a new, revitalized Peter who responded, "We
must obey God rather than men" (v. 29).

What an important reminder to us as we live in a postmodern culture
where Christianity is despised. We must have similar resolve. These men were
fearless. After they were admonished and flogged and warned not to speak in
the name of Jesus any longer, they went on their way rejoicing that they were
counted worthy to suffer for Christ and they continued every day proclaiming
Jesus as the promised Messiah.

CONSIDER: *In our postmodern culture we must resolve to remain steadfast and
fearless in telling others about Jesus Christ—no matter the repercussions.*

MINISTRY TO WIDOWS = PURE RELIGION

ACTS 6:1–7:1

Widows were being overlooked in the daily serving of food. (Acts 6:1)

M y mother was only forty-six years old when my father died. They had enjoyed a wonderful fellowship in the local church. Every Sunday afternoon five families would gather at one of the homes and visit. But when my father died, they dropped my mother. As a young boy, I remember my mother sitting at home Sunday afternoon, crying. She was all alone. Neglected by the church.

As the infant church began to grow, it also needed to organize. They quickly discovered that the Grecian Jewish widows were being overlooked. These were Jewish homes that had adopted Grecian culture. They were being discriminated against by native Hebrews. As a result, the apostles, the leaders in the early church, instructed the Christians to select seven men to serve the widows. But these men were to be qualified: having a good reputation, being full of the Holy Spirit, and wise, so that they would be able to make sound judgments, not allowing prejudice or discrimination.

While the term "deacon" doesn't occur in this passage, it is commonly concluded that this refers to the initiation of the office of deacon. The qualifications of a deacon are given in 1 Timothy 3:8–13. Their ministry to widows is significant. James reminds us, "Pure and undefiled religion in the sight of our God and Father is this: to visit orphans and widows in their distress . . ." (James 1:27).

As a result of selecting these men to care for the widows, the apostles—the leaders in the early church—could devote themselves "to prayer and to the ministry of the word" (Acts 6:4).

The early church chose seven men to fulfill the ministry to widows, but one man was singled out: Stephen, "a man full of faith and of the Holy Spirit" (v. 5). All the men had Greek names, indicating they would be especially conscientious in ministering to the Grecian widows.

Stephen was performing "great wonders and signs," validating the message of Christ so that many came to faith in Christ. But opposition arose from libertine Jews who were once slaves of Rome but had now been set free (A. T. Robertson, *Word Pictures of the New Testament*). They were unable to cope with the power of the Spirit in Stephen, however, so they stirred up the people and brought false witnesses to accuse him. Yet even amid the accusation, Stephen reflected the power of God, "with face aglow, as one who stood in the presence of God" (F. F. Bruce, *Book of Acts*).

CONSIDER: *Ministry to widows is a distinct obligation of the church. Do you know of a widow that you can help?*

REBELLING AGAINST GRACE

ACTS 7:2–60

---

*"You men who are stiff-necked and uncircumcised in heart
and ears are always resisting the Holy Spirit; you are
doing just as your fathers did." (Acts 7:51)*

We live in a politically correct society, where the emphasis is to tolerate all views, no matter how divergent, how false they may be. Even Christian leaders have fallen into this philosophy where they frown on other Christians who take a firm stand on truth.

Stephen would not have been accepted in our postmodern society (and not in some Christian circles) because he spoke bluntly and forcefully—but he spoke the truth. Stephen traced Israel's history, showing how God continued to extend His grace to the people and how they resisted but with dire consequences.

Israel's rebellion began with Abraham (Acts 7:2–7). God called the patriarch from Ur, promising him the land of Canaan (Gen. 12:1–3). What did Abraham do? He delayed. He settled in Haran. So God delayed the inheritance. Abraham never saw it; furthermore, his descendants were enslaved in Egypt for 400 years (Acts 7:6).

God extended His grace through Joseph (vv. 8–16). But resistance came through Joseph's brothers who were jealous and sold Joseph into Egypt. Instead of a blessing, God sent famine and suffering to the Israelites.

Now God raised up a deliverer, revealing His grace through Moses (vv. 17–37). But the people rejected Moses—despite God's having anointed him—and he fled to Midian. The rejection of Moses anticipated the rejection of Jesus Christ. As a prophet, Moses prefigured Christ who would be The Prophet (v. 37).

God continued to exhibit His grace, giving Israel the Law on Sinai (vv. 38–44). But once more Israel rejected God's revelation, imploring Aaron to make them the molten calf. So God turned away from them and judged them with the Babylonian exile.

When Israel entered the land and God gave them a monarchy, He extended His grace by having Solomon build a temple (v. 47). But Israel rebelled, refusing to let go of the temple when the glory of God had departed from it (Ezek. 11:23). The consequences were dire: the Romans destroyed the temple in A.D. 70.

God's ultimate extension of grace was sending Jesus, the Righteous One (v. 52). But what did Israel do? They killed Jesus. They stood in the lineage of those who continually rejected God's grace—they acted just like their forefathers. The Jews could no longer listen to Stephen. They rose up and stoned him to death.

CONSIDER: *When God extends His grace, it is imperative to respond in obedience to avoid His discipline.*

May 18

BEYOND THE BOUNDARIES

ACTS 8:1–25

*Therefore, those who had been scattered went about
preaching the word. (Acts 8:4)*

China remains one of the great, modern success stories in the spread of Christianity. When the communists took over in 1948, Mao Tse-tung and others sought to eliminate Christianity. But they didn't succeed. At the beginning of the twenty-first century China has approached or even surpassed 100 million Christians! Persecution doesn't stamp out Christianity—persecution spreads Christiantiy.

And so it was in the early church. After the stoning of Stephen persecution expanded against believers in Jerusalem. Saul began "ravaging" the church—picturesque since it envisions a wild beast mangling its enemy (Cleon Rogers Jr. and Cleon Rogers III, *The New Linguistic and Exegetical Key to the Greek New Testament*). He entered house after house, dragging believers to jail.

But what did the believers do? Give up? No. They spread the word! In fact, the persecution intensified the evangelism. It resulted in believers going beyond Jerusalem to neighboring Samaria—where Jews would not normally travel. Philip, one of the original deacons, went to Samaria and preached Christ to them. As in the first century, the message was corroborated by signs. This gift was given to the apostles and those immediately under the apostles.

Simon Magus, who practiced the magical arts and conjuring of demons heard Philip preach and he too believed the gospel. When the apostles in Jerusalem heard of the Samaritans coming to faith in Christ, they came to Samaria and laid hands on them that they would receive the Holy Spirit. Does the Holy Spirit come through laying on hands? Does the Holy Spirit come subsequent to salvation? No. This was a unique incident that accomplished three things. First, it served as a reminder to the Samaritans that "salvation is from the Jews" (John 4:22). Further, it showed the Jews that Samaritans also receive the Holy Spirit. Finally, it prevented a schism of the church, into a "Samaritan church" and a "Jewish church."

When Simon sought the gift of bestowing the Holy Spirit, Peter rebuked him, severely, warning him to repent—which Simon did. Assuming that Simon had genuinely believed, it is a reminder that Christians don't change overnight.

Nonetheless, the gospel had extended beyond Jerusalem; it was impacting Samaria, a region despised by the Jews because the Samaritans were "half-breeds"—part Jew, part Gentile. Opponents will never succeed in stamping out the gospel of Christ, now matter how harsh the opposition.

CONSIDER: *Persecution, rather than destroying the church, enlivens it and causes the spread of the gospel.*

ENCOUNTERING A EUNUCH

ACTS 8:26–40

---

*"Of whom does the prophet say this? . . ." Then Philip opened
his mouth, and . . . preached Jesus to him. (Acts 8:34–35)*

An angel appeared to Philip, directing him to go down to Gaza, on the Mediterranean coast. As he went, he met an official from Ethiopia who was returning from Jerusalem where he had gone to worship. He was an official of Candace, the title given to the queen mother in the royal court. The king of Ethiopia was regarded as the child of the sun and, as such, too sacred to perform secular functions of royalty (F. F. Bruce, *Book of Acts*).

As a eunuch, he would have been forbidden to enter the Lord's assembly (Deut. 23:1), but as a Gentile he may have gathered with others in the Court of the Gentiles (1 Kings 8:41–43). The man was clearly on a quest for truth—similar to the Queen of Sheba who came to visit King Solomon (1 Kings 10:1–9). The man was reading Isaiah on a scroll he probably purchased in Jerusalem. Philip heard him because he was reading aloud. Philip had run to apprehend the official. In the sovereign purpose of God the official was reading Isaiah 53. Bishop Taylor Smith (1860–1938) said, if Philip hadn't run, the eunuch would have been reading Isaiah 54!

Philip questioned the official: "Do you understand what you are reading?" (Acts 8:30). The official confessed his need of someone to interpret the passage for him. He probably recognized Philip as a Jew and invited him to join him in the chariot. The man was reading Isaiah 53:7–8 and was obviously absorbed in the passage—and recognized its significance. "Of whom does the prophet say this? Of himself or of someone else?" the official asked. He knew Isaiah 53 spoke of a person. But of whom?

Philip had the obvious opportunity: "Philip opened his mouth, and beginning from this Scripture he preached Jesus to him" (v. 35). Philip explained the meaning of Isaiah 53, a seven-hundred-year-old prophecy literally fulfilled in the crucifixion of Christ. Philip will have told the official of Christ's substitutionary atonement for sin: "*He* was pierced through for *our* transgressions, He was crushed for *our* iniquities . . . and by *His* scourging *we* are healed" (Isa. 53:5, emphasis added).

The official's heart had been prepared. As he listened to Philip, he responded. When they came to water, he begged Philip to baptize him. When the Lord snatched Philip away, the official returned to Ethiopia rejoicing. Why? He had peace. He had forgiveness. He had Christ! Irenaeus (second century A.D.) tells us he became a missionary to his own people.

CONSIDER: *Our meetings with unbelievers are not accidental; they are "divine appointments," opportunities to tell them about Jesus.*

May 20

CONVERSION OF AN ENEMY

ACTS 9:1–25

"He is a chosen instrument of Mine, to bear My name before the Gentiles and kings and the sons of Israel." (Acts 9:15)

John Newton (1725–1807) was an infamous individual, deeply involved in sin. But when a sudden storm descended on his ship, he cried out to the Lord and was gloriously saved. His life changed dramatically. Encouraged by the great evangelist George Whitefield (1714–1770), he pursued the ministry and served the Lord for forty-three years.

As Paul (then known as Saul) comes on the scene, he was aggressively persecuting Christians, sending them to prison and casting his vote for their death (Acts 9:1–2; 26:10). Paul obtained permission from the ruling Sanhedrin (whose authority was recognized by the Romans) to pursue the Jews who had identified themselves with "the Way," a reference to Jesus' exclusive statement about salvation found in John 14:6. While traveling to Damascus, Paul was stopped by the brilliant light of God's glory. A voice identified itself as, "Jesus whom you are persecuting" (Acts 9:5). Jesus identified Himself with the suffering church. He commanded Paul to go into Damascus where "it will be told you what you must do" (v. 6). Entering Damascus, Paul remained blind for three days—enabling him to reflect on what was happening.

Ananias would be God's instrument in bringing Paul into fellowship with believers. Furthermore, God would commission Paul as His chosen instrument to carry the good news to Gentiles, kings, and Hebrew people. But more, Paul would suffer for Christ; the man who had been a persecutor of the church would himself now be persecuted. (See the synopsis of his sufferings in 2 Corinthians 11:23–28!)

Ananias identified himself to Paul and laid his hands on him, identifying himself with Paul and recognizing Paul as a brother in Christ.

Paul's change was immediate. His sight returned and "immediately he began to proclaim Jesus in the synagogues saying, 'He is the Son of God'" (Acts 9:20). His conversion was profound and thorough; so much so that his former associates now sought to kill him. God was going to uniquely use this chosen apostle to spread the gospel through the Mediterranean world.

CONSIDER: *No matter what a person's background may be, God can dramatically convert and completely change a person, and then use that one for the gospel.*

PEACE AFTER PERSECUTION

ACTS 9:26–43

So the church throughout all Judea and Galilee and Samaria enjoyed peace, being built up; and going on in the fear of the Lord and in the comfort of the Holy Spirit, it continued to increase. (Acts 9:31)

Although Paul had been preaching for three years by the time he came to Jerusalem, the disciples were afraid of him. It took Barnabas ("which translated means 'son of encouragement'" [Acts 4:36]) to bring him into the Christian fellowship as he told them about Paul's boldness in proclaiming Jesus. Then the disciples welcomed him. Paul continued to proclaim the good news in Jerusalem, inciting opposition from the Hellenistic Jews who then sought to kill him. To spare his life, the disciples sent Paul to Tarsus.

Since Paul had been the leader in persecuting the church—and apparently with influence that extended throughout the land of Israel and beyond—the believers now enjoyed peace and rest.

The apostles continued to proclaim the good news of Christ. Peter traveled to Lydda, some twenty-five miles west of Jerusalem where he encountered Aeneas, who had been paralyzed for eight years. "Aeneas, Jesus Christ heals you; get up and make your bed" (Acts 9:34). Aeneas's healing resulted in many people turning to the Lord in faith. The Lord had given Peter and the apostles the unique gift of healing to corroborate the good news of Jesus Christ.

The news of Aeneas's healing probably reached the coastal town of Joppa where another crisis occurred. Dorcas, a faithful disciple known for her deeds of kindness, had died. When Peter arrived, the widows stood around, showing him the garments she had made for them. Sending them out of the room, Peter kneeled and prayed, then simply spoke the words, "Tabitha, arise." She opened her eyes and Peter took her hand and raised her up, presenting her alive to the widows. What joy there must have been!

The result was similar to what happened at Lydda. Many people came to faith in the Lord. And Peter continued his ministry, staying with Simon, a tanner—something Peter previously would not have done since, by Jewish Law, a tanner was considered unclean.

CONSIDER: *The gospel cannot be contained; it spreads amid persecution and it spreads amid peace.*

THE GOSPEL GOES TO THE GENTILES

ACTS 10:1–22

"What God has cleansed, no longer consider unholy." (Acts 10:15)

It is exciting to see the gospel spreading to other countries today. Where has the gospel not gone? It has spread through North and South America, Europe, Africa, and Asia. From villages in Sudan to cities in China. Men like David Brainerd (1718–1747), David Livingstone (1813–1873), and Hudson Taylor (1832–1905) have pioneered modern missions—but it began with the apostles in the first century.

God revealed Himself to a Gentile, a Roman centurion named Cornelius. He was a "God-fearer," a Gentile who had embraced the Hebrew faith but had not followed through to become a full-fledged proselyte. The Lord responded to his prayers and instructed him to send messengers to Joppa, a coastal city, to get Peter who was staying with Simon, a tanner. That in itself was unusual since Peter would have been rendered ceremonially unclean by residing with a tanner. It reflects the progress in Peter's life in embracing Gentiles—something he previously would not have done.

As the men went to Joppa, Peter went up on the rooftop of the house to pray. Roofs were flat and an ideal place for meditation and prayer. Peter became hungry and, falling into a trance, saw a sheet, like an awning, being lowered to the ground. On the sheet were all types of birds and animals, clean and unclean (see Leviticus 11 for the laws about animals). Then Peter heard a command from the Lord, "Get up, Peter, kill and eat!" (Acts 10:13). But Peter's strict adherence to the Law prohibited him and he answered, "By no means, Lord, for I have never eaten anything unholy and unclean" (v. 14). Peter was thinking about forbidden food like pork. The interaction continued three times. And the Lord answered Peter, "What God has cleansed, no longer consider unholy" (v. 15).

As Peter reflected on what he had seen, the men Cornelius had sent appeared at the gate. (God's timing is always right!) God had just taught Peter a spiritual truth and now He would give Peter the opportunity to implement that truth. He invited the men into his house where they explained their mission. Cornelius had sent for Peter who was to deliver a message in his (a Gentile's) house. Peter had never gone down this road before. But the Lord had prepared his heart. The vision of food was a lesson about Gentiles. Peter would embark on a mission leading to an influx of Gentiles into faith in Christ. What a momentous event!

CONSIDER: *God prepares our hearts and directs our steps.*

ACCEPTING ALL PEOPLE

ACTS 10:23–48

"God is not one to show partiality, but in every nation the man who fears Him and does what is right is welcome to Him." (Acts 10:34–35)

When Peter came to Caesarea, Cornelius was waiting for him—and he had invited friends and relatives in anticipation of what would transpire. When they met, Cornelius prostrated himself before Peter but the apostle reprimanded him, "Stand up; I too am just a man" (Acts 10:26). What an important reminder that God alone is to be worshiped.

Peter knew immediately for what purpose he had come. He reminded them of his background, that it is unlawful for a Jew to associate with a Gentile. The Lord's lesson with the sheet of unclean animals had captured Peter. He understood—and he made the transference: "God has shown me that I should not call any man unholy or unclean" (v. 28). What a milestone! The Jews had enacted many laws prohibiting relationships with Gentiles. "Three days before a heathen festival all transactions with Gentiles were forbidden . . . to enter the house of a heathen defiled [the person] until the evening. . . . A Jewess was actually forbidden to give help to her heathen neighbour, when about to become a mother! Milk drawn from a cow by heathen hands, bread and oil prepared by them, might indeed be sold to strangers, but not used by Israelites" (Alfred Edersheim, *Sketches of Social Life in the Days of Christ*). Separation of Jew and Gentile was intense.

Cornelius explained to Peter about the vision he had seen. But God had revealed Himself to Peter as well, so now the apostle spoke boldly on the new truth he had discovered. He began with his thesis, "I most certainly understand now that God is not one to show partiality" (v. 34). He immediately reminded the gathering that God welcomed people from every nation if they feared (revered) Him and did what was right. Then Peter launched into his message, "preaching peace through Jesus Christ" (v. 36). He told them of Christ's earthly life and ministry culminating with His atoning death and bodily resurrection—verifiable by the witnesses that had seen Him. Peter climaxed his message with the all-encompassing invitation, "everyone who believes in Him receives forgiveness of sins" (v. 43). To validate the authenticity of the Gentiles' acceptance by God, Peter saw that they too had received the Holy Spirit. He was amazed! The good news is indeed for everyone!

CONSIDER: *The invitation of the gospel is universal—there are no restrictions— it is available to all people.*

CONTENDING FOR THE PURITY OF THE GOSPEL
ACTS 11:1–18

---

*"If God gave to them the same gift as He gave to us also
after believing in the Lord Jesus Christ, who was I
that I could stand in God's way?" (Acts 11:17)*

One day when I came home I found a homemade gospel tract, crudely lettered, on my door. It explained salvation in this way: "Believe in Jesus Christ as your Lord, be baptized by immersion, receive the Holy Spirit and speak in tongues." Was that message accurate? It referenced four things that had to happen before one could become a Christian. Of course it was a false message. In every age the enemy seeks to corrupt the purity and simplicity of the gospel. That was Peter's experience when he returned to face the Jewish believers in Jerusalem.

Coming from Caesarea, Peter encountered the Jewish Christians in Jerusalem who "took issue with him" (Acts 11:2). They were upset because Peter had entered the home of an uncircumcised Gentile and had fellowship with Gentiles. During that time Jews believed that Gentiles had to become Jewish proselytes through baptism, circumcision, and the presentation of an offering; then they could become true believers.

These Jewish Christians did not understand that this was a new dispensation—the age of the church in which Jews and Gentiles are one body in Christ (1 Cor. 12:13). This one body is the church (Eph. 1:22–23). Gentiles as well as Jews receive the Holy Spirit in this present church age (Acts 11:17).

Peter rehearsed his experience on the rooftop in Joppa when God taught Peter the important lesson through the vision of the variety of animals let down on a sheet. Peter explained how the Lord showed him that the variety of animals, some previously considered unclean, illustrated that in this present age God was accepting Jews and Gentiles alike. The significant point of Peter's message was that the Holy Spirit fell on these Gentiles *just as* He had on the Twelve on the day of Pentecost. What had they done? They had believed in the Lord Jesus Christ. They had not been baptized; they had not been circumcised. But they received the Holy Spirit simply by believing in Jesus Christ. Peter accepted that message and so did the disputants. And that simple message hasn't changed.

CONSIDER: *God accepts all people when they put their trust in Jesus Christ and Him alone for their salvation.*

May 25

Witness in Antioch

Acts 11:19–30

> *[They] came to Antioch and began speaking to the Greeks
> [Gentiles] also, preaching the Lord Jesus. . . . And the disciples
> were first called Christians in Antioch. (Acts 11:20, 26)*

God uses unique ways to spread the good news of Jesus Christ. Persecution is one method. We wouldn't think this is a reasonable or appropriate method but God views things from an eternal perspective—and so should we. In the early morning sun, sounds of laughter are heard as 5,000 children attend Bible camps in Vietnam. Last year, 927 young people in these camps trusted Jesus as their Savior. Persecution doesn't stop the spread of the gospel.

God wanted to uproot the believers from clustering around Jerusalem so He allowed persecution, which scattered the believers to the outlying islands of the Mediterranean. Beginning at Phoenicia, north on the coast of Israel, they expanded to the island of Cyprus and to Antioch, in the interior of Asia Minor. But when they began their missionary endeavor, they only preached to the Jews. Yet some of them expanded their ministry to the Greeks (Gentiles)—a new venture and an expansion of the good news.

What was God's evaluation of this turn of events? "The hand of the Lord was with them, and a large number who believed turned to the Lord" (Acts 11:21). God blessed the missionary venture to the Gentiles. When the church in Jerusalem heard of the mission to the Gentiles, they sent Barnabas, a leader and an encourager, to investigate the reality of the Gentile conversions. What did he do? Seeing what had happened, "he rejoiced and began to encourage them all with resolute heart to remain true to the Lord" (v. 23).

Then Barnabas left for Tarsus to search for Saul/Paul. Apparently Paul was not in his ancestral home, indicating he had been rejected (F. F. Bruce, *Book of Acts*). When Barnabas found Paul, he brought him to Antioch where Paul taught the believers for a year, resulting in them being called "Christians"—a designation likely given by pagans. As an Antiochene would say, "O, these are the people who are always talking about Christos, the Christ-people, the Christians" (F. F. Bruce, *Book of Acts*). They didn't realize it but they were paying the believers the highest compliment.

CONSIDER: *The good news of Christ cannot be restrained; amid persecution and suffering the gospel continues to spread to all races and people groups.*

May 26

PERSECUTION IN JERUSALEM

ACTS 12:1–11

So Peter was kept in the prison, but prayer for him was
being made fervently by the church to God. (Acts 12:5)

On October 20, 2008, as Gayle Williams, a Christian aid worker in Kabul, Afghanistan, was walking to work, two Taliban militia on a motorbike shot and killed her. They shot her because she was spreading Christianity. "Our [leaders] issued a decree to kill this woman," spokesman Zabiullah Mujahid told the Associated Press. "This morning our people killed her in Kabul" (*World*, Nov. 1/8, 2008).

Persecuting and killing Christians is nothing new. It began when they rejected and crucified Christ and it has continued into the twenty-first century. In A.D. 44, Herod Agrippa I, grandson of Herod the Great, began to persecute the church. He was politically motivated to do this but he may also have had "aspirations to be recognized as a messianic ruler" (Cleon Rogers Jr. and Cleon Rogers III, *The New Linguistic and Exegetical Key to the Greek New Testament*). He began with brutality—he had James, one of the apostles, put to death. His political motivation is evident: when he saw it pleased the Jews, he arrested Peter as well. Why were the Jews pleased? Because Peter had fraternized with the Gentiles. Since this was during the Feast of Unleavened Bread, the Jews would have been particularly upset at any association with a Gentile.

Peter was imprisoned and guarded by four "quaternions" of soldiers—four groups of four, sixteen soldiers in all. Each group alternated in shifts of three hours each. Two would be chained to Peter while the other two guarded him. But as Peter was kept in prison, the church was praying for him. The language is graphic: Peter was *continually being kept in prison* and the believers were *continually praying* for him. It was a spiritual battle.

On the precise night that Herod was going to execute Peter, an angel appeared with a blazing light reflecting the presence of God from where he had come. God may not be early but He is never late. The angel struck Peter's side and immediately Peter's chains fell off. Amid all this—the light, the angel speaking to Peter—the guards did not wake up. God was and always is in control. The angel escorted Peter past two guarded gates and then vanished. Peter now realized that this was not a vision—God had accomplished his release. Amid persecution and suffering, God is with His people.

CONSIDER: *A believer's life is a spiritual battle between good and evil because of the enemy's opposition to the gospel of Christ.*

PRAYER FOR THE PERSECUTED

ACTS 12:12–25

Many were gathered together and were praying. (Acts 12:12)

When my uncle confronted my brother with the gospel in a crude and dictatorial way, my brother became hardened to the gospel. I prayed for him for years, all the time thinking that while God saved others, my brother wouldn't be saved. Thankfully, God overruled and my college friend, Wayne, led my brother to faith in Christ.

This event is a reminder that believers can pray fervently—amid unbelief that God will answer their request. When Peter was released from prison he made his way to the home of John Mark's mother, Mary. She apparently was wealthy since her home was where the church had gathered. It was a large upper room and may have been the upper room where the apostles and others had gathered (Acts 1:13). The believers are pictured being in continuous prayer. The fact that this is between 3:00 and 6:00 A.M. demonstrates their fervency. It was a critical time; Peter was scheduled for execution this new day.

As Peter knocked on the courtyard door, Rhoda, the servant girl, answered. Astonished as she recognized Peter's voice, she left Peter outside and ran and told the believers it was Peter! What was their response? Unbelief! They had prayed for days and, at this point, for hours on end, but they didn't believe God answered their prayer! They had a heated exchange. They accused Rhoda of being insane but she kept insisting it was Peter—and Peter kept on knocking! The guards would soon be coming! The believers may have thought the one outside was the "death angel," ready to transport Peter to heaven—they thought he was dead.

When they finally opened the door, they saw it was Peter. He quickly motioned for them to be quiet, and he explained to them what had happened. He told them to report this to James, the Lord's half-brother who was the head of the Jerusalem church. Then Peter quickly departed because the authorities would soon be looking for him.

There was turmoil among the authorities and when Herod discovered what had transpired, he had the guards executed. But when Herod went down to Caesarea and accepted the people's acclaim of deity, the Lord struck him and he died. Meanwhile, the word of the Lord kept on growing and multiplying in the lives of people. Despite opposition and persecution, people were coming to faith in Christ.

CONSIDER: *God responds to the prayers of His people—despite our unbelief.*

THE REGIONS BEYOND!

ACTS 13:1–12

Then the proconsul believed when he saw what had happened,
being amazed at the teaching of the Lord. (Acts 13:12)

L iving in England in the late 1700s, William Carey sensed the Holy Spirit's urging to go to the Far East and spread the gospel of Jesus Christ. But when he shared his vision with the elders in his church, they rebuked him and told him if God wanted those people saved He would accomplish it without Carey. But Carey remained determined and gave his life to bringing the gospel to India.

Acts 13 marks a major new event in the life of the church. Until this time the church had focused on Jews in the land of Israel. But now that would all change. As the church was meeting in Antioch, prophets and teachers, the leaders in the church, were ministering to the people. A prophet was one who received direct revelation from God and communicated that to the people. The Holy Spirit directed them to set apart Barnabas and Saul/Paul for a new ministry. The believers must have been sensitive to the Holy Spirit's ministry because they responded in obedience. But they fasted and prayed before they took action—a wise decision. Then they laid hands on Barnabas and Saul and sent them away. Why did they lay their hands on them? It did not impart anything; it meant identification—they were identifying with Barnabas and Saul in the ministry.

From the seaport of Seleucia they sailed to Cyprus, and in the city of Salamis they began to proclaim the good news. To whom? To the Jews. The church had not yet expanded its ministry beyond the Jews. It is significant that they went to the Jews and proclaimed Jesus as the Messiah. What they were doing was biblical; the gospel was to come to the Jews first (Rom. 1:16).

At Paphos, the seat of the provincial government, they met Sergius Paulus, a proconsul (the title of a Roman governor) who had summoned Barnabas and Saul to hear their message. But accompanying Sergius Paulus was Bar-Jesus (Elymas), a magician and false prophet. He was constantly opposing the ministry and message of Barnabas and Saul. He tried to disrupt the meeting and sought to discourage the proconsul from believing the gospel. But Saul confronted him. Rather than being a "son of Jesus" as his name indicated, he was really a "son of the devil." Saul judged him by announcing that he would be struck with blindness for a time—and he became blind. The event impacted the proconsul so that he believed. Despite opposition, the good news of Jesus Christ was moving beyond the land of Israel.

CONSIDER: *When God's people are doing the work of God they can expect the enemy to oppose them and their ministry.*

THE GOSPEL EXPANDS TO THE GENTILES

ACTS 13:13–52

---

*"It was necessary that the word of God be spoken to you first; since
you repudiate it and judge yourselves unworthy of eternal
life, behold, we are turning to the Gentiles." (Acts 13:46)*

This morning I shared the gospel with my Iranian Muslim lawn man. I've
talked to him a number of times and reminded him that only Jesus—not
Mohammed—was raised from the dead to authenticate His messiahship. He
alone is the way to God (John 14:6). I explained the new birth and he listened
intently and interacted with me.

Acts 13 brings a turning point in the expansion of the gospel. Paul and
Barnabas left Cyprus and sailed north to Asia Minor and trekked inland to
Antioch of Pisidia. At this point they still focused their evangelism on the
Jewish people as they entered the synagogue on the Sabbath. Two groups
were present: "Men of Israel" and "you who fear God"—both Jews and Gentile
converts to Judaism (v. 16). The synagogue service followed a distinct format
(see January 16 devotional): invitation to prayer, lifting up hands in prayer,
reading from the Mosaic Law and the Prophets as well as an exposition of the
passage. Then, if there was a competent visitor present, the synagogue ruler
invited the visitor to give an exhortation (Bruce Metzger, *The New Testament:
Its Background, Growth, and Content*). Paul took the stand.

Paul began by tracing God's dealing with Israel, ultimately focusing on
Christ's descent from the lineage of David. From the seed of David came the
Savior, Jesus, bringing salvation. But they rejected the Savior, just as the proph-
ets had predicted. Yet His messiahship was demonstrated in that He rose from
the dead, authenticated by the many witnesses who saw Him. The Messiah's
resurrection had been announced a thousand years earlier, however, through
David (in Acts 13:33–35, Paul is shown quoting Psalms 2:7 and 16:10). It wasn't
David whose body would not undergo decay, but Jesus.

And this was the good news that Paul now proclaimed! Those who believe
in Him would receive forgiveness of sins and be set free from the bondage
of the Law (vv. 38–39). Paul concluded his message by warning them not to
scoff. The response was strong—in both directions. When Paul met with the
people again the next Sabbath, the Jews became jealous and contradicted
and blasphemed. This was a turning point. Since the Jews rejected the gospel,
Paul would now focus on the Gentiles—as the Scriptures had commanded in
Isaiah 49:6. And the word continued to spread—not only to Jews now but to
Gentiles as well.

CONSIDER: *The gospel is for all people—for the Jews first, but ultimately for all
people, tongues, and nations.*

May 30

*R*ESPONSE AND *O*PPOSITION

Acts 14:1–18

Therefore they spent a long time there speaking boldly with reliance upon the Lord, who was testifying to the word of His grace, granting that signs and wonders be done by their hands. (Acts 14:3)

Leaving Antioch, Paul and Barnabas journeyed some ninety miles east on the main east-west highway, to Iconium which lay at the foot of the Taurus Mountains. At that time Iconium was part of the Roman province of Galatia. As was their custom, Paul and Barnabas went to the synagogue to present the good news first to the Jewish people. Gentiles, too, responded to that message. These may have been Gentile converts to Judaism but likely there were other Gentiles that came, having heard of Paul's preaching. The result was that many Jews and Gentiles believed.

But the unbelieving Jews stirred up the Gentiles, painting Paul and Barnabas as evildoers. Yet Paul and Barnabas remained faithful, proclaiming the good news with boldness in dependence on the Lord who verified their message with miracles. Eventually the city of Iconium became divided, with the Jewish opposition joining forces with the unbelieving Gentiles to incite mob violence against Paul and Barnabas. When the mob determined to stone them, Paul and Barnabas fled from the city.

The missionaries headed south to Lystra (the home of Timothy). When they encountered a crippled man Paul challenged the man, "Stand upright on your feet!" (Acts 14:10). When the man leaped up and began to walk, the Lycaonians were shocked, believing the gods had taken on human form and had come to visit them. "Barnabas may have been identified with Zeus because of his more dignified bearing; Paul, the more animated of the two, was called Hermes 'because he was the chief speaker'" (F. F. Bruce, *Book of Acts*). Soon the priest of Zeus prepared to sacrifice oxen to Paul and Barnabas! Alarmed, Paul began to address the crowd. It is noteworthy that Paul spoke differently to these Gentiles. To the Jews Paul used the Old Testament Scriptures; with the Gentiles he invoked general revelation, reminding them of the living God, who created the heavens and the earth, giving them rain and fruitful seasons. For this reason, they should "turn from these vain things to a living God" (v. 15). Paul's presentation is a reminder that we must know our audience and—while not diminishing the gospel—know how to approach different people.

CONSIDER: *The proclamation of the good news may bring varying undesirable responses—it may bring opposition and persecution or it may bring "deification" of the messenger. In all instances we must remain faithful to the Word of God.*

May 31

A LESSON IN COURAGE

ACTS 14:19–28

> *They returned . . . strengthening the souls of the disciples, encouraging them to continue in the faith, and saying, "Through many tribulations we must enter the kingdom of God." (Acts 14:21–22)*

Today's hero is tomorrow's villain. Ask some major sports figures. If a quarterback has a great season, he is popular and enthusiastically acclaimed. If he throws interceptions and loses several games, he is the villain. An audience is fickle.

The Jews who had opposed Paul came from Antioch and Iconium. Their hatred must have been severe for them to travel over a hundred miles just to attack him. They manipulated the audience, won them over, then stoned Paul, leaving him for dead. Paul was singled out because he was the chief speaker.

The text is not entirely clear, but it seems this was a miracle. Paul had been stoned on the spot where they engaged him, then he was dragged out of the city and left for dead. While the disciples stood around Paul, no doubt grieving, thinking he was dead, Paul got up and entered the city. The next day, Paul journeyed thirty miles to Derbe and then on to Lystra, Iconium, and Antioch. It is doubtful Paul could have done this had he not been healed supernaturally.

When Paul suffered physically (in 2 Corinthians 11:25 he specifically mentions his stoning), he was suffering for God's truth—bearing the physical "brand-marks of Jesus" (Gal. 6:17). But Paul was not discouraged—what a lesson for us! He didn't brood or withdraw from ministry because of what had happened. Just the opposite. Paul returned to the very cities that had troubled him, again preaching the gospel and strengthening and encouraging the believers. "These recent converts from heathenism were ill-informed, were persecuted, had broken family and social ties, greatly needed encouragement if they were to hold out" (A. T. Robertson, *Word Pictures of the New Testament*). Paul also helped organize the fledgling church by appointing elders in every church. Then, with prayer and fasting, they commended the young church to the Lord for His care.

Having completed the first missionary journey, Paul and Barnabas left Asia Minor and sailed back to Antioch where their missionary journey began. They reported to the leadership how God had opened the door to the Gentiles. The spread of the gospel to the nations of the world had begun!

CONSIDER: *Staying focused on the Lord, rather than on self, is crucial in remaining faithful and successful in ministry.*

DEFENDING THE PURITY OF THE GOSPEL

ACTS 15:1–21

"But we believe that we are saved through the grace of the Lord Jesus, in the same way as they also are." (Acts 15:11)

It was a momentous event when my wife and I visited the church in Wittenberg, Germany, where in 1517 Martin Luther posted his Ninety-five Theses on the church door, sparking the Protestant Reformation. Luther defended the supreme biblical truth that salvation is by grace, through faith, plus nothing.

Steeped in the Mosaic Law, it was extremely difficult for some of the Jews to accept the gospel of grace that set aside the Law. They still wanted to keep the Law. They wanted to combine Law and grace—an impossible scenario. When Paul and Barnabas returned from their mission trip, explaining how Gentiles had been saved, they were confronted by some Jews who warned that unless the Christian believers were circumcised they would not be saved. This caused a significant debate—and it was a critical issue—the gospel would be corrupted if they added prerequisites to salvation.

The issue reached its climax when Paul and Barnabas came to report to the church in Jerusalem. Pharisees who had believed the gospel provoked the issue, thinking adhererence to the Law was still essential. Perhaps the controversy was due to the success of the missionary journey, with many Gentiles believing the gospel. The apostles and elders collaborated on the issue. Peter reminded them of his visit with Cornelius some ten years earlier (Acts 10), how God gave these uncircumcised Gentiles the Holy Spirit "just as He also did to us; and He made no distinction between us and them, cleansing their hearts by faith" (Acts 15:8–9). That resolved the issue. God accepted the uncircumcised Gentiles, making no distinction between them. By demanding circumcision for the Gentiles, they would be placing a burdensome yoke on the Gentiles. Peter concluded by reminding them that Jews are saved by grace as well as Gentiles (v. 11); why then put a yoke around the Gentiles' necks? Paul and Barnabas were vindicated.

After hearing Paul and Barnabas explain the response and conversion of the Gentiles, James (the half-brother of Jesus), the leader of the Jerusalem church, spoke. He cited Amos 9:11–12 to show that the Old Testament foretold the Gentiles' inclusion in God's program—without submitting to circumcision. He concluded that the Gentiles should not be troubled with the Law. To avoid offending Jews, he urged the Gentiles to abstain from things contaminated by idols, from fornication, and from eating the meat of animals that had not had their blood properly drained. This was not a legal issue. A major victory had been won—the purity of the gospel would be maintained.

CONSIDER: *The purity of the gospel—salvation by grace through faith plus nothing—must be constantly defended.*

A LETTER OF GOOD NEWS!

ACTS 15:22–35

They delivered the letter. When they had read it, they
rejoiced because of its encouragement. (Acts 15:30–31)

When we go to the mailbox we get a variety of letters—good news, bad news, no news. Certain letters we have received remain strong in our memory because of the good news they contained. Six months after I had made a manuscript proposal to a publisher, I received a contract in the mail. That was exciting news!

The apostles, elders, and the entire church agreed to send a letter to encourage the Gentiles. Moreover, two other men, Judas Barsabbas and Silas would accompany Paul and Barnabas. What was the point? Perhaps these men represented the two groups: Hebrews and Hellenists (Everett Harrison, *Interpreting Acts*). Their word would have been authoritative in bringing the message of grace to the church in Antioch.

The Jerusalem church leaders disassociated themselves from the legalistic troublemakers who had upset the Gentiles (Acts 15:24). The obligation of circumcision and adherence to the Law (Acts 15:5) had not been sanctioned by the Jerusalem church.

What was the purpose of the letter?

1. The gospel of divine grace was reaffirmed.
2. The unity of the church was safeguarded (preventing a split into a Jewish church and a Gentile church).
3. The evangelism of the Gentiles could proceed without hindrance.
4. The Gentile churches which had already been established would be given encouragement (see 16:4–5).
5. The future of the church as a whole was guaranteed. (Everett Harrison, *Interpreting Acts*)

The instruction to avoid things sacrificed to idols, blood, things strangled, and fornication were *moral* issues. Paul warned believers not to participate in immoral pagan practices that were common in those days (Stanley Toussaint, "Acts," *Bible Knowledge Commentary*). When Paul and the other men delivered the letter in Antioch, the Gentile believers rejoiced at the encouraging good news. To further encourage the Gentiles, Judas and Silas remained in Antioch for a time, strengthening the believers in their teaching. Paul and Barnabas remained in Antioch longer, teaching and preaching—no doubt further encouraging the Gentile believers.

CONSIDER: *How can you encourage someone today? Can you send an encouraging letter, a note to bless someone?*

DISAGREEMENT AMONG BELIEVERS

ACTS 15:36–41

*And there occurred such a sharp disagreement that
they separated from one another. (Acts 15:39)*

Martin Luther and Huldrych Zwingli were two giants during the Reformation, leading the church out of bondage. Both were advocates of salvation by faith alone. In 1529 they met at the Marburg Castle to discuss their views. They agreed on fourteen of fifteen issues but they disagreed on the Lord's Supper. Zwingli taught that it was a memorial of the death of Christ while Luther taught there was a real presence of Christ. The result ended with Luther refusing to shake Zwingli's hand and they parted company.

Believers throughout the ages have disagreed with one another. Here Paul and his mentor and traveling companion, Barnabas, had a strong disagreement. They were about to embark on their second missionary journey. The Jerusalem Council had recognized the right of Gentiles to become Christians without submitting to the Law. The time was ripe for renewed missionary activity; Paul suggested that they revisit the churches in the cities of their first journey. However, Barnabas wanted to take John Mark, his cousin (Col. 4:10). Since Mark had deserted them on the first trip, Paul refused to take him. Their disagreement was sharp. Barnabas apparently stuck to his decision to take John Mark, while Paul "kept insisting that they should not take him along who had deserted them in Pamphylia" (Acts 15:38). The disagreement was so sharp that Barnabas left Paul and sailed to Cyprus with John Mark.

Who was right? What were the issues? (1) As an encourager, Barnabas probably saw potential in John Mark and wanted to help him. (2) John Mark may have wanted to redeem himself—which, in fact, he did. Paul later wrote that Mark "is useful to me for service" (2 Tim. 4:11). (3) John Mark may have brought a detrimental report to the Jerusalem church, jeopardizing Paul's work. (4) Paul put "principle above the closest friendship and the will of God above personal relationships" (Everett Harrison, *Interpreting Acts*).

After they separated, Paul chose Silas and the two men were sent off by the church at Antioch as Paul and Barnabas had previously experienced (Acts 13:3). Paul changed his plans and traveled overland to Tarsus and then on to Derbe and Lystra. It should be noted that the separation was not permanent. Paul later spoke of his association with Barnabas (1 Cor. 9:6). Although they separated, God used the disagreement to create two missionary endeavors rather than one.

CONSIDER: *Christians may disagree amicably and both be used by God.*

CHOOSING AN ASSOCIATE

ACTS 16:1–5

And a disciple was there, named Timothy. . . . Paul
wanted this man to go with him. (Acts 16:1, 3)

Billy Graham and George Beverly Shea; D. L. Moody and Ira Sankey—the names are connected. It is difficult to think of one name without thinking of the other. We think of the Spirit-filled preaching of Billy Graham but we also think of George Beverly Shea's singing, so used by the Holy Spirit to prepare the hearts of the people. Throughout history God has used associates in service for Him.

Traveling with Silas, Paul came to Derbe and Lystra where he met a young convert named Timothy. Paul and Barnabas had visited these cities previously and it is likely Timothy became a believer at that time. He was the son of a mixed marriage, his mother being Jewish, while his father was a Gentile. His mother was Eunice and his grandmother was Lois—both believers (2 Tim. 1:5). His mother had faithfully taught Timothy the Scriptures. Since it simply says "his father was a Greek," it appears his father was an unbeliever.

Timothy had demonstrated his faithfulness and perhaps his spiritual gifts in the local church so that the Christians in Lystra and Iconium spoke well of him. Paul also recognized Timothy's faithfulness and realized he would be a helpful companion on his missionary journey so he endeavored to take Timothy with him. So Paul did something unusual; he had Timothy circumcised. Why? "In the eyes of Jews, Timothy was a Gentile because he was the uncircumcised son of a Greek. In Gentile eyes, however, he was practically a Jew, having been brought up in his mother's religion. Paul therefore regularized his status (and, in Jewish eyes, legitimized him) by circumcising him. . . . It was simple expediency that suggested the circumcising of one who was already a half-Jew with a view to his greater usefulness in the ministry of the gospel" (F. F. Bruce, *Book of Acts*). Timothy's circumcision will have avoided offense to the Jews. Consider 1 Corinthians 9:20–23, where Paul speaks of himself. Among Jews, Paul's ministry would have been hindered had Timothy not been circumcised.

God's blessing was on the trio as they continued traveling in Asia Minor "so the churches were being strengthened in the faith, and were increasing in number daily" (Acts 16:5).

CONSIDER: *God uniquely joins two servants together for greater, more effective service in communicating the gospel.*

June 5

THE GOSPEL EXPANDS TO EUROPE

ACTS 16:6–15

A vision appeared to Paul in the night: a man of Macedonia was standing and appealing to him, and saying, "Come over to Macedonia and help us." (Acts 16:9)

When God called William Carey to bring the gospel to India, the leaders in his church did not understand and rebuked him for it, telling him that if the Lord wanted those Asian people converted He could do it without Carey's help. Yet William Carey went and God used him mightily, despite enormous hardships. Christians do not always understand how God leads His servants.

Acts 16 marks a turning point in Paul's missionary ministry—God directed Paul to take the gospel westward, to Europe. How does this happen? "The missionary journeys of Paul exhibit an extraordinary combination of strategic planning and keen sensitiveness to the guidance of the Spirit of God, whether that guidance took the form of inward prompting or the overruling of external circumstances" (F. F. Bruce, *Book of Acts*). Both are important: planning and guidance by the Holy Spirit.

The missionaries traveled westward and northward through central Asia Minor. When Paul and his party attempted to travel northward into northern Asia, they were prohibited by the Holy Spirit. When they tried to go north to Bithynia, where there were significant cities and Jewish colonies, they were again forbidden by the Holy Spirit.

They finally came to the busy port city of Troas which linked Asia with Europe. Here a man from Macedonia appeared to Paul in a vision, appealing to Paul, "Come over to Macedonia and help us." This was a supernatural event. *God* was directing Paul to Europe. The Holy Spirit prevented them from going north (Acts 16:6); the Spirit of Jesus (probably a reference to Jesus Himself) also prohibited them (v. 7).

Luke joined them (notice the "we" in verse 10) as they set out for Philippi, the "leading city" of Macedonia, lying on the Egnatian Way which linked the Aegean Sea with the Adriatic Sea.

Paul customarily went to the synagogue on the Sabbath but here went to the riverside where some women had assembled. Jewish law required ten men present for a synagogue service, and so there likely was a scarcity of Jews in this area. As Paul spoke, a woman who traded in purple dye, which was in demand by the wealthy people, responded. As a "worshiper of God" she was an Old Testament believer, one who had faith based on God's revelation of Himself through the early Scriptures. Now God opened her heart to believe the message about Jesus Christ. Paul probably had no realization how vast the missionary venture to Europe would become after this humble beginning.

CONSIDER: *God leads His people in unique ways—through circumstances and through the promptings of the Holy Spirit.*

CONVERSION OF A JAILER

ACTS 16:16–40

*"Believe in the Lord Jesus, and you will be saved,
you and your household." (Acts 16:31)*

The gospel is powerful. It reaches every strata of society: the rich, the poor, the educated, the uneducated, the nobility, and the common man. Charles Colson, once a prominent adviser to government leaders, came to faith in Christ. Now he ministers in prisons and sees down-and-outers come to faith in the same Christ.

Earlier in Acts 16, we saw Lydia, a wealthy woman in Philippi, come to faith in Christ. Now we see several people from the other side of the social register who came to believe in Christ. As Paul and Silas were going to a prayer meeting, a slave girl with a "spirit of divination" (allowing her to foretell the future) accosted them. She was involved with Pythian Apollo, a Greek god who had killed a python. This god was worshiped at the temple of Apollo in Delphi. In plain words, she was demon possessed. In the name of Christ, Paul exorcised the demon.

But the masters of the slave girl now lost their lucrative business and brought Paul and Silas before the magistrates who ordered them beaten with rods. What was the charge? Proselytizing Romans. Although Judaism was a legitimate religion, they were not allowed to proselytize Romans (A. T. Robertson, *Word Pictures of the New Testament*). Stripped naked, Paul and Silas were severely beaten in the public square then thrown into prison. Their feet were forced painfully far apart and then fastened in stocks (F. F. Bruce, *Book of Acts*).

What was their response? Praying and singing hymns! Normally prisoners would have cursed God and man, but Paul and Silas continued praying and singing while the prisoners were listening. It was dramatic! Then God answered their prayers with a great earthquake; the jail doors opened and the prisoners' chains fell off. When the jailer saw this he attempted to commit suicide, but Paul cried out to him to avert the suicide. Trembling, the man came to Paul and Silas. No doubt he had heard their praying and singing and he asked the right question, "What must I do to be saved?" Paul and Silas answered, "Believe in the Lord Jesus, and you will be saved, you and your household." As with Lydia, God opened the jailer's heart and he and his family members believed and he was baptized that night. The power of Christ was operative in saving both the elite and the ordinary. Every person needs Christ.

CONSIDER: *Never doubt the power of Christ to save—from every strata of society. Never give up praying, trusting for Christ to save a loved one.*

PENETRATING EUROPE WITH THE GOSPEL

ACTS 17:1–14

*For three Sabbaths [Paul] reasoned with them from the Scriptures,
explaining and giving evidence that the Christ had to suffer and
rise again from the dead, and saying, "This Jesus whom I am
proclaiming to you is the Christ." (Acts 17:2–3)*

It was a momentous occasion when I, along with many others, arrived in Thessaloniki. We walked amid the ruins of the ancient biblical site, read the Scriptures, and reflected. This was the site of the early church of Thessalonica, where Paul proclaimed the gospel, bringing the gospel to Europe and the west.

Traveling along the historic military highway, the Egnatian Way, which connected the eastern province of Thrace with the western provinces of Illyricum and Macedonia, Paul and Silas traveled westward. It would have taken three days to travel over ninety miles to Thessalonica, a city of two hundred thousand inhabitants, the largest and most significant city of Macedonia. Since it was a cosmopolitan and commercial city, there were numerous Jews in Thessalonica. According to his custom, Paul went to the synagogue on the Sabbath. Paul was aggressive. For three Sabbaths, he expounded the Old Testament Scriptures, debating and showing their prophetic fulfillment in the life, death, and resurrection of Christ.

People from different backgrounds responded: Jews, a great number of Gentiles who were converts to Judaism ("God-fearing Greeks"), and leading women. This infuriated the Jews who immediately created mob violence. They were jealous, and wanted to get Paul and Silas in trouble with the Roman authorities. They incited the rabble from the public marketplace who, when they couldn't find Paul and Silas, dragged Jason and other believers before the authorities, charging them with upsetting the peace of the Roman Empire and acting contrary to the decrees of Caesar while proclaiming another king, Jesus. When Jason gave a pledge, perhaps promising that Paul would leave the city, they released him. Immediately that night the believers sent Paul and Silas to Berea. Here the Jewish believers were different, having a gracious spirit but also carefully studying the Scriptures that Paul shared with them. Many more believed. But opposition again set in, necessitating that Paul, the leader and object of opposition, be sent to the seacoast.

CONSIDER: *Response to Christian witness will always be mixed; some will accept the message while others may be hostile and incite opposition.*

CONFRONTING PAGAN CULTURE

ACTS 17:15–34

---

*"Therefore what you worship in ignorance, this
I proclaim to you. . . . God is now declaring to men that
all people everywhere should repent." (Acts 17:23, 30)*

One of the challenges Christians face today is understanding and confronting our culture. Nancy Pearcey has written an excellent book, *Total Truth*, identifying our culture, tracing it to the philosopher Jean-Jacques Rousseau who sought to restore people to their "true nature," creating "autonomous individuals." But that meant removing oppressive relationships like "marriage, family, church, and workplace" to "free" people to live independent of any moral structure or guidelines. This worldview has impacted our society in the twenty-first century.

Paul understood and challenged the culture of his day. Philosophy was the focus at Athens—the city of intellectuals like Socrates, Plato, and Aristotle. Arriving there, Paul immediately went to the synagogue and the marketplace, reasoning and challenging the people. Debating with Paul were the Epicureans who, rejecting any afterlife, taught that pleasure was man's highest goal. Stoics taught the opposite, emphasizing self-control and a life of emotional detachment.

Taking Paul to the Areopagus ("Mars Hill"), Paul was called to give an account for his strange teaching. Paul began by reminding the Athenians they were "very religious"—the Athenians had thirty thousand gods, indicating they did not know the true God. Fearing they might overlook some deity, they addressed one altar "to an unknown god." But now Paul would proclaim the true God to them. Recognizing he was speaking to a Gentile audience rather than Jewish people, Paul did not quote the Old Testament to show how Christ fulfilled the prophecies. Instead, Paul identified God as the Creator of the world—in contrast to Greek philosophy, which taught that matter was eternal. He reminded them that the true God does not live in temples made by humans—the Athenians had beautiful temples but they were empty. In a rebuke to their idea of Greek superiority, Paul reminded them that God has made all nations from one common origin—and God is in control of the destiny of nations.

But God's purpose for the nations was that they should seek God. Now that God had revealed Himself in Jesus Christ, He was calling on people everywhere to repent because He had fixed a day wherein He would judge all people through Christ. When Paul spoke of the resurrection, the Athenians scorned his words and left. A few believed.

CONSIDER: *Believers should be bold in proclaiming and defending the truth about Christ in the public arena while knowing there may be ridicule.*

CONFRONTATION IN CORINTH

ACTS 18:1–17

*"Your blood be on your own heads! I am clean. From
now on I will go to the Gentiles." (Acts 18:6)*

Leaving Athens, Paul came to Corinth, a major cosmopolitan center of four
hundred thousand people and capital of Achaia. Boasting three harbors
Corinth was a major commercial center with people from the entire Mediterranean area visiting the city. The city had one thousand temple prostitutes
serving in their idolatrous and immoral worship of Astarte, the goddess of
fertility. Young girls were required to serve as temple prostitutes at least once
in their lives. The verb *korinthiazo* meant "to act the Corinthian" and came to
mean "to practice fornication."

In Corinth Paul met a believing couple, Aquila and Priscilla, who were
tentmakers by trade. They had been expelled from Rome during the reign of
Claudius because they were Jews. Paul joined them in the trade of tent making.

Paul went to the synagogue and proclaimed the gospel to Jews and Gentiles alike, later to be joined by Silas and Timothy. Timothy brought news of
the persecution the Thessalonian believers were experiencing and, as a result,
Paul was prompted to write the two Thessalonian letters in quick succession.
Silas and Timothy also brought Paul a monetary gift from Philippi (as Paul
mentions in 2 Corinthians 11:9 and Philippians 4:15), enabling him to devote
himself entirely to preaching the good news.

When the Jews rejected Paul's message, slandering and blaspheming, he
turned to the Gentiles, going to the home of Titius Justus ("a worshiper of God"
in Acts 18:7 indicates that he believed in the God of the Scriptures) who lived
next to the synagogue. Titius Justus, along with many others, including Crispus,
the leader of the synagogue, believed the gospel and were baptized.

This was a critical time in Paul's life. He had been imprisoned, tortured,
and driven from Philippi; chased out of Thessalonica; persecuted and driven
from Berea; and ridiculed in Athens. He was in need of encouragement. It
came. The Lord spoke to Paul in a vision, encouraging him to continue preaching the gospel. So Paul stayed in Corinth one and a half years, proclaiming
the gospel.

But the Jews were upset at Paul's preaching and brought Paul to the judgment seat, but Gallio refused to listen to their charge and finally drove them
away.

CONSIDER: *Despite our faithfulness in proclaiming the gospel, opposition will
come and it will call for our faithfulness and steadfastness amid opposition.*

TRANSITION FROM LAW TO GRACE

ACTS 18:18–28

He powerfully refuted the Jews in public, demonstrating by the
Scriptures that Jesus was the Christ. (Acts 18:28)

Transitions can be difficult. When Christ died on the cross, the veil in the temple was torn from top to bottom, reminding the people that the age of the Law was over. Paul reminds us, "you are not under law but under grace" (Rom. 6:14). Yet, in practice, this did not come quickly or immediately. Peter and the apostles probably felt uncomfortable eating ham sandwiches! The transition from law to grace took time.

Paul remained in Corinth for a year and a half, probably until spring, A.D. 52. At Cenchrea, the eastern seaport of Corinth, Paul "had his hair cut, for he was keeping a vow" (Acts 18:18). Why had Paul taken a vow? He may have been ill; according to Josephus, vows were sometimes taken for thirty days during illness. Or it may have been a Nazirite vow (Num. 6:1–21), which ended with cutting one's hair. "Acts describes a period of transition, and it should not surprise us to find Christian Jews still observing Jewish ritual as a matter of choice" (Homer Kent Jr., *From Jerusalem to Rome*).

When Paul came to Ephesus he entered the synagogue and debated with the Jews but soon left the city. He may have been in a hurry to be in Jerusalem for a feast (as seen in Acts 20:16) or simply to greet the church in Jerusalem. Going on to Antioch, Paul began his third missionary journey (A.D. 53–57), returning to Galatia and Phrygia, revisiting the churches to strengthen the believers.

Between Paul's first and second visits to Ephesus, another teacher, Apollos, had visited the city. Apollos was "mighty" (powerful) in the Scriptures. But what was Apollos's message? He was "teaching accurately the things concerning Jesus, being acquainted only with the baptism of John" (v. 25). John had introduced Christ to the nation but was incarcerated and killed shortly afterward. John did not know about Jesus' rejection, crucifixion, resurrection, and the descent of the Holy Spirit and the birth of the church. Priscilla and Aquila filled in these details of the life of Christ to Apollos. Apollos accepted the instruction and traveled on to Achaia (specifically, to its capital, Corinth) where he powerfully refuted the Jews, demonstrating that Jesus was the Messiah.

CONSIDER: *It is a challenge—and essential—to keep grace clear and clean, without corruption by mixing it with law.*

VERIFICATION OF THE NEW MESSAGE

ACTS 19:1–20

*So the word of the Lord was growing
mightily and prevailing. (Acts 19:20)*

Does the Holy Spirit come to the believer at a "second blessing," subsequent to salvation? What about "speaking in tongues"? Do believers speak in tongues after a so-called second blessing? These are controversial issues that this chapter of Acts raises.

When Paul came to Ephesus, he encountered Apollos's disciples who had not heard that the Holy Spirit had been poured out at Pentecost—they didn't even know about the Holy Spirit. These people were Old Testament saints, they believed in the God of the Scriptures but, without the Bible, had not yet received God's entire revelation. After Paul explained Jesus' coming, they were baptized in the name of Jesus. What followed is unique to the transition period when people who were Old Testament believers had not yet heard about Christ. After believing, these people began speaking in tongues. Why? The tongues (languages) authenticated the message Paul preached. The visible sign of the Holy Spirit demonstrated the reception of these Ephesian believers into the body of Christ. In this transition period from Jew to Gentile, it was a sign that God was receiving Jews and Gentiles into one body (preventing a schism into a Jewish church and a Gentile church).

Paul continued proclaiming Christ in the synagogue for three months but when they opposed him, he withdrew to the school of Tyrannus where he remained for two years. As a result, the word spread. Probably the churches mentioned in Revelation 1–3 as well as Colossae and Hierapolis were founded during this time although Paul himself did not visit them (Col. 2:1; 4:13). Paul also penned the first letter to the Corinthians at this time (A.D. 54). As in the first century, prior to the canonization of Scripture, the miracles authenticated the message. Many believed, in fact, "fear fell upon them all and the name of the Lord Jesus was being magnified" (Acts 19:17). When Jewish exorcists attempted to use the name of Jesus in casting out demons, the demons refused to recognize the Jewish exorcists!

Fear came upon the people as they recognized the power of Christ through Paul. As a result, they "cleaned house," burning their magical books, and the word of God continued to grow mightily.

CONSIDER: *When we truly get right with the Lord, we will fear and reverence His name and remove from our lives the things displeasing to Him.*

June 12

OPPOSITION TO THE MESSAGE
ACTS 19:21–41

*About that time there occurred no small
disturbance concerning the Way. (Acts 19:23)*

Having been in Ephesus for two years, Paul purposed to go to Jerusalem, sending Timothy and Erastus ahead of him to Macedonia while he stayed in Ephesus a while longer. Paul's stay in Ephesus had made an impact. People were believing the gospel; new believers were abandoning idolatry. As a result, there was an uproar among the idolaters. Demetrius, a silversmith, led the charge among the tradesmen against Paul. His "workshop manufactured hundreds of small shrines which were miniatures of the temple and enclosed a small statue of the goddess" (Merrill Unger, *Archaeology and the New Testament*). He charged that Paul was ruining their business (Acts 19:24–27) and that Paul was turning people away from worshiping Artemis (v. 27). To the idolaters, this was serious. "Those who worshiped Artemis of Ephesus called her the Lady, Saviour, heavenly goddess, Queen of the Cosmos and looked to her for safety, health, protection, deliverance, answers to their prayers, and general benevolence" (Cleon Rogers Jr. and Cleon Rogers III, *The New Linguistic and Exegetical Key to the Greek New Testament*).

Shouting "Great is Artemis of the Ephesians," the people rushed to the theater, which held twenty-five thousand people. Unable to find Paul, the rioters dragged Gaius and Aristarchus along into the theater. The Asiarchs (leading citizens of the city) who were friendly to Paul urged him not to go. Meanwhile, there was shouting and enormous confusion: "the majority did not know for what reason they had come together" (v. 32).

When the Jews saw it was Christians that had instigated the conflict they wanted to disassociate themselves but when Alexander, a Jew, attempted to speak, the crowd didn't let him and continued to cry out, "Great is Artemis of the Ephesians!" The town clerk, who was the official liaison between the civil authorities and Rome, quieted the crowd, warning them against undue rebellion—they stood in danger of Rome with their rioting. And recognizing Paul and his people were innocent, he dismissed the assembly.

CONSIDER: *Are you making an impact with your life that causes a response among unbelievers—either positive or negative?*

STRENGTHENING BELIEVERS

ACTS 20:1–12

*On the first day of the week, when we were gathered together
to break bread, Paul began talking to them, intending to leave the
next day, and he prolonged his message until midnight. (Acts 20:7)*

When I and several others took a mission trip to Ukraine, we visited several churches in Kiev. Being used to the worship services in America, we encountered a distinct difference. They were not bound by the rigidity of a one-hour worship service. They had three lengthy speakers, interspersed with a considerable number of musical selections. And the people were accustomed to it and entered into it.

After the uproar at Ephesus ceased, Paul departed for Macedonia. During this time he wrote 2 Corinthians (A.D. 56). From Macedonia, Paul returned to Greece (Corinth) where he spent three months and also wrote the epistle to the Romans. Paul planned to sail for Jerusalem but when he received word of a plot to kill him when he boarded the ship, he returned to Macedonia to sail from there instead. Paul was carrying a contribution from the churches to the Jerusalem church which had suffered from famine. Luke joined the party at Philippi (seen by the "we" statements in verse 6).

Arriving at Troas, they gathered for worship ("to break bread") on the first day of the week—a reminder of the transition from worshiping on the Sabbath (seventh day) to Sunday (first day). Breaking bread involved a fellowship meal called the Agape Feast. The believers brought their own food to the meal which sometimes resulted in some going hungry while others gorged themselves (which Paul mentions in 1 Corinthians 11:20–22). "This was probably a carry-over from the Last Supper when a complete meal took place between the bread and cup sayings" (G. F. Hawthorne, *The Zondervan Pictorial Encyclopedia of the Bible*).

The meal was followed by a period of self-examination (1 Cor. 11:28). "It may have been strictly personal, or it may have involved individual public confession in the church, or corporate confession . . ." (G. F. Hawthorne, *The Zondervan Pictorial Encyclopedia of the Bible*). The gathering concluded with the Lord's Supper when they remembered the body and blood of Christ which was given for them.

Since Paul was leaving the next day he prolonged his message until midnight. A young man, Eutychus, was overcome by sleep and fell from the third floor window and was "picked up dead." Paul fell on him, performing a miracle similar to Elijah in 1 Kings 17:21 and Elisha in 2 Kings 4:34. Eutychus was restored to life. But then Paul continued to talk until daybreak!

CONSIDER: *Perhaps we have lost something in our precise and concise worship services; perhaps we have forfeited fellowship with others and with our Lord.*

WARNING ABOUT WOLVES

ACTS 20:13–38

"But I do not consider my life of any account as dear to myself, so that I may finish my course and the ministry which I received from the Lord Jesus, to testify solemnly of the gospel of the grace of God." (Acts 20:24)

This week I received a mailing from an evangelical leader that stated: "But the Lord Jesus never said that in order to be born again one must believe in His deity, His death, or His resurrection." I was shocked. Of course this is a heretical statement—from within evangelicalism. Paul predicted false teaching would come from within.

At Troas Paul's companions boarded the ship while Paul walked to Assos alone. Why did Paul walk alone? Perhaps he had unfinished business in Troas; perhaps he paid a visit to Eutychus; maybe he wanted to be alone. At Assos Paul joined the group and they sailed south to Miletus, just south of Ephesus. Paul did not want to stop at Ephesus since he was hurrying to be in Jerusalem for the Feast of Pentecost. We see the transition from law to grace, from Israel to the church. In this transition period the Christian leaders still observed the Jewish feasts. No doubt, a key reason was to bring the gospel to the Jews and bring the Old Testament saints into faith in Christ.

At Miletus Paul called the elders to come to him where he could instruct them. The elders (*presbuteros*) signified older persons, leaders in the church. It is used synonymously with "overseers" (v. 28), which views the work of shepherding and feeding the flock. The term "pastor" would relate to both of these terms and is a synonym of overseer.

Paul bared his soul to them, explaining his suffering and his diligence in service. He had not compromised the truth. He had taught in public discourses and homes. Paul had a singular message: "repentance toward God and faith in our Lord Jesus Christ" (v. 21). This summarizes the gospel message. Both repentance and faith are involved in a single transaction. Repentance (*metanoian*) means "change of mind" toward God, recognizing Him as holy and righteous and oneself as a needy sinner. When a person believes in Christ there is also repentance.

Paul recognized that hardship and suffering awaited him yet he did not shrink from his God-ordained task. Then he exhorted the leaders to be diligently on the alert against false teachers who would come from within the church fellowship. Paul prayed for them and then, amid the elders' tears because they wouldn't see him again, he departed.

CONSIDER: *In this postmodern world, it is incumbent on us to stand strong for the historic truth of God's Word.*

June 15

COMMITTED TO SUFFERING

ACTS 21:1–16

*"What are you doing, weeping and breaking my heart?
For I am ready not only to be bound, but even to die at
Jerusalem for the name of the Lord Jesus." (Acts 21:13)*

On January 8, 1956, Jim Elliot, Pete Fleming, Ed McCully, Nate Saint, and Roger Youderian were killed, speared to death, while attempting to bring the gospel to the fierce Auca Indians in Ecuador. Jim Elliot was fearless, committed to telling others the liberating good news of Jesus Christ. He made the classic statement, "That man is no fool who gives up that which he cannot keep to gain that which he cannot lose."

The apostle Paul was of the same mind. On the way back to Israel from his third missionary journey, Paul and the others landed at Tyre. Paul found the believers but when they discovered his determination to go to Jerusalem, "they kept telling Paul through the Spirit not to set foot in Jerusalem" (Acts 21:4). Was Paul disobeying the Spirit? The believers undoubtedly saw the danger and the suffering if Paul went to Jerusalem. But Paul was sensitive to the Spirit (16:6–10) and he was willing to suffer (20:24). He knew what was involved in his commission (9:16). So the believers escorted Paul to the beach, knelt, and prayed, committing him to the Lord.

Sailing south, Paul arrived at Caesarea, coming to the home of Philip the evangelist. Here they encountered a prophet named Agabus. Using a belt as an object lesson, Agabus took the belt, bound his own hands and feet, and prophesied, "In this way the Jews at Jerusalem will bind the man who owns this belt and deliver him into the hands of the Gentiles" (21:11).

Was Paul disobedient in going to Jerusalem? No. Was Agabus telling Paul not to go to Jerusalem? No. Agabus prophesied what would happen to Paul; he was not prohibiting Paul from going to Jerusalem. Paul was fully aware that he was going to suffer for the cause of Christ. When the people begged Paul not to go, he was moved, telling them they were breaking his heart. He was not afraid of laying down his life for the Lord. He was prepared to be imprisoned in Jerusalem and even to die for the name of the Lord Jesus. When they heard his heart, they committed him to the Lord and Paul left for Jerusalem—and the suffering that awaited him.

CONSIDER: *Suffering for the cause of Christ does not necessarily mean we are not doing the will of God—it may be precisely the will of God.*

GRACE PLUS LAW?

ACTS 21:17–36

"They have been told about you, that you are teaching all the Jews who are among the Gentiles to forsake Moses, telling them not to circumcise their children nor to walk according to the customs." (Acts 21:21)

The issue of law and grace was a problem in the first century and it remains a problem in the twenty-first century. Some groups teach it is imperative for salvation to keep the Sabbath. Is the law—all or part—incumbent on New Testament believers?

It was an issue when Paul came to Jerusalem. The third missionary journey had now come to an end. With Acts 21:17 the first stage of the ultimate movement to Rome had begun. Paul would be arrested and spirited out of Jerusalem and brought to Rome. But it was important for Paul to go to Jerusalem: (1) He would bear witness at the Feast of Pentecost; (2) he was bringing the money for the poor believers (Rom. 15:25–27); (3) he would tell them of his missionary travels and the conversion of the Gentiles (Acts 21:19, 28); (4) he would visit the church for mutual blessing (Acts 21:17).

In Jerusalem Paul was met by James and the elders. When they heard of Paul's success among the Gentiles, they praised God. But they also expressed concern. Among the thousands of Jewish Christians in Jerusalem, it was reported that Paul was discouraging Jewish and Gentile converts from adhering to the Law of Moses. This was upsetting the Jewish believers—and it raised a problem.

To avert the problem the elders suggested Paul show his support for the Law by joining four men who were going to the temple for purification in relation to a temporary Nazirite vow (as described in Numbers 6:1–21). Was Paul mixing law and grace? No. Paul lived as a Jew that he might win the Jews (1 Cor. 9:20–23). This reflects the transitional nature of Acts. While the transition from law to grace was immediate, experientially it took a generation, certainly until the temple was destroyed in A.D. 70. "As long as [Paul's purification] was voluntary and not imposed upon gentiles, Paul nowhere teaches that such activity was wrong for Jews" (Homer Kent Jr., *From Jerusalem to Rome*).

The Jews from Ephesus came to Jerusalem, aroused the people against Paul, and created a violent mob. The Jews quickly attacked Paul, dragging him out of the temple with the intention of killing him. Roman soldiers finally rescued Paul, binding him with chains (fulfilling Agabus's prophecy in Acts 21:11). The hostile legalists attempted to stifle Paul's message of grace.

CONSIDER: *The purity of the gospel is critical; there is no mixing of law and grace. Salvation is by grace through faith alone, without the works of the law.*

June 17

CONFRONTING A MOB

ACTS 21:37–22:29

---

*"And He said to me, 'Go! For I will send you
far away to the Gentiles.'" (Acts 22:21)*

When I was preaching in a church in Kiev, Ukraine, through an interpreter, I explained the "cessationist position"—that the gift of speaking in tongues was restricted to the first century. Immediately, I heard "Nyet! Nyet!" all over the auditorium. The female leader in the church told me to stop. It was over. They threw me out of the church. But a large group followed me outside and I continued to talk to them outside.

A single statement can change the direction of a speech, and so it was with Paul. After the Jewish crowd attacked Paul, the Roman commander rescued him but he didn't understand the situation. He thought Paul was an Egyptian Messiah-pretender who had led an unsuccessful revolt against the Romans. When Paul spoke Greek, the commander was astonished and realized he was wrong in his assessment of Paul. Paul then asked permission to address the people. Having received it, Paul spoke in the "Hebrew dialect," likely Aramaic, which gave him a responsive audience. Paul proceeded to defend his credentials as a Jew—brought up in Jerusalem, trained by the respected and renowned Gamaliel of the school of Hillel. In his zeal, Paul had persecuted Christians. Even Jewish leaders, members of the Sanhedrin, could attest to Paul's zeal for Judaism.

But then something happened. On the way to Damascus to imprison Christians, a bright light from heaven flashed around Paul. Then a voice: "I am Jesus the Nazarene, whom you are persecuting" (Acts 22:8). Paul was bewildered. What should he do? Jesus instructed him to go to Damascus where he would meet Ananias, a devout Jew who kept the Law. It was from "the Righteous One" that Paul would receive his mandate and commission. He was to be a witness "to all men" (v. 15). Then Paul was baptized. Falling into a trance, the Lord told him to leave Jerusalem quickly because his message would not be accepted. With that the Lord commissioned Paul, "Go! For I will send you far away to the Gentiles!" When Paul mentioned the word "Gentiles," his speech was over. While there were Gentile converts to Judaism, they kept the Law. But Paul was bringing Gentiles to Christ without imposing the legalism of the Law on them.

Once more, the Roman commander had to rescue Paul. When he found out Paul was a Roman citizen he released him. But a hostile reaction had been created; many Jews opposed Paul's bringing the gospel of grace to the Gentiles.

CONSIDER: *A single word we speak about Christ may upset people and create a hostile reaction—but it is not about us—it is their response to Christ.*

June 18

A BELIEVER'S DEFENSE AGAINST OPPOSITION

ACTS 22:30–23:11

*"I am a Pharisee, a son of Pharisees; I am on trial for
the hope and resurrection of the dead!" (Acts 23:6)*

The Roman commander was still puzzled over the conflict between Paul and the Jews and was determined to resolve the problem. He called a meeting with the Sanhedrin ("Council") and Paul. The Sanhedrin was Israel's "Supreme Court"—seventy members with a high priest—the ruling body of elders, scribes, Pharisees, and Sadducees, with the Sadducees making up the majority.

Addressing the Sanhedrin, Paul reminded them that he had lived his life with a good conscience. Paul's statement "is a pointed disclaimer against the charge that he is a renegade Jew, an opposer of the law, the people, the temple" (A. T. Robertson, *Word Pictures of the New Testament*). Ananias, the high priest, ordered Paul struck across the mouth. Ananias had disgraced and profaned the high priest's office. He took tithes for himself, becoming very wealthy, and he resorted to violence and assassination when he was opposed (F. F. Bruce, *Book of Acts*).

Paul responded vigorously, "God is going to strike you, you whitewashed wall!" (v. 3). He was reminding Ananias that his action against Paul was unjustified because Paul had not yet made his case and Ananias was already judging him. Jesus Himself called the scribes and Pharisees "whitewashed tombs" (Matt. 23:27). When bystanders pointed out to Paul that he was addressing the high priest, Paul apologized.

When Paul realized that with Ananias, the corrupt high priest, there would be no possibility for a fair trial, Paul brought division to the Council by his remark, "I am a Pharisee, a son of Pharisees; I am on trial for the hope and resurrection of the dead!" The high priest and the majority on the Council were Sadducees who rejected the doctrine of the resurrection. This was a major issue. Immediately there was a division.

Was Paul correct in his approach? The Council needed to be in agreement in determining Paul's guilt. Paul realized that in asserting his belief in the resurrection there would be no unity among the Council members. Paul's life and ministry were at stake. Should they find him guilty, his life and ministry could be terminated.

The text affirms that Paul did the right thing at this critical time in his life. The Lord came to Paul at night, encouraging him with assurance that he would come safely to Rome and testify for His Lord in the imperial city.

CONSIDER: *Believers need to live with wisdom in this world so that the ministry will not be curtailed.*

June 19

GOD'S SOVEREIGNTY IN BELIEVERS

ACTS 23:12–35

*But the son of Paul's sister heard of their ambush, and he
came and entered the barracks and told Paul. (Acts 23:16)*

June 6, 1944, was a historic, memorable day. The allies under General Dwight
Eisenhower were launching an assault on Nazi Germany which occupied
western Europe. The Germans had broken the code and knew the invasion was
coming. But Erwin Rommel, leader of the German forces, was going home to
celebrate his wife's birthday. As a result, the message didn't get passed along
and the allies were victorious. What was the key? The sovereignty of God in
having Rommel go home for his wife's birthday.

We see the sovereignty of God operative in protecting his servant Paul.
Forty Jews had put themselves under an oath (*anathematisan*) meaning "to
place oneself under a curse, to invoke divine harm if what is said is not true
or if one does not carry out what has been promised" (Cleon Rogers Jr. and
Cleon Rogers III, *The New Linguistic and Exegetical Key to the Greek New Testament*). They would neither eat nor drink until they had killed Paul. The plot
was hatched with the help of the chief priests and elders. They would employ
deception, pretending to hold an investigation of Paul—then they would kill
him. How phenomenal! The religious leaders helped plot the murder of a man!

But . . . Paul's nephew heard about the plot. What was Paul's nephew doing
there? How did he come to hear about the plot? We don't know. Perhaps he
was studying in Jerusalem as Paul had done earlier. In any case, he was courageous in seeking out Paul to tell him what he had heard and then informing
the commander.

The commander determined to save Paul and planned to send him to
Caesarea, some 60 miles distant, with 200 soldiers, 200 spearmen, and 70
horsemen. Unquestionably, it reflects the serious situation. He was determined Paul would be protected. Perhaps Paul's Roman citizenship was also a
factor. Meanwhile, the commander wrote a letter to Felix the governor, slanting the letter to make himself look good. He failed to mention that he had
chained Paul or that he wanted to examine Paul by scourging. But the letter
also exonerated Paul, stating that there was no legitimate charge deserving
of death or imprisonment.

So the soldiers brought Paul safely to Caesarea. Paul did not fall prey to
the evil scheming of his opponents. He would live to testify to the gospel of
Christ in Rome. God is sovereign.

CONSIDER: *The sovereignty of God in our lives is a profound truth; God sovereignly cares for His people.*

June 20

RESPONDING TO FALSE CHARGES
ACTS 24:1–27

*"For the resurrection of the dead I am on
trial before you today." (Acts 24:21)*

It is not uncommon to read newspaper articles or hear news commentators report on an evangelical only to find the facts have been twisted. There is a decided bias against evangelicals in the media. But this is not something begun in the twenty-first century; it was there in the first century.

While Paul was detained in Caesarea, Ananias and the elders came from Jerusalem and brought charges against Paul. Tertullus, a Hellenistic Jew who understood Roman law, served as their attorney and brought the formal charges before Felix. Tertullus leveled three charges against Paul (Homer Kent Jr., *From Jerusalem to Rome*). (1) He charged Paul with treason (v. 5). Calling Paul a pest, he accused Paul of spreading the "plague" through his preaching, stirring up strife. (2) He accused Paul of heresy as a ringleader of the Nazarenes (v. 5). (3) He accused Paul of temple desecration (v. 6), likely a reference to the false suggestion that Paul tried to take Trophimus into the temple (21:29). The Jews noisily added to Tertullus's charges.

When Paul was asked to respond to the charges, he avoided the false flattery that Tertullus employed. Paul denied the validity of the charge of treason (24:11–13). He could not have stirred up an insurrection; he had only been in Jerusalem twelve days. Prior to that, he had been absent from Jerusalem for several years. Further, he did nothing in the temple, nor in the synagogue, nor in the city to create dissension. Paul admitted to the second charge (vv. 14–16), but what they called a sect was actually the accurate Way according to the Law and the Prophets. He reminded them that the Old Testament taught the resurrection (as seen in Isaiah 26:19 and Daniel 12:2)—and that was the message Paul taught. Paul denied the third charge (Acts 24:17–18). Paul had come to the temple to worship, bringing alms and presenting offerings.

Then Paul countercharged (vv. 18–21). First, the Jews who had made the original charge were from Ephesus but they were not there to make the accusation. Second, the Sanhedrin should bring a legitimate charge. The only statement he could be guilty of was his belief in the resurrection.

Felix delayed his decision but kept Paul in custody. When Felix again heard Paul and Paul spoke of righteousness and judgment, Felix became agitated and dismissed Paul. Yet he kept Paul in custody for two years, hoping to get money from Paul.

CONSIDER: *The world stands opposed to God's people. How do we respond to false charges that are made against us?*

Before the VIPs

Acts 25:1–27

"If, then, I am a wrongdoer and have committed anything worthy of death, I do not refuse to die; but if none of those things is true of which these men accuse me, no one can hand me over to them. I appeal to Caesar." (Acts 25:11)

Festus succeeded Felix as the Roman governor of Judea and began his tenure by going to Jerusalem to acquaint himself with the Jews. While he was there, the Jewish leaders brought charges against Paul and urged Festus to have Paul stand trial in Jerusalem. Their motive, however, was to kill Paul. Instead, Festus demanded they come to Caesarea to bring their charges against Paul. So Paul's case was reopened. Paul should have been released by Felix but was not because Felix was corrupt. Festus, too, allowed the Jews to manipulate him, perhaps fearing they would report him to the emperor.

Luke emphasizes the apologetic nature of his writing, showing that while the Jews brought serious charges against Paul, they couldn't be proven. Paul again defended himself against the original charges (Acts 24:5–6). The ineptitude of Festus is evident as he, like Felix, made a decision based on his fear of the Jews (25:9; 24:27).

Paul indicated that he was willing to die if he was judged guilty of the charges, but argued that if the charges were untrue, then he should not be handed over to the Jews. Hence, Paul appealed to Caesar. This was the right and privilege of a Roman citizen if his case was not being properly processed. Ironically, Nero was the Roman emperor at this time, yet, under the tutelage of Seneca, the philosopher, these years were called the "golden years."

With Paul's appeal to Caesar, the responsibility was removed from Festus. Several days later, King Agrippa II and Bernice (who was his sister, living in an incestuous relationship with him) arrived in Caesarea to pay his respects to Festus, since he wanted to express his loyalty to Rome. Festus explained the situation to King Agrippa and that Paul had appealed to Caesar. Since Agrippa understood the Jewish issues, perhaps he could be of help to Festus who was at a loss in dealing with Jewish matters. Agrippa expressed interest in hearing Paul so they arranged for a meeting. The following day the dignitaries arrived amid great pageantry. The word *pomp (phantasia)* pictures a showy parade with all the colorful uniforms of the leading people. This would be God's way of spreading the gospel to this august group of VIPs.

CONSIDER: *God may lead us into unusual circumstances that we may not understand, yet God uses them to disseminate His Word.*

June 22

DEFENDING THE RESURRECTION
ACTS 26:1–23

*"The Christ was to suffer, and . . . by reason of His resurrection
from the dead He would be the first to proclaim light both to
the Jewish people and to the Gentiles." (Acts 26:23)*

Since Paul had appealed to Caesar, this was an informal questioning, not a trial. Yet God used this to fulfill the promise of Acts 9:15—Paul would bear witness before kings—and this was indeed an august group. Saluting the king, Paul began his speech, declaring that he was fortunate to make his presentation before King Agrippa, who was familiar with Jewish customs. But there was another reason. Paul had opportunity to present the gospel to this group of nobility.

Paul reminded them of his heritage as a Pharisee. Raised in Jerusalem, he exhibited faithfulness to Judaism and the external demands of the Law. Paul lived as a Pharisee with its strict legislation. Paul was blameless as a Pharisee (see also Phil. 3:5–6). But now Paul was on trial for the hope of every true Israelite, those of the twelve tribes of Israel —particularly the Pharisees—the hope of the resurrection (Acts 26:8). Paul was emphatic: he was being accused by the Jews for holding a fundamental doctrine of the Jews!

Paul showed his patriotism to Judaism through his fierce persecution of the Christians. He locked them up in prison and cast his vote for their death; he punished them in the synagogues, pursued them to foreign cities, and even tried to force them to blaspheme. He had been loyal to Judaism. But then something happened. En route to Damascus he was struck down by the brilliant light. Then a voice challenged him, "It is hard for you to kick against the goads" (v. 14). A goad was a sharp pointed stick used to drive cattle. A stubborn animal would kick at the pointed stick and receive a severe wound. Paul was kicking against the divine will. Jesus, who identified Himself, commissioned Paul to minister to the Gentiles as a witness who had now seen the Lord.

Paul had made his point. He had received a heavenly vision and he had obeyed. This explained why Paul had changed—the risen Lord had commissioned him to preach to the Gentiles. Having received this command from the Lord, Paul had not been disobedient; he immediately began to proclaim to both Jews and Gentiles that they should repent and turn to God. Yet, for this very reason, the Jews attacked him and sought his death. However, Paul was teaching nothing that was not in accord with the Old Testament. And what was that message? The Old Testament in the Law and the Prophets prophesied the death and resurrection of Christ, and that message of the resurrection should be proclaimed to the Gentiles.

CONSIDER: *The climactic summation of the Old Testament points to the atoning death and bodily resurrection of Jesus Christ—a message for Jews and Gentiles alike.*

ALMOST PERSUADED

ACTS 26:24–32

"In a short time you will persuade me to
become a Christian." (Acts 26:28)

Mark was a young architect, entirely self-assured and with strong opinions. I had the opportunity to share the gospel of Christ with him but when I concluded, he only grinned and ridiculed the faith. He thought it was foolish and beneath him. Laughing, he left me and didn't give it a moment's serious thought.

Festus, the Roman governor of Judea, recognized Paul's great knowledge but thought that all his learning had driven him mad. Festus loudly interrupted Paul's defense, telling Paul he was out of his mind. Paul had talked about visions and the resurrection; he had exhibited enthusiasm for repentance. And so Festus ridiculed Paul, accusing him of spending too much time studying the Law.

But Festus was wrong. Paul reminded Festus that he was of sound mind; he was speaking "words of sober truth" (v. 25). "Paul says he is speaking words which are understandable and capable of being proven, which do not have to do with ecstasy" (Cleon Rogers Jr. and Cleon Rogers III, *The New Linguistic and Exegetical Key to the Greek New Testament*). Paul's statement was significant, reminding Festus that the gospel of Christ is based on fact. The New Testament records the life, death, and resurrection of Christ. The numerous witnesses to the resurrection of Christ validate its historicity. The resurrection of Christ is a *historical fact.*

To alert Festus to the truthfulness of Christianity, Paul zeroed in on Agrippa, reminding him that he knew about these things; they had not escaped his notice. Paul was referring to the events of the life of Christ and the birth and growth of the church. Agrippa knew about these things. Paul challenged Agrippa concerning the Prophets—Agrippa surely believed the Prophets!

This was probably an embarrassing moment for Agrippa and he responded sarcastically: "In a short time you will persuade me to become a Christian" (v. 28). Perhaps Agrippa was more concerned with his social status and perception by the socialites than giving serious consideration to the claims of the gospel.

CONSIDER: *Response to the gospel of Christ may mean ridicule by the world—am I willing to accept identification with Christ at the expense of the world?*

SOVEREIGN SEA VOYAGE

ACTS 27:1–44

*"Do not be afraid, Paul; you must stand before Caesar; and behold,
God has granted you all those who are sailing with you." (Acts 27:24)*

No Jew would have written Acts 27. The Jews had an unusual fear of the
sea, partially because of "leviathan" and other sea monsters living in their
mythology. But Luke was a Gentile and his love of the sea is apparent from his
extensive description of their journey to Rome. But was Luke only describing
a trip to Rome? No. This unusual voyage was sovereignly directed by God. God
wanted Paul to bear witness in Rome, and to Rome Paul would go.

Since Paul had made an appeal to the emperor, the apostle was now being
sent to Rome under escort, along with other prisoners. They embarked on
an Adramyttian ship, calling on various ports in the province of Asia. Luke
and Aristarchus traveled as Paul's slaves, granting Paul considerable importance in the eyes of the centurion (W. M. Ramsey, *St. Paul the Traveler and the
Roman Citizen*). This would explain the kind treatment Paul received from the
centurion (v. 3).

The ship sailed along the east side of Cyprus to avoid the danger of being
driven ashore by the westerly winds. At Myra they changed ships, Julius having found an Egyptian grain ship from Alexandria bound for Rome. The north-
westerly wind was still blowing, making travel difficult. The ship finally arrived
at Cnidus and then Fair Havens.

But this was the dangerous season for sailing when travel on the open
sea terminated until the end of winter. Paul warned them to remain in Fair
Havens but the council overruled and the voyage continued. Suddenly, an
Euraquilo ("a northeaster"), a violent wind, began to drive the ship along. They
let down the sea anchor, which served as a brake, slowing the drift of the ship.
They finally had to jettison the cargo to spare the ship. Hope for survival was
diminishing.

"I told you so!" Paul began his chastisement. But he went on to encourage
them. An angel had appeared to Paul, telling him there would be no loss of
life. What was the reason? Paul. God had appointed Paul to bear witness in the
imperial city of Rome. Ultimately, they ran the ship aground on the beach and
all 276 people reached the shore safely. Many lives were saved because God
had appointed one man—Paul—to bear witness in Rome.

CONSIDER: *God will sovereignly direct the life of His servant, even through difficult circumstances, to the place of his divine appointment.*

June 25

THE APPOINTED PLACE

ACTS 28:1–15

There we found some brethren, and were invited to stay with them for seven days; and thus we came to Rome. (Acts 28:14)

God leads His people in unusual ways and unusual circumstances. Along the journey we may wonder why certain things happen to us; we may question the path. Why the death of a spouse? Why the loneliness? Yet God sovereignly directs and controls our lives, bringing us to our appointed place.

Following the shipwreck, the crew finally arrived at Malta or "Melita," meaning refuge, which is what the port became for them. The Greek word translated "natives" in Acts 28:2, 4 is the same word translated "barbarians" in Romans 1:14. The natives were termed "barbarians" by Greeks because they did not speak Greek.

Paul continued to demonstrate his leadership. They gathered firewood, laying it on the fire, when suddenly a snake from amid the wood bit Paul and clung to him with its fangs in his hand. The natives quickly concluded that Paul was a murderer and that justice would judge Paul. These Maltese knew the effect of a snake bite and expected Paul to die momentarily. Luke reveals his medical knowledge as he records the common result that occurred from a snake bite. These people expected Paul's hand to swell with inflammation or for him to suddenly drop dead. When nothing happened, they changed their minds about Paul and began to say he was a god. This is the opposite of what happened to Paul at Lystra (Acts 14:11, 19).

Publius, the leading man of the estate, extended his kindness to the 276 voyagers. It became known to Paul that Publius's father was afflicted with fever and dysentery. (Luke, the physician in the party, would have been able to provide an accurate medical diagnosis.) When Paul saw Publius's father, he prayed, laid his hands on him, and healed him. When the word spread about the man being healed, other people came for healing and they were "getting cured" (the imperfect tense in Greek indicates the healing was constant and ongoing).

While Luke does not mention that Paul preached, it is inconceivable that Paul would *not* have preached the gospel. The gift of healing validated the messenger and his message. Paul would have used the healing to proclaim the gospel.

Having wintered in Malta for three months, Paul and his party resumed their voyage to Rome, arriving at Rhegium and then Puteoli. Finally, Paul entered Rome. What had Christ promised the disciples just before He ascended to heaven? They would bear witness to the remotest part of the earth (Acts 1:8). Rome was the climactic location to bear witness. God brought Paul to the appointed place. Rome! And Paul thanked God.

CONSIDER: *God is sovereign and calls us to trust Him when we encounter unusual events.*

RESPONSE IN ROME

ACTS 28:16–31

*Paul . . . was explaining to them by solemnly testifying about the
kingdom of God and trying to persuade them concerning Jesus. . . .
Some were being persuaded by the things spoken, but others
would not believe. (Acts 28:23–24)*

Although Paul was brought to Rome as a prisoner, he was allowed considerable freedom. "Paul was treated in Rome with the utmost leniency. He was allowed to hire a house or a lodging in the city, and live there at his own convenience under the surveillance of a soldier who was responsible for his presence when required. A light chain fastened Paul's wrist to that of the soldier. No hindrance was offered to his inviting friends into his house, or to his preaching to all who came in to him; but he was not allowed to go out freely" (W. M. Ramsey, *St. Paul the Traveller and the Roman Citizen*).

Since Paul was confined to his house, he invited the Jewish leaders to come to him, enabling him to explain his dilemma to them. He told them of his innocence concerning the crimes with which the Jews had charged him. The Romans had found him innocent (28:18; see also 23:29; 26:32), yet because of the pressure of the Jews, Paul was forced to appeal to Caesar. The handcuffs he wore were for the sake of the hope of Israel—the Messianic hope.

The Jews expressed ignorance of Paul's case. They had received no letters concerning Paul, nor had any Jews come to Rome to accuse Paul. Perhaps the Jews actually knew something but were afraid to admit it for fear of reprisal from the Romans. The Christians had been expelled from Rome in A.D. 49 and had only recently been permitted to return. That fear may also have dictated their rejection of Christ.

On an appointed day they came together and Paul spoke of the kingdom of God, seeking to persuade them about Jesus, showing how He fulfilled the Old Testament prophecies.

The result was similar to Paul's experiences elsewhere: some were persuaded and believed; others refused to believe. Like Jesus did (Matt. 13:14–15), Paul quotes Isaiah 6:9–10, reminding the unbelievers that they were responding just like their forefathers 700 years earlier. And now the gospel would be extended to the Gentiles—and they would respond. Unabashed, Paul continued his ministry, proclaiming the gospel unhindered for two years at which time he was released.

CONSIDER: *God calls us to faithfulness in our service for Him, amid adversity and despite ridicule and rejection.*

June 27

THE THEME OF ROMANS

ROMANS 1:1–17

For I am not ashamed of the gospel, for it is the
power of God for salvation to everyone who believes,
to the Jew first and also to the Greek. (Romans 1:16)

The city of Rome was the foremost metropolis of Paul's day. Founded in 753 B.C., the population was one to two million, although an inscription dating A.D. 14 infers a population of over four million. The majority of people were slaves and most others were poor; the people's main interests were food, gladiator fights, and the circus games. Morally and spiritually Rome was bankrupt, with the games contributing to the corruption and devaluation of human life. Religiously, Romans worshiped the Egyptian gods Isis and Serapis as well as the goddess Astarte with over 420 pagan temples.

The church at Rome was probably founded by Roman Jews who were converted through Peter's preaching when they visited Jerusalem on Pentecost (Acts 2:10). Paul wrote to the Christians in Rome, especially because it would be strategic for Paul to come to Rome. If the gospel penetrated Rome, it could spread throughout the Roman Empire.

Romans is a logically arranged book developing the theme of 1:17, "the righteousness of God is revealed. . . ." Paul relates the righteousness of Christ to the problem of *sin* (1:18–3:20), then resolves the problem with *salvation* (3:21–5:21), and the believer's progress in *sanctification* (6:1–8:39). He explains how Israel fits into the picture with God's *sovereignty* (9:1–11:36), and closes with how a believer will ultimately *serve* God (12:1–15:13).

Paul begins his letter by explaining the uniqueness of Jesus Christ: He is both man ("born of a descendant of David according to the flesh," 1:3) and God ("declared the Son of God with power," v. 4). Paul's purpose in writing is to see Gentiles come to faith in Jesus Christ (v. 5). And while they exercise faith, on the divine side they are the "called of Jesus Christ" and "beloved of God" (vv. 6–7). What an encouraging introduction!

Despite Paul's absence, the Roman believers had been vigorous in spreading the good news of Jesus Christ. But now Paul longs to come to them that he might share his gift of teaching with them, that they may be mutually encouraged. He is eager to proclaim the saving gospel of Jesus Christ to those in Rome and see it spread through the Roman Empire. Paul's desire must ultimately be our desire.

CONSIDER: *Living in the postmodern world with moral relativism, we must never be afraid nor ashamed of the gospel of Christ. It is still the power of God for salvation.*

THE HUMAN DILEMMA

ROMANS 1:18–32

For the wrath of God is revealed from heaven against
all ungodliness and unrighteousness of men who
suppress the truth in unrighteousness. (Romans 1:18)

Our Western culture is changing—dramatically. Nations like Belgium, the Netherlands, Canada, and others have changed their laws, validating homosexual marriages. Other nations are following suit. Public schools in America are teaching young children that some homes have two daddies and some have two mommies. Jocelyn Elders, Surgeon General under Bill Clinton, endorsed homosexuality as a valid lifestyle and even encouraged adoptions by homosexuals (*Washington Times*, Mar. 19, 1994). The traditional, biblical view of marriage (among other issues) is being rejected.

The Bible is not silent concerning these topics. The book of Romans speaks to the human dilemma of sin (1:18–3:20). The universal dilemma is that all humanity—*everyone*—Jew, Gentile, the entire world—stands guilty and condemned before God.

Romans begins with the guilt of the Gentiles. God is a holy God and reveals His wrath against humanity; although people know they stand guilty before God, they nonetheless are indifferent about their sin. God has revealed His attributes and His judgments in nature; this is His general revelation. Every hurricane, every tornado, every flood, every tsunami is a reminder that God is a God of judgment and there is a day of judgment coming.

Humanity has deliberately turned away from God, refusing to honor Him; instead, mankind has indulged in futility and vanity—worthless things, such as teaching evolution in public schools and militantly crusading for homosexuality in the public arena. Why? Because "their foolish heart was darkened" (v. 21). They abandoned the normal life that God has ordained for mankind: one man and one woman in marriage.

As a result, "God gave them over" (vv. 24, 26, 28) to their depravity. God was not only withdrawing His grace but also was putting them under His judicial judgment. Why? People distorted God's normal creative functioning in marriage; men committed immoral acts with men, and women committed sinful acts with women. Yet, while recognizing God and being fully aware that they stand under His judgment for death on these issues, they not only practiced these things, but encouraged others in the same sinful pursuit.

CONSIDER: *All humanity stands guilty, under the judgment of the Holy God. Only His grace through Jesus Christ will resolve the dilemma.*

GUILT OF THE JEWS

ROMANS 2:1–16

*For all who have sinned without the Law will also
perish without the Law, and all who have sinned under
the Law will be judged by the Law. (Romans 2:12)*

As my wife and I were visiting an antique shop, I engaged the young owner in a conversation and began sharing the gospel with him. When I broached the subject of sin, he exclaimed, "Oh, I have never sinned." He was adamant. As a result, the conversation shifted and then he casually mentioned that his girlfriend was living with him although they were not married.

Our modern culture has a low view of sin, yet the book of Romans speaks directly to that faulty mind-set. Paul established the guilt of the Gentiles in Romans 1:18–32; now he proceeds to affirm the guilt of the Jews. While embracing the Mosaic Law and sitting in judgment of the Gentiles, Paul concludes that the Jews stand similarly guilty—they were guilty of the very same things they accused the Gentiles of doing. For this, they would not escape the judgment of God; yet, it was their stubbornness and their unrepentant heart that would ultimately bring down the judgment of God upon them. They believed that their forefather Abraham sat at the gate of Sheol and would not allow a son of Abraham to pass into hell. But they were wrong.

A day of wrath is coming, Paul reminded them, pointing to the future tribulation period when the righteous judgment of God would be revealed—and enacted. Their deeds would ultimately reflect whether they were a believer or an unbeliever. While works play no part in salvation, works are the evidence of a believer (see James 2:18). Those who would reflect the genuineness of their faith would reveal it in doing good; these believers "seek for glory and honor and immorality" and they would ultimately receive "eternal life" (Rom. 2:7).

There will indeed be "payday someday" for those "who are selfishly ambitious and do not obey the truth"—they will receive "wrath and indignation" (v. 8). Sobering thoughts. God is impartial. He will judge Jew and Gentile alike. The Jews have received enlightenment through the Mosaic Law; the Gentiles, who have not received the Law, will nonetheless have the law of God written on their conscience. Both groups will be judged accordingly. The inference is that neither group will meet God's standard. The avenue of faith is the only possibility of receiving the grace of God. But the message is also clear: greater revelation (through the Scriptures) demands greater responsibility.

CONSIDER: *Do you recognize the privileged revelation you have received through the Scriptures? Have you responded accordingly, with your heart focused on the things of God rather than on the world?*

June 30

FAILURE OF THE JEWS

ROMANS 2:17–29

*For indeed circumcision is of value if you practice
the Law; but if you are a transgressor of the Law, your
circumcision has become uncircumcision. (Romans 2:25)*

Of all the ethnic groups and people on this earth, the Jewish people are the most unique—they are the special people of God, chosen by Him. Despite hostility against them over the centuries and millennia, God has preserved them.

Paul lists nine things about the Jewish people in which they prided themselves: (1) The name "Jew." They prided themselves: "We are Jews by nature, and not sinners from among the Gentiles" (Gal. 2:15). (2) They "rely upon the Law." This was a false assurance that God would bless them because they were the recipients of the Law—regardless whether they kept the Law. (3) They "boast in God." They had reason to boast in God but they abused it by not keeping the Law and instead continuing in sin. (4) They "know His will." They knew His will because it was revealed in Scripture. (5) They "approve the things that are essential." They prided themselves on debating details of the Law. The Talmud provided many intricate interpretations. (6) They were "instructed out of the Law." The priests publicly instructed the people. (7) They were a "guide to the blind, a light to those who are in darkness." God's original intention was that salvation should come through the Jewish nation. They were a light to the Gentiles, to bring them salvation. (8) They were "a corrector of the foolish, a teacher of the immature." They were to train the immature and bring them to maturity in morals and faith. (9) They had "in the Law the embodiment of knowledge and of the truth." They had the truth in the written Scriptures.

Paul challenged them. Having all these privileges—did they adhere to them? Did they commit adultery? Did they break the Law? In boasting that they had the Law, did they violate the Law and dishonor God? Serious questions. Valid questions. Paul reminded them that the real Jew, the "fulfilled Jew" was one who obeyed the Law—he obeyed the revelation of God. Ethnically a Jew is always a Jew but the true Jew is one who honors God by walking in faith (Gal. 6:16).

CONSIDER: *We Gentiles can also, like the Jews of old, pride ourselves in having the Scriptures, and yet fail to act on them.*

July 1

UNIVERSAL GUILT

ROMANS 3:1–20

---

*"THERE IS NONE RIGHTEOUS, NOT EVEN ONE; THERE IS NONE
WHO UNDERSTANDS, THERE IS NONE WHO SEEKS FOR GOD; . . . THERE
IS NONE WHO DOES GOOD, THERE IS NOT EVEN ONE." (Romans 3:10–12)*

It is common to see a sticker on the window of a pickup truck reading "No Fear." It portrays much of the contemporary mind-set. Modern man, with a haughty spirit, stands opposed to God. Hollywood movies and contemporary books like *Religulous* ridicule God, Jesus Christ, and believers in God. There is no fear of God. Yet, before God, all humanity stands guilty.

But do the Jews have a privileged position? Absolutely. It was through the Hebrew people that the word of God came to humanity. If the Jew sins like the Gentile, and if his circumcision doesn't help him when he sins, does that negate his covenant relationship with God? No. In fact, Paul makes the strongest negative assertion (*me genoito*) "May it never be!" (Rom. 3:4; Paul uses this emphatic phrase ten times in Romans). May "every man be found a liar" if they suggest that God does not fulfill His promises—in this case, to His covenant people Israel.

What conclusion then should we draw? "What then? Are we [Jews] better than they [Gentiles]?" (v. 9). Paul answers the question in the same verse: "Not at all." And he draws a conclusion: all are under sin—Jews and Gentiles alike. All are under the penalty and guilt of sin; all are under the power of sin. All stand guilty and condemned before God. There are no exceptions. All humanity lies under a burden of guilt.

Paul details the universality of guilt: "none righteous . . . none who understands . . . none who seeks for God . . . none who does good." As an act of the will, all have inclined away from God. Their spoken words "are like the odor of a tomb" (William Shedd, *Commentary on Romans*). They speak lying, deceiving words as though the poison of a cobra is under their lips. Ultimately, they have no fear of God.

What is the conclusion? All humanity—without exception—stands guilty before God. Jew and Gentile alike. Paul concludes, "whatever the Law says, it speaks to those who are under the Law, so that every mouth may be closed and *all the world* may become accountable to God" (v. 19, emphasis added). Since Paul emphasizes "all the world," it indicates "Law" is used in a broader sense: "It is that which binds the reason, the conscience, the heart, and the life, whether it be revealed in the constitution of our nature, or in the decalogue, or in the law of Moses, or in the Scriptures" (Charles Hodge, *Commentary on the Epistle to the Romans*).

CONSIDER: *All humanity—Jews and Gentiles alike—stand guilty before a holy God.*

DECLARED RIGHTEOUS BY FAITH

ROMANS 3:21–31

---

*. . . being justified as a gift by His grace through the
redemption which is in Christ Jesus; whom God displayed publicly
as a propitiation in His blood through faith. (Romans 3:24–25)*

My father was a jeweler. When someone's watch was broken, they would bring it to my father to repair. After he repaired the broken watch, the customer would come back, pay the price for the repair, and receive the watch that was now repaired and running. The customer had redeemed the watch. He paid the price to repair the broken watch.

In the preceding verses, Paul painted a dilemma for all humanity: guilt. What was the resolution? The resolution would clearly be apart from the Law. The Law could not justify anyone. But Paul reminds the reader that this sublime truth—"the righteousness of God through faith in Jesus Christ for all those who believe" (Rom. 3:22)—is not new. It was reported in the Law (Gen. 15:6) and by the prophets (Hab. 2:4).

Since all humanity (Jews and Gentiles) have sinned, salvation is available to all (Jews and Gentiles) who believe. Through faith, believers are justified. This is an important word, emphasizing both a legal acquittal of sin and a declaration of righteousness. The believer is *declared righteous*. What a phenomenal transaction! Moreover, this justification is a *gift*—it cannot be earned. The believer cannot pay for it. It does not come through adherence to the Law. It is *by His grace*. Grace reflects the unmerited, undeserving favor of God to a sinful, repentant humanity.

How does this grace come to us? It comes "through the redemption which is in Christ Jesus." Redemption pictures the release of prisoners and slaves through the payment of money. For us, this pictures the release of sinners from the condemnation and judgment by divine justice. How is this resolved? Through the substitutionary atonement of Jesus Christ. The death of Christ on behalf of guilty sinners satisfied the holiness of God. And this redemption and declaration of righteousness is available to Jews and Gentiles alike. What a phenomenal transaction! What an outpouring of the mercy and grace of God! Have you availed yourself of this expression of grace?

CONSIDER: *Christ died as a substitute for sinners, providing acceptable atonement to God, satisfying His holiness so that we can be declared righteous.*

By Grace in Every Age

Romans 4:1–8

*"Abraham believed God, and it was credited
to him as righteousness." (Romans 4:3)*

When I was a student in seminary, my family and I worked with a very meager budget. One day I received a statement from the bank indicating that $28,000 had been credited to my account. $28,000! We couldn't believe it! That was more money than we could fathom. Unfortunately, when I inquired about it at the bank, they informed me that it was an error.

Spiritually, God has credited to our account an amount that none of us could ever pay. It is beyond us. But is this something new? What about ancient Abraham? What about David? Paul uses two illustrations—Abraham and David—to show that believers were declared righteous on the basis of faith in the Old Testament.

If Abraham (or anyone else) was justified by works, then they had reason to boast—but not before God. However, Genesis 15:3 clearly resolves the issue: "Abraham believed God, and it was credited to him as righteousness." No human being is ever justified by works. Abraham *believed* God. "Believed" stands in the emphatic position in the original text. When Abraham believed God, it was credited to his account. This is a banking term, referring to making an entry in an account book.

What is the result? "The man who trusts in Christ becomes 'the righteousness of God in Him,' 2 Cor. 5:21, becomes in Christ all that God requires a man to be" (W. E. Vine, *Epistle to the Romans*). But how is this righteousness credited to the believer's account? By grace. If God had counted Abraham righteous because Abraham fulfilled the works of the Law, then the righteousness would not have been of grace but of debt.

David himself spoke of the blessing of forgiveness and righteousness apart from works in Psalm 32:1, "Blessed is he whose transgresion is forgiven, whose sin is covered!" (Rom. 4:7). Through faith in Christ, a believer's lawless deeds are "forgiven"—they are let go, released, and dismissed. They are also "covered," meaning there is a removal of guilt and a removal of divine wrath from the sinner. Israel's greatest patriarch and Israel's greatest king both affirm salvation is by grace through faith alone.

CONSIDER: *Both the Old and New Testaments strongly affirm that salvation is by grace through faith in Christ alone—apart from any works.*

EXPLANATION OF JUSTIFICATION

ROMANS 4:9–25

---

*For this reason it is by faith, in order that it may
be in accordance with grace. (Romans 4:16)*

Within the heart of the natural man is the inclination that we must do
something for our salvation. One group says we must keep the Sabbath;
another says it is not only believing in Christ but immersion baptism that
saves us; another says we must keep the seven sacraments . . . the list is endless. But the book of Romans clarifies the issue.

Is circumcision necessary for justification? No. Abraham's faith resulted in
righteousness being credited to his spiritual account (Gen. 15:6). But when did
this happen? It was before he was circumcised. Had it been after he was circumcised, then righteousness would have been restricted to the covenanted
people of Israel. The early church resolved that Gentiles did not have to be
circumcised (recall our earlier discussion of Acts 15).

But what is the relationship of justification to the Law? Must one keep the
Mosaic Law to be saved? No, the Abrahamic covenant was given 430 years
prior to the giving of the Law (see Galatians 3:17). Further, this promised that
Abraham would be "heir of the world" (Rom. 4:13), in other words, it was for all
people, including Gentiles. Since it is by grace through faith (v. 16), it cannot
involve the Law, otherwise faith "is made void" (v. 14), "emptied of all meaning" (A. T. Robertson, *Word Pictures of the New Testament*). The Law brings
wrath, not justification.

Paul concludes justification is by faith "in accordance with grace" (v. 16).
"Accordance with grace" emphasizes that it is not through the merit or works
of man; neither is the faith itself meritorious. It is all of grace—God's undeserving favor to mankind. For that reason, all descendants of Abraham—Jews and
Gentiles alike—may receive the promise of justification by faith.

Humanly speaking, it was impossible for Abraham and Sarah to have a
child; they were both old and impotent. But Abraham exhibited "hope against
hope" (v. 18). He believed God could (and would) do the impossible. Though
Abraham was weak in body, he was not weak in faith. Abraham was "fully
assured" that what God had promised, He would perform. Abraham *believed
God.* God rewarded Abraham's faith so that he became the father of a multitude as God had promised.

But the promise of God does not stop with Abraham. Paul concludes it
was "for our sake also" (v. 24). The promise of justification by grace through
faith is for Jews and Gentiles alike. Justification is credited to the account
of all "who believe in Him who raised Jesus our Lord from the dead" (v. 24).
The resurrection of Christ is the reminder that the Father accepted the Son's
sacrifice for our justification.

CONSIDER: *Justification is by grace through faith, without any works; otherwise,
grace is nullified and meaningless.*

July 5

PEACE WITH GOD

ROMANS 5:1–5

---

*Therefore, having been justified by faith, we have peace
with God through our Lord Jesus Christ. (Romans 5:1)*

On August 15, 1945, Emperor Hirohito of Japan announced the acceptance of the Potsdam Declaration, surrendering to the Allied forces, bringing an official end to World War II. The surrender was signed aboard the battleship USS *Missouri* in Tokyo Bay on September 2, 1945, with President Harry Truman declaring that date to be V-J Day. Nations that had been at war with each other were now at peace.

Paul now develops the implications of justification by faith. Will this justification uphold the believer in the presence of the Lord? Paul draws a strong conclusion of the certainty of our salvation. Because we have been justified by faith, "we have peace with God." The Greek manuscripts give two possible readings: "we have peace" or "let us have peace." There is not a great deal of difference. In either case, we should enjoy the peace that we have with God through Christ. It may read, "let us go on enjoying the peace we now have" (Curtis Vaughan and Bruce Corley, *Romans*). This peace looks at our position before God. "Man's relationship to God has been altered in justification from one who is a rebel against the law of God to one who is fully acquitted, forgiven, and empowered to a new life" (Alan Johnson, *Romans: The Freedom Letter*). God's wrath has been removed. Man has been reconciled to God. God's justice has been met through Jesus Christ.

Moreover, through Christ "we have obtained our introduction by faith into this grace in which we stand" (Rom. 5:2). Paul paints a beautiful picture. We needed an introducer to the Father. Through Christ we have been acquitted, we have received His righteousness, and we have access to the presence of the Father. It is all through Christ. We now "stand in grace." The permanency of our position in grace is pictured.

What is our response? We triumphantly and confidently rejoice in our new position—looking forward in confident hope to the future manifestation of the glory of God. And that hope sustains us in the present so that we can rejoice in our present tribulations, knowing that tribulations develop us spiritually, producing patient endurance amid the storms of life, which in turn develop proven character, the quality of a person tested amid trials. It is all based on hope—confident trust—that will not disappoint because of the love of God which overwhelms our hearts.

CONSIDER: *Through our justification by Christ, we have peace with God, enabling us to endure tribulations in the present.*

July 6

DYING FOR THE UNGODLY

ROMANS 5:6–11

*God demonstrates His own love toward us, in that while
we were yet sinners, Christ died for us. (Romans 5:8)*

Helen and I honeymooned in the Rockies in Banff, Alberta, Canada. Among
the many beautiful sites we enjoyed was the rushing Bow River. Coming
down from the mountain with its clear, cold water, the powerful river was
evident with its forceful current.

The Bow River, with its rushing torrent, is a picture of the overwhelming
love of God displayed to all humanity. Paul explains the enormous love of God
in verses 6–8. It is seen in the death of Christ—the Righteous One dying for the
unrighteous. And that occurred while we were helpless, entirely powerless to
resolve our deepest need. Yet, at the right time, "Christ died for the ungodly"
(Rom. 5:6). The little word "for" (*huper*) is significant; it means "in behalf of;
instead of" (A. T. Robertson, *Word Pictures of the New Testament*). Christ died
as our *substitute*. He did not merely die as an example of bravery or love. He
died in our place.

Christ's love is contrasted with human love. On a human plane, scarcely
anyone would choose to die for a righteous man or a good man. But Christ did
more than that; He died for the ungodly. God gave proof of His love for fallen
humanity by having Christ die for us even though we were sinners (v. 8). This
is an unusual love, a supernatural love. It is "His own love," divine in origin and
entirely unique to God Himself. And it is a conspicuous love because Christ
did not die for righteous or good men. He died for sinners.

What is the result? Much more then—Paul argues from the greater to the
lesser—if God did the greater (Christ died for the ungodly), He will surely do
the lesser (rescue believers from the coming tribulation). Because we are justified by the blood of Christ, "we shall be saved from the wrath of God through
Him" (v. 9). "The wrath" (*tes orges*) identifies this as the coming great tribulation. The coming tribulation will be an outpouring of the wrath of God (see, for
example, Revelation 11:18; 15:1, 7; and 16:1). But believers are spared the wrath
of God; Christ took our punishment upon Himself, enduring the wrath of God.
Now that we are reconciled to God, we will be saved by His life. Since Christ
lives, we can look with joyous expectation to our future completed salvation
at His return and our transformation into His likeness.

CONSIDER: *Christ died as our substitute while we were enemies; now that we
are reconciled, we will be saved from the future tribulation.*

July 7

CONTRASTS

ROMANS 5:12–21

*For if by the transgression of the one the many died, much
more did the grace of God and the gift by the grace of the
one Man, Jesus Christ, abound to the many. (Romans 5:15)*

Throughout history we see contrasts in people, contrasts between good and
evil. Contrast Tetzel and Luther. In the Middle Ages, corruption had spread
in the hierarchy of the Catholic Church. It resulted in Johann Tetzel selling
indulgences which enabled a person to pay ahead of time for a sin he planned
to commit later. Martin Luther opposed this vigorously, finally protesting with
the historic Ninety-five Theses against the abuse of these indulgences.

Paul contrasts and summarizes what Adam brought to the human race—
sin and death—with what Christ brought—grace and life. Through Adam
sin entered into the world which would affect the entire human race. As
descendants of Adam, all humanity participated in Adam's sin and therefore all humanity is guilty. And sin brought death. Death is threefold and
all-encompassing: (1) Spiritual death is the separation of the soul from God.
Chronologically, spiritual death precedes physical death (see Ephesians 2:1).
(2) Physical death is the penalty of sin (Rom. 5:14). (3) Eternal death is the
final separation of the soul from God, though in continued existence in torment (Rev. 20:14).

Emphasizing the term "one," Paul shows that through the sin of one man,
many (all) died and, by contrast, by one Man, the gift of grace was given
to many (those who trust Him). Adam and Christ stand in contrast. One is
unlike the other. Through one came death and through One came life (Rom.
5:17). Through the sin of one man came judgment (v. 16). Adam's singular sin
brought judgment to the entire human race. And from judgment proceeds condemnation which anticipates execution. Judgment implies "sentence"—which
will be carried out in "condemnation" unless grace averts the judgment and
condemnation.

But Jesus Christ has resolved the dilemma. He has brought the free gift of
justification of life to all men. "All men" includes those who respond in faith
and trust in the completed work of Jesus Christ. Although sin was intensified
through the Law, "grace abounded all the more" (v. 20). Grace far surpasses
sin. Christ has defeated sin and death for those who respond to Him in faith.

CONSIDER: *One man, Adam, brought death, judgment, and condemnation to the
human race; one Man, Jesus Christ, brought grace, life, and immortality.*

CONTINUE LIVING IN SIN?

ROMANS 6:1–5

Are we to continue in sin so that grace may increase? May it never be! How shall we who died to sin still live in it? (Romans 6:1–2)

Grigori Yefimovich Rasputin was a mystical Russian monk who held an unusual influence over Czar Nicholas II and his family. He had a reputation as a holy man, a healer, and also as an immoral charlatan. His life of sexual immorality was well known. Rasputin taught that in order to experience repentance and salvation it was necessary to sin deeply with alcohol and immorality. Only through enormous sin would the sinner experience enormous grace.

Of course, Scripture teaches the opposite. Having emphasized grace and justification in Romans 5:12–21, Paul raises the hypothetical question, If sin magnifies grace, why not sin more and therefore magnify grace still further? Paul answers the supposed question: "May it never be!" Unthinkable! Perish the thought! The problem of sin as guilt has been resolved. Paul now deals with sin as a power in the believer's life. Since believers are joined to Christ in His death, it is impossible for the believer to continue living in sin. We died to sin when we died with Christ. "Death to sin is separation from sin's power, not the extinction of sin. Being dead to sin means being 'set free from sin' (vv. 18, 22)" (John Witmer, "Romans," *Bible Knowledge Commentary*).

Paul explains: "all of us who have been baptized into Christ Jesus have been baptized into His death" (v. 3). This is not referring to water baptism; water cannot accomplish death to sin. It is a reference to Spirit baptism which occurs at the moment of salvation for all believers (as described in 1 Corinthians 12:13). Spirit baptism does two things: it places us in union with Christ—"in Christ"—and it unites us with other believers as the body of Christ.

The purpose of our union with Christ in death is "so that as Christ was raised from the dead . . . so we too might walk in newness of life" (Rom. 6:4). The believer lives in a new state of life—it is new in quality. It is a supernatural life. It is a *changed* life.

The believer is "united with Him" (v. 5), meaning we have been grafted to Christ like a limb on a tree. As a branch draws nourishment from the tree so the believer now draws new life from Christ, through union with Him, enabling the believer to live a new life.

CONSIDER: *As Christ died and rose again to a new life, so the believer is united with Christ, having died to a life of sin and risen to a new life of righteous living.*

DEAD YET ALIVE

ROMANS 6:6–11

Knowing this, that our old self was crucified with Him, in order that our body of sin might be done away with, so that we would no longer be slaves to sin. (Romans 6:6)

Fred was an elderly bachelor in the country church I served early in my ministry. When I visited him I was surprised to see he didn't have electricity in his home. Fred was cautious with his money in every way. He would ride his bicycle ten miles into the city to buy day-old bread for a dime a loaf. He pinched his pennies. But when Fred died, they discovered he was a wealthy man. He had not appropriated the wealth that he had.

Some Christians are similar to Fred, failing to appropriate the spiritual blessings and victory that is rightly theirs. In a dramatic statement, Paul reminds us that "our old self was crucified with Him [Christ]" (v. 6). What is the "old self"? It refers to the lifestyle we were under in our unregenerate lives; it reflects all that we were as an unsaved person. It is a "corrupted" way of life (Eph. 4:22).

What has happened? Our old self was "crucified with Him." It means that when Christ died He took our sin upon Himself. As believers, we are identified with Him in death. All that we were as unsaved people is placed on Christ; there is a transfer of our sins to Christ. The result is that "our body of sin might be done away with," which means sin becomes *inoperative* in us. The power of sin is broken.

The dramatic result is that we are no longer slaves to sin. In our unsaved estate we were slaves to sin but no longer. We have been released from bondage. We have been freed from sin. And this has wonderful ramifications. Since we have died together with Christ, we will also live together with Him. And the new life in Christ begins immediately. Just as Christ died and death no longer has any dominion or mastery over Him, even so the believer has died and risen to a new life in Christ. Christ broke the guilt of sin and He broke the power of sin.

But now the application. We are to consider ourselves "dead to sin." This is a command. We are to live each day reminding ourselves that we are united with Christ in His death with regard to sin's guilt and power and we are united with Christ to a new life. What is the critical point? We must *reckon* it as having happened to make the victory over sin operative in our lives. Have I considered myself dead to sin and alive to Christ?

CONSIDER: *The believer is united to Christ in both death and resurrection, giving us the victory and enabling us to walk in newness of life.*

July 10

WHO IS RULING OVER ME?

Therefore do not let sin reign in your mortal
body so that you obey its lusts. (Romans 6:12)

Juan Peron was the highly controversial president and dictator of Argentina from 1946–1955 and 1973–1974. Amid corruption and controversy with the Catholic Church, he was overthrown in 1955 and went into exile in Madrid, Spain. His dictatorship ended in 1955, yet pro-Peron groups continued to be strong. The people had a choice. They could live in liberty, or they could still submit to Peron's authority—even though he had been deposed. It was a choice.

In light of the believer's union with Christ, Paul draws a conclusion. The believer is no longer to allow sin to reign or rule as king in his body (Fritz Rienecker and Cleon Rogers, *Linguistic Key to the Greek New Testament*). A king has authority and power to rule over a country. Paul says we are not to allow sin to have authority and the rule over us as a king rules over a country. Paul's command is strong. It may mean "stop" or "do not continue" to let sin reign in your body. It is abnormal for the believer to continue living in sin because of his union with Christ and his power through Christ to have victory over sin. Even though we are united with Christ, we still retain the old nature which has evil desires and lusts that can lead us into sin. We are not to obey or listen to the desires of the old nature.

What is the resolution? Paul explains: "Present yourselves to God as those alive from the dead, and your members as instruments of righteousness to God" (v. 13). Paul presents a forceful, military picture. The verb "present" is dramatic. It is a decisive act, a break with the past. It sees the believer as turning around and walking in a new direction. The believer no longer lives as he formerly lived. The members of our body now become instruments that are used for righteousness, not evil. "Instruments" is pictured as a tool or weapon. "Sin is regarded as a sovereign (v. 12), who demands the military service of its subjects, levys their quota of arms (v. 13), and gives them their soldier's-pay of death (v. 23)" (Fritz Rienecker and Cleon Rogers, *Linguistic Key to the Greek New Testament*).

Yes, the believer is set free from sin's domination—but the believer must make a choice. Will sin reign over me or will righteousness reign supreme? Since we are no longer under the law but under grace, sin need not have mastery over us.

CONSIDER: *Because of our union with Christ, we can no longer go on living in sin but we must once-for-all dedicate our bodies to Christ for His glory.*

July 11

SET FREE!

ROMANS 6:15–23

*For the wages of sin is death, but the free gift of God is
eternal life in Christ Jesus our Lord. (Romans 6:23)*

A prominent Hollywood actor made some classic films and achieved great
fame and popularity. He was a great actor but he had a drinking problem,
and eventually became an alcoholic who was constantly drunk. One day he
fell while drunk, hitting his head on the edge of a coffee table, and he bled to
death. Tragically, the end result of his life of sin was both physical death and
eternal death.

Paul draws a contrast he began in verses 1–2. He reminds us that we are
the slaves of the one to whom we present ourselves, whether to sin—resulting
in death—or to obedience—resulting in righteousness. We are the slaves of
the one whom we obey—that is Paul's message. A slave can only belong to one
master. To choose sin would mean sin is the master over us, resulting in physical and spiritual death (as it first began in Genesis 2:17). To choose obedience
to God results in righteousness, culminating in life—eternal life.

But Paul reminds his readers that they once were slaves to sin, but no
longer. "From the heart" (v. 17)—as a decisive act of the will—they became
obedient to the truth. They heard the teaching and responded in faith, turning from sin to righteousness. By an act of the will they were freed from the
tyranny of sin. And the result is they have become "slaves of righteousness"
(v. 18). But it still necessitates a volitional choice to live a righteous life. As he
had in verse 13, Paul again challenges the believer: "present your members
as slaves to righteousness" (v. 19). Paul again anticipates a decisive action.

Paul asks, Was there any benefit to the old life of living in sin? No. The
end result of a life of sin is death, both physical and eternal. The testimony of
various people who have achieved fame, wealth, and notoriety by living for
themselves is that they come to the end of their life empty. There is no earthly
or eternal benefit that a life of sin can bring.

But now Paul draws a contrast. Having been freed from sin and being
enslaved to God there is great benefit: eternal life. It is both a qualitative and
quantitative life. Paul is emphatic: we have *eternal life!* That is the fruit. That
is the benefit.

CONSIDER: *The life of sin and righteousness is set in contrast: the life of sin is
empty, resulting in death, but the life of righteousness derives eternal benefit.*

July 12

Freedom from the Law

ROMANS 7:1–6

*But now we have been released from the Law, having died to
that by which we were bound, so that we serve in newness
of the Spirit and not in oldness of the letter. (Romans 7:6)*

When my wife and I visited Berlin in 2004, we walked past the Brandenburg Gate which was the division between East and West Berlin, between communism and freedom. Parts of the Berlin wall remain as a reminder of a decadent era when people were enslaved under communism. But many people scaled the wall, seeking freedom. When they were able to escape to the eastern zone, they were no longer under communism. They were free.

Paul pictures the believer in Christ having been set free from the Law's domination. Paul amplifies the argument begun in Romans 6:14. Since we have died to the Law in union with Christ, the Law no longer has jurisdiction over us. We are now under grace, not the Law. Some may fail to recognize this phenomenal transaction and may still attempt to live under the Law—but that is erroneous.

Paul illustrates this with marriage. A married woman is bound to her husband by law as long as he lives. But when the husband dies, she is released from the law regarding her husband. The law which stated she was bound to her husband has no more authority over her. One woman's husband severely restricted her spending. When he died, she bought expensive furniture, new carpeting, and much more. Her husband no longer had authority over her spending!

Using the marriage illustration, Paul makes the application. As in marriage, the wife is set free to marry another man when her husband dies, so the believer has died to the Law in order that he may be set free to be joined to Christ and bear fruit.

Only under grace can the believer properly bear fruit for God. A fruitful life is not possible under the Law since it is a life "in the flesh." All the Law could do was arouse the sinful passions. Thankfully, the believer has been released from the Law so that we can now serve God in the newness of the Spirit.

CONSIDER: *The believer has been released from the Law and has been united to Christ to bear fruit for God.*

REBELLION!

ROMANS 7:7–11

---

*What shall we say then? Is the Law sin? May it never be! On
the contrary, I would not have come to know sin except
through the Law; for I would not have known about coveting
if the Law had not said, "YOU SHALL NOT COVET." (Romans 7:7)*

When my family and I visited Disneyland, we took a ride in which a sign was
posted: "Keep arms inside the car." Immediately a teenage girl began putting her arm outside the car. Had the sign not been there she likely would not
have even thought to extend her arm. Her action reflected a natural, human
disposition to disobey the law, whether it is a "No Talking" sign in a library or
a speed limit posted on a highway.

Since it is a natural human tendency to disobey the Law of God, is there
a problem with the Law? Is the Law at fault since it apparently causes people
to sin? "May it never be!" Paul answers. There is nothing wrong with the Law;
the problem is with sinful humanity.

Paul explains the purpose of the Law: it was given to expose sin. When
Paul read the statement, "You shall not covet," it created within him a desire
to rebel and disobey the commandment. The Law exposed sin. It created an
inward lust to rebel against God. It is a graphic picture. "Sin launched an attack
against man and viciously and deceptively used the commandment as a foothold for the advance" (Alan Johnson, *Romans: The Freedom Letter*).

When the commandment came, the sin nature responded in rebellion
against God. God's commandment triggered sin within the unbeliever. When
this happened, Paul exclaimed, "I died" (v. 9). What does he mean? Paul is
referring to spiritual death, separation and alienation from God. Paul died
subjectively. He was spiritually separated from God. The Law had exposed
him and his need for righteousness.

As a Pharisee, Paul attempted to obtain righteousness through the Law
but found that the Law brought death instead of life. How then could the commandment bring life (v. 10)? Life in the Old Testament could only come by the
principle of faith as Abraham discovered (Gen. 15:6) and as David realized (Ps.
32:1–2). Faith would result in salvation, enabling the believer to keep the Law.

CONSIDER: *The Law exposes sin, and the sin nature within the unbeliever rebels
against the Law of God, creating an inner warfare.*

THE WAR OF THE TWO NATURES

ROMANS 7:12–25

*Wretched man that I am! Who will set me free from the body
of this death? Thanks be to God through Jesus Christ our Lord! So then,
on the one hand I myself with my mind am serving the law of God,
but on the other, with my flesh the law of sin. (Romans 7:24–25)*

An old Indian proverb tells of a warfare within the person. The Indian explains that there is an inner battle, two wolves are fighting within him, one to do the right thing, the other to do the wrong thing. "Which wolf wins?" asked a friend. "The one I feed," answered the Indian.

Indeed, everyone will acknowledge the inner warfare that people experience. Paul continues his explanation. The problem is not with the Law. He reminds the reader "the Law is holy, and the commandment is holy and righteous and good" (v. 12). There is nothing wrong with the commandment. By these three statements the Law reveals the character and nature of the Lawgiver—God—He is holy, righteous, and good.

Is the Law then the cause of death? Absolutely not (v. 13). The Law cannot be blamed for death. It was not the Law that was the cause of death; rather it was sin. The Law is spiritual—it has its origin from God. The Law is caused by the Spirit of God. The Law is good; it directs the person to do the right thing. On the contrary, Paul exclaims that he is unspiritual, "of the flesh" (v. 14). He is under the domination of sin.

And the conflict continues. Paul does not practice what he would like to do and he is doing the thing he hates. It is "sin" within him (v. 17). This may be called the "sin nature," "the principle that evil is present in me" (v. 21)—whatever terminology one may use, there is a disposition to sin within every human being. No one is exempt.

Paul draws a conclusion. He readily acknowledges the goodness of the Law yet he experiences a conflict. There is another law waging war against the Law of God in the mind. It is "sin which dwells in me" (vv. 17, 20), "my flesh," (vv. 18, 25).

Yet there is victory "through Jesus Christ our Lord!" (v. 25). While the battle remains in this present life, yet Paul can look ahead to the triumphant return of Jesus Christ when believers will receive glorified bodies as the final resolution to the conflict with the sin nature (as Paul describes in Philippians 3:20–21).

CONSIDER: *In this present life we experience an inner conflict between the old nature and the new nature yet we can serve the Law of God, focusing our mind on Him. What are you focusing your mind on?*

July 15

No Condemnation

ROMANS 8:1–8

---

*Therefore there is now no condemnation for
those who are in Christ Jesus. (Romans 8:1)*

Condemned! It is a harsh term. It looks at both the pronouncement of guilt and the ultimate execution of the sentence. A man condemned for a heinous crime can expect to pay the ultimate price: execution.

Paul introduces this most beloved of all chapters in the Bible with a great message of comfort: *No condemnation.* Paul explains the resolution to the conflict between the two natures described in Romans 7—victory comes through the power of the Holy Spirit. "No condemnation" emphasizes that we are set free from the Law's condemning curse. We are free from both the guilt and the enslaving power of sin. Why? Because we are "in Christ Jesus." The Holy Spirit has regenerated the believer, setting him free from the principle of sin and death. We have new life in Christ and this new life gives us victory—something the Law could not do.

What the Law could not achieve, God did through His Son. When Christ came, He offered Himself as a sin offering, a propitiation, a satisfaction to God for the penalty of sin and so He condemned sin. In that divine transaction, Christ broke sin's power over humanity for all who identify with Him, that we may enjoy a life of victory over sin. Through our identification with Christ, the requirement of the Law is fulfilled in us.

How is this evident? In verses 5–8 Paul draws a contrast between those who live according to the flesh and those who live according to the Spirit. The unregenerate person lives his life with his mind set on the flesh; he is dominated by the sin principle. The mind set on the flesh is at war with God and unable to please God. The one who is in Christ Jesus is dominated by the Spirit; his mind is set on life and peace. The believer in Christ walks in victory through the indwelling Spirit of God.

CONSIDER: *There is no condemnation for the believer in Christ Jesus who walks in victory according to the Spirit.*

July 16

ADOPTED INTO THE FAMILY OF GOD

ROMANS 8:9–17

You have received a spirit of adoption as sons by which we
cry out, "Abba! Father!" The Spirit Himself testifies with our spirit
that we are children of God, and if children, heirs also, heirs
of God and fellow heirs with Christ. (Romans 8:15–17)

My grandniece and her husband adopted a boy and a girl from Ethiopia. They have a natural born daughter as well but now they have three children. Do the children from Ethiopia have an inferior position? No. They have been adopted into the family and have all the rights and privileges exclusive to that family.

Through Christ we are adopted into the family of God and enjoy an entirely unique position. We are children of God. In that marvelous transaction, the triune God has come to indwell the believer. The Holy Spirit indwells us (v. 9), Christ indwells us (v. 10), and the Father indwell us (v. 11). For this reason we enjoy a new life—we no longer live according to the impulses and desires of the old nature. Someone living in that fashion gives evidence he is on the road to death. But the believer's spirit has been regenerated; it has been "powered up!" We have *life!* God has given us a new life, not dictated by the old nature. We have a new nature, a new capacity for living that is directed and governed by the Holy Spirit.

This new life is a sign of sonship. Believers are led, directed in life by the Spirit of God, reflecting we are "sons of God" (v. 14). We have new desires, new initiatives that we did not have before. They are impulses given to us by the Holy Spirit. We are no longer slaves of a harsh slave-master. We have received the "adoption as sons," being placed into the family of God. What does this mean? "The adopted person lost all rights in his old family, and gained all the rights of a fully legitimate son in his new family. . . . He became heir to his new father's estate. . . . In law, the old life of the adopted person was completely wiped out . . . legally all debts were cancelled . . . In the eyes of the law the adopted person was literally and absolutely the son of his new father" (William Barclay, *Letter to the Romans*).

We have a new intimate relationship with God. We can call him "Abba! Father!" And as sons we have privileges. We have fellowship and empowerment with the triune God, now enabling us to live victoriously over the old nature. But we also have a future. We are heirs of God and joint heirs with Christ. We will receive glorified, incorruptible bodies. Rejoice, believer, in your present position and your phenomenal future!

CONSIDER: *In our new relationship as sons of God, being adopted into God's family, we are empowered to live according to the Spirit and not according to the old nature.*

LOOK UP! LOOK AHEAD!

ROMANS 8:18–30

*And we know that God causes all things to work together
for good to those who love God, to those who are
called according to His purpose. (Romans 8:28)*

The brilliant red bougainvillea in my front yard require constant pruning because they grow so fast. They are beautiful but the branches have sharp thorns, so each time I trim the bushes, my arms are covered with blood where the thorns have left their marks. But a day is coming when bougainvillea will not longer torment people with its thorns.

Nature is graphically pictured actively seeking, anxiously longing for its restoration and freedom from corruption (vv. 19–21). Through Adam's transgression, all of creation was subjected to futility resulting in earthquakes, hurricanes, floods, droughts—the list is endless. But all creation awaits the day of restoration, graphically pictured as a mother, experiencing the pain of childbirth, eagerly awaiting delivery from suffering to bring forth a healthy child.

Believers also groan, awaiting our completed redemption and placement as sons where we will be set free from corruption. Will it come? Yes! We have received the down payment—the indwelling Holy Spirit—as a reminder of our ultimate, complete redemption. For this reason we hope for that future day; we trust and patiently wait for that great day when mortal will put on immortality. And we remind ourselves that our present suffering cannot compare with the ultimate glory we will enjoy. Meanwhile, the Spirit helps us in our present weakness since we do not even know how to pray correctly. Not knowing how we should pray amid our sufferings, the Holy Spirit takes our inept prayers, corrects them, and carries them to the Father. Then the Father answers the corrected prayer which specifies our real need. What is the result? Notice Romans 8:28. God then causes all things to work together for our good, for what we really need, for what we really should have prayed for in the beginning. He will bring it all to pass, from the past to the future. The One who foreknew us, predestined us, and called us is also the One who justified us in Christ, and is the One who will ultimately bring us home to glory in the future, when this mortal will put on immortality.

Dear suffering believer, take courage! Your suffering cannot be compared with the ultimate, eternal glory you will enjoy forever and ever. Look ahead!

CONSIDER: *Living in a fallen world, we groan, anticipating the future day of glory but the Holy Spirit carries our corrected petitions to the Father who works all things for our good.*

Overwhelming Love, Overwhelming Victory
Romans 8:31–39

If God is for us, who is against us? He who did not spare His
own Son, but delivered Him over for us all, how will He
not also with Him freely give us all things? (Romans 8:31–32)

Dwight L. Moody once remarked that if his friend Mr. Tiffany had offered him as a gift a large, beautiful diamond, he would not hesitate to ask Mr. Tiffany for some brown paper to wrap up the diamond" (quoted from Alan Johnson, *Romans: The Freedom Letter*).

These verses have been building like a crescendo. If God is the One who foreknew, predestined, called, justified, and will glorify us, who can possibly lay a charge against us? Who can accuse us before God? If God, the Sovereign One, is for us, no one of note can be against us. Certainly, it would be pointless. If God has given us the greater gifts (salvation and glorification), He will also give us the lesser (help in our suffering).

The ultimate proof that God is for us is seen in that He delivered up His Son for us all. We can therefore count on God to give us "all things." The context identifies all things as help in our weakness (v. 26). You and I can count on God in whatever we are suffering—loneliness, sickness, financial hardship, or other troubles. These are the "all things" in which He will help you. Amid the difficulties of life, count on God.

What about the adversary? Can he bring a formal accusation against us in court? Although Satan is the accuser of believers, can he bring a charge against us? No, his charges are invalid. "Satan's accusations will be thrown out of court, because it is God who justifies" (John Witmer, "Romans," *Bible Knowledge Commentary*).

Who will condemn us? No one. No condemning action against us will stand because Christ is with us through His death and He is with us in His resurrection life. He continually intercedes for us. We can rest secure! Nothing can separate us from the love of Christ. *Nothing!* The love of Christ is so certain and constant, it gives us courage in all circumstances, making us victorious.

Paul lists ten things in speculating what could separate us from the love of God. But nothing—not even death—can separate us. Are you appropriating by faith the victory that is already yours because you are kept in the love of God?

CONSIDER: *Because Christ died for us and because He intercedes for us we can face any trial in life and overwhelmingly conquer through Christ.*

July 19

GOD'S CHOSEN PEOPLE

ROMANS 9:1–13

For though the twins were not yet born and had not done anything good or bad, so that God's purpose according to His choice would stand, . . . it is written, "JACOB I LOVED, BUT ESAU I HATED." (Romans 9:11, 13)

On one of my visits to Israel I encountered a local Israeli in Jerusalem who exclaimed to me, "You think this is a holy city? You will find it is a very unholy city." I was stunned. I also discovered that some 85 percent of the Israelis consider themselves "secular Jews." They recognize their Jewish ethnicity but they are not practicing Jews by religion. They neither believe in Jesus as their Messiah nor do they practice the Mosaic Law.

This raises a question. Are the Jews God's chosen people? If so, why are they in unbelief? Isn't the gospel for the Jews as well? Yes, Paul stated that at the outset of the book of Romans (1:16). In chapters 9–11 Paul will show that God has not been unfaithful to Israel. Rather, it is because of their unbelief that they have not entered into the blessings God promised them.

Paul has great grief and sorrow over Israel's unbelief. If it were possible, he would wish himself "accursed, separated from Christ" for the sake of his people (v. 3). Consider their privileged position: adopted as sons, they can lay claim to the glory of God's presence, the covenants, the Law, the temple service, the promises, the fathers, and Christ the Messiah.

What then? Why hasn't Israel entered into these blessings? Has God's word failed? No, God's word has not failed. Not all who have descended from Abraham—not everyone who can claim to be a Jew—will enter into the blessings. It is through Isaac's lineage (not Ishmael's) that the blessings will come. And not all of Isaac's descendants will be blessed, rather God's sovereign choice was through Jacob, not Esau. The phrase "Jacob I loved, but Esau I hated" should not be understood as hateful. This is a Hebrew idiom meaning, "I preferred Jacob to Esau" (C. K. Barrett, *The Epistle to the Romans*). "The word 'hate' is here used in the Hebrew sense of 'loving less,' or 'showing less favor towards'" (William Shedd, *Commentary on Romans*).

God's sovereign purpose and choice concerning Israel remains. They are God's chosen people despite their unbelief in this present age.

CONSIDER: *God sovereignly chose Israel and despite their unbelief, they remain God's chosen people.*

July 20

Sovereignty and Responsibility

Romans 9:14–33

So then He has mercy on whom He desires, and He hardens whom He desires. . . . They did not pursue it by faith. (Romans 9:18, 32)

I stood outside a shop in Bethlehem, watching the potter create a vessel. He pumped the paddle with his feet, spinning the basin that contained the clay. Meanwhile, with his hands he was shaping the vessel. Soon it took on a specific shape as he carefully formed it with his hands. The potter had complete control over the vessel.

If God, in His sovereignty, chose Jacob over Esau, is He then unfair? No! Again Paul exclaims, "May it never be!" No way! God illustrated the truth from Moses and Pharaoh. God told Moses, "I will have mercy on whom I have mercy" (v. 15). God has the freedom to show mercy however He chooses. Ultimately, God—in His absolute perfection—can do no wrong. God's mercy is not dependent on human will nor human effort. "If God does anything at all for sinful man, it is of his mercy. If he does nothing, he is not unjust, for man deserves nothing" (C. K. Barrett, *The Epistle to the Romans*).

So God shows mercy on whom He desires and He hardens whom He desires. This raises a difficult question: Does God actively harden people? To answer that, we must refer back to what we know from elsewhere in Scripture. Unregenerate man's heart is naturally hard (Ezek. 36:26). "To harden is not to soften. . . . The agency of God in hardening is inaction, rather than action" (William Shedd, *Commentary on Romans*). Man cannot blame God. Man is responsible to respond to God (Rom. 2:5).

The debater then argues in Romans 9:19, Who then can resist His will? Paul doesn't answer the question; rather, he rebukes the man for asking the question! "Man's position as a creature does not qualify him to contradict the Creator (vv. 20, 21). Man must be silent!" (Alan Johnson, *Romans: The Freedom Letter*). A potter may use a piece of clay in any way that he wishes, fashioning one for honorable use while passing over the other.

Paul makes a significant statement. God actively prepares vessels for glory fitting people for heaven. But it says, "vessels of wrath prepared for destruction" (v. 22). The statement is passive; it does not say God actively prepares vessels for destruction.

Are people then not responsible? Yes, they are responsible. Paul concludes by saying Israel did not enter into blessing because they did not seek it by faith (vv. 30, 31).

This illustrates two parallel truths: God is sovereign *and* people are responsible.

With our finite minds we cannot reconcile these two truths.

CONSIDER: *God is sovereign in bringing Israel and Gentiles to salvation, yet people are responsible to believe and can never accuse God of being unfair.*

FOR JEWS AND GENTILES

ROMANS 10:1–21

---

*If you confess with your mouth Jesus as Lord, and believe in your heart
that God raised Him from the dead, you will be saved . . . "WHOEVER
BELIEVES IN HIM WILL NOT BE DISAPPOINTED." (Romans 10:9, 11)*

While evangelicals strongly support the State of Israel, considerable tension exists because evangelicals also share the gospel, wanting to see
Jewish people come to faith in Christ. J. Lee Grady, editor of *Charisma*, has said
"some Jews believe that Christian evangelism is a form of anti-Semitism—as if
converting a person to faith in Jesus strips them of their Jewishness." This has
caused some evangelicals to stop evangelizing the Jewish people. A prominent
evangelical pastor spoke at Shabat services at Sinai Temple and "managed to
speak for the entire evening without once mentioning Jesus."

But was this Paul's heart? Was Paul concerned for Israel's salvation?
Indeed, Paul's desire and prayer for them was for their salvation. His concern
for them was that while having zeal, it was misdirected. They had a misconcep-
tion about God's righteousness, seeking it through works rather than through
grace. But their attempt to establish their own righteousness failed because
there was no atonement for sin and there was no perfect obedience to satisfy
the demands of the Law (William Shedd, *Commentary on Romans*). Christ is
"the end of the law" (v. 4). This means Christ terminated the Law—as a system
it is over (cf. Rom. 6:14). It also means that Christ is the goal of the law in its
ceremonial and moral precepts. And Christ has completed the Law; He has
met all the requirements of the Law (William Shedd, *Commentary on Romans*).

So how is this righteousness then received? It does not come through the
law; it comes through faith. It is received by acknowledging Jesus as Lord—
He is God incarnate. It is a decision of the heart, a moving of the will. And it
involves believing that God raised Him from the dead. The resurrection is the
completion of the redemption transaction. And the one who believes in Christ
will never be disappointed—salvation is real and genuine. It relates to both
Jew and Gentile: "whoever [Jew or Gentile] will call upon the name of the Lord
will be saved" (v. 13). The gospel is universal; Christ came for both Jews and
Gentiles.

What then? The responsibility is to tell the good news. How can they
believe if they haven't heard? How can they hear if no one tells them? The
question then becomes personal: do I faithfully and consistently share the
gospel with others—Jews andGentiles?

CONSIDER: *The gospel of Christ is for both Jews and Gentiles but for them to
hear, the gospel must be proclaimed.*

July 22

HAS GOD REJECTED ISRAEL?

ROMANS 11:1–10

I say then, God has not rejected His people, has He? May
it never be! . . . God has not rejected His people
whom He foreknew. (Romans 11:1–2)

Israel stands as a miracle among all the nations of the world, in the entire history of the world. Removed from their homeland by the Babylonians in 586 B.C., they never again lived independently in their own land until 1948—a period of two and a half millennia. The Jewish people are back in their homeland, despite enormous opposition by their enemies.

Has God rejected His people Israel? "May it never be!" Unthinkable! Paul states the negative in the strongest term. Even to this day some groups teach that the church has replaced Israel, calling it "replacement theology" but Paul answers that erroneous teaching in the opening statement. Paul cites himself as an example that God has not rejected the Hebrew people. Paul too is an Israelite. Then he emphatically states, "God has not rejected His people whom He foreknew" (v. 2).

Paul demonstrates the principle of a believing remnant throughout Israel's history—even during times of national apostasy. Elijah thought he alone was a believer but God showed him there were seven thousand others that had remained true to their God. In the same way, God has kept a faithful remnant in Paul's day. In fact, thousands of Jews in Paul's day had believed in Christ (Acts 21:20). What was the reason? There was "a remnant according to God's gracious choice" (Rom. 11:5). They were not better than the nation but God chose them out of His grace.

Israel sought righteousness and acceptance by God but did not attain to it because they sought it through works and not faith (as seen in Romans 9:31–32 and 10:3). A remnant obtained it because they were chosen; the rest of Israel did not obtain it because they were hardened. (Recall the discussion of *harden* in the July 20 devotional.) Citing Isaiah 29:10, Paul explains that God had given Israel over to a spirit of stupor—"God has ceased to strive with the man [Israel], and has left him to himself" (William Shedd, *Commentary on Romans*). But hardening does not come without reason. God judged the nation because of their unbelief. Rejection of God's grace resulted in unbelief, bringing God's discipline and thereby hardening.

There is a tension between God's sovereignty—His choosing us—and human responsibility—us choosing Him. Both are true, yet our limited human thinking does not enable us to reconcile the two truths. But opposition to and rejection of God's grace has drastic results.

CONSIDER: *The Jewish people remain God's chosen people, even amid unbelief.*

ISRAEL'S ULTIMATE SALVATION

ROMANS 11:11–36

*A partial hardening has happened to Israel until the fullness of the Gentiles
has come in; and so all Israel will be saved. (Romans 11:25–26)*

E vangelism in Israel is not easy. It may be opposed by the authorities or by
groups or individuals. One local Israeli said, "It is illegal in Israel to provide
material goods as a way to persuade Israelis to change their religion." In Arad,
a small group of believers has been harassed with death threats and destruction of property. Yet some, but not many, come to faith in Christ.

Israel has "stumbled" but they have not "fallen." There is a difference.
Theirs is not an irrevocable fall; they will be restored in the future. But through
Israel's stumbling, salvation has come to the Gentiles. When the Jews rejected
the message of the gospel, Paul turned to the Gentiles (see Acts 13:46). What
was the purpose? To provoke the Jews to jealousy. Furthermore, if Jewish
rejection of the gospel resulted in the riches of God's grace extending to the
Gentiles, how much greater will be the blessings to the Gentiles at the future
restoration and conversion of the Jewish people?

Paul warns the Gentiles—seen as a wild olive branch that was grafted
into the olive tree (Israel)—that they should not be arrogant toward the
Jews, since the root supports the branches, not vice versa. The Gentiles were
grafted in because of faith; they should not boast since they could also be cut
off. In God's kindness He had grafted them in.

But Israel's blindness is temporary, not permanent. Their hardening is
"until the fullness of the Gentiles has come in." When the full number of Gentiles has come to faith in this present age, then Israel will again turn to the
Lord and "all Israel will be saved." This dramatic event refers to a national
turning of Israel in repentance to God (as seen in Zechariah 12:10–14). "All
Israel" in Romans 11:26 refers to the believing remnant at the end of the tribulation. The Redeemer—Christ—will come and turn the hearts of the Hebrew
people back to their Lord. This is a reminder that "the gifts and the calling
of God are irrevocable" (v. 29). God chose Israel long ago and God does not
renege on His promises.

As Paul considers the conversion and restoration of Israel, he breaks into a
doxology (vv. 33–36). Indeed, God's ways are unsearchable and unfathomable!
Who can comprehend the faithfulness and loving-kindness of God?

CONSIDER: *The Hebrew people remain the chosen people of God and in the
fullness of time, God will restore their hearts to Christ.*

July 24

SERVING OTHERS

ROMANS 12:1–8

---

*Therefore I urge you, brethren, by the mercies of God, to present
your bodies a living and holy sacrifice, acceptable to God, which
is your spiritual service of worship. And do not be conformed to this
world, but be transformed by the renewing of your mind, so that
you may prove what the will of God is, that which is good and
acceptable and perfect. (Romans 12:1–2)*

Having built a strong doctrinal foundation in chapters 1–11, Paul now directs
the Roman believers to live as Christians in the world and to help other
believers in the fellowship. The foundation is Romans 12:1–2. Knowing that
Christ has made atonement for us and that we are called to sanctification, Paul
calls on the believers to once-and-for-all present their bodies a living sacrifice
to God. Instead of a dead animal sacrifice as in the Old Testament, we are
called to be a *living* sacrifice. We are not being conformed to the philosophy
and mind-set of the world. We are called to have a renewed mind—Christ is
to control our thoughts, attitudes, and actions. Only in this way will we know
the will of God.

Because Christ extended His grace to us, we are warned not to have a
haughty opinion of ourselves. It is important that we have the right evaluation
of ourselves, recognizing that we all have different functions within the body
of Christ. And we are not in competition; we are members of one another, just
as the various parts of the human body do their individual tasks for the good
of the whole body.

Since we have all received spiritual gifts according to the grace given to
us, we are called to exercise our gifts in agreement with the faith. In other
words, we should be building up one another. The first gift mentioned in this
passage, the gift of prophecy, foretelling the future, was a foundational gift
in the early church, to build it up before the Scriptures were complete. Since
we have the written Scriptures, this gift is no longer operative. The remaining
gifts listed are still applicable to us. The gift of service is a basic gift of serving
others, particularly those in need, meeting physical needs, helping the poor
and widows. The gift of teaching involves explaining Christian truth and applying it. Exhortation is related to teaching and speaks to the heart; it involves
both consolation and confrontation. Giving means "to share with someone,"
liberally and without selfishness. Leading suggests a "take-charge person."
Showing mercy means relieving distress, as in ministering to the sick, poor,
widowed, and bereaved. The message is clear: having a knowledge of what
Christ has done for us, we are called to serve others.

CONSIDER: *Are you exercising your spiritual gift in unity with others for the
spiritual upbuilding of the body of Christ?*

DEMONSTRATION OF LOVE

ROMANS 12:9–21

*Be devoted to one another in brotherly love; give
preference to one another in honor. (Romans 12:10)*

When Helen heard our neighbor lady was sick, she baked a pie for her, then she washed her kitchen floor. The neighbor lady cried in appreciation for the love Helen demonstrated.

Above all else, believers are called to practice love toward one another. Love is the hallmark of the Christian. Building on the doctrinal foundation he has established, Paul directs believers toward demonstrations of love in the Christian fellowship. This love is not merely an emotion. Love (*agape*) is a reasoned-out love; it is a volitional decision to love the other person, regardless of whether the love is reciprocated.

This love is not a stage act; there is no element of hypocrisy. It is genuine. It is practiced out of devotion to others, seeking to honor others rather than honoring self. This love is a result of the energizing of the Holy Spirit. Agape love is *active*.

How does this love manifest itself? It is reflected in sharing the sorrows and joys of others. We are called to weep with those who weep and rejoice with those who rejoice. It is sympathy and empathy toward others. But this can only happen when we are "of the same mind toward one another" (v. 16). What does this mean? We enter into their grief and their joy. Can we do that? Yes, we are called to have the mind and attitude of Jesus Christ (Phil. 2:5). He did not seek His own interest but the interests of others. This is also our call.

But the call to love is even broader—it extends outside the Christian fellowship. We are called to exhibit love in the world. How is this seen? The Christian does not retaliate or show vengeance; instead, we are exhorted to "be at peace with all men" (Rom. 12:18). When this isn't possible, it shouldn't be the result of our failure. We should seek every avenue to live at peace with others. Our demonstration of love to others can bring about their remorse and repentance. This demands serious introspection: Do I genuinely love others? Do I live at peace with unbelievers?

CONSIDER: *We are called to exhibit selfless love to believers, sharing their sorrows and joys while living at peace with unbelievers in the world.*

Submission to the Government

Romans 13:1–14

*Owe nothing to anyone except to love one another; for he
who loves his neighbor has fulfilled the law. (Romans 13:8)*

What is the Christian's relationship to the government? In China the government forces a mother to have an abortion if she has two children. Our own government does not permit corporal punishment of children yet the Bible speaks to this. The government is considering imposing the "Fairness Doctrine," in which radio programs would have to give equal time to opposing views. What should a Christian do?

It was during Nero's reign as emperor of the Roman Empire that Paul commanded the believers, "Every person is to be in subjection to the governing authorities" (Rom. 13:1). Paul then cites the reason: "For there is no authority except from God." The governments that exist have their power from God and they are established by God. It is God who "removes kings and establishes kings" (Dan. 2:21). Hence, to resist the government is to resist God. The ultimate purpose of government is to punish evil, hence, the believer should not have cause to fear the government while living an upright, law-abiding life. Paul summarizes that believers are to give honor and reverence—and pay taxes! Yet we are also reminded that in a conflict (and they may come) between God and government, "we must obey God rather than men" (Acts 5:29).

Paul broadens the believer's obligations: "love one another" (Rom. 13:8). This is one area in which we will never fulfill our obligation. Loving one another is the sum total of the Law. While the Mosaic Law can be codified into 613 laws, it is fulfilled in this: love God, love your neighbor. This is one debt we will never completely pay.

Paul cites the necessity and motivation for loving one another: the any-moment return of Jesus Christ. We are called to awaken out of our lethargy because the day of Christ's return is near. What is the believer to do? Since the "day" of Christ is approaching and the "night" of Satan's domain is coming to an end, we are urged to display that we are children of light by living respectfully, avoiding the immorality of the world. How do we do that? We "put on the Lord Jesus Christ" (v. 14). Since we have entered into union with Christ, the life of Christ should be reflected in our lives.

CONSIDER: *The believer is called to submission to the government and, above all, to display love toward others, reflecting the love of Christ.*

July 27

THE DILEMMA OF DOUBTFUL THINGS

ROMANS 14:1–12

But you, why do you judge your brother? Or you again, why do you regard your brother with contempt? For we will all stand before the judgment seat of God. (Romans 14:10)

Doubtful things. Gray areas. What are they? Different people would have different lists. City folks will differ from country folks. Doubtful things are not sinful things; they are things that cause other believers to stumble. Some of the following may be cited: washing the car on Sunday, listening to certain kinds of music, issues in clothing (like wearing shorts to church), sporting tattoos or various body piercings, playing cards . . . the list is endless (and different for different people).

Paul warns the Roman believers concerning things that are in the gray area. One person has freedom to do certain things, another does not have the liberty. The issue is that the one having freedom will cause the weaker brother to stumble when he sees the strong brother doing something and his conscience smites him if he does the same.

Paul provides principles regarding doubtful things. The strong brother is to accept the weak brother in fellowship but not to criticize him. There will be no fellowship when one brother tries to reform the other! The issue in biblical times was the diet. The strong brother had freedom to eat all foods; the weak brother was a vegetarian. Neither one should judge the other. Acceptance or rejection comes in the believer's stand before God, not before man.

Some regarded days differently. The weaker brother may still cling to the Sabbath while the stronger brother regards every day as belonging to the Lord. What is the resolution? Each one should be fully convinced in his own mind concerning his responsibility to the Lord. In all cases, whether observing a special day, whether eating or abstaining from eating, it is for one purpose: it is for the Lord. "All parts of believers' lives—their thoughts, actions, ambitions, decisions—are to be carried out with a view to what pleases and glorifies the Lord" (Douglas Moo, *Epistle to the Romans*).

Paul repeats: don't judge the other person. Why? Because each one of us will stand before the judgment seat of Christ and give an account of ourselves—but not of our neighbors. This is the Bema Seat where the believer's works will be evaluated and rewarded.

To summarize: we will give account to God, not man. Therefore, we should be concerned for our own spiritual integrity and faithfulness and not sit in judgment of our fellow believer.

CONSIDER: *Since we will give account of our lives to God, we should not sit in judgment of others.*

July 28

PURSUE PEACE

ROMANS 14:13–23

---

*So then we pursue the things which make for peace
and the building up of one another. (Romans 14:19)*

Paul Little tells of going to a conference where they had time to fit in a major league baseball game. One of the men became upset. When they quizzed him, they found he was a new Christian. Previously, his entire life was wrapped up in baseball; there was no room for God. When he became a Christian, he gave up baseball because it had been his idol. He didn't realize others could be neutral toward the game without making it an idol.

For unity among believers, Paul warns us not to put a stumbling block in a brother's path. It pictures a log fallen across the road that makes the traveler stumble. For example, all food is clean, yet the weaker brother, coming out of Judaism, could not eat pork. To him it was unclean. If the stronger brother would eat pork and thus offend and hurt his weaker brother, he was not walking in love. Yet, that is to be a governing principle: walk in love. If the stronger brother indulges in something that he knows will offend the weaker brother, then that is wrong.

The kingdom of God—the fellowship of believers—produces unity, not separation. The result of living under the guidance of the Holy Spirit will produce righteousness, joy, and peace—but not disunity. Paul warns: don't destroy the unity because of food! The one who is guided by the Holy Spirit in these issues is accepted by God and approved by men, producing unity with believers.

Romans 14:19 challenges us: pursue the things that produce peace. If what we do in the area of doubtful things produces dissention, it is wrong. Whatever we do should result in peace and build up fellow believers. Our actions should help others, not hinder them. By insisting on our own rights we may destroy the work of God—a solemn thought. Eating pork in front of a Jewish believer, causing him to stumble, tears down the work of God instead of building it up.

Verse 21 summarizes: don't do things that cause others to stumble. If something hurts others, abstain from it. Ultimately, it becomes an issue of faith. We should have peace in whatever we do. If we are doubtful about what we do, we stand condemned because our actions are not a result of faith.

CONSIDER: *We should be led by the Holy Spirit in whatever we do, walking in faith and in consideration of others—and above all, we must walk in love.*

*Now we who are strong ought to bear the weaknesses of those
without strength and not just please ourselves. (Romans 15:1)*

A church fellowship decided to have a Christmas banquet. Should they cater the banquet or should the church ladies serve? They discussed and debated the issue. It became very divisive; ultimately the church split over the issue and many left the church. How could this happen? People were thinking of themselves and not others.

Scripture provides principles that will prevent division. The one who is strong with respect to doubtful things cannot live for himself alone—he must live in consideration of others, namely, the weaker believers who are overly scrupulous in nonessentials. Why? For their spiritual development; for their edification. If our living becomes a stumbling block to other believers, we hinder their spiritual growth. Christ is our example. He did not please Himself—He accepted the reproach and hostility of men because it was for the good of others. What does my life reflect? Do I live for myself without caring what effect it has on others or do I take others into consideration?

Scripture gives us direction in how to live. The strong brother is to persevere in patience while the weaker brother receives comfort and encouragement. What is the result? Unity. Through perseverance and encouragement by both parties, unity will result. We are called "to be of the same mind with one another according to Christ Jesus" (v. 5). Only then will God the Father be glorified. God is dishonored in disunity.

Rather than seeking our own selfish ways, we are exhorted to accept one another. Christ is the example—He accepted us—Jews and Gentiles. Christ came to fulfill the promises made to the Jewish people but God also provided for the Gentiles. Paul quotes from several Old Testament passages, reminding us that Gentiles are included in the promises of God. Rejoice, Gentiles! God has united Jews and Gentiles in one body in Christ. Since God is the God of hope for both Jews and Gentiles, we can have joy and peace. Although we are different within the body of Christ, as we seek to please others, we will be filled with joy, peace, and hope through the Holy Spirit.

CONSIDER: *Christ has united Jews and Gentiles in one body, reminding us that we need to nurture unity in the body by seeking the good of others.*

July 30

VISION

ROMANS 15:14–16:27

---

*And thus I aspired to preach the gospel, not where
Christ was already named, so that I would not
build on another man's foundation. (Romans 15:20)*

From an early age, William Carey (1761–1834) had a heart ablaze for missions. However, Carey lived before missionary societies were in vogue. When he shared his passion for missions with ministers, Dr. Ryland shouted, "Young man, sit down; when God pleases to convert the heathen, He will do it without your aid or mine." Despite opposition and ridicule, Carey persisted and spent his life in India where he served as a college professor and saw the Scriptures translated into forty languages.

Carey had a passion like the apostle Paul, who wrote Romans while on his third missionary journey. Considering the mode of travel at that time, Paul was undoubtedly tired. But was he ready to retire? No. Paul had plans. He was writing to the church at Rome, the capital of the Gentile world, because God had set Paul apart as "a minister of Christ Jesus to the Gentiles" (15:16).

Christ has worked through Paul with power, signs, and wonders as he preached the gospel from Jerusalem to Illyricum. He could boast in his accomplishments—but it was what Christ had accomplished through Paul. The apostle had one burning passion—to preach the gospel where it had never been preached before (thereby fulfilling the prophecy of Isaiah 52:15). Paul had not come to Rome because they had already heard the gospel, as had the people in Asia Minor, so Paul determined to go to Spain, the westernmost region of the Mediterranean. There he would proclaim the good news to those who had never heard.

But meanwhile, Paul was on his way to Jerusalem to bring a gift of money from the Macedonian believers to the poor people in Jerusalem. Since the Gentiles were indebted to the Jews for their salvation, they were eager to share their material means with the poor of Jerusalem.

Paul concludes this remarkable letter by greeting numerous people by name (he focused on people) and reminding them to strive together (pictured as wrestling) in prayer for Paul. A concluding question: Do you have a vision for sharing the gospel? You may not need to go around the world—perhaps you need to go across the street and talk to your neighbor.

CONSIDER: *Paul's passion was to preach the gospel where people had never heard of Christ.*

CORINTHIAN CULTURE AND THE CHURCH

1 CORINTHIANS 1:10; 3:1–3; 5:1

*And I, brethren, could not speak to you as to spiritual men, but
as to men of flesh, as to infants in Christ. (1 Corinthians 3:1)*

The church in the city. Does a church affect a city by its presence or does a
city impact the church? Does the lifestyle of a city influence the lifestyle of
a church? This is an important question since urbanization has taken place in
America. The majority of people have moved from a rural setting to an urban
setting—and frequently "gotten lost" in the process. The extended family no
longer affects individuals living in the city.

Corinth was a significant city, situated in a strategic location. It lay on an
isthmus connecting two large bodies of water, some four to six miles wide. Its
high elevation afforded it important protection and for this reason the site was
settled early. The city that Paul knew was relatively new and was well known
for its commerce. "Its location at the head of the Corinthian isthmus gave it
control over the only route for merchandise between the peninsula and the
mainland of Greece" (D. Edmond Hiebert, *Pauline Epistles*).

Because of its location, Corinth was a cosmopolitan city; in addition to
Romans, it hosted Greeks and also Jews engaged in business—as well as a
variety of other nationalities. The city boasted 600,000 to 700,000 people
of whom various accounts report from one-third to two-thirds were slaves.
The city had developed a reputation for moral laxity so that the term "to
Corinthianize" meant "to act like a native Corinthian." "The immorality of
Corinth was fostered by the degrading worship of the goddess Aphrodite,
the goddess of love. In the old city of Corinth, situated on the topmost peak
of Acrocorinthus, was a magnificent temple to this goddess with a thousand
female *Hieroduli* (consecrated prostitutes) for the free use of the visitors to
the temple" (D. Edmond Hiebert, *Pauline Epistles*).

A major problem in the church at Corinth pertained to the city itself. Some
of the new converts had not been able to completely sever their old way of
life. As we will see as we read through Corinthians, there was a divisive spirit
(1:10–17; 3:1–15); immorality existed with incest taking place (5:1–13); and
believers were initiating lawsuits against one another in heathen courts (6:1–
11). Paul addressed numerous issues related to their contact with the culture
in Corinth. The pagan culture had seriously impacted the church at Corinth.
As a result, the church was weak and carnal.

CONSIDER: *The church exists in the world, yet the world is not to be the moral
determinant for believers. Has the world impacted your life in a negative way?*

GOD'S FAITHFULNESS DESPITE HUMAN FACTIONS

1 CORINTHIANS 1:1–17

*God is faithful, through whom you were called into fellowship
with His Son, Jesus Christ our Lord. (1 Corinthians 1:9)*

Although the Corinthian church had severe problems, Paul nonetheless
gives a glowing introduction, reminding them of their status in Christ.
While their lives may not reflect it, they are sanctified, set apart in Christ
and for Christ. Although they may not appear as such, positionally they are
"saints" (1 Cor. 1:2).

Paul is thankful for the Corinthian believers because they had been made
spiritually rich, in speech (outward) and knowledge (inward). This, no doubt,
reflects on their spiritual gifts, which Paul will later discuss. Everything they
needed spiritually had been supplied to them. The result was that they were
"not lacking in any [spiritual] gift" (v. 7). "What saddened Paul was that the
Corinthians had everything in which to do a work for Christ while they waited
for Him, but they had failed to do so" (Robert Gromacki, *Called to Be Saints*).
Paul concludes the introduction by reminding them of God's faithfulness—He
sovereignly called them into fellowship with His Son, Jesus Christ. It is the
ninth time in as many verses that Paul has invoked the name of Christ; it
reflects the centrality of Christ to Paul's message.

Yet, despite their spiritual richness, Paul begins with a rebuke. He appeals
to them and warns them that there should be no divisions in the assembly. It
is a graphic picture. "Divisions" (*schisma*) depicts a tear in a garment. Just as
clothing can be torn, so the local church can be torn apart. Paul exhorts them
to "mend the garment" spiritually by reflecting unity in mind and judgment.
"The unity which Paul desired was a union in faith and love" (Charles Hodge,
1 Corinthians).

But the Corinthians' disunity was real and Paul elaborated on the problem. People from Chloe's household had informed Paul of the quarrels in the
Corinthian church, observed in factions in which some were taking sides,
identifying themselves "of Paul" or "of Apollos" or "of Peter." Paul considered
it shameful and strongly rebuked them: Is Christ divided? Did Paul or Peter
provide their salvation? Were they baptized in Apollos's name? The Corinthians' focus—and ours—ought to be Christ, not men.

CONSIDER: *Despite the riches we enjoy in Christ, it is possible to act in a carnal
manner, creating factions and bringing disunity among believers. Are you guilty
of this?*

FOOLISHNESS OF THE CROSS

1 CORINTHIANS 1:18–31

For the word of the cross is foolishness to those who are perishing, but to us who are being saved it is the power of God. (1 Corinthians 1:18)

"John Derbyshire, journalist, author, and math aficionado, is also the resident skeptic among contributors to *National Revue*. . . . He accuses Christianity of being anti-science. Why? Most religions make supernatural claims, but Christianity establishes itself on a 'historical' event that defies reality, namely the incarnation. We are asked to believe that a human female was impregnated by a nonhuman spirit and gave birth to a God-man. How ridiculous is that?" (*World*, Dec. 27, 2008).

At the outset of today's Scripture reading, Paul delineates two kinds of people: the perishing and the saved. To the perishing the cross is foolishness. But "the unsaved are not perishing because they regard the cross to be foolishness; rather, they treat it with mental disgust because they are already perishing" (Robert Gromacki, *Called to Be Saints*). To the saved, on the other hand, the cross is the power of God in changing lives. The message of the cross changed Corinthians from adulterers, homosexuals, thieves, and drunkards into cleansed, sanctified, justified believers (look ahead to 1 Corinthians 6:9–11). Through the preaching of the cross God renders foolishness the wisdom of the world (1 Cor. 1:20). Worldly wisdom does not change lives; the preaching of the cross brings salvation and changed lives.

Worldly wisdom does not lead people to God. The Jews sought a knowledge of God through signs, basing everything on miracles; hence, they demanded signs from Jesus (see, for example, John 6:30). The Greeks sought wisdom through philosophy. Neither group arrived at a knowledge of God; both Jews and Greeks rejected the simple message of Jesus Christ crucified. But it is precisely in this simple message of Christ crucified that both the power and wisdom of God are manifested.

Not many from the ranks of society's elite—the aristocratic, powerful, and politically influential—are chosen. God confounds the worldly wise by choosing those from the lower ranks of society. What is the point? We can't boast of our status or worldly position before God. Our boasting is in the Lord—and we rejoice at our profound spiritual position. The Christ the world repudiates is our wisdom, righteousness, sanctification, and redemption!

CONSIDER: *Jesus Christ and the message of Him crucified—something the world scorns and repudiates—is the power and wisdom of God to the believer.*

WORLDLY WISDOM VERSUS GOD'S WISDOM

1 CORINTHIANS 2:1–16

But a natural man does not accept the things of the Spirit of God,
for they are foolishness to him; and he cannot understand them,
because they are spiritually appraised. But he who is spiritual
appraises all things. (1 Corinthians 2:14–15)

Recently I spoke to a lady on our street and in the ensuing conversation I was able to share the gospel of Christ with her. She dismissed the gospel, giving no response, but focused on berating one of the political leaders. As I attempted to calm her and talk about spiritual issues, she only continued her anger at a political leader.

In this chapter Paul vigorously contrasts worldly wisdom with God's wisdom. They differ significantly. The tragedy is that believers may become so engrossed in this world's system that they may function by worldly wisdom rather than God's wisdom. That was the problem with the Corinthians. Paul had not come to them with eloquent speech. He came to them amid fear and anxiety—so much so that they were not impressed with Paul (as he will later mention in 2 Corinthians 10:10). But he came with a simple, straightforward message: Jesus Christ, crucified and risen. That was the message that reflected the wisdom of God and the power of God.

Paul's purpose was to ground the Corinthians in the power of God rather than in the wisdom of the world (v. 5). That is the road to spiritual maturity. God's wisdom transcends the wisdom of this world. The wisdom of civil leaders passes away—what they endorse today is changed and gone tomorrow. But God's truth and wisdom are eternal, unrelated to this temporal age. Worldly leaders and philosophers cannot comprehend God's wisdom; it is hidden to them. But what is hidden to the world is revealed to God's people by His Spirit (v. 10). God has given us His Spirit so that the Spirit might teach us the things of God; otherwise, the things of God would be unknown to us.

These are things the "natural man" (v. 14), the unsaved individual, cannot comprehend. They remain foolishness to him because he does not have the Holy Spirit, God's divine Teacher indwelling him. He functions by the old nature. By contrast, "he who is spiritual" is able to appraise all things. He functions and evaluates and appraises all things by the Divine Teacher, the Holy Spirit. And because believers have the indwelling Holy Spirit Paul can exclaim, "we have the mind of Christ."

CONSIDER: *As believers, we have the indwelling Holy Spirit, enabling us to properly appraise life, making sound decisions, enabling us to live pleasing to God. Are you living your life by worldly wisdom or by God's divine wisdom?*

THE CARNAL BELIEVER

1 CORINTHIANS 3:1–17

For no man can lay a foundation other than the one
which is laid, which is Jesus Christ. (1 Corinthians 3:11)

A prominent evangelical church, led by a dynamic preacher, grew to over five thousand members but after the preacher died, the church dwindled to a few hundred. Why? The church was built on the wrong foundation; it was built on a man rather than on Jesus Christ.

Having explained the contrast between a natural man (unsaved) and a spiritual man (saved), Paul delineated a third category: "men of flesh"—a carnal believer. Paul rebuked the Corinthians for not developing spiritually. They were still "fleshly" (*sarkikos*). "Flesh is the outlook orientated toward the self, that which pursues its own ends in self-sufficient independence of God" (Cleon Rogers Jr. and Cleon Rogers III, *The New Linguistic and Exegetical Key to the Greek New Testament*).

The Corinthians' carnal life was evident in their jealousy and fighting. They were envious of one another and in that, they exhibited worldly traits—they were living like ordinary, unsaved individuals. Rather than focusing on Christ, they focused on men. They aligned themselves under human leaders: "I am of Paul" or "I am of Apollos." They had a wrong perspective of these leaders. Paul and Apollos were merely servants through whom the Corinthians had come to faith. The Corinthians had sinned by idolizing human leaders, causing a rupture in Christian unity. Paul explained that he and Apollos planted and watered but it was God who gave the increase. God, not human leaders, was the important one. Three times Paul emphasizes this: We are God's *fellow-workers;* you are God's *field; God's building.*

While the Corinthians were dividing their loyalties and dividing the body of Christ, Paul explains that he and Apollos worked together as one. The Corinthians' focus was wrong; it was on men when it should have been on God. They were building on the wrong foundation.

But there is only one foundation: Christ—and at the judgment seat of Christ the believer's works will be evaluated by fire. If they stand the test, the believer will be rewarded; if they fail the test the believer will be saved but his works will be burned up.

The sobering question is: Am I building on carnal, fleshly, selfish desires or am I led by the Spirit, focusing on God?

CONSIDER: *A carnal heart focuses on men and proves divisive; a spiritual heart focuses on God.*

August 5

SERVANTS

1 CORINTHIANS 3:18–4:5

Let a man regard us in this manner, as servants of Christ and stewards of the mysteries of God. (1 Corinthians 4:1)

Following my graduation from seminary I had accepted a faculty position in another state. I rented a truck and, with my wife and two sons, was prepared to load the U-Haul. The morning of our move, the doorbell rang. Dr. Dwight Pentecost, my professor, stood at the door and asked, "Where is the truck?" Dr. Pentecost spent the day perspiring while loading the truck with the rest of us. He taught me by example the meaning of "servant."

The Corinthian believers had adopted a worldly philosophy in priding themselves in their alignment with men. Paul rebuked them. The Corinthians were absorbed in worldly wisdom but that had only led to strife. It was not the answer. The answer was in becoming a fool (in the eyes of the world) by becoming a Christian. There is a stigma attached to becoming a Christian. Worldly wisdom is ultimately foolishness because God will catch people in their craftiness. "His point is that God knows the thoughts of every man. Nothing can be hid from Him. Moreover, He knows the emptiness of such thoughts" (Leon Morris, *First Epistle of Paul to the Corinthians*). The thoughts of the worldly wise are fruitless. So Paul admonishes the carnality of the Corinthians. They are thinking like non-Christians and it will come to nothing.

Paul draws a conclusion: don't boast or glory in men. It is carnal and sinful to pride oneself on being a follower of a man. Because of Christ, *all* things "belong to" the believers; the teachers, the world, life (Phil. 1:21) and death (1 Cor. 15:55–57), the present and the future. And all believers belong to Christ.

Paul goes on to explain the importance of the ministry and the position of the minister. Ministers are servants (*huperetas*), pictured as an "underrower of a large ship"; hence, it suggested lowly service. Ministers are also stewards (*oikonomoi*), seen as an overseer or administrator of a large estate who would be responsible to give an account to his master for his oversight and faithfulness.

The primary importance of a steward is faithfulness because the lord would examine him and judge him. But Paul warned them not to judge others for the Lord alone can judge the motives of men's hearts—which He will do on the day of judgment.

CONSIDER: *Worldly wisdom looks on the external but godly wisdom recognizes that we belong to Christ and, as such, we are servants, seeking to be found faithful.*

IMITATORS

1 CORINTHIANS 4:6–21

Therefore I exhort you, be imitators of me. (1 Corinthians 4:16)

Growing up in western Canada, we saw a lot of snow. Walking through freshly fallen snow, we made big tracks. I recall trying to follow my brother, who was six years older than me, who made big footprints in the snow. I tried to walk in his steps, but it was difficult. I had to take large steps and then I couldn't fill his footprints.

It is not unusual for us, consciously or unconsciously, to imitate others. We may do it in a variety of ways—and often in the wrong ways. Since the Corinthians were arrogant, aligning themselves in factions dubbed "of Paul," or "of Apollos," Paul sought to show them who they really were. In their worldly philosophy they had become arrogant, puffed up with pride. But how could they boast in their cliques? While they were glorying in self, Paul reminded them that everything they possessed, they had received from God. So what was the legitimacy of their boasting?

Since they were boasting in being of Paul or of Apollos, Paul determined to show them who he and Apollos really were. The Corinthians saw themselves as "already filled," "rich," and "kings." What was the basis of their boasting? Pride. Arrogance. By contrast, Paul shows the apostles are "last of all, as men condemned to death . . . a spectacle to the world" (1 Cor. 4:9). The imagery is from the Roman arena, where those condemned to a public death were a spectacle in the arena. As those identified with the rejected Christ, Paul and the apostles were "fools for Christ's sake" (v. 10). The Corinthians had a high opinion of themselves; Paul had a low opinion of himself. "Before the world, Paul viewed himself and the apostles as nothing, yet the Corinthians prided themselves on their acceptance in the world" (Robert Gromacki, *Called to Be Saints*).

Paul admonished them for their carnal, worldly philosophy and purposed to correct them as a father would his children. He reminded them that he was their father in the gospel and, as a father, he exhorted them to imitate him. This is a strong statement. How should they imitate (*mimetes*) or mimic Paul? In precisely the ways he mentioned: when reviled, he blessed; in persecution, he endured; when slandered, he tried to conciliate. He was a spectacle to the world, a fool for Christ's sake.

CONSIDER: *Are you walking in pride, with a worldly philosophy, or are you living amid rejection by the world as a believer in Jesus Christ?*

DEALING WITH IMMORALITY

1 CORINTHIANS 5:1–13

Do you not judge those who are within the church? . . . REMOVE THE WICKED MAN FROM AMONG YOURSELVES. (1 Corinthians 5:12–13)

Does the culture impact us as Christians? A woman who served as a professor in an evangelical seminary was improperly involved with a male faculty member. They both left the seminary and she ultimately divorced her husband and married a pastor. The church accepted her and the pastor despite their immorality.

Paul had sharp words for the church at Corinth in their acceptance of incest in their assembly. They knew about the sexual sin and yet they did nothing about it; in fact, they prided themselves about it. They had become arrogant about the issue. Paul rebuked them. They were allowing sin in their assembly of such a nature that even the pagan Gentiles did not experience—a man was living with his father's wife—incest. The Old Testament, the rabbis, and Roman law all prohibited such unions (Cleon Rogers Jr. and Cleon Rogers III, *The New Linguistic and Exegetical Key to the Greek New Testament*).

What should they have done? Paul is clear in his answer. They should have mourned over the sin the man perpetrated and then they should have disciplined him by removing him from the church fellowship. The Lord Himself outlined the process in issues like this (Matt. 18:15–19). Paul spoke of the discipline as delivering the man to Satan (1 Cor. 5:5). What does this mean? By excommunicating the man from the fellowship, they would deliver the man into the world, the domain of Satan (1 John 5:19). This was designed to bring the man to repentance so he could be restored to fellowship.

Why was this necessary? Because by permitting the immoral behavior within the assembly, it would spread like a cancer to others: as a bit of leaven affects the whole lump of dough, so this man's behavior would affect others.

Paul warned them not to associate with believers who were living in immorality. Paul was not suggesting they isolate themselves from the world, but that they should separate themselves from believers who were not walking in moral integrity. They had a responsibility: to judge believers within the assembly—not outsiders, but believers. Perhaps this is a distinct failure in the modern evangelical church—the failure to discipline and judge immorality within the church.

CONSIDER: *We must discipline immorality within the church in order to bring the immoral person to repentance.*

August 8

Lawsuit Against a Brother

1 Corinthians 6:1–11

Does any one of you, when he has a case against his neighbor, dare to go to law before the unrighteous and not before the saints? . . . Why not rather be wronged? Why not rather be defrauded? (1 Corinthians 6:1, 7)

My father-in-law was a successful grain farmer. His land produced lush crops. Later in life he decided to rent some of his land to two professing Christians. They worked the land and they too had an excellent crop in the fall. But they refused to pay my father-in-law the rental fee, which amounted to several thousand dollars. When others suggested my father-in-law sue them, he refused. He was a Christian and he walked away from the issue—at a significant personal financial loss.

Should a Christian take another Christian to court? Can one Christian sue another Christian? The believers in Corinth were taking one another to court in lawsuits. Paul rebuked them for this. The issue was that they, as believers, were parading their differences before the world and allowing unbelievers to settle their issues. In his rebuke Paul reminded them of their ignorance: "do you not know . . ." (1 Cor. 6:2–3, 9). Paul reminded them that when Christ returns believers will judge the world and angels. How then could they allow unbelievers to settle their differences in this life? It was a spiritual failure on their part. If they would one day judge the world, why could they not now do the lesser—resolve their differences with other believers? What they were doing was a shame and a spiritual embarrassment. They were looking for a victory in a public court but by their lawsuit against a Christian brother they had already suffered a defeat.

So what should they do? Paul is explicit: "Why not rather be wronged? Why not rather be defrauded?" Paul exhorted them: rather than taking a Christian brother to court in a lawsuit they should rather accept the financial loss or defeat. If they did otherwise, taking their brother to court, *they* were guilty of wronging and defrauding their brother. A serious thought. Jesus taught similarly, telling His hearers that if someone wanted to sue them, they should give him their coat (Matt. 5:40).

Paul concludes with a solemn thought. Why would they go before unbelievers in a court of law when unbelievers will not inherit the kingdom of God? God had rescued them from a sordid past; they were washed, sanctified, and justified. Resorting to unbelievers for help in a case against a brother was a serious spiritual failure.

CONSIDER: *Rather than taking another believer to a public court in a lawsuit, the believer should rather suffer the personal loss.*

IMMORALITY

1 CORINTHIANS 6:12–20

Do you not know that your body is a temple of the Holy Spirit
who is in you, whom you have from God, and that you
are not your own? (1 Corinthians 6:19)

I received an e-mail today from an unknown source, asking if the gay lifestyle was acceptable. He asked what our church taught about homosexuals living together and practicing their lifestyle. From the way the e-mail was worded, it was evident the person was practicing homosexuality and he wanted a confirmation that it was acceptable.

Paul has already discussed the subject of immorality in this letter to the Corinthians (1 Cor. 5:1–13), but now he develops it further. People in the Corinthian church had developed a slogan to cloak their immorality: "all things are lawful for me." They used it as license to live as they pleased. Paul rebuts their statement with the response: "not all things are profitable. . . . I will not be mastered by anything." Apparently the Corinthians assumed that since eating was for the body and yet it was not unlawful, therefore, other physical activity such as immorality was not unlawful; it was just like eating. In the process, they were being mastered by immorality.

Paul condemned their faulty conclusion. One day God would eliminate eating and the need for eating. But Paul reminds them "the body is not for immorality, but for the Lord" (v. 13). The body is not to be abused in immoral sexual activity; rather, it is to honor and glorify the Lord through service for Him.

The apostle shows the paradox: How can they take their bodies, which are members of the body of Christ, and unite them with a prostitute? Paul responds with a resounding negative: "May it never be!" If they indulged in sexual immorality, they were becoming one flesh with the prostitute. But God had reserved that special one-flesh union for a husband and wife in marriage (Gen. 2:24).

Because of the corrupt Corinthian environment Paul warns them, "flee immorality" (1 Cor. 6:18). This sin "strikes at the very roots of man's being. . . . Other sins against the body, e.g. drunkenness or gluttony, involve the use of that which comes from without the body. The sexual appetite rises from within. . . . This has no other purpose than the gratification of the lusts. They are sinful in the excess" (Leon Morris, *First Epistle of Paul to the Corinthians*). Hence, the sobering question I must ask is: Are you keeping your body for the Lord and sexually pure?

CONSIDER: *The body is the temple of the Holy Spirit; it is for the Lord and therefore the believer is to keep the body morally pure.*

MARRIAGE DIRECTIVES

1 CORINTHIANS 7:1–24

But to the married I give instructions, not I, but the Lord, that the wife should not leave her husband (but if she does leave, she must remain unmarried, or else be reconciled to her husband), and that the husband should not divorce his wife. (1 Corinthians 7:10–11)

The American culture assaults the mind of man with a sexual agenda that is evident in every venue. Provocative billboards display their product; print ads and now Internet pop-ups advertise with seductive illustrations; television programming—even baseball and football—run ads that neither children nor adults should watch. We are bombarded with sexual motifs everywhere.

So how should we live, faced with a sex-saturated culture? Paul tells the Corinthians that since people have a propensity for sexual immorality, it is appropriate for a man and woman to marry. Within the context of marriage a husband and wife can fulfill their sexual obligations and needs. In fact, they should not deprive each other sexually unless they do it by agreement, for a brief time, for prayer. Otherwise, Satan will entice them to sin through immorality to fulfill their lusts.

In this chapter, Paul will remind them that it is good for the unmarried and widows to remain single so they can single-mindedly serve the Lord; yet, it is also acceptable for them to marry if they desire. But if believers marry, the wife should not leave her husband. If she does, she is to remain unmarried or else be reconciled to her husband. Those are the only options. And the husband is not to leave [divorce] his wife. The command is clear: a believing husband and wife are not to divorce.

In a mixed marriage, where a believer has an unbelieving wife, he is not to send her away, nor is a believing wife to send an unbelieving husband away. Yet, when the unbelieving one leaves, the believer is not under bondage.

What then? Paul provides an overarching principle relating to single/married, slave/free: "Each one is to remain with God in that condition in which he was called" (1 Cor. 7:24; see also vv. 17, 20). Contrary to our culture, God calls us to permanence in our marriage. Are you committed to doing what's necessary to make that a reality in your marriage?

CONSIDER: *God's plan for marriage is one man and one woman for life; the couple should remain together.*

FOCUSED: SINGLE OR MARRIED

1 CORINTHIANS 7:25–40

It is good for a man to remain as he is. Are you bound to a wife?
Do not seek to be released. Are you released from a wife?
Do not seek a wife. (1 Corinthians 7:26–27)

I know several men and women who have volitionally chosen to remain single for the sake of ministry. Some have been college and seminary professors, training many people for ministry. Some have written books. Some have been active in missionary work overseas, giving their lives for significant ministry that has changed the lives of many people. How did this happen? They *chose* to stay single to serve the Lord in a significant way.

Paul speaks to both men and women in this passage but he begins by addressing women ("virgins") in verse 25. Christ did not address this issue but Paul gives his advice on the matter. In view of the present time—viewing the entire age between the first and second comings of Christ, a stressful, calamitous time—it is best for one not to marry. Why? Because they will be diverted from the singular focus of serving Christ. So he counsels the believer to remain in his present situation. Is he married? Remain married. Is he single? Stay single. Yet if a single person marries, they have not sinned but they will experience difficulties in this present life. The single person can give "undistracted devotion to the Lord" (1 Cor. 7:35) while the married believer will have divided loyalties because he will seek to please his wife. Yet in summary, Paul gives a strong reminder that the wife is bound in marriage to her husband as long as he lives. They are not to divorce. Marriage is permanent.

In either case, their focus should not be on this life because "the form of this world is passing away" (v. 31). "All that makes up the present world, the pomp, splendor, form of government, state, condition" it is all passing away (Cleon Rogers Jr. and Cleon Rogers III, *The New Linguistic and Exegetical Key to the Greek New Testament*). The believer doesn't set his or her hope on this world.

So how should the believer live in a world that is passing away? Because of the brevity of time, "believers should not be preoccupied with earthly circumstances. They should not permit the life of this world to determine and control their spiritual development (Heb. 11:13–16, 24–26)" (Robert Gromacki, *Called to Be Saints*). The point is that the world is not to control our thinking, life, and service for the Lord.

CONSIDER: *A single person can give undistracted devotion to the Lord; nonetheless, single or married, the believer should live to please the Lord since this world is passing away.*

A STUMBLING BLOCK

1 CORINTHIANS 8:1–13

*Take care that this liberty of yours does not somehow
become a stumbling block to the weak. (1 Corinthians 8:9)*

One Sunday morning after the worship service in a church I formerly attended, I started to talk to one of the leaders in the church. He stopped me while I was in mid-sentence and said, "I can't talk to you now. I'm going to the football game." And he left. I was surprised. He didn't want to talk to a fellow Christian because he was in a hurry to go to an NFL game. Is it wrong to go to an NFL game on Sunday? This is a question that falls into the "gray area" of Christian living. There are numerous questions we have on issues that are not black-and-white—questions for which we don't have a clear answer. Stealing, lying, adultery—these are issues clearly prohibited by Scripture. But in this chapter Paul speaks of questionable areas, as he also did in Romans 14, and he provides us with some principles.

The question confronting the Corinthian believers was whether it was acceptable to eat meat that was sacrificed to pagan idols. After the offering, some of the meat was sold in the public marketplace. Was it acceptable to eat this meat? The Corinthians had the knowledge that the idols were not gods; there is but one God. They recognized the Father, the source of all things and believers exist for Him and they realized there is only one Lord—Jesus Christ through whom believers have their very existence.

So they had freedom to eat the meat offered to an idol. Yet this knowledge could cause pride on their part. Paul pinpoints the key issue: love. Love for God and love for others—and love for others should prevent them from causing others to stumble. Some, having a background in idolatry, saw this differently. Because of their past, they saw this nonmoral issue as a moral issue—as sin—and they "stumbled" when another believer ate meat that had been offered to idols. These believers were not better before God by abstaining from eating this meat. But Paul provided a principle to the stronger believer who had freedom to eat: don't become a stumbling block to other believers. Otherwise the weak believer sees the one eating the meat and he is spiritually ruined. Hence, what is a nonmoral issue becomes sin when we make a believer stumble.

Returning to the opening story, was the church leader in error when he rushed off to the game? Attending the game on a Sunday wasn't the issue; the problem lay in his refusal to talk with a fellow believer. In the church age we are not under the Law, but it is possible for us to abuse the liberty that we have in Christ.

CONSIDER: *A believer may be involved in a nonmoral issue that causes a weak believer to stumble and thereby the nonmoral issue becomes sin. Are you doing something to cause a fellow believer to stumble spiritually?*

THE SERVANT'S RIGHTS

1 CORINTHIANS 9:1–14

*So also the Lord directed those who proclaim the gospel to
get their living from the gospel. (1 Corinthians 9:14)*

I once heard a man suggest that a church should have a collection jar in the foyer. Whatever money was in the jar was what the pastor should receive for his income and livelihood. That may sound humorous but the individual was serious! Should pastors receive a regular income for their ministry? Paul addresses this issue.

The Corinthian believers had challenged Paul's rights, even questioning his apostleship—which he capably defended (2 Cor. 12:12). Now Paul defended his rights in Christian liberty concerning nonmoral issues, beginning his defense with a series of questions—all expecting an affirmative answer. In his defense he was reminding the Corinthians of his legitimate apostleship—he had seen the Lord (described in Acts 9:1–9).

Paul defended his rights in Christian liberty by referring to the basics: the right to eat and drink, the right to take along a wife, and the right to refrain from working in order to serve in the ministry. Paul had the right (*exousian*; same word translated "liberty" in 1 Cor. 8:9). It appeared that only Paul and Barnabas refrained from receiving remuneration for their work in the churches.

Paul questioned the validity of their challenges concerning him receiving money from the churches. A soldier didn't serve at his own expense; an orchardist ate the fruit from his vineyard; a shepherd drank the milk from the flock. The point was pertinent: by working in the church he should receive remuneration from the church.

But what did the Scriptures say? Paul pointed to the Mosaic Law where the Lord said, "You shall not muzzle the ox while he is threshing" (1 Cor. 9:9; Deut. 25:4). Paul reminded them that the main focus was not oxen—it meant that God's servants should be paid for their service. Was it not reasonable that one who taught them the Word of God would also receive material benefits? Again, Paul reminded them of the Old Testament priests who served in the temple—they received the material benefits. So Paul concludes "the Lord directed those who proclaim the gospel to get their living from the gospel" (v. 14). Nonetheless, Paul reminds them, "we did not use this right" so that the furtherance of the gospel would not be hindered.

CONSIDER: *God has ordained that those who serve in the ministry should receive remuneration from the ministry.*

The Servant's Discipline

1 Corinthians 9:15–27

*I have become all things to all men, so that I may
by all means save some. (1 Corinthians 9:22)*

The world of television viewers watched awestruck as American Michael Phelps won a record-setting eight gold medals at the Summer Olympics in Beijing, China, in 2008. How did Phelps do it? His powerful arms slicing through the water, his focus and energy to the very end, told the story. Discipline of his body. Serious discipline.

In the ministry, Paul exercised discipline. Paul set aside his rights in living off the gospel even though he preached the gospel and had that right. Because he was not financially obligated to the Corinthians, they had no right to question his motives. His only motive was to preach the gospel and he did this voluntarily, without charge. He knew that he would have his reward from the Lord. While Paul had the right to expect remuneration, he chose to forgo it—his reward was simply in offering the gospel for free. "Paul's pay is that he preaches the gospel as a servant for no pay" (Cleon Rogers Jr. and Cleon Rogers III, *The New Linguistic and Exegetical Key to the Greek New Testament*).

Although Paul was a Roman citizen, functionally he made himself a slave to all so that he might win more people to faith in Christ. Although Paul (and all New Testament believers) was not under the Law of Moses (Rom. 6:14), he put himself under the Law so that he might win the Jews. To the Gentiles, he exhibited freedom from the Law and did not put the constraints of the Law on them. Yet, he himself was "under the law of Christ," meaning Paul had "the intimacy of a relation and union established in the loyalty of a will devoted to Christ" (D. Edmond Hiebert, *Pauline Epistles*).

Paul pictures his life in Olympian language. He runs a disciplined race, as in the Olympics, knowing that only the winner receives a prize. He boxes, not merely beating the air; he disciplines his body, lest, like a losing Olympian, he is disqualified in the race of life.

Paul had a purpose. He had become all things to all men that he might by all means save some. This is a sobering thought. What is reflected in my life? Do I live for myself? For selfish, self-centered purposes? Or do I live out of consideration for the lost, that by my disciplined life there will be no obstacles for them—and, as a result, some will come to faith in Christ?

CONSIDER: *Paul lived a disciplined life so that he could impact Jews and Gentiles alike, so that there would be no stumbling block to their salvation.*

TEMPTED TO SIN

1 CORINTHIANS 10:1–13

---

*No temptation has overtaken you but such as is common to man;
and God is faithful, who will not allow you to be tempted beyond what
you are able, but with the temptation will provide the way of escape also,
so that you will be able to endure it. (1 Corinthians 10:13)*

A professor in a Christian college invited a young female student to live in his home. Soon the professor began a polygamous, immoral relationship in his home. He tried to justify it by appealing to David's multiple wives. It wasn't long before his home, his life, and his ministry were destroyed.

Can a believer fall into heinous sin? Yes. Did the Israelites who had been redeemed and rescued out of Egypt fall into sin? Yes. Paul rehearses their privileged position. God had protected them from the Egyptians, safely leading them by a pillar of cloud (Exod. 13:21). He brought them safely through the Red Sea while the Egyptians drowned (Exod. 14:22). He fed them with manna, a supernatural food (Exod. 16:4). In the desert God provided water from the rock for them (Exod. 17:6), and the rock prefigured Christ, who would give them supernatural drink whereby they would never thirst (as Jesus teaches in John 6:35).

Yet they failed. And they sinned. God judged them by death in the wilderness, setting them as an example or "type" (*tupoi*) for us, a warning for us to sit up and take notice. Israel's failure in the past is a lesson for Christians in the present "so that we would not crave evil things" (1 Cor. 10:6). Israel's history is a serious reminder that God hates sin. He does not take it lightly; He does not overlook it. When the Israelites became idolaters and committed immorality, God judged them in death. And grumbling and complaining? Yes, that too is sin! God hates sin!

We should learn from Israel's history and evil practices. They are lessons for us—negative lessons that contain a warning. God hasn't changed; He still hates sin. And, since pride can cause us to think we can't fall, we are warned "let him who thinks he stands take heed that he does not fall" (v. 12).

But there is a strong word of encouragement. God does not allow believers to be tested beyond their capability to resist and conquer the temptation. He is faithful. He provides the spiritual way out of our dilemma.

CONSIDER: *God takes sin seriously and He is faithful, having provided the spiritual resources to give us victory over temptation.*

FELLOWSHIP WITH DEMONS?

1 CORINTHIANS 10:14–11:1

Whether, then, you eat or drink or whatever you do,
do all to the glory of God. (1 Corinthians 10:31)

A Christian missionary to the far east was invited by a Buddhist to join him in a fellowship meal in the Buddhist temple. The Christian accepted. Was it biblically right for the Christian to eat a meal in the Buddhist temple?

Paul was writing to believers living among unbelievers where pagan, idolatrous worship was taking place. How should believers relate to this? In speaking to this, "Paul wanted to demonstrate that participation in the pagan feasts within the temple actually was a misuse of Christian liberty and really involved them in fellowship with the evil world of demons" (Robert Gromacki, *Called to Be Saints*). This is a strong statement, yet it is true. In 1 Corinthians 10:16, Paul reminds them that in the Lord's Supper, the cup is a sharing (*koinonia*), a fellowship in the blood of Christ; the bread is a sharing (*koinonia*), a fellowship in the body of Christ.

What then is the effect of eating in a pagan temple? It is sharing (*koinonous* = same word) fellowship with demons (v. 20). Since Gentiles sacrifice to idols, they are really sacrificing to demons. If, then, a Christian joins the pagan in the event, the Christian is fellowshiping with demons. And the believer can't do both—fellowship with Christ and fellowship with demons (v. 21). The Lord is jealous for His people and for singular, loyal worship to Him. Israel had provoked the Lord to jealousy in the Old Testament and these believers were on the verge of provoking the Lord as well.

The Corinthians said, "All things are lawful" but Paul responded "not all things are profitable . . . not all things edify" (v. 23; also see 6:12). He reminds them not to seek their own good, but the good of the other believers. Paul illustrates this: if an unbeliever invites them to dinner and then someone says the meat they are about to eat has been sacrificed to idols, to avoid harming the believer who told him, he should avoid eating it.

Paul concludes with the principle: whatever we do, it should be for God's glory, not for selfish reasons. We should not offend either fellow believers or unbelievers. This means that I cannot live for myself; I live my life in consideration of others.

CONSIDER: *Whatever we do in the realm of nonmoral issues should not be a stumbling block to other believers but should be for the glory of God.*

Headship and Interdependence

1 Corinthians 11:2–16

Christ is the head of every man, and the man is the head of a woman, and God is the head of Christ. (1 Corinthians 11:3)

On an Easter Sunday edition, a newspaper carried remarks from women who enjoyed wearing hats to church. They commented: "When you're wearing a hat, you feel like you own the world." "I love coming to church, and you get so many ideas about hats. People admire your hat; you admire their hat." "I think hats make a woman look more distinguished. I don't go any Sunday without wearing a hat."

These comments indicate the biblical meaning of a woman's head covering is lost in today's use of the hat. But Paul begins by teaching the functional authority: God is the head of Christ, Christ is the head of man, and man is the head of woman. The key word is "head" (*kephale*). Feminists have argued that *kephale* means source in order to teach that man is simply the source of the woman. However, this creates a heretical teaching, inferring that God is the source of Christ—which would mean Christ had a beginning. That would deny His deity, destroying His person and His work.

Paul is referring to function. Within the Godhead, Christ, the God-Man, submits to the authority of the Father, but Christ is no less deity. Similarly, in marriage, the woman submits to the man in function but spiritually they are equal (as Paul clearly teaches in Galatians 3:28). Paul's statement does not denigrate the position of the woman.

When praying or prophesying, a man was not to have his head covered. Having the head covered was a sign of subjection to authority. Conversely, if the woman removed the veil covering her head in the assembly, it was a sign that she was not under the authority of her husband. If she refused to wear the veil, then Paul said she should have her head shorn like a prostitute or slave.

What was the significance? Paul takes the discussion back to creation. Man was created in the image and glory of God; the woman was created for the glory of man. And the woman was created for man, not man for the woman. Yet, before God, neither is independent and both are spiritually equal.

This text is a reminder of the distinct function of the man and woman (just as Christ and the Father), yet also of the interdependence of man and woman—in function they need each other and spiritually they are equal before God.

CONSIDER: *God has established man as the head of the woman in function, yet spiritually they are equal before God.*

OBSERVING THE LORD'S SUPPER

1 CORINTHIANS 11:17–34

The Lord Jesus in the night in which He was betrayed took bread; and when He had given thanks, He broke it and said, "This is My body, which is for you; do this in remembrance of Me." In the same way He took the cup also after supper, saying, "This cup is the new covenant in My blood; do this, as often as you drink it, in remembrance of Me." (1 Corinthians 11:23–25)

Unquestionably, my most memorable participation in the Lord's Supper was in Jerusalem. It was an emotional time. We were sitting in the actual city where Jesus inaugurated the Lord's Supper—Jerusalem. It was special for us as we prayed and meditated in the city where Jesus atoned for our sins on the cross, making our salvation possible.

Paul begins today's Scripture passage with a thesis statement (11:17) that he's going to address over the next several chapters, admonishing the Corinthians for both their carelessness in taking the Lord's Supper (11:17–34) and their confusion about spiritual gifts (chs. 12–14). When the Corinthians gathered for the Lord's Supper it resulted in factions. The early church gathered to eat a meal together first (known as the Agape Feast), which was then followed by the Lord's Supper. But some among them were poor and had little to eat, while others ate sumptuously, resulting in divisiveness in the church. Paul rebuked them. Speaking primarily to the wealthy, he admonished them—they should have eaten at home. By gorging themselves in the church fellowship they showed disdain for the poor among them.

This was serious. Paul rehearsed the Lord's Supper: Jesus Himself instituted it, breaking the bread and reminding them, "This is My body, which is for you." He gave His body as a sacrifice for believers on the cross. Similarly, the cup represented His blood shed for sins, initiating the new covenant. When they participated in the Lord's Supper they were to look back, remembering His substitutionary atonement on their behalf.

But first they were to examine themselves to see if they were spiritually prepared to participate. They needed to confess sin and make sure they were in right relationship with other believers. If they were alienated from fellowship with other believers, that would first need to be resolved. Failure to do this was serious—it would bring judgment from God. In fact, God had already judged some in their midst with sickness and death (1 Cor. 11:30). To avert this, self-judgment was necessary before participating in the Lord's Supper.

CONSIDER: *The Lord's Supper, remembering the Lord's substitutionary atonement for us, should be taken seriously, with self-examination and reconciliation with fellow believers.*

Sovereignly Given Spiritual Gifts

1 Corinthians 12:1–11

But one and the same Spirit works all these things, distributing to each one individually just as He wills. (1 Corinthians 12:11)

The health and wealth movement is a highly controversial group with serious deviation from biblical teaching. One of their leaders has written that if Jesus was a firstborn, there must have been a second born and a third born. In other words, Jesus was not unique. He claims a similar position to Jesus. He said when he reads that Jesus said, "I AM," he says, "Yes, and I am too!" He claims that believers are "little gods."

Paul begins by reminding the Corinthians of their pagan past when they worshiped idols. It was not simply dead stones they were worshiping; they were being led astray by Satan. This was evidenced when some cursed Jesus. The Spirit of God would never lead them to curse Jesus; on the contrary, only the Spirit of God would lead them to confess the unique deity of Christ.

Now Paul reminds them of the diversity of spiritual gifts, invoking the Trinity in the process, mentioning the Spirit (v. 4), the Lord (Jesus; v. 5), and God (the Father; v. 6). The triune God brought variety as well as diversity to the gifts believers possess. Then Paul emphasizes that spiritual gifts are given "to each one." No one is exempt. Every believer has one or more spiritual gifts. Moreover, the gifts are not to arouse jealousy; they are given "for the common good" (v. 7), meaning spiritual gifts should be advantageous, bringing believers together to profit them all.

Paul delineated some of the gifts. Some had the "word of wisdom," signifying receiving direct revelation from God; "word of knowledge" was receiving direct revelation and teaching the people; "faith" was also a unique gift even though all are called to walk by faith. Bible scholars believe that gifts such as healing, miracles, prophecy, tongues, and interpretation of tongues were restricted to the apostolic era to validate the message of Christ before the canon of Scripture was fully written and compiled.

The Holy Spirit was the One giving the gifts to each individual believer "just as He wills." The believer does not have the right nor the ability to chose a gift. They are sovereignly given by the Holy Spirit to build up the body of believers.

CONSIDER: *The Holy Spirit has sovereignly given every believer one or more spiritual gifts. Have you discovered your gift(s) and are you using it for the good of the body of Christ?*

MANY MEMBERS, ONE BODY

1 CORINTHIANS 12:12–31

*For by one Spirit we were all baptized into one body, whether
Jews or Greeks, whether slaves or free, and we were all
made to drink of one Spirit. (1 Corinthians 12:13)*

After the Lord suddenly and unexpectedly took my wife to heaven, I thought God brought me to Idlewild Baptist Church for such a time as this. The people rallied around me, loved me, helped me—showed me the love of Christ and the unity of the body of Christ. I never learned to cook and over the course of two years the people either took me to dinner or brought me food nearly three hundred times! I have seen the love of Christ and the unity of the body caring for one another in countless ways. This is a picture of the one body.

No matter what our background may be—English, German, African American, Latino, Asian—we have all been placed into one body—the body of Christ. We are one! We belong to Christ and we belong to each other. We all have the identifying seal of the Holy Spirit.

Paul illustrates the unity of the body with the human body. The foot is as important as the hand and the ear is as important as the eye. It would be difficult to drive our car without one of these members: We need the foot to hit the accelerator, the hand to hold the steering wheel, the eye to see the traffic, the ear to listen for a siren. The body functions in unity and so does the body of Christ. Every member of the human body is important and every member of the body of Christ is important. Even those members that are not visibly displayed—all are important.

That produces a warning: there should be "no division in the body" (1 Cor. 12:25). Why? Because if one member suffers, all suffer. One of our men has pancreatic cancer and we have rallied around him. We share his hurt; we suffer with him. That is the body of Christ.

Paul concludes by reminding us that God has appointed leaders in the body—apostles, prophets, and teachers—and then distributed other spiritual gifts. We all differ in our giftedness, and we should not covet other believers' gifts. However, he reminds us to "desire the greater gifts" (v. 31), that is, in the assembly we should emphasize the primary gifts of pastor and teacher (also see Ephesians 4:11–13). The challenge, then, is for each of us to function according to our giftedness to promote the unity of the body.

CONSIDER: *God has uniquely gifted each of us to produce maturity and unity of the body of believers in Christ. What are you doing to promote the unity of the body?*

August 21

THE GREATEST OF THESE

1 CORINTHIANS 13:1–13

[Love] bears all things, believes all things, hopes all things, endures all things. . . . But now faith, hope, love, abide these three; but the greatest of these is love. (1 Corinthians 13:7, 13)

We watched Jerry as he brought his wife to church, as they sat up front together. She had Alzheimer's disease and it wasn't easy for him, having to help dress her and assist her with mundane things. Then the time came when she couldn't even feed herself so Jerry sat with her throughout the day, taking care of her, feeding her, helping her in everything pertaining to the ordinary things in life. Why? Jerry loved his wife.

This chapter is sandwiched between two chapters dealing with spiritual gifts. Why? It reminds us that our gifts, our ministry should be enshrouded in love. It also provokes us to remember that love is central, superior, and permanent; gifts are temporary.

The Corinthians quarreled about the primacy of certain spiritual gifts so Paul begins by striking at the heart of the Corinthian controversy: tongues. He reminds them that the one speaking in tongues but devoid of love is only a noisy gong or a loud cymbal as in heathen worship. Similarly, one having the highly regarded gift of prophecy, having all knowledge and all faith but devoid of love is "an absolute zero" (A. T. Robertson, *Word Pictures of the New Testament*). It is even possible to feed the poor and be a martyr, and yet fail to love. A life lived without love is without profit.

What is love? Love is patient and long-suffering; it does not quickly retaliate when opposed or confronted. Love is gracious, reflecting kindness toward others, serving others. Love doesn't boast, isn't puffed up in arrogance.

Love is unique. Love looks at the other person, not self. Hence, love protects others, covering for them; love patiently bears with difficulties, love endures amid the most trying circumstances. *Love never fails—everything else does.* Even the high profile gifts like prophecy and tongues will pass away, but not love. Love endures.

This passage is a sober reminder of the primacy of love. Do I exemplify love amid the crises of life? Do I display love when I am harshly treated? Is love at the *core* of my life?

CONSIDER: *Love is of greater importance than the greatest spiritual gifts. It is primary in our daily lives. Is love seen in your associations with others?*

BIBLICAL TONGUES

1 CORINTHIANS 14:1–25

*So then tongues are for a sign, not to those who believe
but to unbelievers. (1 Corinthians 14:22)*

A missionary who had studied foreign languages and was able to diagram the sounds of foreign languages and categorize them even though he didn't know them, attended a session where people would be "speaking in tongues" and recorded it. When he attempted to diagram the tongues into a foreign language, it failed to exhibit language structure. He concluded the "tongues" being spoken was not a language; it was simply gibberish.

Paul has sharp, instructive words to the Corinthians who were abusing speaking in tongues. He began by reminding them of their erroneous practice. By speaking in tongues they were indulging in the babbling common in idol worship. As a result, they were edifying themselves (falsely) and not the church.

Rather than speaking in tongues, Paul urged them to emphasize teaching in the assembly; otherwise, there was no profit. Tongues was like the indistinct sound of a bugle—no one would understand—and Paul wanted them to understand God's truth. And that occurred only through normal speaking, not pagan tongues. Paul reminded them it is better to speak five words that can be understood than ten thousand words that can't be understood. The focus was on their maturity; when they focused on tongues, they were reflecting immaturity.

What then was the purpose of tongues? Paul quotes Isaiah 28:11 to remind them that as the Jewish people heard the foreign Babylonian language when the Babylonians invaded Judah, the foreign language was a sign of judgment. Similarly, foreign languages spoken in the assembly were a sign to unbelieving Jews who knew the prophecy of Isaiah 28 that God was doing a work in their midst. But if Gentiles, who did not know Isaiah 28, came into the assembly and heard the foreign languages being spoken, they would think the people were crazy (1 Cor. 14:23).

It is evident, then, that tongues was a sign for Jewish people, foreign languages used as an evangelistic tool for the Jews who knew the Old Testament. In the book of Acts, every occurrence of tongues is in the presence of Jewish people (Acts 10:28, 46; 19:6). Tongues was a sign to the Jews that Gentiles also received the Spirit and it was a sign to the Gentiles that authority came from the Jews.

CONSIDER: *Biblical tongues are languages used as an evangelistic tool during the first century.*

August 23

SPEAKING IN TONGUES

1 CORINTHIANS 14:26–40

If anyone speaks in a tongue, it should be by two or at the most three, and each in turn, and one must interpret; but if there is no interpreter, he must keep silent in the church. . . . The women are to keep silent in the churches. (1 Corinthians 14:27–28, 34)

When I was working in architecture, there was a fellow draftsman who was also a Pentecostal deacon. He was a fine Christian man and we had good fellowship. One day we discussed the issue of tongues and I mentioned the directives that Scripture gives in this section. He chuckled and exclaimed, "Oh, we break those all the time!"

The Corinthian church was chaotic not only in the manifestation of tongues but in their assemblies. Paul rebuked them. When they gathered, one had a psalm, another a teaching, a revelation, a tongue—there was confusion. Paul warned them: "Let all things be done for edification" (1 Cor. 14:26). Hence, when tongues were in use, there was to be order. There should be no more than three speaking in tongues and they were to speak in turn; there had to be an interpreter, and if there was no interpreter, there was to be silence; and women were not allowed to speak in tongues (vv. 27–28, 34). These are the biblical directives.

Prophets, too, were given restrictions—a reminder once more of the chaos in the Corinthian church. (Prophecy involved receiving direct revelation from God—another gift that ceased when the canon of Scripture was complete. Nothing is being added to Scripture.) Only two or three were permitted to speak; those with discerning of spirits were to judge them; they were to prophesy in order.

Women were to keep silent in the church. In the context, it indicates they were not to speak in tongues or prophesy in the regular meetings. It may also refer to asking questions in a public context. However, women were permitted to pray and prophesy (look back at 1 Cor. 11:5), probably in a nonformal situation.

Paul cited these directives because of the confusion in the Corinthian church; he affirmed that God is not a God of confusion (v. 33). Although the sign gifts of the first century are no longer in use today, these Scriptures are still a serious application for all that we practice in the local church today. Is there confusion in the church? Chaos? Is everything done decently and in order so that it is God-honoring?

CONSIDER: *God is not a God of confusion, but of peace.*

THE RESURRECTION OF CHRIST

1 CORINTHIANS 15:1–19

If Christ has not been raised, your faith is worthless;
you are still in your sins. (1 Corinthians 15:17)

A prominent Episcopal bishop exclaimed, "It wouldn't hurt my faith if they found the bones of Jesus." Ironically, this bishop who denied the bodily resurrection of Christ decided to write about the life of Christ. To research, he traveled to Israel and took an excursion into the desert. His car broke down, and then he and his wife separated to look for help. When a search party finally found him, he was lying dead in the desert.

The fundamentals of the Christian faith—including the resurrection of Christ—continue to be attacked. In this crucial chapter, Paul provides a clear statement of the gospel. The gospel is that Christ died for our sins, that He was buried, and that He was raised on the third day. That is the gospel. One evangelical said we only need to ask people to believe in Jesus; we don't need to mention His death and resurrection. But is that what this passage teaches? Paul said this is "the gospel . . . by which also you are saved" (vv. 1–2). What is the gospel? That Jesus died for our sins, was buried, and rose from the dead. That is the gospel. Nothing more; nothing less.

Proclaiming the resurrection is crucial. The Christian faith is based on a historical event—Jesus Christ, who was crucified and died, and then rose bodily from the grave. It is a historical fact. Numerous witnesses testify to that fact: Peter, the Twelve, five hundred believers, James, the apostles. Hundreds of people saw the resurrected Christ. Even Paul.

Is belief in the resurrection crucial? Absolutely. Yet some Corinthians denied the resurrection. Paul points out the tragic results if Christ did not rise from the dead: their faith is worthless, completely meaningless. In other words, it is a non-faith. Furthermore, then Paul has been a false witness, a liar, since he has been preaching that Christ did rise from the dead. And if Christ was not raised, "you are still in your sins" (v. 17); the sin problem remains unresolved. Paul concludes that if it is only in this life that we have hope in Christ we are to be most pitied. What hopelessness—if Christ was not raised. But praise God—Jesus Christ has risen from the dead!

CONSIDER: *Jesus Christ rose bodily from the grave; the resurrection of Christ is a historical fact and the foundation of the Christian faith.*

THE RESURRECTION OF EVERYONE

1 CORINTHIANS 15:20–34

But now Christ has been raised from the dead, the first
fruits of those who are asleep. (1 Corinthians 15:20)

Since my wife Helen's homegoing to heaven, I have changed the way I witness. Dining in a restaurant, I ask, "May I tell you a story?" Then I tell the waitress about the good marriage I had and that, although I live with a broken heart, Jesus has resolved our problem. He atoned for our sins on the cross and He rose from the dead. Because of that, I will be reunited with my wife—all because of the resurrection of Christ.

No secular philosophy has a response to the resurrection of Christ. It is a historical fact. In contrast to the preceding section, Paul begins with an exclamatory statement: "*But now* Christ has been raised from the dead." Christ is the solution to the greatest human dilemma: death. As Adam brought sin and death into the human race, so Christ has brought life to all humanity, some to everlasting joy and some to everlasting punishment.

But there is an order to the resurrections. Paul presents a military picture of a body of troops according to their ranking. Christ is "the first fruits," meaning He is the first in the order of resurrections. Next to be resurrected are those at Christ's coming (*parousia*), the resurrection of the church age believers at the rapture (described in 1 Thessalonians 4:13–18). Old Testament saints and tribulation saints will be resurrected at the second coming of Christ (Rev. 20:4). "Then comes the end" (v. 24) anticipates the third phase of the resurrections, which sees the unsaved of all ages resurrected after the millennial kingdom reign.

Revelation 20 depicts these end-time events. At the second coming, Christ will establish His millennial reign as king over all the earth; everyone will be subject to Christ. At the end of the millennium, He will put down Satan's final rebellion and then, with finality, death will forever be abolished. The unsaved dead will be raised to face Christ at the great white throne judgment. Then, all will be subject to Christ in His rule in the eternal kingdom on the new earth.

This blessed truth ought to be a motivator for holy living. Worldliness and wrong thinking will deter believers from this central, motivating, and real hope.

CONSIDER: *Everyone will one day be resurrected from the dead; the righteous to everlasting life and the unbelieving to everlasting punishment.*

A NEW BODY OF POWER AND GLORY

1 CORINTHIANS 15:35–57

This perishable must put on the imperishable, and this mortal must put on immortality. . . . Thanks be to God, who gives us the victory through our Lord Jesus Christ. (1 Corinthians 15:53, 57)

Joe Louis was one of the greatest heavyweight boxing champions. He defended his title twenty-five times while reigning as champion for twelve years. Yet at the end of his boxing career second-rate fighters were defeating him. And his life took a downward turn from there. The weakness and frailty of his declining body became evident—and so it is with everyone. We await the resurrection for the restoration of our bodies.

Paul admonished the Corinthian skeptics concerning the resurrection. They were trying to make sense of the resurrection in relation to their present bodies, and he explained that the resurrection body was different. When a kernel of wheat was sown, a stalk of wheat would spring forth. And even among earthly bodies, there are differences: humans, animals, birds, and fish—each group is distinct.

So Paul draws a distinction between our present earthly body and our resurrection body. The present body is perishable, subject to corruption and decay. But the resurrection body is imperishable, not subject to decay or control by sin. The present body is sown in dishonor, in humiliation and weakness, but it is raised in glory and power. As Christ's body radiated glory, so the believer's body will be raised in the image of Christ's body, reflecting glory (Phil. 3:21) and power. The body enters the grave a natural body, subject to death and decay; the resurrection body is raised a spiritual body, meaning it is never again subject to death—yet it remains a corporeal body, a body of flesh and bones. The resurrection body will never tire, never weaken, never diminish in strength. It won't age, hair won't turn gray, skin won't sag, the mind will never lose memory—the resurrection body will be eternally perfect.

At the rapture these mortal bodies will be transformed to immortality in a moment (in the twinkling of an eye, as quick as one can cast a glance) as the trumpet calls church age believers to Christ (1 Thess. 4:16). God's people will no longer be subject to death—the sting is gone. Christ has given us the victory! This most glorious truth should forever be an intensely motivating force in our lives to steadfastness and persistent faithfulness because we know the glorious future that awaits us!

CONSIDER: *Christ has won the victory over sin and death whereby we will forever enjoy an imperishable, resurrection body of power.*

Personal Plans

Be on the alert, stand firm in the faith, act like men, be strong.
Let all that you do be done in love. (1 Corinthians 16:13–14)

Although I was just a young boy when my father died, I treasure the letters that he wrote my mother and the rest of us from his hospital bed. My father normally had wise words of instruction and commendation for all of us. Best of all, he expressed his love for us, calling my mother, *"Mein Schatz"*— "My Treasure!" What a blessing to read those letters.

As Paul concluded his letter to the Corinthians he had a number of personal items to share with them. But first, he instructed them concerning giving— a needed instruction that Paul included in both letters. He reminded them to set aside money on the first day of the week, that is, Sunday, as God had prospered them in business, that they would be ready to give to Paul when he came to Corinth. The collection was for the poor people in Jerusalem, which Paul would bring to them. Agabus had foretold a famine that would come (Acts 11:27–30). Christians especially will have suffered because of hatred toward them. Since Jerusalem was where Christianity had begun, it was important for the Gentile churches to show their love for the believers in Jerusalem.

Paul expressed his love for the Corinthians, wanting to visit them on his way to the Macedonian churches. In fact, Paul would consider visiting them for the entire winter. Yet Paul reminded them that he would be spending time in Ephesus and, while a door for effective service had opened for him there, the opposition was strong. This is a reminder that while we labor success- fully for the Lord, the enemy is actively opposing the ministry. We can expect opposition.

Paul exhorted the Corinthians to treat Timothy well if he should come to them—knowing that some among the Corinthians could create difficulties for him. Yet he was doing the Lord's work and they should not despise him. In fact, they should recognize and honor and be subject to those men that served in the ministry (1 Cor. 16:15–18).

In summary, Paul exhorted them to be on the alert—no doubt concerning moral issues—and to stand strong in the faith, because they had a tendency to laxity. "Maranatha!" ("O Lord, come!") These exhortations are for every believer to be expectantly anticipating the Lord's return.

CONSIDER: *As a spiritual father, Paul exhorts the church to spiritual and moral maturity by being alert and living in expectation of the Lord's return.*

GOD'S COMFORT

2 CORINTHIANS 1:1–2:4

---

*Blessed be the God and Father of our Lord Jesus Christ, the
Father of mercies and God of all comfort, who comforts us in
all our affliction so that we will be able to comfort those who are
in any affliction with the comfort with which we ourselves
are comforted by God. (2 Corinthians 1:3–4)*

I just hung up the phone from talking to a lady who was widowed two weeks ago. She was weeping, having a difficult time adjusting; she had had such a good marriage. Since I have walked the same path, I spoke to her about the adjustment of living alone and offered her words of comfort.

In 2 Corinthians, Paul defends his apostleship and ministry, which the Corinthians had challenged. Toward the end of the letter, Paul will remind them that the signs of a true apostle—signs, wonders, miracles—were evident in his ministry (2 Cor. 12:12), and that he came to them with the authority of the Lord, but for the purpose of building up, not tearing down (13:10).

Paul opens this epistle with some of the most comforting words found in Scripture. He praises God for being the "Father of mercies and God of all comfort" (1:3). He mentions the word "comfort" nine times in four verses. "Comfort" is a marvelous word, the translation of *paraklesis*, meaning "one called alongside to help"; hence, here it means "the standing beside a person to encourage him when he is undergoing severe testing" (Cleon Rogers Jr. and Cleon Rogers III, *The New Linguistic and Exegetical Key to the Greek New Testament*). God Himself stands with us amid our testing and comforts us. But it doesn't stop there. He comforts us so that we can comfort others. God gives us His divine comfort and we share that comfort with others who are suffering.

Our sufferings can take us to what we would see as our absolute limit in suffering. Paul said he "despaired even of life" and he had the "sentence of death" within himself (vv. 8–9). Yet, amid the suffering, we don't walk alone. Even though we have abundant sufferings, we also receive abundant comfort through Christ. And even though we don't begin to understand "why," in glory we will. Sometimes our affliction is for the comfort of others as they observe the supernatural strength the Lord gives us.

What is the result? God's supernatural comfort enables us to patiently endure our trials and bring glory to His name. "God is faithful" (v. 18). Our hope and confidence must be in Him; He will ultimately deliver us from our peril.

CONSIDER: *God comforts us in our suffering so that we can, in turn, comfort others who are suffering with the comfort we receive from God.*

August 29

Triumphant Victory in Christ

2 Corinthians 2:5–3:3

But thanks be to God, who always leads us in triumph in Christ, and manifests through us the sweet aroma of the knowledge of Him in every place. (2 Corinthians 2:14)

On May 7, 1945, Col. Gen. Gustaf Jodl, chief of staff for the German army, surrendered to the Western allies, ending the bloodiest war in history, with over forty million casualties. There was celebrating throughout the Western world, with victory parades.

The letter Paul mentions in 2 Corinthians 2:9 (written following 1 Corinthians but lost) had caused him pain and anguish. Apparently an individual in the Corinthian assembly had caused trouble. It is unclear what this was. Was it the man guilty of incest mentioned in 1 Corinthians 5:1–13? Possibly. Or it may also have been someone challenging Paul's authority. In any case, the church had disciplined him so now Paul was calling on them to forgive him and comfort him and restore him to fellowship.

Paul was involved since he reminds them that he also forgave him. Forgiveness is important to prevent Satan's schemes from prevailing. Satan uses bitterness and an unforgiving spirit to create dissension and disunity in the church. Paul's admonition is important in every generation. Sin must be dealt with in the church but when genuine repentance takes place there must also be forgiveness, comfort, and restoration of the individual. Otherwise Satan, with his scheming, will gain the victory.

Paul paints a beautiful picture of the victory that comes through Christ. Paul pictures the Roman armies returning to Rome, victorious in battle. The conquered prisoners lead in the parade while the victorious Roman military follows and the aroma of perfume permeates the parade route. The aroma of victory. Similarly, Paul reminds them that believers are the fragrant aroma of Christ. Just as the aroma of the victorious Roman armies was the aroma of death to the conquered captives, to unbelievers, we are the aroma of death; to those being saved, the aroma of life.

Moreover, the Corinthians themselves were Paul's aroma of life. He had invested in them and rather than Paul providing a letter of recommendation for himself, the Corinthians themselves were his letter of recommendation!

CONSIDER: *It is a provocative thought to realize that we effuse the aroma of Christ—either of life or of death—to those with whom we interact.*

TRANSFORMED INTO GLORY

2 CORINTHIANS 3:4–18

But we all, with unveiled face, beholding as in a mirror the glory
of the Lord, are being transformed into the same image from
glory to glory, just as from the Lord, the Spirit. (2 Corinthians 3:18)

When we read through Exodus, Leviticus, and Deuteronomy we are over-whelmed by the many commandments. Organized and listed topically, they amount to 613 commandments: 365 negative commands (one for each day of the year) and 248 positive commands (supposedly one for each bone in our body). But the commandments would have been even more overwhelming for those under the Law who faced their obligation to keep the 613 command-ments of the Mosaic covenant.

In this section Paul speaks of the glory of the *new* covenant. Paul tells of the privilege of being a servant of the new covenant: we are no longer under the letter of the Law which kills; but rather, we are servants of the new cov-enant which is of the Spirit, giving life. The new covenant "was inaugurated by Christ in His sacrifice on the cross (Luke 22:20), and is entered into by faith (Phil. 3:9) and lived out in dependence on the Spirit (Rom. 7:6; 8:4)" (David Lowery, "2 Corinthians," *Bible Knowledge Commentary*).

While the old covenant came with glory—as exhibited by the glory shin-ing forth from Moses' face—how much more does the new covenant, brought about by Christ, reflect the glory of God! The glory seen in Moses' face faded, but the glory in the new covenant is eternal. And the new covenant brings boldness. We have a message of glory! With courage and candid speech we bring others the message of glory. While the people under the old covenant were blinded, the veil of blindness is removed through Christ. Then the Spirit brings liberty—no longer is the believer under the domination of the Law—that domination has ended.

The veil of blindness is lifted when we become a believer. Then the trans-formation into the glory and image of Christ begins—and continues. We undergo a metamorphosis (the word *transformed* is the Greek word *metamor-phao*), being changed from one image to another (see Rom. 12:2), growing into the likeness of Christ, producing the fruit of the Spirit (Gal. 5:22–23). Are you growing into the likeness of Christ?

CONSIDER: *The new covenant, inaugurated by Christ and administered through the Holy Spirit, produces a transformed life, reflecting the glory of God. Are you daily reflecting the glory of the Lord in the transformation of your life through the new covenant?*

August 31

SUFFERING WITH AN ETERNAL PERSPECTIVE

2 CORINTHIANS 4:1–18

For momentary, light affliction is producing for us an eternal weight of glory far beyond all comparison, while we look not at the things which are seen, but at the things which are not seen; for the things which are seen are temporal, but the things which are not seen are eternal. (2 Corinthians 4:17–18)

The first three centuries saw fierce persecution. "Some of the Christians, so Tacitus declares, were wrapped in the hides of wild beasts and were then torn to pieces by dogs. Others, fastened to crosses, were set on fire to illuminate a circus which Nero staged for the crowds in his own gardens" (K. S. Latourette, *A History of Christianity*). Amid the persecution the believers did not lose heart; they continued to "point out the weaknesses in the pagan religions and [gave] positive reasons for holding to Christianity" (K. S. Latourette, *A History of Christianity*).

Their focus was biblical—like the apostle Paul. Having the ministry of proclaiming the good news of Christ, Paul did not lose heart. He proclaimed the gospel fearlessly and truthfully, without deceit. Yet not everyone responded to the gospel. Why? Satan, the god of this age, has blinded the unbelievers' minds and their ability to think and reason.

But that did not diminish Paul's focus: he proclaimed Christ as Lord. Paul was emboldened because Christ had enlightened Paul and He would also enlighten those who responded to the gospel. The light from heaven had literally shone upon Paul on the road to Damascus (Acts 9:1–9)—he knew the reality of Christ.

Now, despite his suffering, Paul proclaimed Christ. Paul had this glorious message, this treasure, in a fragile, weak body—like a common, breakable jar. This was to demonstrate the power of God. So despite being afflicted, perplexed, persecuted, and struck, Paul did not give up. In his persistence Paul portrayed the life of Christ in him. Paul was "always carrying about in the body the dying of Jesus, so that the life of Jesus also may be manifested in [his] body" (2 Cor. 4:10). Paul's perspective was eternal. Any present suffering was light compared with the "eternal weight of glory."

Paul did not lose heart in serving Christ because he was looking to the glory of heaven; hence, he endured suffering in the present.

CONSIDER: *How do you fare under suffering for Christ? Are you able to look beyond the present sufferings? Do you have an eternal perspective?*

MOTIVATED BY THE PRESENT AND THE FUTURE

2 CORINTHIANS 5:1–21

We . . . prefer rather to be absent from the body and to be at home
with the Lord. . . . Therefore, we are ambassadors for Christ, as though
God were making an appeal through us. (2 Corinthians 5:8, 20)

I recently returned from the Shepherds' Conference led by John MacArthur at Grace Community Church in Sun Valley, California. I was moved by the intensely courageous and forthright speakers. They exemplified a fearless devotion to Christ and the Scriptures, standing strong for God's truth amid our decaying culture. They proclaimed the truth about Christ with vigor and devotion. Why? Because they have a strong hope in Christ for the present and the future. Their faith is solid.

That was Paul's motivation. He longed for the future when this temporary tent would be shed and he would receive a new and greater "building"—his new body. Paul portrayed our present body as a tent. What is a tent? A temporary dwelling. Paul was longing for his permanent body and his permanent home—to be with Christ. Moreover, he was filled with courage because he recognized this mortal life would one day transfer to immortality. And that was his excited anticipation: at home with the Lord. For that reason, Paul sought to please the Lord—especially since he (and we all) would give account at the judgment seat of Christ.

Hence, whether looking ahead to heaven or looking at his ministry in this life, Paul sought to please the Lord. In this present life, Paul was motivated by Christ's love, recognizing Christ died as a substitutionary atonement for all (2 Cor. 5:14–15). And God had given him the ministry of reconciliation. As sinners, we were alienated from the God who is holy, but now Christ, through His atonement, reconciled us to God. "Reconciliation indicates that Christ's death removed God's enmity against man" (Cleon Rogers Jr. and Cleon Rogers III, *The New Linguistic and Exegetical Key to the Greek New Testament*). What a phenomenal truth! Do you grasp it? We who were enemies of God are now made friends of God through Christ's atonement. And He has made us new creatures. In effect, we are a new creation (v. 17)!

How can we respond? Can we keep silent about this good news? No. God has "committed to us the word of reconciliation . . . we are ambassadors for Christ" (vv. 19, 20). God uses *us—ordinary people*—to announce this good news to others. Through us, God urges people to be reconciled to Him.

Recognizing that the sinless, righteous Christ had our sin charged to Him, that we could have the righteousness of Christ imputed to us—how does that perception motivate you as His ambassador in a troubled, needy world?

CONSIDER: *Paul was motivated to ministry by both the future and the present—anticipating being at home with the Lord but in the present being motivated by the love of Christ.*

REPENTANCE LEADING TO LIFE

2 CORINTHIANS 6:1–7:16

*For the sorrow that is according to the will of God produces
a repentance without regret, leading to salvation, but the
sorrow of the world produces death. (2 Corinthians 7:10)*

A young lady stood in front of the congregation, confessing that she had
been living in immorality. She begged the believers for forgiveness and
restoration. The congregation acknowledged her repentance, standing to show
their acceptance of her repentance. She was restored and went on to live faithfully for Christ.

Paul warns the Corinthians concerning their union with unbelievers,
reminding them that a believer cannot have an intimate relationship with an
unbeliever. To illustrate his admonition, Paul reminds them that Christ can
have no fellowship with Satan. A believer has nothing in common with an unbeliever. Why unite with an unbeliever in marriage, in business? It is an unequal
partnership that has no commonality. Light and darkness have nothing in common. Believers who are overtly involved with unbelievers in any form of union
are headed for disaster. Scripture is clear: "'Come out from their midst and be
separate,' says the Lord" (2 Cor. 6:17). Only then can the believer have a whole-
some relationship with the Lord.

Paul had been forthright with the Corinthians, but they criticized him and
even questioned his authority. There had been false accusations against Paul
and the Corinthians had fallen prey to the gossip. It grieved the apostle. "Make
room for us in your hearts," he urged them (7:2). While the Corinthians were
lacking in love, Paul was ready to live and die together with them. But the
Spirit of God was working in them and Paul took delight in that, overflowing
with joy on their behalf.

When Paul was stressed with conflicts and fears, God sent Titus to the
apostle, bringing him the news of the Corinthians' genuine repentance. Paul's
admonition to them had resulted in their sorrow—a sorrow that led to genuine
repentance and salvation. Sorrow alone is inadequate. Genuine sorrow will
produce repentance, *metanoia* meaning "change of mind," that will result in
change of behavior. Paul could rejoice because their repentance was genuine,
reflected in their obedience. Now Paul could have confidence in them.

This is a solemn word. Is there anything in your life that necessitates
repentance to enable you to live in obedience to the Scriptures?

CONSIDER: *The Corinthians had been living carelessly, in close association with
unbelievers, but through Paul's rebuke, they repented and became obedient.*

September 3

THE GRACE OF GIVING

2 CORINTHIANS 8:1–9:15

---

*For you know the grace of our Lord Jesus Christ, that though
He was rich, yet for your sake He became poor, so that you
through His poverty might become rich. (2 Corinthians 8:9)*

The president of a Christian college was raising funds for the college and
met with a Christian businessman who was a multimillionaire. He had
given several million dollars to a secular university. Over lunch the president explained the needs of the Christian college and asked the businessman, "Would you commit to helping us?" "Yes," replied the businessman. "How
much can I put you down for?" asked the president. "Twenty-five dollars a
month," replied the multimillionaire.

The Corinthian believers had not followed through in giving to the poor
in Jerusalem for whom Paul was taking up a collection. Had the false teachers in Corinth discouraged the Corinthian believers from giving? Perhaps.
Paul had instructed the Corinthians about giving in a previous letter. Now
Paul reminded the Corinthians about the abundant giving of the Macedonian
churches (Phillipi, Thessalonica, Berea) who gave liberally with joy, even
beyond their ability. And that was of their own volition; no one coerced them.
But the foundation of their giving was that they first had given themselves to
the Lord.

Since the Corinthians had progressed spiritually, Paul exhorted them to
overflow in giving as well. But Paul was not issuing a command; rather, their
giving would reflect an overflow of love. And from where? From Christ! He
is the ultimate expression of giving since He laid aside His riches, taking on
humanity in the incarnation and becoming poor by going to the cross in order
that we, through His poverty, would become spiritually rich.

With that reminder, Paul urged the Corinthians to follow through in giving for the poor in Jerusalem. Titus would be coming to Corinth to receive
their donation. Paul urged them not to disappoint nor shame him; rather, they
should reflect their love by giving generously the gift they had previously
promised, when Titus would come. Paul reminded them that should they give
miserly, they would reap accordingly. And he reminded them that God would
make it possible: He would shower His grace on them, enabling them to have
an abundance for every need—and for giving.

Giving is a reflection of the heart—and thus ultimately an evidence of our
love for the Lord and for one another. Does your giving reflect joy, liberality,
and an overflow of love?

CONSIDER: *Christ is the ultimate example of giving: He who was rich became
poor by going to the cross, that we might become spiritually rich.*

CRITIQUING CRITICISM

2 CORINTHIANS 10:1–18

We are taking every thought captive to the obedience of Christ. . . .
HE WHO BOASTS IS TO BOAST IN THE LORD. (2 Corinthians 10:5, 17)

When an evangelical pastor was on a major television program, explaining Christianity and that Jesus is the only way of salvation, he received a call from a Hollywood celebrity asking him to come to his home. When the pastor visited the celebrity, the man proceeded to rebuke him for his narrow position and offered eastern mysticism as the alternative. The pastor remained gracious but firm in his response.

Paul faced enormous criticism from the Corinthians. They accused him of duplicity—he exhibited meekness and humility when in their presence but he was bold and courageous when he was absent! Were that indeed true, Paul would be walking "according to the flesh." Paul countered that while he walked "in the flesh"—in humanity—he did not walk "according to the flesh"—controlled by the sin nature. Paul's weapons were not worldly; they were spiritual, divinely powerful. (See the list in Ephesians 6:10–18 of divine weaponry available to the believer.)

Paul's spiritual weapons were powerful, destroying worldly philosophy and speculation as though they were towers and fortresses to be torn down. How would this happen? By "taking every thought captive to the obedience of Christ" (2 Cor. 10:5). "Paul is the most daring of thinkers, but he lays all his thoughts at the feet of Jesus" (A. T. Robertson, *Word Pictures of the New Testament*). As believers, we are called to set our minds on things above (Col. 3:2), and so we discipline our thinking to think things that are true, honorable, right, pure, admirable, and praiseworthy (Phil. 4:8).

The Corinthians' error was that they were evaluating things outwardly, externally—they were looking at the surface. They criticized Paul's letters, saying they were weighty and strong but his presence was contemptible. But their judgment was wrong; Paul was the same whether absent or present.

The false apostles had influenced the Corinthians against Paul, so Paul reminded them that he was indeed the apostle to the Gentiles and in this, he was their father in the gospel. But he was bringing the gospel "to the regions beyond" (v. 16), so that he would not boast in the work of others. Regardless, boasting should not be in man but in the Lord.

CONSIDER: *Uncontrolled in their thought life, the Corinthians depreciated Paul, an apostle of Christ, who was their father in the gospel. What are you doing to daily discipline and control your thinking?*

September 5

Suffering as a Servant

2 Corinthians 11:1–12:13

And He has said to me, "My grace is sufficient for you, for power is perfected in weakness." Most gladly, therefore, I will rather boast about my weaknesses, so that the power of Christ may dwell in me. (2 Corinthians 12:9)

Graham Scroggie was a great British Bible expositor and author, yet he was turned out of the first two churches he served because of his opposition to modernism in one and worldliness in the other. During World War II he was bombed out of three houses and his historic church burned down—all within a six-month period.

Paul suffered significantly as an apostle—especially through the Corinthian believers. The Corinthians were being swayed by false apostles and in serious danger. Paul was jealous for their purity; he wanted to present them as a virgin presented to Christ. Yet they were weak, capable of being led astray by false teaching.

Paul reminded them of his faithfulness and integrity toward them, accepting wages from others in order to preach the gospel to them without charge. Why? Because he loved them. But they were in danger of being subverted by false apostles, servants of Satan, disguised as angels of light.

If they wanted to look at things in a worldly way, Paul would help them! He spoke facetiously in reminding them of his credentials. Could the false teachers boast? He could boast even more. Since the Corinthians apprized these false teachers by their credentials, Paul would delineate his credentials. He was a Hebrew, an Israelite, a descendant of Abraham, and a servant of Christ.

But Paul could also boast in his sufferings. He was imprisoned, beaten countless times, beaten five times with thirty-nine lashes, shipwrecked, in countless dangers, exposure to cold, without food, and pressured with concern for the churches—the list was endless. Paul especially experienced the spiritual issues, identifying with the weak with concern for those in sin.

Paul reminded them of his authenticity as an apostle in that he had visions and revelations, being caught up into the third heaven—an indescribable event of which it was not permissible to speak. Because of the magnitude of the revelation, Paul received a thorn in the flesh, some physical ailment to prevent him from exalting himself. Yet amid this God gave him sufficient grace to bear it, revealing the power of Christ in him. This is a serious reminder that we may suffer extensively in life, yet receive grace to bear it.

CONSIDER: *The servant of God may suffer significantly, yet God's grace is always sufficient to enable us to bear up under the suffering.*

September 6

Challenged for Maturity

2 Corinthians 12:14–13:14

*Finally, brethren, rejoice, be made complete, be comforted,
be like-minded, live in peace; and the God of love and
peace will be with you. (2 Corinthians 13:11)*

A pastor began a new ministry in a country church only to discover there had been terrible bickering and fighting in the church so that it had split into two major factions. Some left the church, others stayed but were at odds with others in the church. The pastor devoted himself to reconciling the factions to bring unity and harmony to the church.

The church at Corinth was beset with numerous problems. Now in concluding his second inspired epistle to them (and planning a third visit), Paul came to them as a father to "gladly spend and be expended" for them (2 Cor. 12:15).

Paul is speaking facetiously to them as he reminds them that he did not take advantage of them, nor did Titus. Paul and his protégés were circumspect in all their association with the Corinthians. The Corinthians, in fact, misunderstood Paul's ministry to them, thinking Paul was defending himself. What Paul wanted was their upbuilding, their spiritual maturity. He was fearful that if he should come he would find the same sinful behavior: strife, jealousy, slander, gossip, and arrogance. How disappointed he would be! He would, in fact, be humiliated and mourn when he would see those who were continuing in their sin without repentance.

Paul expected to come to them again soon and when he would come, he would not spare them. He had been disappointed in his second visit to them since there had been immorality in the assembly; in his third coming he would confront the unrepentant ones, giving the proof that they were looking for to show that Christ was speaking through him. He would demonstrate the power of the risen Christ.

Paul challenged them: "test yourselves to see if you are in the faith" (13:5). Ultimately, someone who continues to live in immorality will not inherit the kingdom of God (see 1 Cor. 6:9–10; Gal. 5:19–21; Eph. 5:5). The issue was serious. They wanted proof of Paul's apostolic authority but he wanted proof of their salvation.

The apostle concluded his letter expressing his desire that they "be made complete." He wanted to see them unified and growing in holiness. He wanted them to be built up in the faith, living in unity and peace.

CONSIDER: *Paul grieved at the disunity and immorality of the Corinthians; he sought their unity, holiness, and spiritual maturity.*

CORRECT OR CURSED GOSPEL?

GALATIANS 1:1–10

*As we have said before, so I say again now, if any
man is preaching to you a gospel contrary to what
you received, he is to be accursed! (Galatians 1:9)*

As I sat in the car repair shop in Riverside, California, studying my Greek
New Testament, a man initiated a conversation. He was interested in what
I was reading. I quickly discovered he was involved with a denomination that,
while they proclaimed salvation by grace through faith (according to him), yet
they were kept saved by works, including keeping the Sabbath. Keeping the
Sabbath was essential for salvation; without it, they were lost.

Paul addresses precisely this issue in Galatians. Paul was writing to the
churches in south Galatia, the churches mentioned in Acts 14–15. Following
the visit by Paul and Barnabas, Judaizers had entered the assembly and corrupted the faith of the believers. They thought they would gain perfection
through the Law. They had abandoned the gospel of grace for "another" gospel. They depreciated Paul's ministry, even questioning his apostolic authority. They sought perfection through the Law (Gal. 3:3); they were reverting to
circumcision (5:2–4); they observed Jewish festivals and seasons (4:10). They
had "fallen from grace" (5:4). Paul denounced this "sanctification through the
Law" as heresy.

There are no complimentary remarks at the beginning of this letter as is
so common in Paul's other letters. He begins his letter abruptly, reminding
them of the substitutionary atonement of Christ that we may be delivered out
of this evil world. Paul is making a point. If the Law could bring righteousness,
delivering believers from the world, then Christ died needlessly (2:21).

Paul launches into a terse rebuke of the Galatians. Their acceptance of
sanctification through the Law is "another" gospel—a different kind of gospel.
It denotes military desertion—they have deserted Christ. They have been led
astray by Judaizers who have distorted the gospel.

Paul concludes: whether Paul himself or even an angel would preach a
different gospel, may he be accursed (*anathema*)! In case they missed it, Paul
repeats his statement, "he is to be accursed" (vv. 8, 9)! The purity of the gospel
is a singularly significant issue. Those who distort the gospel are alienated
from God and devoted to destruction.

CONSIDER: *The pure gospel of grace brings righteousness to the believer through
the substitutionary atonement of Christ without the works of the Law.*

COMMISSIONED BY CHRIST

GALATIANS 1:11–24

For I would have you know, brethren, that the gospel
which was preached by me is not according to man. For
I neither received it from man, nor was I taught it, but I received
it through a revelation of Jesus Christ. (Galatians 1:11–12)

Kenneth Copeland infers Jesus spoke to him: "You are the very image and the very copy of that one [Jesus]." (Copeland to Jesus): "I could have done the same thing?" (Jesus to Copeland): "Oh, yeah, if you'd had the knowledge of the Word of God that He did, you could've done the same thing, 'cause you're a reborn man, too" (Michael Horton, *The Agony of Deceit*).

Many false teachers over the centuries have indicated that God or Christ spoke to them. But these are false messages. Paul the apostle was different. His apostleship was authenticated by the direct revelation he received from God. In vindicating his apostleship to the Galatians, he reminds them that he did not construct the gospel he proclaimed to them; he received it directly from Jesus Christ. Christ abruptly stopped the apostle when he was on his way to Damascus to continue aggressively persecuting the church. Christ appeared to Paul, commissioning him to minister to the Gentiles.

God had set Paul apart from birth and on the road to Damascus called him both to salvation and to a ministry to the Gentiles. This divine transaction was "to reveal His Son in me" (Gal. 1:16). Paul was changed. Others would now see Christ in the apostle. After this occurred, Paul did not go to Jerusalem to meet with the apostles, rather he went away to Arabia. Why? Most probably he went to meditate, study, and receive further revelation from the Lord. The point Paul was making is that he did not proclaim a gospel received from man. His message was the result of direct revelation from God.

Only three years later did Paul finally go to Jerusalem to meet briefly with Peter and James (who was the head of the church in Jerusalem). After that Paul went to Syria and Cilicia, partly because his life was in danger in Judea.

Paul's new life in Christ impacted the believers in Judea as they heard about his dramatic conversion—the one who formerly persecuted believers was now preaching the faith he once tried to destroy. And they glorified God because of Paul. Christ had confronted Paul directly and Paul was a changed man.

CONSIDER: *Paul did not receive his message from men; he received his message of the gospel of grace by direct revelation from Christ.*

September 9

JUSTIFIED BY FAITH—ALONE
GALATIANS 2:1–21

*Nevertheless knowing that a man is not justified by the works
of the Law but through faith in Christ Jesus, even we have believed
in Christ Jesus, so that we may be justified by faith in Christ and
not by the works of the Law; since by the works of the Law
no flesh will be justified. (Galatians 2:16)*

A group of us gathered for fellowship at a restaurant after the Sunday evening service. A lady with a different background joined us. She was filled with questions. Wasn't baptism necessary for salvation? Isn't that what Acts 2:38 taught? Her denomination taught "baptismal regeneration," that baptism was essential for salvation. This raises a serious question: Is there *anything* in addition to faith required for salvation?

After fourteen years Paul went back to Jerusalem and related the gospel message that he was preaching to the Gentiles. Judaizers had created trouble in Jerusalem, attempting to bring believers into the bondage of the Law (Gal. 2:4). Was it necessary for Gentiles to keep the Law? Did Gentiles have to be circumcised? These were serious issues for the church in transitioning from Judaism to Christianity, from law to grace. But Titus, a Gentile believer, was not required to be circumcised. Paul and his people refused to accede to the Judaizers' demands. The purity of the gospel was at stake.

While Peter was commissioned as the apostle to the Jews, Paul was set apart as the apostle to the Gentiles. Was it a different gospel to the Gentiles? No. It was the same gospel of salvation by grace through faith—plus nothing. The meeting had a positive resolution: James, Peter, and John endorsed Paul's message to the Gentiles.

Nonetheless, in this first century period of transition, there were difficulties. When Peter was alone with Gentiles, he would eat with them. But when Jews from Jerusalem came, Peter separated himself from the Gentiles, creating a class distinction. Paul rebuked Peter for his hypocrisy. Paul would later remind the Galatians, "you are all one in Christ Jesus" (3:28). There are no class distinctions in the gospel. Paul concluded that a person is not justified by the Law but through faith in Christ. Moreover, through Christ, Paul (and all believers) died to the Law, having been "crucified with Christ." In the new life, Christ lives His life through the believer who walks by faith, having died to sin and the Law.

CONSIDER: *Paul preached the pure gospel of grace: justification comes by faith in Christ and not through the works of the Law.*

September 10

THE PURPOSE OF THE LAW

GALATIANS 3:1–25

Therefore the Law has become our tutor to lead us to Christ,
so that we may be justified by faith. (Galatians 3:24)

A gospel tract asks "Are You Going to Heaven?" It then quizzes the reader to check the appropriate answer for how they know they're going to heaven: 1. Keeping the Ten Commandments; 2. Gifts to charity; 3. Doing one's best; 4. Leading a good life; 5. Good works; 6. Trying to obey the Golden Rule. . . . The tract goes on to cite biblical references disproving any need for works in gaining entrance into heaven.

Paul confronts the Galatians with their problem of works: "You foolish Galatians. . . . Are you so foolish?" (Gal. 3:1, 3). The Galatians had been deceived—as though someone had cast a deceptive spell over them, corrupting the gospel. They were not thinking; they failed to recognize the serious spiritual error in their corruption of the gospel. They thought they were saved by faith and sanctified by works. As a result they were observing the Mosaic Law, keeping the festivals, and practicing circumcision.

But Paul reminded them that even Abraham was saved by faith, not works: Abraham believed God, and God "reckoned it to him as righteousness" (Gen. 15:6). People are saved by grace through faith *in every age.* There aren't different ways of salvation in different ages. Moreover, God's blessing of Abraham anticipated the Gentiles coming to faith: "In you all the families of the earth will be blessed" (Gen. 12:3).

Why then the Law? Anyone attempting to live by the Law was obligated to keep all of it. But the Law was not given for salvation; it was given to show man's need of redemption. In effect, it was a curse. But Christ redeemed us from the curse of the Law so that the blessing of faith might come to the Gentiles (Gal. 3:13–14).

The promise of justification by faith came to Abraham prior to the Law. The Law was added 430 years later. Why? "Because of transgressions"—the Law was given to show mankind the need for a Savior. The Law "shut up" all men under sin, pictured as locked up in dungeon (A. T. Robertson, *Word Pictures of the New Testament*). It was a tutor, a custodian to lead people to Christ and justification through faith. The Law's duration was "until the seed would come to whom the promise had been made" (v. 19). So the Law existed from the time of Moses until Christ. Christ fulfilled the Law so those who trust in Him are not under the Law. What a phenomenal truth! Justification is by faith alone—do you rejoice and glory in that sublime truth?

CONSIDER: *Salvation in every age is by grace through faith; the Law existed from Moses until Christ to reveal mankind's sinfulness and need of a Savior.*

FREE IN CHRIST

GALATIANS 3:26–4:7

There is neither Jew nor Greek, there is neither slave nor free man, there is neither male nor female; for you are all one in Christ Jesus. (Galatians 3:28)

When I teach my seminary class, I see a great diversity in the student body: students may be Caucasian, African American, or Hispanic; they may come from Africa, South America, or Canada. Yet there is a wonderful unity—we are one in Christ.

Paul reminds the Galatians—who were prone to put themselves back under slavery, under the Law—you are "sons of God through faith in Christ Jesus" (Gal. 3:26). What a prized position! They have been "baptized into Christ" (v. 27; see also 1 Cor. 12:13)—that is their position and, as such, they have been clothed with Christ. They have been united to Christ and united to one another in the family of God. "In the Roman society when a youth came of age he was given a special toga which admitted him to the full rights of the family and state and indicated he was a grown-up son. So the Galatian believers had laid aside the old garments of the Law and had put on Christ's robe of righteousness which grants full acceptance before God" (Donald Campbell, "Galatians," *Bible Knowledge Commentary*).

In this unique new position there are no class distinctions—neither Jew nor Gentile, slave nor free person, male nor female. All are "in Christ." Spiritually, there are no distinctions; all are one in Christ. (There are, however, still various functions, as Ephesians 5:22–6:4 addresses: an employer is still in authority over the employee, husband is head of the wife, and parents are in authority over children.)

Since Christ is the seed (physical descendant) of Abraham (as Galatians 3:16 clarifies), and since believers are in Christ, they are also heirs. But if they are like children—still under the Law—then they are unable to access their inheritance and aren't any more free than slaves. But they are sons!

At precisely the right time in history, God sent His Son, born under the Law for the purpose of redeeming those who were in bondage to the Law. Christ redeemed us from enslavement to the Law. Our status is now changed from slave to son! We are in the family of God, endowed with the privilege of calling God "Abba! Father!" Do you rejoice that you have been set free from slavery and brought into the family of God? You are a son!

CONSIDER: *Believers in Christ are sons, and spiritually there are no distinctions; we are one in Christ.*

BE FREE!

GALATIANS 4:8–5:1

*It was for freedom that Christ set us free; therefore keep standing firm
and do not be subject again to a yoke of slavery. (Galatians 5:1)*

I met a unique couple in our church fellowship. They had come out of a cultic
background and were happy to be free in Christ. He attended classes I taught
and was excited about the new truths in Christ he was learning. But she was
unable to make the transition. One day I discovered they had gone back to
their cultic worship. I was sad and disappointed. Why would they go back to a
system of bondage?

Paul reprimanded the Galatians—it was inconceivable! They were going
back "to the weak and worthless elemental things" (Gal. 4:9). They were again
becoming slaves to a faulty system. Was Paul's ministry in vain? The Judaizers had provoked them and they were going back to the Law, observing the
festivals.

Paul appealed to them on a personal level. He had a bodily illness—we are
not told what it was but, based on verse 15, it may have been an eye problem.
The Galatians had shown their love for Paul, receiving him as though they
were receiving Christ; they would have plucked out their eyes and given them
to him. Why had they now changed? Had he become their enemy? Paul agonized over their spiritual vacillation as though he were an expectant mother,
wishing that Christ would be formed in them. Paul was perplexed over their
spiritual ineptitude.

The apostle presented the Galatians with an allegory. Hagar reflected
bondage under the Law, "in slavery with her children" (v. 25). And Sarah,
who bore "children of promise" like Isaac (v. 28) represented freedom. Paul
reminded the Galatians they were like Isaac.

What was the conclusion? "Cast out the bondwoman and her son" (v. 30).
Paul was telling them to reject subservience to the Law. Christ had set them
free; it was folly to return to the bondage of the Law. Paul reminded them, "So
then, brethren, we are not children of a bondwoman, but of the free woman"
(v. 31).

Christ has set us free. There is no element of the Mosaic Law, no legalism,
no maintenance of the Sabbath for salvation or sanctification. We are free in
Christ. May we not look back to any legalism that would nullify the freedom
we have in Christ.

CONSIDER: *Christ has set us free from the bondage of the Law; it is imperative
that we do not return to the Law and become enslaved again.*

CONTROLLED BY THE SPIRIT

GALATIANS 5:2–26

*But I say, walk by the Spirit, and you will not carry
out the desire of the flesh. (Galatians 5:16)*

Seventh-day Adventists believe that anyone who does not keep the Sabbath in the last days will have "the mark of the beast." Those not observing the Sabbath will be lost; keeping the Sabbath is essential to salvation. Ellen White, their founder, said, "In the last days the Sabbath test will be made plain. When this time comes anyone who does not keep the Sabbath will receive the mark of the beast and will be kept from heaven."

Paul addressed those that tried to mingle law and grace, reminding them that if they sought circumcision because of the Law, they were under obligation to keep the *entire* Law—613 commandments! Paul's words are severe—they are "severed from Christ" and have "fallen from grace" (Gal. 5:4) because neither circumcision nor uncircumcision means anything, only faith working through love. They had begun well but Judaizers had led them astray. Paul's words are harsh: these Judaizers, bent on circumcision, may they castrate themselves!

In Christ we are called to freedom and liberty, reflected in serving one another through love since love is the fulfillment of the Law: "You shall love your neighbor as yourself" (v. 14; Lev. 19:18). By biting and devouring each other, we fail to fulfill the consummate Law: love your neighbor.

The ultimate solution for the believer living in love and victory is to "walk by the Spirit" (Gal. 5:16, 25) and be led by the Spirit (v. 18). What is a "walk by the Spirit"? It is being *controlled by the Spirit.* This will prevent the "deeds of the flesh" like immorality, idolatry, strife, and drunkenness (vv. 19–21). It is a serious warning: those who practice these things will not inherit the kingdom of God. A truly sobering thought. On the contrary, walking by the Spirit produces the fruit of the Spirit—"love, joy, peace, patience, kindness, goodness, faithfulness, gentleness, self-control" (vv. 22–23). This is the result of a walk by the Spirit and, through union with Christ, having the passions and desires of the flesh crucified.

Are you daily, consistently, living under the control of the Holy Spirit whereby you are producing the fruit of the Spirit?

CONSIDER: *The life of victory is not lived in adherence to the Mosaic Law but lived under the control of the Holy Spirit, producing the fruit of the Spirit.*

LEGITIMATE BOASTING

GALATIANS 6:1–18

---

*But may it never be that I would boast, except in the cross
of our Lord Jesus Christ, through which the world has been
crucified to me, and I to the world. (Galatians 6:14)*

Legalism will always lead to boasting. These people are "self-justified"
through what they take pride in doing (or not doing). They have a list of
laws that they keep and a list of things they don't do. And they pride themselves in the process.

Paul concludes his epistle to the Galatians with a summary of instructive
words and exhortations. While they are not under the Mosaic Law, they are
under the Law of Christ (Gal. 6:2). Christ did not come to bring another codified law; rather, the believer is called to reflect the love of Christ by loving
one's neighbor, bearing one another's burdens; by so doing we fulfill the Law
of Christ.

Reflecting the love of Christ will also mean that we don't boast. By contrast, we should examine our own works whether they can be approved. Were
they done with the right motive? In addition, we are to assume responsibility,
carrying our own load (v. 5), while helping others bear their heavy burden
(v. 2).

Paul reminds the Galatians of their responsibility in financially support-
ing those who instruct them in the Word. Had the Judaizers led the Galatians
astray in their giving as well? Possibly. The Mosaic Law clearly established
remuneration for the priests and Levites. But Paul expands his comments,
reminding them that they would reap a harvest in proportion to their liberality (or lack of it). And that is always true. Tragically, some Christians are so
focused on this life, busy laying up treasures on earth, that their treasure
in heaven will be meager. Paul encourages the believers not to lose heart or
become tired in giving, but to do good to all, with a focus on helping fellow
believers. Ultimately there will be a heavenly harvest.

Paul concludes his letter dealing with the dominant Galatian theme: legalism. Boasting in circumcision is profitless; there is only one avenue in which
to boast: the cross of Christ. And that takes the focus from self and places it
on Christ—precisely where it should be.

CONSIDER: *Boasting in living a legalistic life is profitless; the only reason for
boasting is the cross of Christ.*

September 15

CHOSEN, REDEEMED, AND SECURED

EPHESIANS 1:1–14

*We have obtained an inheritance, having been predestined
according to His purpose who works all things after
the counsel of His will. (Ephesians 1:11)*

When we were living in Moreno Valley, California, our front yard looked out across the desert toward Mount Gorgonio. One day surveyors came and began surveying the desert, marking out property lines with stakes. Weeks later the contractor came and construction of houses began. Soon beautiful houses replaced the arid desert. Where were the houses built? Precisely where their properties had been marked out beforehand.

Paul wrote to the Ephesian believers (it was probably a circular letter going to other churches as well), extolling the greatness of God. In these verses Paul traces the work of God in the believer's redemption. The Father predestined and chose the believer (Eph. 1:3–6), the Son redeemed us (vv. 7–12), and the Holy Spirit sealed us (vv. 13–14).

Before the foundation of the world, God chose us for salvation, that we should be His special, set apart people to live our lives for Him. He marked us out beforehand that we would be adopted into His family, with all the rights of children belonging to God. He did this not because He foresaw any good in us; it was entirely out of His grace. But it was for the singular purpose that we should give praise to God, living for His glory.

While God chose us for salvation in eternity past, our redemption took place in time and space and history. Christ redeemed us when He shed His blood for sinful humanity on the cross. It is picturesque. He bought us out of the slave market of sin and set us free. His death for us was a *substitutionary atonement*. He, the Righteous One, died for us sinners; He died in our place that we could be forgiven. Forgiveness does not come in any other way—only through the atoning blood of Christ.

Christ's work of redemption anticipates the completion of Christ's work, which will be in the "fullness of time" when Christ will establish His kingdom. At that time Christ will "sum up" all things, "gather again under one head . . . gather up into one" (Cleon Rogers Jr. and Cleon Rogers III, *The New Linguistic and Exegetical Key to the Greek New Testament*). *Everything* in heaven and earth will be renewed when Christ will rule supreme in His kingdom on the new, renovated earth.

The Holy Spirit ensures our security by sealing us, marking us out as belonging to Christ. It is the down payment of our ultimate inheritance in Christ. All of this is done by God "who works all things after the counsel of His will" (v. 11). Surely this should make us stand in awe and live to the glory of His grace.

CONSIDER: *The Father chose and predestined us; the Son redeemed us through His atoning blood; and the Holy Spirit sealed us, showing that we belong to God.*

September 16

RICHES IN CHRIST

EPHESIANS 1:15–23

*. . . the surpassing greatness of His power toward us who
believe. These are in accordance with the working of the
strength of His might which He brought about in Christ, when
He raised Him from the dead. (Ephesians 1:19–20)*

Today wealthy individuals are assessed in billions, not millions, of dollars. This is inconceivable, yet spiritually believers are far richer than any earthly assessment is capable of measuring. The power that raised Christ from the dead is operative in believers! Think of it! Reflect on it! I spoke with someone yesterday who has enormous burdens—yet he too knows the power of Christ that's at work during just such a time.

The apostle Paul was overawed at the greatness of Christ and the blessings that accrue to the believer—he wrote verses 15–23 in one sentence in the Greek text! He was carried away with joy at what Christ has wrought for us. Paul frequently begins with the trilogy "faith, hope, love" which expresses the believer's maturity in Christ. Here he mentions their faith and love. These believers had a faith that was genuine—it was "in the Lord Jesus." The object of one's faith is of prime importance. Faith is "an activity which takes men right out of themselves and makes them one with Christ" (Leon Morris, *Gospel According to John*). By exhibiting "love for all the saints" (Eph. 1:15), these believers fulfilled the summation of the Law: love God (Deut. 6:5) and love others (Lev. 19:18).

Paul continuously thanked God for them, praying that God would give them wisdom and knowledge—that they would know God, His character and will, personally and intimately (Harold Hoehner, "Ephesians," *Bible Knowledge Commentary*). What a phenomenal privilege!

But now Paul prays that they would be enlightened and know (1) the hope of His calling—this is the confident trust that patiently waits for a certain future; (2) the glory that we are *God's inheritance*; and (3) the enormous power God has made available to believers. How great is this power? It is the enormous power in accordance with the power that raised Christ from the dead and seated Him at the Father's right hand and subjected all things to Him. This is the power that works in believers! This is inconceivable! And all things are subjected to Christ and He gives guidance to the church, which is His body. We have been privileged beyond comprehension. Take time to reflect on the riches of your inheritance in Christ. We are rich *in Christ!*

CONSIDER: *Believers have an enormously great power—the very power that raised Christ from the dead is operative in believers.*

September 17

A Poem of God

EPHESIANS 2:1–10

*For by grace you have been saved through faith; and that
not of yourselves, it is the gift of God; not as a result of works,
so that no one may boast. For we are His workmanship, created
in Christ Jesus for good works, which God prepared beforehand
so that we would walk in them. (Ephesians 2:8–10)*

Pete was one of the strongest, most faithful Christians I ever met. Pete had a rough background but he was gloriously saved as an adult and his life turned around dramatically. He devoured the Scriptures and grew spiritually. He became the superintendent of the Union Gospel Mission, spending the rest of his life helping men come to faith in Christ and seeing their lives changed. Pete was a *poiema* of God.

But Pete didn't begin there. In our unsaved estate we were constantly in a state of being dead in sin. That was our condition. That was our life and lifestyle. Unbelievers conduct their lives according to the philosophy of this world. What is that? It is according to "the prince of the power of the air," that is, the devil. According to 1 John 5:19, the whole world lies in the power of the devil. He promotes evil in this world and people respond and follow his directives. That once *was* the lifestyle of believers, but no more. We *formerly* indulged the desires of the flesh, but that is past.

"But God" (Eph. 2:4). These two words reflect the dramatic change that has occurred in believers. God took pity on us, extending His mercy, which resulted in the outpouring of His love. He "made us alive together with Christ" (v. 5). When we were spiritually dead and headed for destruction, God gave us spiritual life by uniting us to Christ. What a wonderful truth! We are alive and we are forever united to Christ! Note the emphasis in verses 5–6: "with Christ . . . with Him . . . with Him . . . in Christ Jesus." We have been joined to Christ and are already seated in the heavenlies together with Christ!

How did this come about? All through God's grace. Not one element of human merit enters the transaction. The glory goes to God, not us. And for all eternity it will display the outstanding riches of God's grace.

God did this that we might be His "workmanship," His *poiema*, His "poem," His "work of art" (Cleon Rogers Jr. and Cleon Rogers III, *The New Linguistic and Exegetical Key to the Greek New Testament*). Our transformed lives from what we once were to what we now are in Christ reveal God's work of art. Are you a poem of God?

CONSIDER: *Although we were dead in sin, God, through His mercy and grace, made us alive in Christ that we might reflect His workmanship.*

Reconciled—In God's Family!

EPHESIANS 2:11–22

---

*But now in Christ Jesus you who formerly were far off have
been brought near by the blood of Christ. (Ephesians 2:13)*

Helen and I were sitting on a park bench in Mondsee, Austria, when a bridal couple led a parade and entered the reception building. We wandered over to the building and when the host recognized us as Americans, he exclaimed, "You are President Bush's delegates to our wedding!" He left the room and returned with the bridal couple, snapping pictures of the four of us. Americans and Austrians and Germans, now friends. After the enmity of World War II, reconciliation has been established.

Paul addresses the Gentiles, reminding them of their former position, "uncircumcised," a significant term designating those outside of the covenant promises of God. They were "separate from Christ"—without Him. They were alienated and estranged. They were, in fact, "without God" (*astheneia*), a term from which we get "atheist." Truly strong terms to remind them of their former isolation from God's promises and blessings. Remember, Paul says—keep on remembering your past when you were outside of the grace of God so that you will value your present position.

"But now" (Eph. 2:13). A change has occurred! "In Christ Jesus" the Gentiles have been brought near. How did that happen? "By the blood of Christ" (v. 13). It was through the substitutionary atonement Christ made when He shed His blood on the cross. That is the transaction that brought peace with God. Previously there was a division, a barrier between Gentiles and Jews. No longer. Christ has brought Gentiles into the family of God. Christ fulfilled the Law and thereby nullified the Law. As a result Christ made Jew and Gentile into one in the body of Christ. Where there was alienation, Christ brought reconciliation and peace.

What a privileged position! The same message of peace through Christ has gone to both Gentiles (far away) and Jews (nearby). We all now have "access in one Spirit to the Father" (v. 18), access to the throne of God, access to the King. We are in God's family, fellow citizens. Does that capture your heart? Does it provoke excitement and joy? It should! Now, in Christ, we—Jews and Gentiles alike—are being built up in the faith, having been firmly established on the foundation of the apostles and prophets. We have enormous reason to rejoice!

CONSIDER: *Gentiles, who were outside of the covenant promises of God, have been reconciled into one body with the Jews through the blood of Christ.*

A Revealed Mystery

Ephesians 3:1–13

By revelation there was made known to me the mystery . . . that the Gentiles are fellow heirs and fellow members of the body, and fellow partakers of the promise in Christ Jesus through the gospel. (Ephesians 3:3, 6)

Over my years of teaching I have encountered a number of Jewish believers. Recognizing that they are God's chosen people, it has always been special to have them in my classes. Yet in the New Testament era, we are one body in Christ—Jews and Gentiles are one.

In the Old Testament economy, Gentiles were required to become Jewish proselytes to worship and approach God. But now God has revealed a new stewardship, a new *oikonomia*, an "administrative responsibility given to a servant over a household" (Cleon Rogers Jr. and Cleon Rogers III, *The New Linguistic and Exegetical Key to the Greek New Testament*). The gospel of God's grace, uniting Jew and Gentile in one body, was a sacred trust, a stewardship, given to Paul. This was new. Paul refers to it as a *mystery*, something that no one can know unless God reveals it to them. It "cannot be unraveled or understood by human ingenuity or study. It is not something that is mysterious but rather a revealed secret [by God] to be understood by all believing people" (Harold Hoehner, *Ephesians: An Exegetical Commentary*). God gave this to Paul through direct revelation.

What is the mystery? In the body of Christ there is equality of Jews and Gentiles. They are equal. Gentiles are also fellow heirs—they share in the hope of Jesus as their Messiah. They now inherit salvation (Heb. 1:14), glorification (Rom. 8:17), grace (1 Peter 3:7), blessing (1 Peter 3:9), eternal life (Titus 3:7), and an eternal reign with Christ (Rev. 22:5). They are also fellow members of the body, the church, as are the Jews. There is not a Jewish church and a Gentile church. Gentiles are also fellow partakers of the promise of Christ. While Jews are Abraham's descendants physically, Gentiles who trust in Christ are Abraham's descendants spiritually (Gal. 3:6–29).

God appointed Paul a minister to the Gentiles, to preach the unfathomable riches of Christ and to announce the new message which had never been known before—Gentiles are fellow heirs of Christ! And this message isn't restricted to earth; it is made known in the angelic realm in the heavenlies!

What is the result? We may have boldness and confident access to God through faith in Christ. And because this message results in Jews and Gentiles alike coming to faith in Christ, we should not lose heart.

CONSIDER: *God revealed a new message, previously unknown, namely, that Gentiles are fellow heirs, fellow members, and fellow partakers of Christ.*

September 20

SURPASSING LOVE AND STRENGTH
EPHESIANS 3:14–21

*[I pray] that Christ may dwell in your hearts through faith; and that
you, being rooted and grounded in love, may be able to comprehend
with all the saints what is the breadth and length and height and depth,
and to know the love of Christ which surpasses knowledge, that you
may be filled up to all the fullness of God. (Ephesians 3:17–19)*

Paul resumes the thought he began in Ephesians 3:1. He bows in prayer to
the Father, exhibiting humility and adoration, especially as he considers
God is Father over "every family in heaven and on earth" (v. 15). This signifies
that "God the Father is the one who creates (3:9) and thus names every family
in heaven and on earth. . . . God's ability to create and name every family in
heaven and on earth stresses his sovereignty and his fatherhood. He is the
one who is able to perform more than we ask or think . . ." (Harold Hoehner,
Ephesians: An Exegetical Commentary).

Paul encourages the believers. He wants them to know the strength that
Christ will give them so that they can live exemplary lives for Him. He prays
that they may be "strengthened with power through His Spirit" (v. 16). It is
picturesque, as rafters on a roof are braced with boards so the roof will remain
in place, so believers can be braced up "in the inner man." This was a promise
Jesus had given the disciples earlier (Acts 1:8). In this way Christ will dwell in
their hearts through faith; that is, Christ will "be at home in, at the very center
of or deeply rooted in, believers' lives. Christ must become the controlling factor in their attitudes and conduct" (Harold Hoehner, *Ephesians: An Exegetical
Commentary*).

With Christ as the center of their lives, believers are to be rooted firmly
in love as a plant is rooted in the ground and they are to be grounded, firmly
established as a foundation—in love. Thereby, they will know the surpassing greatness of Christ's love (Phil. 4:7). Yet, Christ's love is so immense, it
surpasses knowledge. In their position in Christ, Paul prays that they may
experientially know the fullness of Christ in their lives.

Paul is so provoked by the magnitude of Christ's love he breaks into a
doxology, reminding us that Christ is "able to do far more abundantly beyond
all that we ask or think." That covers everything. What is there in my life for
which I need to trust Him? What is there that you need to remove from your
worry list and submit to Christ, allowing Him to resolve it through the power
He has given you?

CONSIDER: *Paul is overwhelmed by the magnitude of Christ's love and the power
He has given to His people.*

September 21

UNITY IN LOVE AND MINISTRY

EPHESIANS 4:1–16

> *And He gave some as apostles, and some as prophets,*
> *and some as evangelists, and some as pastors and teachers,*
> *for the equipping of the saints for the work of service, to the*
> *building up of the body of Christ. (Ephesians 4:11–12)*

A church was well known for its faithful Bible exposition. The pastor was a humble, godly man who faithfully expounded God's Word. Yet there were cliques in the church and the church was governed by wealthy businessmen who didn't condescend to even talk to ordinary believers. Eventually they dismissed the godly pastor and destroyed the church. Unity in love and ministry was missing.

Having completed the doctrinal section of Ephesians 1–3, Paul begins his practical application of doctrinal truth. He begins by exhorting believers to walk worthy of their calling to salvation, defining it as humility, gentleness, and patience—surrounded with love. All of these terms relate to association with other believers and result in Paul's plea to "preserve the unity of the Spirit" (Eph. 4:3). Why is this necessary? Because there is one body of believers, not two. There is one Lord, one faith, one baptism, one God and Father. *One*. Not two. We are called to *unity*. We not only belong to Christ; we also belong to each other and need to preserve unity.

How is this accomplished? Unity of believers is achieved through the ministry of spiritual gifts to one another in love. Every believer has received one or more grace gifts at the discretion of the Holy Spirit (1 Cor. 12:11) to serve the body of Christ. The foundational gifts are apostles, prophets, evangelists, pastors, and teachers. The gift of apostle was restricted to the Twelve and they were given a unique authority (Matt. 10:1–8), laying the foundation of the church (Eph. 2:20). Prophets received direct revelation from God and the gift ceased after the completion of the canon of Scripture. Thus, the gifts of apostle and prophet were temporary, restricted to what is known as the apostolic age. Pastors and teachers shepherd God's people, instructing them in the Word, while evangelists proclaim the good news to the world. These foundational gifts are to equip believers to do the work of service, so that the body of Christ is built up. The result is unity, love, and maturity in Christ.

When believers are all exercising their spiritual gift in the church fellowship, believers will be built up in the faith; there will be unity, and love will permeate the fellowship.

CONSIDER: *Are you exercising your spiritual gifts for the unity and upbuilding of the body of Christ?*

September 22

THE NEW LIFE

EPHESIANS 4:17–5:2

*Put on the new self, which in the likeness of God has been created
in righteousness and holiness of the truth. (Ephesians 4:24)*

The founder of Radio Bible Class (RBC Ministries), M. R. DeHaan, was also a pastor and was rather straightforward. While preaching one Sunday he asked the people to read the book of Hezekiah for the following week. Next Sunday he asked how many had read Hezekiah. Several people raised their hands. Then Dr. DeHaan explained there was no book of Hezekiah but he would preach on "lie not one to another."

The believer in Christ has entered a new life that also calls for the believer to actively pursue the new life. Paul exhorts the believers to no longer conduct their lives like pagan unbelievers who live in spiritual darkness, having no understanding of God. Their hearts are calloused and spiritually insensitive. They embrace every form of impurity. Sound like Western culture?

But "truth is in Jesus" (Eph. 4:21). When we came to know Christ we were taught "in Him"—we have been united to Christ; we are called to live a new life. Therefore, we are exhorted to "put on the new self" (v. 24). The old self was the old lifestyle under sin and all we were as unsaved persons. Like dirty clothes, we are instructed to take off the old clothes of the old life and put on the new clothing of the new life.

The new life begins with a renewal of the mind. Some former vocabulary is gone; some previous habits and activities are gone. New thoughts now pervade the mind. The new mind is a creation of God in "righteousness and holiness" (v. 24). The new life has practical ramifications. The believer no longer tells lies but rather speaks the truth. Anger and bitterness are not left to simmer. Disagreements are resolved before sunset. Instead of stealing, the believer works. Above all, gracious words flow from the believer's mouth, words that encourage and build up the fellow believer.

In summary, sin grieves the Holy Spirit who now indwells us. He is our seal of redemption but He is grieved when we sin. Hence, we are challenged to lay aside all anger, bitterness, yelling, and hatred. Instead, we are to display a forgiving spirit toward others. That is the sign of a new person. Since we have been forgiven so much, why can we not forgive others?

CONSIDER: *The believer is challenged to lay aside the old, unsaved lifestyle and put on the new self which has been created in righteousness and holiness.*

September 23

CONTROLLED BY THE HOLY SPIRIT

Ephesians 5:3–20

Do not get drunk with wine, for that is dissipation,
but be filled with the Spirit. (Ephesians 5:18)

These are critical days for Christians. How do we live in the world? A generation ago preachers spoke on separation from the world. That topic is largely avoided today. But what is the result? It is no longer unusual to hear Christians take the Lord's name in vain. Christians watch immorality on TV and movies—undoubtedly, that affects their vocabulary and also their home life. Evangelicals divorce at a rate equal to non-Christians. Some professing Christians live together without being married. So does the Bible have anything to say about how a Christian should live in the world?

The Scriptures warn against immorality—any form of it. It should not even be named (Eph. 5:3, 12). Paul is saying "these sins should be so universally absent from the body of believers that there should be no occasion to associate them with the church" (Harold Hoehner, *Ephesians: An Exegetical Commentary*). Sexual immorality, impurity, greed, obscene speech, foolish talk—these are inappropriate and contradictory for Christians. It is probably correct to say that some believers know too much of what is going on in unbelievers' lives.

Why is this so significant? The Scriptures provide a sobering reminder that those who engage in immorality or covetousness will not inherit the kingdom of God (Eph. 5:5). In Matthew 7:21, Jesus reminded His listeners that not everyone who says "Lord, Lord" will enter the kingdom. God will expose unbelievers one day—in judgment. And the wrath of God will ultimately judge all immorality, hence, a believer can have no part of that. Believers were formerly children of darkness but that life is gone; we are now light in the Lord and need to walk according to our new status in Christ, pleasing Him in our daily living.

How is the new life in Christ accomplished? As we "walk as children of Light" (v. 8)—living under the daily, moment-by-moment control of the Holy Spirit. Through God's Word, the Holy Spirit will direct and control our lives so that we will live with a thankful heart, pleasing to the Lord.

How are you living? In speech? In conduct? Is it pleasing to the Lord? Do you exhibit new life in Christ?

CONSIDER: *Living under the control of the Holy Spirit, the believer is no longer to walk in darkness, in any association with sin.*

September 24

SUBJECT TO ONE ANOTHER

EPHESIANS 5:21–6:9

Wives, be subject to your own husbands, as to the Lord. . . .
Husbands, love your wives, just as Christ also loved the
church and gave Himself up for her. (Ephesians 5:22, 25)

Some eight-year-olds were asked, "What is the best age to get married?" One girl replied, "Eighty-four!" "Why?" "Because when you're eighty-four you don't have to work anymore and you can just spend time loving each other." Good advice!

This section of Scripture deals with three relationship areas: husband and wife, children and parents, employee and employer. The thesis statement teaches these three areas of submission: "be subject to one another in the fear of Christ" (Eph. 5:21).

First, wives are to be subject to their husbands "as to the Lord" (v. 22). The latter phrase removes the issue from simply being "cultural." The wife's submission to her husband is her response of obedience to the Lord since that is the Lord's will. The reason for the submission is that the husband is the head of the wife—he has authority over her. It is analogous to the relationship of the church to Christ. Christ is the head of the church. And husbands are to love their wives as Christ loved the church. How is that? Christ died for the church. It means the husband *loves* his wife; he doesn't lord authority over her. It means he continually seeks her highest good. Just as he cares for his own body, so he nourishes and cherishes his wife. If the husband fulfills his obligation, the wife will not have difficulty fulfilling her obligation. Yet one cannot wait for the other; each is obligated to fulfill their biblical injunction.

Second, children are to obey their parents "in the Lord" (6:1). The phrase pictures the quality of obedience children give their parents. And the "honor" of parents (v. 2) is lifelong; it is the first command on the second table of the Law (see Exodus 20:12). Fathers are instructed to discipline and instruct their children "in . . . the Lord" (Eph. 6:4), training their children through act and word.

Third, employees are to be subject to employers "as to Christ" (v. 5). They are to serve their masters "as to the Lord and not to men"—a significant instruction! And employers are to "do the same things" (v. 9) for their employees.

Our modern culture encourages rebellion rather than submission in every area of these three biblical directives. Yet, as we obey God's Word, we will always discover God's way is right and best—and it brings blessing.

CONSIDER: *God's Word directs wives, children, and employees to be subject to their husbands, parents, and employers; and it directs husbands, parents, and employers to be self-sacrificing.*

September 25

STRONG IN THE LORD

EPHESIANS 6:10–24

Finally, be strong in the Lord and in the
strength of His might. (Ephesians 6:10)

God has given significant instruction concerning marriage, family, and the workplace. But how is this accomplished? How do we have the strength to fulfill these biblical obligations? Paul provides the answer in these verses. Like a soldier donning his military armor and equipment, preparing for an intense battle, so the believer is given directives for the spiritual warfare in which we are engaged: "be strong in the Lord and in the strength of His might."

"How do I do that?" you say. The answer is, you don't. God does it. We are supernaturally empowered for battle by the Lord. You and I do not have the capacity to strengthen ourselves. "Be strong" is in the passive form in the Greek text: "let yourself be strengthened in the Lord." God must do the strengthening in our battle with the enemy. Three terms are used in 6:10 to describe the believer's strength.

Paul pictures a warrior equipped for warfare—that is the imagery for us. We are to put on the spiritual armor for our spiritual battle with the enemy, enabling us to stand firm against the schemes (*methodeia*)—the subtlety and trickery—of the devil.

Like the Roman soldier who puts on a wide leather belt to protect his abdomen, so the believer envelopes himself with the belt of truth: this is both God's objective truths themselves, as laid out in the Scriptures, as well as a willingness on the believer's part to faithfully live in accordance with those truths. As the Roman soldier wore a piece of metal covering his chest and hips, so the believer appropriates God's righteousness and acts righteously in daily living (Harold Hoehner, *Ephesians: An Exegetical Commentary*). Like the Roman soldier wore shoes thickly studded with hobnails (Cleon Rogers Jr. and Cleon Rogers III, *The New Linguistic and Exegetical Key to the Greek New Testament*), so the believer advances with the message of the gospel (Rom. 10:15). The soldier's protective shield was 4' x 2-1/2', deflecting the arrows of the enemy. Faith is the spiritual shield of believers. The Roman helmet was so strong, virtually nothing could inflict damage. Spiritually, salvation is the believer's helmet; nothing can pierce the believer's helmet to destroy his salvation. Finally, the double-edged sword is the offensive weapon—spiritually, the preached Word of God is the believer's weapon. Prayer in the Spirit consummates the believer's protection against the enemy.

The Lord has provided equipment for us to win the spiritual battle against the enemy. Have you put on the spiritual armor? Are you victorious in your spiritual warfare?

CONSIDER: *The believer is strengthened by God against the schemes of the devil by putting on the spiritual armor of God.*

September 26

JOY IN BELIEVERS

PHILIPPIANS 1:1–11

*I thank my God in all my remembrance of you, always offering
prayer with joy in my every prayer for you all. (Philippians 1:3–4)*

Philippians, along with Ephesians, Colossians, and Philemon, make up the
"Prison Epistles"—letters written by Paul during his first imprisonment
in Rome (Acts 28:30–31) in A.D. 61–63. Paul's visit to Philippi was a dramatic
change in his plan. Paul had wanted to go north in Asia Minor but the Holy
Spirit prohibited him (Acts 16:6–7) so Paul turned westward—to Europe. Paul
responded to the man from Macedonia, calling for him to come to help them
(Acts 16:9–10). Paul concluded that God was calling him to preach the gospel
in Europe.

Today we are the beneficiaries of Paul's movement to the west. This initiated the proclamation of the gospel throughout Europe. It began in Philippi,
a "leading city" of Macedonia, a Roman colony (Acts 16:12). Geographically,
Philippi was the first town of Macedonia. Apparently there was no synagogue
in the town since Paul met with some women to pray at the riverbank (Acts
16:13). From this simple, small beginning grew a strong church, sharing in
Paul's missionary endeavors.

The theme of Philippians is joy; the terms *joy* and *rejoice are* found some
sixteen times. The key verse is 4:4: "Rejoice in the Lord always; again I will
say, rejoice!"

Paul immediately exhibits joy as he begins with tender words of affection
for the Philippian believers. As he remembers his fellowship with them, he is
provoked to pray for all of them. With great gratitude, Paul remembered their
participation (*koinonia*) in the gospel. *Koinonia* means "fellowship" or "sharing." The Philippians had helped Paul financially in spreading the gospel and
he was deeply grateful to them for this expressive fellowship. From the first
day they met Paul on the riverbank, they had helped him. Paul was confident
that this good work which the Lord had begun in them would be brought to
completion at the return of Christ.

The Philippians were in Paul's heart. The Philippian believers responded
immediately to the gospel, exhibiting love for Paul in sharing in the proclamation of the gospel. They had stood with him in his imprisonment and defense
of the gospel. Paul recognized their spiritual development and prayed that
their love amid genuine knowledge and spiritual discernment would continue
so that they would stand blameless before Christ, bringing glory to His name.

What a heartwarming encouragement—to go on faithfully from the first
day.

CONSIDER: *Have you slowed in your zeal for Christ and your love for others, or
is that intensity continuing?*

JOY IN SUFFERING

PHILIPPIANS 1:12–30

For to me, to live is Christ and to die is gain. (Philippians 1:21)

I visited with Skip an hour or two before his homegoing to heaven. He was excited, a broad smile sweeping his face. When the moment came, he told his wife, "Cheryl, I'm going now. I love you." And Skip entered heaven. How could Skip transition so easily? Because Skip had lived righteously; Christ was preeminent in his life.

Although Paul suffered imprisonment because of the gospel, he reminded the Philippians that this had resulted in the greater spread of the gospel. Paul is picturesque: "Progress" views an army of woodcutters cutting a road through an impenetrable forest (Kenneth Wuest, *Wuests's Word Studies from the Greek New Testament*). Paul had blazed a trail for the gospel in the royal courts of Rome! The praetorian guard, special Roman soldiers, now heard the gospel. Since Paul was chained to a guard twenty-four hours a day, they heard his prayers, conversations with other Christians, letters dictated. . . . God used these events to spread the good news! Perhaps we ought to consider our unusual paths as being God-ordained for the spread of the gospel.

While some used Paul's imprisonment for selfish motives because of jealousy, Paul was still grateful that they preached the gospel. Others took courage by Paul's imprisonment and proclaimed the good news with boldness. Either way, Paul was grateful the gospel was being proclaimed. He was neither bitter nor angry.

Yet Paul was encouraged, expecting to be released from prison because of their prayers. Paul was not fearful—whether he would be released or whether he would be executed by the Romans. Living, for Paul, meant fellowship with Christ and service for Christ—he was occupied with Christ. Yet, to die was "gain," advantageous because he would be with Christ—and that would be much better than this present life. But Paul recognized his need to remain for their sake so he could help them develop spiritually. In either case—whether in life or death—Paul wanted Christ exalted.

So Paul reminded the Philippians not to fear suffering that would come to them, since believers have been destined for suffering. In Philippians 1:28, Paul alludes to the gladiator: the sign of a thumbs-up called for sparing the life of the warrior, while thumbs-down called for his death. "The Christian gladiator does not anxiously await the signal of life or death from the fickle crown" (J. B. Lightfoot, *Commentary on the Epistle of St. Paul to the Philippians*).

"To die is gain" can only be said if I first say "For to me, to live is Christ" (v. 21). If I would say "to live is wealth, business, success, sports, fame" I could never say "to die is gain" (G. Campbell Morgan, *How to Live*). To die right, one must live right.

CONSIDER: *The believer is victorious in both life and death; life means living for Christ; death is to be in His presence.*

September 28

Joy in Humility

PHILIPPIANS 2:1–11

Have this attitude in yourselves which was also in Christ Jesus,
who, although He existed in the form of God, did not regard equality
with God a thing to be grasped, but emptied Himself, taking
the form of a bond-servant. (Philippians 2:5–7)

Who is Jesus Christ? That is the most critical, most important question each one of us will ever answer. Some say He was a great teacher, some say He was a son of God but not equal with the Father. These are inadequate and false statements. But what does it mean when it says He "emptied himself"?

Paul begins by exhorting the Philippians to unity. Through their union with Christ and fellowship of the Holy Spirit, they have encouragement to walk in love, humility, and unity. Their motivation is Christ. Paul reminds them that the ultimate example of humility is Christ. They are to have the attitude that Christ exhibited.

Christ existed in the "form of God," which is a strong statement of the deity of Jesus Christ. Christ exhibited the attributes of God in His being and also performed the works of God. Jesus could say, "He who has seen Me has seen the Father" (John 14:9). But what does it mean when Scripture says that He "emptied Himself" (Phil. 2:7)? Did He empty Himself of His deity? No. Jesus exhibited His deity throughout His earthly ministry through His words (John 10:11, 30, 36) and His works (John 5:21–27).

The phrases that follow "emptied" explain the emptying of Christ. It was not a subtraction but an addition. He did not subtract His deity; rather, He added humanity: ". . . taking the form of a bond-servant, and being made in the likeness of men. Being found in appearance as a man . . ." (vv. 7–8). These three phrases explain that Christ emptied Himself by taking on an additional nature—humanity. Jesus' emptying culminated in humbling Himself "by becoming obedient to the point of death, even death on a cross" (v. 8). The statement reminds us of the extent of Christ's humiliation—dying on the cross. It is the strongest exhortation for believers to walk in humility.

Christ could only make atonement for sin as the God-Man. He had to be man to represent humanity and He had to be God for His death to have infinite value. But the period of Christ's humiliation is over. He is exalted in glory, where every creature in heaven, on earth, and under the earth will bow in recognition that Jesus is Lord—deity. Only God is to be worshiped. Can I fathom the depth of the humiliation of Christ that He would procure my salvation? Does that leave any allowance for pride?

CONSIDER: *Christ humbled Himself by taking on humanity that He might atone for sins as the God-Man and thereafter be exalted in heaven as Lord.*

EXAMPLES OF HUMILITY

PHILIPPIANS 2:12–30

---

*Prove yourselves to be blameless and innocent, children of God
above reproach in the midst of a crooked and perverse generation,
among whom you appear as lights in the world, holding
fast the word of life. (Philippians 2:15–16)*

As my wife and I were traveling in Germany with our friends, John and Heidi, John was trying to locate the place where he lived after Word War II. On that Sunday afternoon we saw a well-dressed couple walking along the street. After we told them what we were looking for, he and his wife took us to the site and spent three hours answering our questions! A complete stranger—but to our joy we discovered he was a believer with a servant mentality.

The Scriptures do indeed teach servanthood and humility. Paul delineates several prime examples. First, Paul emphasizes the need for unity and humility. Paul addresses the church—they are to work hard at effecting unity with one another. And when this happens, it is God who is energizing them in their work. Their unity, love, and humility are a testimony to the world where they are to be blameless and innocent, spotless and pure, above reproach. Only then will the light of the gospel shine in a sin-darkened world.

Paul reminds them to be "above reproach"—without blemish in a crooked and perverse generation. This is a somber reminder that we live in a world of distorted and twisted moral and spiritual values. We are to "hold forth" the word of life—offering salvation to those who are lost.

While challenging the Philippians to walk in humility, Paul himself is an example. He is ready to forfeit his life for the cause of Christ; he is ready to be poured out as a drink offering. But amid suffering and even death—rejoice! Suffering and death should not rob Christians of their joy.

With concern for the Philippians, Paul planned to send Timothy to encourage their hearts. There was no one else more suited to minister to them. Yet Paul hoped to come to Philippi himself, but he first needed to see how his situation would be resolved.

Paul also determined to send Epaphroditus, whom Paul termed a "fellow-worker and fellow-soldier," who had been sick and nearly died in commitment to the cause of Christ. He exemplified humility. He longed to see the Philippians; he had the heart of Christ in his love for the Philippian believers.

Men like this, who have risked their lives and suffered for the gospel, are to be held in high regard. These men—and others like them—serve as examples of humility.

CONSIDER: *We are challenged to walk in humility while living in a decadent world.*

Joy in the Lord

Philippians 3:1–11

> *. . . that I may know Him and the power of His*
> *resurrection and the fellowship of His sufferings,*
> *being conformed to His death. (Philippians 3:10)*

Charles Colson was a significant name in the Nixon administration. He was dubbed the "hatchet man" for his ruthless dealings with any opposition. But Jesus Christ changed Charles Colson. After serving time in prison, Mr. Colson launched Prison Fellowship, conducting Bible studies for prisoners and other ministries.

Amid suffering, while in prison, Paul enjoins, "rejoice in the Lord." Amid sadness, amid suffering: rejoice! Why? It is a safeguard from error and foolish thinking—thinking as Judaizers and evil workers. Are they in our midst? Absolutely. They knock on your door on Saturday morning, expounding a works salvation while denying the deity of Christ. These are the false teachers who boast "in the flesh"—the works they perform. Paul could boast in the flesh—he had the best credentials of all: circumcised the eighth day, nation of Israel, tribe of Benjamin, a Hebrew of Hebrews, a Pharisee, and persecutor of the church. Strictly adhering to the Law—blameless.

Paul had a remarkable pedigree but he counted it one huge loss—worthless "in view of the surpassing value of knowing Christ Jesus" (Phil. 3:8). And Paul's thought hasn't changed. He still counts them "rubbish"—refuse. That was Paul's evaluation of human attainment and high position apart from Christ. He forfeited all human endeavor in order that he might "gain Christ."

Paul no longer sought righteousness through the Law. His righteousness was now found in Christ! He looked for the day when he could stand before Christ and be accounted righteous through the imputed righteousness of Christ through faith in Him.

Paul's goal was the intimate knowledge of Christ: "that I may know Him and the power of His resurrection and the fellowship of His sufferings." What a challenge! Like Paul, we need to seek the intimate fellowship with Christ (through His Word) and His resurrection power in our lives (see Ephesians 1:18–21). But there are also sufferings that drive us to Christ for strength. We live in dependence on Him.

What is your emphasis? Do you take pride in your worldly position? You may need to evaluate if there is something you need to set aside so that you may know Christ.

CONSIDER: *Although Paul had premier credentials, he considered them a total loss for the high value of knowing Jesus Christ through faith.*

October 1

JOY IN ANTICIPATING HEAVEN

PHILIPPIANS 3:12–4:1

*For our citizenship is in heaven, from which also we eagerly
wait for a Savior, the Lord Jesus Christ. (Philippians 3:20)*

In *Mere Christianity* C. S. Lewis noted, "If you read history you will find that the Christians who did most for the present world were just those who thought most of the next. The Apostles themselves, who set on foot the conversion of the Roman Empire, the great men who built up the Middle Ages, the English Evangelicals who abolished the Slave Trade, all left their mark on Earth, precisely because their minds were occupied with Heaven. It is since Christians have largely ceased to think of the other world that they have become so ineffective in this. Aim at Heaven and you will get earth 'thrown in': aim at earth and you will get neither."

With heaven and Christ in view, Paul was pressing on. His eyes were on the goal. Like a Greek Olympic runner being pursued and streaking down the race course to the finish line, Paul's eyes were on the goal. Why? Paul sought to know Christ experientially. God had captured Paul's heart on the Damascus road so that Paul would reflect Christ in his life—and that was the reason Paul now sought intimate fellowship with Christ.

The past with its prominence was no longer important; Paul makes a point of forgetting the past. What did he forget? Past failures. Paul did not dwell on how he persecuted the church or hindered the Lord's work. Past accomplishments. Paul no longer dwelt on his past achievements in Judaism. They were no longer important. Like a runner, Paul was straining "toward the goal for the prize of the upward call of God in Christ Jesus" (Phil. 3:14). Like the victor in the Olympics heard his name, his father's name, and his country announced and the charioteer would arrive to place a palm branch in his hands, so Paul sought the prize: Christ Himself. "The high calling of God is to be like His Son. . . . Everything God brings into our experience He brings to conform us to the image of His Son. . . . Paul drives himself because he wants to accomplish that purpose Christ had for him when He saved him, and separated him to Himself" (J. Dwight Pentecost, *Joy of Living*).

Warning them against the false teachers, Paul focuses on heaven. He reminds us that our citizenship (*politeuma*) is in heaven. We have a dual citizenship: one is on this old earth and it is temporary; the other is in heaven (the new earth) and it is permanent. For this reason we "eagerly wait for a Savior, the Lord Jesus Christ" (v. 20) from heaven. At that moment these corruptible bodies will be transformed into incorruptible bodies, fit for eternity! Are you joyfully anticipating heaven?

CONSIDER: *Forgetting the past, Paul pressed on to intimately know Christ, eagerly anticipating the Savior's return from heaven.*

JOY IN WORRY-FREE LIVING

PHILIPPIANS 4:2–23

Be anxious for nothing, but in everything by prayer and supplication with thanksgiving let your requests be made known to God. And the peace of God, which surpasses all comprehension, will guard your hearts and your minds in Christ Jesus. (Philippians 4:6–7)

As a pastor, I have visited numerous believers in the hospital when they have received the harsh news of terminal cancer. Yet they have consistently reflected the joy of the Lord that has given them peace. Amid the sobering news of a terminal illness they retained the peace and joy of the Lord.

The theme of Philippians surfaces once more: "Rejoice in the Lord always" (4:4). This is a command to be continually, at all times rejoicing. As the Philippians lived in a hostile world, so in the twenty-first century we live in a world that is increasingly hostile to Christianity. The solution? Rejoice in the Lord. And we are to display "a humble, patient steadfastness, which is able to submit to injustice, disgrace, and maltreatment without hatred and malice, trusting in God in spite of all of it" (Cleon Rogers Jr. and Cleon Rogers III, *The New Linguistic and Exegetical Key to the Greek New Testament*).

Rejoicing and worry cannot coexist, so Paul exhorts the Philippians not to worry or be anxious about anything. Anxiety comes over things that we cannot control—but Paul tells us to stop being anxious. Instead, we are challenged to pray. We should pray to God, making request for our specific needs. It is foolish to carry the burden ourselves when we can give the burden to God. The result will be supernatural. As God's peace guards our heart like soldiers guarding a city gate, worry will not be able to enter; instead, God's peace will flood our hearts.

But to further avert worry, Paul exhorts the believers to control their thinking. What do I think about throughout the day? That will affect whether or not I worry. We are to let our mind dwell on good things—things that are true, honorable, right, pure, lovely, reputable, excellent, and praiseworthy. This will also lead to contentment whether our circumstances are meager or extravagant. The secret lies in the indwelling Christ who strengthens us. He gives us the strength we need.

So how do you live? Is your life filled with worry? Is your thinking focused on worldly things, financial issues? Learn to rest. Give your burdens to the Lord.

CONSIDER: *We are to rejoice in the Lord through committing our concerns to Him in prayer and thinking righteously.*

PREEMINENCE OF LIFE IN CHRIST

COLOSSIANS 1:1–14

We . . . [are] praying always for you, since we heard of your faith
in Christ Jesus and the love which you have for all the saints;
because of the hope laid up for you in heaven. (Colossians 1:3–5)

When Abe met Jesus Christ, God totally transformed him. He was physically strong and had been brutal to some people. Abe made a list of the people he had troubled and he went to each one of them, telling them of his new faith in Christ and asking their forgiveness. From day one, Abe was a new man.

Paul addresses the believers at Colossae with joy and thanksgiving while praying for them. They were robust in their new faith in Christ. The trilogy of faith, love, and hope are indicators of spiritual development. From the first day the Colossians heard the gospel, they displayed *faith* in Christ and *love* for one another, all because of the *hope* laid up for them in heaven.

The Colossian believers had a genuine faith; it was "constantly bearing fruit and increasing" (1:6). What a wonderful testimony! They heard and they understood. This was more than merely receiving information; they consciously recognized the truth of the gospel and they embraced the gospel experientially in their lives. The reality of the gospel was evidenced in their "love in the Spirit" (v. 8). The Holy Spirit empowered them to walk in the Spirit, producing love for one another (see Galatians 5:22, which points out that love is one evidence [fruit] of the Spirit in the believer's life).

Should they stop at this point? No. Paul continued to pray for them to be filled with the full knowledge of God's will. The beautiful result of this would be living their lives pleasing to the Lord and bearing fruit. And they would be strengthened with power—God Himself would empower them. And the result? Steadfastness and patience. "Steadfastness" means "to remain under." God gives us strength to remain "steadfast under the difficult pressures of life" (Robert Gromacki, *Stand Perfect in Wisdom*). These promises are important reminders that the Christian life is a supernatural life. We don't live it on our own; we don't have the power on our own. Christ gives us the strength.

In all of this we give thanks to the Father who has qualified and authorized us to share in heaven's glories. All of grace! We are no longer in darkness; we are citizens of the kingdom of God's Son! And all this because Christ has provided our redemption. What a blessing! What a privilege! Have you entered into your victorious walk in Christ?

CONSIDER: *Our victorious walk will exhibit faith, love, and hope as we constantly progress in our knowledge of God's will.*

October 4

PREEMINENCE OF CHRIST

COLOSSIANS 1:15–23

*And He is the image of the invisible God, the firstborn
of all creation. For by Him all things were created,
both in the heavens and on earth, visible and invisible,
whether thrones or dominions or rulers or authorities—all things
have been created through Him and for Him. (Colossians 1:15–16)*

Who is Christ? That is the cental issue everyone faces. Liberals are quick to say He was a great teacher, but they deny His deity. Cultists regularly deny the deity of Jesus Christ in promoting their false gospel.

Colossians establishes a grandiose picture of the person of Christ. Who is He? Christ is "the image of the invisible God." *Image (eikon)* denotes the picture of the ruler on a coin. The image shows exactly what the ruler looks like. None of us has ever seen George Washington but we know what he looks like because of his image on a quarter. No one has ever seen God the Father but we can know what He is like because Jesus Christ is the exact image of the invisible God.

Christ is also the "firstborn of all creation." *Firstborn* "emphasizes the pre-existence and uniqueness of Christ as well as His superiority over creation. The term does not indicate that Christ was a creation or a created being" (Cleon Rogers Jr. and Cleon Rogers III, *The New Linguistic and Exegetical Key to the Greek New Testament*). Psalm 89:27 explains the meaning: "My firstborn, the highest of the kings of the earth." He is preeminent in dignity, position, and authority.

Jesus is deity—the second person of the Godhead. As God, He has created all things—the heavens, the earth, the visible, the invisible, thrones, dominions, rulers, and authorities (John 1:3; Heb. 1:2). This includes the angelic realm. And if Jesus has created all things, then He is the uncreated one. He is eternal. He is God.

Christ existed before all things and through Him all things hold together. He is the cohesive force of the universe (Heb. 1:3) and He carries all of history forward to its predetermined conclusion.

As Creator, the head of the church, and the firstborn, Christ is "preeminent over the realms of men and angels, both good and evil, throughout eternity" (Robert Gromacki, *Stand Perfect in Wisdom*). And He is preeminent over my life.

CONSIDER: *Jesus Christ is God of very God, the precise image of the Father; having created all things, He is uncreated and He is preeminent over all things and every sphere.*

Upholding His Preeminence

Colossians 1:24–2:7

*We proclaim Him, admonishing every man and teaching every man
with all wisdom, so that we may present every man complete
in Christ. . . . In whom are hidden all the treasures
of wisdom and knowledge. (Colossians 1:28; 2:3)*

The false message of the "Health and Wealth Gospel" has penetrated many Christians' lives. Why? Because some Christians desire to be wealthy. One preacher proclaimed that we have the right to expect a return of one thousand dollars on a ten dollar contribution.

Some believers mistakenly seek for earthly wealth. They have no apparent knowledge of the riches they have in Christ. Paul determined to make that known to the Colossians: he proclaimed the preeminence of Christ. This was not revealed in the Old Testament; this was new revelation. Jew and Gentile, united in one body, the church, accomplished through Christ indwelling every believer: "Christ in you, the hope of glory" (1:27). What an astonishing truth! He is not only the God of the Jews, but also of the Gentiles. Christ is in you Gentiles! And Christ is our hope of glory. When Christ returns in His glorious splendor, our hope will be realized as we will reign with Him.

Paul admonishes and instructs them to present themselves "complete in Christ." Positionally, believers are already complete in Christ, as Colossians 2:10 makes clear; but in practice, there remains a need for growth. And that's the purpose behind Paul's work.

When truth is taught, the enemy doesn't take a vacation; there is an assault. As in an athletic contest, Paul was in a spiritual warfare with false teachers. Paul's desire was for the Colossians to be encouraged and knit together in love so they would be able to grasp a full understanding and true knowledge of Christ. This is more than intellectual knowledge—it is knowing Christ by experience. And Christ is the storehouse of wisdom and knowledge: "It is in Christ that all the treasures of divine wisdom and knowledge have been stored up—stored up in hiding formerly, but now displayed to those who have come to know Christ" (Cleon Rogers Jr. and Cleon Rogers III, *The New Linguistic and Exegetical Key to the Greek New Testament*).

"So walk in Him . . . being built up in Him" (2:6, 7). Like a building under construction, we are to grow to completion in Christ.

CONSIDER: *Previously unrevealed, now Christ indwells Jews and Gentiles alike, and we are complete in Him who is the epitome of wisdom and knowledge.*

October 6

DEFENDING CHRIST'S PREEMINENCE
COLOSSIANS 2:8–23

See to it that no one takes you captive through philosophy and empty deception, according to the tradition of men, according to the elementary principles of the world, rather than according to Christ. For in Him all the fullness of Deity dwells in bodily form, and in Him you have been made complete. (Colossians 2:8–10)

Figurines are sold in stores. Bumper stickers read: "Angels are watching over me." People pray to guardian angels. Angels have become the new mediators between man and God. With unsuspecting people, angels have replaced Christ.

The Scriptures warn us against being taken captive through philosophy and deception by false teachers. Cultists have led numerous people astray. Any philosophy that is not centered on Christ is wrong. God's final and complete revelation is in Christ! The fullness of deity dwells in Christ—in bodily form. The ascetic heretics believed the spirit was good but matter was evil; however, the fullness of God dwells in bodily form in Christ. Moreover, in Him we have been made complete. Because the fullness of deity dwells in Christ and since we are united in Him, we are complete in Him who is head over all authority. Christ is not merely an angelic being, He is in authority over the entire angelic realm.

"In Him . . . in Him . . . in Him." Paul continues to remind believers of their unique position of being "in Christ." What a sublime truth! Does it capture your heart? We have been united with Him, buried and raised up to a new life in Him. And we are now alive in Christ! United with Him we have been forgiven though an outporing of God's grace. How much? *All* our transgressions—past, present, and future. We stand forgiven in Christ. The debt that we could never pay has been cancelled, erased, wiped out. The IOU of indebtedness that we had is gone forever. It was nailed to the cross. Christ has conquered Satan and his domain and has made a public spectacle of them.

Now the challenge for believers is not to be led astray by deceivers. Paul warns against legalism—things that are a mere shadow. The reality is in Christ. Paul also warns against worship of angels and asceticism. Paul concludes these are all of "no value." They are teachings of men and not of God.

So how should we live? Appropriate the blessings that are ours in our position in Christ. Stand fast in the truth, defend the truth. Keep fixated on Christ and our glorious position in Him.

CONSIDER: *The fullness of deity dwells in Christ and we are complete in Him. Stand fast against false teachings.*

LIVING CHRIST'S PREEMINENCE

COLOSSIANS 3:1–4:6

*Therefore if you have been raised up with Christ, keep
seeking the things above, where Christ is, seated at the
right hand of God. (Colossians 3:1)*

In *One Month to Live*, Kerry and Chris Shook state, "Just as some people live like there's no tomorrow, others use their faith to live like there's no today. They're always thinking about heaven 'someday' instead of fully engaging in life today." Yet the Scriptures admonish us to stay focused on heaven (see, for example, Colossians 3:1; Titus 2:13; and 1 Peter 1:13). It is as we live with a heaven mind-set that we will have an impact on earth.

A strong doctrinal foundation has been laid for us. We are forgiven, united to Christ; we are complete in Him. Now Paul draws practical applications. Since we have been raised to a new life, we are to keep habitually seeking the things above. Daily. Constantly. We are to keep focused on Christ and heaven. This is another way of saying, "seek first His kingdom" (Matt. 6:33), or praying, "Your kingdom come" (Matt. 6:10). We are to focus on the spiritual blessings in the heavenly places in Christ (Eph. 1:3).

This is a challenge. We are warned to set our mind on the things above, not on things that are on earth. An earthly focus does not produce spirituality (see 1 John 2:15). Is it possible to keep a heavenly focus? Yes. It is possible since we have died with Christ and our life is "hidden with Christ in God" (Col. 3:3). Our anticipation is that glorious day when Christ is revealed, transforming us into the likeness of Christ.

Meanwhile we live for His glory. Since we have died with Christ and been raised to a new life, we are to consider the members of our earthly bodies as dead to sin. These bodies that once served sin now serve Christ. Appropriation is the key. We receive what Christ has done. We have been positionally crucified with Christ—now we apply it. We are dead to the old life of immorality, anger, and evil speaking. This is the former life; it is not the new life in Christ. We are to "put them all aside" (v. 8), like taking off old, dirty clothes. We have been washed and we put on the new life like new clothing.

We walk a new path. Where there was formerly a hard heart there is now a heart of compassion, kindness, and humility. The consummating credential is love. Love is the cement that produces maturity in Christian fellowship. Then peace will pervade our hearts with a thankful spirit. Finally, we are instructed: "Whatever you do in word or deed, do all in the name of the Lord Jesus, giving thanks through Him to God the Father" (3:17). That is the new standard by which we live.

CONSIDER: *United with Christ, we are challenged to seek the things above, focused on Christ, while putting on the new self and allowing Christ to reign supreme.*

October 8

Names . . . Names

Colossians 4:7–18

---

*As to all my affairs, Tychicus, our beloved brother
and faithful servant and fellow bond-servant in the Lord,
will bring you information. (Colossians 4:7)*

We know the high profile ancient and modern names: Abraham, Moses, Peter, Paul, John . . . Martin Luther, Jonathan Edwards, Billy Graham, Chuck Colson. . . . But the Bible contains names of individuals about whom we know very little, yet they are on the register of God—and important. Paul concludes his letter to the Colossians with a lengthy list of individuals who are largely unknown.

Tychicus was unique in that he delivered the epistles to the Ephesian and Colossian believers (Eph. 6:21–22). Was he useful to Paul? Significantly so! Paul refers to him as "beloved brother and faithful servant and fellow bond-servant in the Lord." This is a strong commendation. He was beloved and exhibited faithfulness as a servant of the Lord. Furthermore, he came to encourage and comfort the Colossians, telling them what had happened to Paul.

Onesimus was the runaway slave, belonging to Philemon, who was converted through Paul's ministry and was now returning to his master. But Paul doesn't refer to him as a slave—even though he still is one—he calls him faithful and beloved. Only now could he be called faithful, since previously he was unfaithful, running from his master.

Aristarchus had been a traveler with Paul (Acts 19:29) and was now a fellow prisoner with Paul in Rome.

Mark, who had once turned back from traveling with Paul on the first missionary journey ("John" in Acts 13:13 was also called Mark), was again with Paul, this time visiting him in prison in Rome. On Paul's final imprisonment, he called Mark "useful for service" (2 Tim. 4:11).

Jesus Justus, a Jewish believer, was Paul's fellow worker in the kingdom of God and an encouragement to Paul. Epaphras, a bondslave of Christ, labored energetically for them in his prayers. Luke and Demas also sent greetings.

Why did Paul mention all these people? They were important, yet unknown. May that be a reminder to you and me that while our names may be relatively unknown on this earth, we are known to God and important to God.

CONSIDER: *Paul mentions numerous individuals by name; although relatively unknown, they are important in the ministry and important to God.*

DRAMATIC CHANGE

1 THESSALONIANS 1:1–10

*For they themselves report about us what kind of a reception
we had with you, and how you turned to God from idols to
serve a living and true God, and to wait for His Son
from heaven. (1 Thessalonians 1:9–10)*

Erik is a remarkable young man. Since he came to faith in Christ two years ago, his life has evidenced a dramatic change. He has completed a Bible institute program and is busily involved in helping and ministering to others. Erik exhibits the joy of Christ in his heart—it is evident in his face, his speech, and his life.

The church at Thessalonica was founded when Paul visited the city on his second missionary journey (see Acts 17:1–10). Although Paul only spent three weeks there, a large number of Jews and Gentiles came to faith in Christ. Paul was writing them to remind them of his prayers and to commend them. Although young in the faith, they exhibited the trilogy of maturity: faith, love, and hope (1 Thess. 1:3).

The gospel had come to them in power through the Holy Spirit, having penetrated their hearts "with full conviction" (v. 5). The Thessalonians had "a deep inward persuasion of the truth of the gospel, a token of the Holy Spirit's work in their hearts" (F. F. Bruce, *1 & 2 Thessalonians: Word Biblical Commentary*). They recognized the truth of the gospel and the integrity of Paul and Silas.

But their response to the gospel was costly: they received the word "in much tribulation" (v. 6). They were persecuted when they came to faith in Christ. We don't see this to any significant degree in America, yet in many parts of the world people pay a dear price for believing in Christ. But amid their persecution, the Thessalonians nonetheless had the "joy of the Holy Spirit" (v. 6). Both? Yes. It is possible to have the joy of Christ while suffering persecution. In their stalwart faith, they became an encouragement and testimony to believers throughout the land. Word about them spread. They had turned away from idolatry to serve the living and true God and to wait expectantly and patiently for the return of Jesus Christ. Even in their infant faith, they knew that the coming of Christ for His own would precede the intense judgment that would be meted out to an unbelieving world.

What an encouragement and lesson for us! We can (and should) exhibit joy amid suffering—and we need to have a heavenly focus—waiting for the return of Christ.

CONSIDER: *The Thessalonian believers exhibited a dramatic conversion; amid suffering, they had joy as they expectantly awaited the return of Christ.*

October 10

A CALL TO INTEGRITY

1 THESSALONIANS 2:1–20

*But just as we have been approved by God to be entrusted
with the gospel, so we speak, not as pleasing men, but
God who examines our hearts. (1 Thessalonians 2:4)*

One Christian conference speaker made special arrangements whenever he spoke. The service was to begin prior to his coming. Being chauffeured, he arrived at a reserved parking place in the front of the church. When he walked the aisle, it was a signal that it was the last stanza of the hymn. He got up, spoke, then had someone lead in prayer while he made his exit. When the prayer was over, they heard the roar of his car leaving.

That was not Paul's perception on the ministry. Yet Paul needed to explain his own ministry to the Thessalonians because others had charged him with impure motives. Paul had come to Thessalonica after having been shamefully treated and humiliated in Philippi. But Paul was bold; having been entrusted with the gospel, he spoke the truth with boldness, despite hostility and opposition. He didn't seek to please others. He wanted God's approval, not man's. For that reason, he didn't come with flattering, deceptive speech so people would applaud him.

When Paul taught the Thessalonians, he was gentle with them. Recognizing they were spiritual babies, he ministered to them like a nursing mother caring for her children. As his spiritual children, they were dear to him and he sought to impart his own life to them. Paul worked very hard physically so he wouldn't be a financial burden to them, guiding and directing them like a father guiding his children. And they responded, readily receiving Paul's instruction, recognizing it as "the word of God . . . not as the word of men" (2:13). But they also endured sufferings, from Gentiles and Jews alike. And so Paul reminded them that those who oppose the gospel "fill up the measure of their sins" (v. 16). (When we get to the book of Revelation, we will see that the wrath of God will ultimately fall heavily on those who repudiate the gospel.)

Satan is busy in bringing opposition to the gospel. He did it in the first century and he is doing it in the twenty-first century. Yet, the Lord Jesus will consummate the ages at His coming and Satan will be subdued. So Paul rejoiced in anticipation of that day, when these believers would be his joy in the presence of Christ.

CONSIDER: *In our ministry for Christ we must foremost determine to live and serve with integrity so our actions will not keep others from coming to faith in Christ.*

Excel Still More

1 Thessalonians 3:1–4:12

*Abound in love for one another. . . . Walk and please God [and] . . .
excel still more. . . . You . . . are taught by God to love one another. . . .
But . . . excel still more. (1 Thessalonians 3:12; 4:1, 9–10)*

Some dear friends are going through a difficult time right now. Cancer has invaded their home, and other serious issues impact their lives. Yet, they retain peace and joy amid their trials and difficulties. That is our challenge in the Christian life. Amid trials we are called to exhibit faith and love—and excel still more.

Having spent only three weeks in Thessalonica, Paul was concerned for them, remembering the tumult that existed in the city. So Paul sent Timothy to strengthen and encourage the believers in their faith.

Some people teach that if you just come to Christ, all your problems will be solved. Of course, that is false! Sometimes the trials *begin* when we come to Christ. Paul reminds us that we have been destined for suffering; it is the trials in life that bring spiritual progress and maturity (James 1:2–4; 1 Peter 1:6–7). We don't enjoy trials, but consider this analogy: it is storms that cause a tree to extend its roots and thereby strengthen it.

The Thessalonian believers grew strong amid their trials. Timothy reported of their faith and love. Paul rejoiced to see them standing firm in their faith, yet, it was to be ongoing, "like soldiers repelling an enemy attack" (D. Edmond Hiebert, *The Thessalonian Epistles*). So Paul prayed for them night and day, meaning regularly, that he could come to them and build them up in the faith. What a challenge and reminder that we must be vigilant in praying for believers who are suffering.

Paul puts the challenge to them: amid suffering, "abound in love for one another, and for all people" (1 Thess. 3:12). The reason is significant: that they may be established blameless at the coming of Christ. We don't live for today— we live for tomorrow, anticipating the commendation of Christ at His coming.

Even as we live in a depraved post-Christian era, so Paul challenges believers to "excel still more" (4:1, 10). We must not compromise our Christian beliefs. We are called to live in purity in a decadent world without moral structures. Our commitment to Christ must remain firm, and amid persecution and suffering we are challenged to "excel still more" in love.

CONSIDER: *In a hostile world, believers are called to remain firm in their faith and purity and excel still more in love to one another.*

October 12

THE "ANY MOMENT" RAPTURE

1 THESSALONIANS 4:13–18

The Lord Himself will descend from heaven with a shout, with the voice of the archangel and with the trumpet of God, and the dead in Christ will rise first. Then we who are alive and remain will be caught up together with them in the clouds to meet the Lord in the air, and so we shall always be with the Lord. (1 Thessalonians 4:16–17)

Although Scripture does not tell us when the rapture will occur, numerous people have "prophesied" the event: 87 reasons why Christ will return in 1987. One author wrote "88 Reasons Why the Rapture Will Be in 1988." When that didn't happen, he followed it with "The Final Shout: Rapture Report 1989." Then 1993. Then 1994. The year 2000 was prognosticated by many as the date of Christ's return. Now the self-styled prophets predict 2012. But no one knows.

The rapture is the "catching up," when believers who have died during the church age will be resurrected and, along with living believers, receive glorified bodies and join them in being with Christ. That is our hope and anticipation. For that reason, when a believer dies, we grieve but not without hope; we grieve amid hope. Although the body "sleeps," departed believers are immediately in Christ's presence (notice Jesus' words to the thief on the cross in Luke 23:43). At the rapture, departed believers return with Christ to receive their glorified bodies. They are not at a disadvantage; they will rise first, then we will be reunited with them.

There is no prophecy that needs to be fulfilled prior to the rapture. The rapture is "imminent," meaning it can occur at any moment. Like a general giving orders to his troops, Christ will return from heaven with a shout, a command. The archangel will cry out and God's trumpet will sound; then the believers that have died will respond. Their heavenly form will be reunited with their earthly body and transformed into a glorified body. Then, those believers that are alive when the rapture occurs will receive their glorified bodies and be reunited with their departed loved ones. We will be "caught up together with them"—descriptive of the rapture and reunion with other believers.

What a joyful day that will be! Reunion with loved ones in the presence of Christ. As we are reminded, this is a word of comfort. Do you need comfort today? Look in eager anticipation for the rapture—united to Christ and reunited with loved ones. What a glorious day that will be!

CONSIDER: *The rapture, when Christ returns to catch up living believers to reunite them with departed believers, may occur at any moment.*

October 13

THE DAY OF THE LORD

1 THESSALONIANS 5:1–11

*For you yourselves know full well that the day of the Lord
will come just like a thief in the night. (1 Thessalonians 5:2)*

On most Sundays as we enter the property to our church complex, a man sits outside our gate with a large sign, ridiculing Christ and the church: "Jesus is not coming." Anyone who attempts to talk to him has their ears filled with filth and vitriol. He ridicules the church and rejects the promises Jesus made about His return.

This man's attitude portrays the opinion of people at the end of the age. Paul has described the end times events in sequence. Having explained the rapture in 4:13–18, he now describes subsequent events on earth. Following the rapture, the day of the Lord begins with the tribulation. Like a thief that unexpectedly breaks into a house at night, so the day of the Lord will descend unexpectedly upon unbelievers. They are living in an era of false peace, when the Antichrist has made a peace agreement, guaranteeing the protection of Israel (Dan. 9:27). For three and a half years there will be relative peace. But suddenly, like a mother giving birth to a child, the pain of the tribulation period will descend upon them (Matt. 24:9–31). The wrath of God will be unleashed upon a hostile, decadent world.

Church age believers will not have to endure the trauma of the tribulation. Believers do not look for wrath; they look for the rapture. We are "sons of light and sons of day" (1 Thess. 5:5). Because we know what is coming, we live as children of light, walking in obedience to His Word, putting on the breastplate of faith and love and the helmet of the hope of salvation.

Believers are the objects of the love of God, not the wrath of God. Our destiny is for "obtaining salvation through our Lord Jesus Christ" (v. 9). This means deliverance from the tribulation period that will judge unbelievers.

So whether we are alive ("awake") or have died ("asleep"), we will live "together with Him" (v. 10). We look not for wrath but rapture, for reunion with believing loved ones at Christ's appearing. These are words of encouragement and comfort. Do not fear the world's mockers—live soberly, looking for the return of Christ at the rapture.

CONSIDER: *Following the rapture, unbelievers will have a false sense of peace until suddenly the wrath of God will bring judgment on them during the tribulation.*

October 14

Sanctified Entirely

1 Thessalonians 5:12–28

*Now may the God of peace Himself sanctify you entirely; and may
your spirit and soul and body be preserved complete, without blame
at the coming of our Lord Jesus Christ. (1 Thessalonians 5:23)*

What are the signs of a mature local church? These verses summarize the
spiritual elements in a local church, beginning with respect for the leaders. Those who work hard at teaching and caring for the believers are to be
appreciated and loved. And those who are undisciplined need to be warned
and corrected. Yet there are many others in the church fellowship that need
encouragement and help. Some believers are not strong and need the help and
encouragement of others. We dare not neglect them. Look over your church
fellowship. Are there any who are ill? Have some lost a job? It is our responsibility to encourage them to stimulate their faith.

Revenge and retaliation should never be a believer's behavior, rather we
are to show kindness to others—that is to be our response. In daily issues the
believer is to reflect joy and be in unceasing prayer. We leave matters with our
sovereign God; He can solve our concerns. That in turn will lead to an attitude
of thanksgiving—but only as we leave the issues with the Lord. This doesn't
mean we thank God *for* everything but rather *in* everything. God is in control
of our circumstances.

Believers are warned not to quench the Spirit. We *quench the Spirit* when
"the fervor which He kindles in the heart is dampened by unspiritual attitudes,
criticisms, or actions" (D. Edmond Hiebert, *The Thessalonian Epistles*). But
everything should be tested biblically with a view to being approved by God.
The church should not exhibit chaos. In summary, we are exhorted to "abstain
from every form of evil" (v. 22). Our culture is soft on sin; the believer must
stand strong against sin of any kind. The result will be our sanctification, being
fully set apart for God in body, soul, and spirit so that we can face the Lord
with confidence at His coming.

In our walk with Christ we can trust Him—He is faithful who called us to
salvation. He will "bring it to pass" (v. 24)—God will enable us to stand, fully
sanctified in Christ's presence.

CONSIDER: *Believers are instructed how to live in fellowship with God and one
another, knowing that God is faithful and will sanctify us in preparation for
Christ's return.*

PERSEVERANCE AMID PERSECUTION

2 THESSALONIANS 1:1–12

We ourselves speak proudly of you among the churches of God for your perseverance and faith in the midst of all your persecutions and afflictions which you endure. (2 Thessalonians 1:4)

On April 18, 2007, five young Muslim Turks entered a Christian publishing office in the province of Malatya. They tortured the three Christians in the office and then slit their throats, killing them. One of the Christians was a German missionary. Suzanne, the German missionary's widow, responded, "God forgive them for they know not what they do." Her courage was reported in all the largest newspapers in Turkey.

Persecution of Christians is intensifying around the world (including America). Yet persecution of Christians is not new; it occurred in the early church. So how should Christians respond in persecution? How should they live? What should be their focus? Paul commends the Thessalonian believers because, through their persecution, their faith was growing beyond measure and their love was increasing. Truly a paradox.

So Paul spoke proudly of the Thessalonians because of their perseverance and faith during their persecutions. They remained strong and steadfast, bearing up amid their suffering. Their courage and faith demonstrated their worthiness to enter God's kingdom. It was evidence that they were kingdom citizens.

But the story doesn't end with their suffering. The last chapter hasn't been written. As the persecutors afflicted the believers, so God will afflict the persecutors. That is justice—God's justice. One of the attributes of God is that He is just. Unbelievers will not escape their horrific sin of persecuting believers. Joseph Stalin, Adolph Hitler, Mao Tse-tung—and all the other persecutors of Christianity over the centuries—will be judged by our God who is just. The day of believers' relief is coming when the Lord Jesus comes "with His mighty angels in flaming fire" (v. 7; see also Matthew 25:31–46 and Revelation 19:11–21). Those who have scorned Christ will face "eternal destruction" (not annihilation). But for believers, it will be a day when Christ is glorified and honored among His own. What a day that will be!

CONSIDER: *Amid persecution, believers remain steadfast, awaiting the day of Christ's return when He will judge unbelievers and be glorified among His own.*

THE DAY OF THE LORD

2 THESSALONIANS 2:1–17

*For the mystery of lawlessness is already at work; only he
who now restrains will do so until he is taken out of the way.
Then that lawless one will be revealed whom the Lord will
slay with the breath of His mouth and bring to an end by the
appearance of His coming. (2 Thessalonians 2:7–8)*

Throughout the centuries some believers have speculated that the day of
the Lord had come; they thought they were in the tribulation. Antichrist
figures have appeared, causing further speculation: Is he the Antichrist?

Scripture provides an order of events before the Antichrist will enter
the world stage. Paul explained that to the Thessalonian believers who had
thought the day of the Lord—the tribulation—had already come upon them.
Some sources—speculators—had suggested that to the Thessalonians, but
Paul clarified the future events.

Before the day of the Lord comes, there will first be an "apostasy," a falling
away from the faith, then the Antichrist (who is also called "man of lawlessness" and "son of destruction") will be revealed. He will claim deity, taking
his seat in the temple in Jerusalem as God (Dan. 7:23–25; Rev. 13:1–8). Yet, a
restraining force is hindering the Antichrist from being revealed. Significantly,
the restrainer will continue to restrain the revelation of the Antichrist until the
restrainer is removed. What or who is the restrainer? Many suggestions have
been offered but it is best to understand the restrainer as the Holy Spirit. At
the rapture, the Holy Spirit is removed from the earth, and then His unique
ministry through the church will cease, leaving the Antichrist to rush into the
vacuum. The Antichrist will deceive people through signs and false wonders,
but his rule will be short-lived. At the Second Coming of Christ, the Lord will
slay him with simply a word (Rev. 19:15, 20). His followers will also be judged
because they refused the truth and responded to a lie.

Church age believers will have no part in the tribulation; they have been
chosen for "salvation"—rescue from the tribulation. So amid increasing opposition to the gospel, we are called to stand firm, as we are reminded that God
has given us eternal comfort and good hope by grace.

CONSIDER: *The day of the Lord will not come until the Restrainer, the Holy Spirit,
is removed. Only then will the Antichrist be revealed whom Christ will slay at
His coming.*

PRAY AND WORK

2 THESSALONIANS 3:1–18

Now may the Lord of peace Himself continually grant you peace in every circumstance. The Lord be with you all! (2 Thessalonians 3:16)

When my wife's grandfather turned sixty-five, he received a government pension check like everyone else. When his son handed him the check, he became teary eyed and exclaimed, "I have taken care of myself all my life and now the government will take care of me? No." He refused the check and never accepted one. He was a humble believer who believed in the basic responsibility of work.

As the apostle concludes his letter he reminds the Thessalonians of their responsibility in two areas: prayer and work. He commissions them to pray continually for him, that God's word will spread rapidly—like a running messenger heralding a message—and that Paul would be delivered from outrageous people. Amid the challenges Paul reminds them (and us) of the Lord's faithfulness to strengthen and protect believers. And so we are called to persistence in love and steadfastness—remaining strong in our circumstances.

Paul concludes his letter with lengthy instruction concerning a disciplined life. He warns against association with undisciplined believers—withdraw from those who lead unruly lives. He cites himself as an example. What did Paul do? He worked—hard—night and day so he wouldn't be a burden to others. He was a model for them; he encourages them to follow his example. What a remarkable statement. His conclusion? "If anyone is not willing to work, then he is not to eat, either" (2 Thess. 3:10). Some in their midst were not working but were busybodies. Avoid them, don't associate with them, Paul warned. Instead, the believer is to work quietly and not grow tired of doing good.

In case some took exception to Paul's instruction, he reminded them of his authority—as an apostle he was giving them words from the Lord—and he signed the letter himself to authenticate his words.

Paul encourages them, reminding them of the Lord's peace *in every circumstance.* In what circumstance do you need to trust the Lord today?

CONSIDER: *Paul instructs believers of their responsibility to pray faithfully and to work quietly, disassociating themselves from irresponsible believers.*

October 18

BATTLE FOR TRUTH

1 TIMOTHY 1:1–20

As I urged you upon my departure for Macedonia, remain
on at Ephesus so that you may instruct certain men not
to teach strange doctrines. (1 Timothy 1:3)

Some years ago my family and I were visiting a church with my biblical mentor, Dr. J. Dwight Pentecost, who was the guest speaker. The pastor introduced Dr. Pentecost but began by mentioning Ruth Munce in the congregation who had been Dr. Pentecost's Sunday school teacher, Dr. Pentecost had been my teacher, and I had been the teacher of my son, Terry, who was headed for the ministry. Truth was being passed down four generations.

Passing on the truth of God's Word to the next generation was Paul's purpose in writing Timothy, exhorting him to faithfulness in the ministry. Paul had been released from his first Roman imprisonment, and, coming to Ephesus, found that false teachers had infiltrated the church and were teaching false doctrine. Paul left Timothy in charge while he traveled to Macedonia. Now Paul wrote Timothy, advising him how to deal with the problems in the church.

The false teachers were likely Judaizers who were teaching myths and allegories, which had no practical, spiritual value and did not develop believers in the faith. It was legalistic and fruitless—and the legalists themselves did not even understand the nature of the Law. The Law was given to expose sinners in their sinful behavior.

But Paul had been entrusted with the gospel of Christ because, although he had been a blasphemer and persecutor of the church, he had acted in ignorance. Through His grace, Christ had saved Paul and set him apart to proclaim the gospel of grace, not a gospel of legalism through the Law.

Entrusting this gospel of grace to Timothy, Paul challenged his young disciple to "fight the good fight" (1 Tim. 1:18). This was not a single battle; it was a campaign, a war. Paul strongly exhorts Timothy to persist—to continue the warfare against false teaching. Amid the conflict Paul instructed Timothy to be "keeping faith and a good conscience" (v. 19). His personal faith was to persist along with a good conscience. For victory in battle, the warrior himself must be spiritually strong.

We have an enemy that seeks to corrupt and destroy the gospel of grace, and you and I must stand strong in opposing error and standing for truth.

CONSIDER: *Paul instructs his disciple, Timothy, to constantly wage war against the false teaching of legalism while upholding the gospel of grace.*

October 19

DIRECTIVES IN WORSHIP

1 TIMOTHY 2:1–15

First of all, then, I urge that entreaties and prayers, petitions and thanksgivings, be made on behalf of all men. (1 Timothy 2:1)

How is the church to function in its worship and ministry? Contemporary culture is producing dramatic changes in both styles of worship and concepts of ministry. Much emphasis is placed on the music in worship and the latest forms of media. Worship has almost become a contest to see who can be the "coolest."

The true basis for how we worship and function in ministry, however, should be the Bible, not culture. When Paul directed Timothy concerning worship, he didn't mention music or media—he began with an emphasis on prayer, the one thing that seldom gets top billing in today's church.

Paul's vision for prayer is expansive. We should not just focus on personal needs, but on the "big picture" level. We are to pray for political leaders so that we may lead quiet lives, enabling us to worship God in peace. The primary function of government is to curb lawlessness; when government fulfills this function, then believers are free to spread the good news that God desires all men to be saved. Christ is the only mediator between God and humanity because He gave His life as a ransom—he paid the price to release us from bondage to sin.

In the public worship, men are specifically called upon to lead in prayer, "lifting up holy hands without anger and arguing." If we are to pray for the world to be at peace, then we must be at peace within the church. Personal anger and petty arguments have no place within the family of God. Lifting up one's hands during prayer was a common posture for first-century believers. Paul's concern was that the hands be "holy"—free from sin. We cannot worship God from the heart and yet harbor the sins of resentment or competition. They only lead to dissension and division between believers.

If worship is not a place for competition between leaders, neither is it a contest to see who can show off the latest fashions! The items that Paul mentions—braided hair, gold, pearls, and expensive clothes—indicate considerable wealth, something only a minority possessed. Rather than flaunt their wealth, Paul calls for modesty. The woman who dresses to be seen by God, not by others, will exhibit a sense of what is decent and proper. The best kind of spiritual "clothes" are good deeds. Acts of sacrificial love for others demonstrate a woman's true heart.

There is also peace in the church when God's roles in public ministry are respected: men are to lead in public worship; women are not to assert authority over the men. While not a popular practice in today's church, loving submission to godly roles within the body of Christ is God's plan.

CONSIDER: *Prayer is a vital part of New Testament worship and men are to lead in worship, with women submitting to their leadership in worship and teaching.*

CHURCH LEADERSHIP

1 TIMOTHY 3:1–16

*I write so that you will know how one ought to conduct
himself in the household of God. (1 Timothy 3:15)*

Who are the leaders of the church? There are three terms describing church leaders that are somewhat equivalent. Overseer (*episkopos*; the King James Version translates this "bishop") is the word in 1 Timothy 3:2, describing the function of the leader in superintending, watching, exercising oversight and care of the people. Elder (*presbuteros*) looks at the dignity of the position (and is used synonymously with overseer). Pastor (*poimen*) views the work of a shepherd in caring for the people as a shepherd tends the sheep.

What are the qualifications of an overseer? The qualifications given in this passage are not arbitrary; they are essential. An overseer "must be"—*it is necessary that* he have these qualifications. He must be above reproach; his life can't be censored. He must be without blame; the enemy should not be able to bring any charge against him. He must be the husband of one wife (this excludes a woman from being an overseer); this does not refer to polygamy, which even Roman law opposed, but to divorce and remarriage. His home life must be in order, not chaotic. The overseer must be temperate, sober in judgment, prudent, and discreet, keeping a constant reign on his passions and desires. He must be hospitable and have a concern for people. The overseer must be skilled in teaching. He mustn't linger over wine, and he mustn't be a fighter or quarrelsome; rather, he must be gentle and patient, uncontentious, and not a lover of money. His household must be in order—if he can't control four, how can he control four hundred? He must not be a recent convert and he has to have a good reputation with unbelievers.

Deacons have similar qualifications and they must first be tested—they must be constantly observed to be approved. The qualifications for deacons appear to be interrupted by a reference to women in verse 11; the placement of this verse suggests that it is deacons' wives who are under discussion.

The Scriptures are not unclear in the qualifications for church leaders. When we neglect to impose these qualifications we do great harm to the church and the church will inherently fail. Tragically, for every leader that leaves the church because of doctrinal failure, ten leave because of marital failure. We are obligated to uphold God's standard for church leadership. These instructions are given so that there will be proper behavior and function in the church.

CONSIDER: *Scripture provides qualifications for overseers (elders) and deacons that must be adhered to so that the church will function properly.*

STRIVING FOR TRUTH

1 TIMOTHY 4:1–16

*Pay close attention to yourself and to your teaching; persevere
in these things, for as you do this you will ensure salvation both
for yourself and for those who hear you. (1 Timothy 4:16)*

Elements within evangelicalism are changing. Some among the emerging church take issue with penal substitution—that Christ died as a substitute for the penalty of our sins. One emergent leader stated that if God demanded that Christ die as a substitute for sin to appease His holiness, then the Father is guilty of divine child abuse. Another prominent evangelical has stated, "Jesus never said that in order to be born again one must believe in His deity, His death, or His resurrection." These are serious departures from the historic, biblical faith—and the Scriptures warn about apostasy. In fact, Scripture predicts it will happen, "in later times some will fall away from the faith" (1 Tim. 4:1).

Scripture warns us concerning apostasy with the strongest language: these false teachings are "doctrines of demons"—and they are liars.

What is the solution? It comes through the Word of God, through Scripture. Leaders must warn believers about the false teaching and to facilitate this the leader must be "constantly nourished on the words of the faith and of the sound doctrine" (v. 6). How can a leader discern error? Only through faithful study of Scripture, being established in the truth of God's Word. Like those who discern counterfeit money—they recognize it by studying the real, genuine money. We discern error by studying Scripture. This is not easy; it requires—demands—discipline.

Unlike bodily exercise, which has only temporary value, discipline in the study of Scripture has eternal value. For this reason, Paul would "labor and strive" for biblical truth. Paul admonished Timothy to pursue this course: "Prescribe and teach these things. . . . Give attention to the public reading of Scripture, to exhortation and teaching. . . . Take pains with these things; be absorbed in them. . . . Pay close attention to yourself and to your teaching; persevere in these things" (vv. 11, 13, 15, 16).

These are not suggestions. They are commands. How do we stand against error and apostasy? We must study the Scriptures diligently and faithfully and unapologetically teach them. This is not an option if God's truth is to continue to the next generation. As the book of Judges demonstrates, we are always only one generation away from apostasy.

CONSIDER: *Are you doing your part in standing strong for the Christian faith? Are you disciplined in faithful study of Scripture?*

HONORING OLDER BELIEVERS

1 TIMOTHY 5:1–6:2

Honor widows who are widows indeed. . . . The elders who rule well
are to be considered worthy of double honor, especially those who
work hard at preaching and teaching. (1 Timothy 5:3, 17)

The Bible has a great deal to say about concern and care for widows. They live a difficult life without their husbands to provide for them. We are instructed to "honor widows," meaning "honor, to show respect; the word would also carry the idea of support in this context" (Cleon Rogers Jr. and Cleon Rogers III, *The New Linguistic and Exegetical Key to the Greek New Testament*). "Indeed" emphasizes if the widow is alone, without family, having no way to support herself. If the widow has children or grandchildren, they must assume responsibility in caring for her. Family members who fail to do this have denied the faith and are worse than unbelievers. One who has no relatives to provide for her is to be supported if she exhibits faith in God through prayer but not if she is devoted to a life of pleasure.

Scripture also instructs concerning the ministry by widows (vv. 9–16). She is to be put on the list for ministry if she is sixty years old, having been faithful in marriage and family, having demonstrated a life of good works, including hospitality and helping others. Younger widows are not to be put on the list for service because their inclination is toward marriage. Obviously this refers to ministry rather than support because a young widow with small children would be in desperate need of support. This is a serious issue: Does my church—do I—neglect to help widows?

The support of elders (or overseers) is biblical; they are worthy of "double honor," emphasizing they should be supported financially. It specifies elders that "rule." While this means those who superintend the congregation, it emphasizes those who "work hard at preaching and teaching." This passage does not suggest that there are two kinds of elders; rather, the elder performs pastoral ministry that involves administration but also studyies the Scriptures, preaches, and teaches. It is the same person. Meanwhile, if an accusation against an elder occurs, it should be dealt with cautiously. If true, there should be a public rebuke. Recognition of new elders should come cautiously and young people should not be accepted into this leadership.

Why the stringent guidelines for widows and elders? So widows will be cared for properly and serve in ministry and godly men will be recognized in leadership.

CONSIDER: *The Scriptures provide important directives concerning the care and ministry of widows and the honor and ministry of elders.*

October 23

Contentment

*Godliness actually is a means of great gain when
accompanied by contentment. . . . The love of money
is a root of all sorts of evil. (1 Timothy 6:6, 10)*

When John D. Rockefeller died, one man was curious about how much he
left behind. Determined to find out, he set up an appointment with Rockefeller's highest aides and asked, "How much did Rockefeller leave behind?" The
aide answered, "All of it" (Michael P. Green, *Illustrations for Biblical Preaching*).

Many people are enamored with this world—the things in this world
and the controversies of this world. The result is conflict and turmoil in the
churches. Paul reminded Timothy that the doctrine he had taught would establish believers in godliness. Resistance to sound, doctrinal teaching would have
the opposite effect—it would result in envy, strife, slander, and quarreling;
people who were "giving to get," so to speak.

A key issue in life and ministry is contentment. This is true gain, especially
recognizing we will take nothing with us when we die (unlike the man who was
buried in his classic Cadillac). Having the basics of food and clothing should
bring contentment to the believer. This fits with what Jesus taught concerning
anxiety (Matt. 6:19–34).

In our materialistic world money is a major attraction and lust for many
people—they want to get rich—but wealth is a trap that will destroy. In fact,
the love of money—not money itself—is a root of all sorts of evil. And those
who have made money their focus and objective have wandered away from the
faith and have been struck with multiple sorrows—destroyed relationships
and broken homes.

Believers are warned in strong language: "flee from these things . . . pursue
righteousness, godliness, faith, love, perseverance and gentleness" (1 Tim.
6:11). We are in a cultural war, hence, we are to "fight the good fight of faith"
(v. 12). We are to oppose a worldly, materialistic philosophy. We are challenged
to "keep the commandment" (v. 14), that is, obey God's Word, with a focus
on Christ's return. This world is temporary and those who seek wealth will
discover its emptiness; those who seek eternal life through a focus on heaven
will have a true and lasting treasure—laid up in heaven.

CONSIDER: *Believers are instructed to keep God's Word and stand strong against
false teaching and the pursuit of money.*

LOYALTY AND COURAGE

2 TIMOTHY 1:1–18

God has not given us a spirit of timidity, but of
power and love and discipline. (2 Timothy 1:7)

This is the last letter the apostle Paul will write. It is only a few months
before Paul is executed and the mood of 2 Timothy reflects the somber
spirit. The apostle has served Christ with a clear conscience; he constantly
remembers Timothy in prayer, and longs for his son in the faith. Apparently
Timothy is in despair and Paul writes to challenge him to loyalty and courage.
The apostle reminds Timothy of his genuine faith which was handed down to
him from his mother and grandmother. So Paul charges him, "kindle afresh the
gift of God which is in you" (2 Tim. 1:6). Timothy was discouraged and needed
to "rekindle, stir into flame, keep blazing" (A. T. Robertson, *Word Pictures of
the New Testament*) in ministry for Christ. What an important reminder, that
the fire in our hearts can die down when we become fearful and ashamed of
our Lord.

Paul challenges Timothy anew, reminding him God has not given us the
spirit of cowardice, fear, or timidity; but of power, love, and "self-discipline,
the power to keep oneself in hand" (Cleon Rogers Jr. and Cleon Rogers III, *The
New Linguistic and Exegetical Key to the Greek New Testament*). For this reason
Paul instructs him, "do not be ashamed of the testimony of our Lord" (v. 8).
Timothy's life could be on the line. Would he be ashamed? Would *I* be ashamed
of Christ if my life were on the line? At those moments, the Lord gives us the
strength we need. And what a phenomenal calling! He saved us and called us
with a holy calling through "our Savior Christ Jesus, who abolished death and
brought life and immortality to light through the gospel" (v. 10). That is the
message! That is our confidence! That is our message to a lost world!

Paul reminds Timothy that he suffers on behalf of this message—but he
is not ashamed and neither should Timothy be ashamed—and neither should
you or I ever be ashamed of Jesus Christ. The exhortation to Timothy is emotional: "Retain the standard of sound words. . . . Guard . . . the treasure which
has been entrusted to you" (vv. 13–14).

You and I are the means God uses to convey His message to a lost world.
Don't be ashamed. Don't exhibit timidity or fear. Be strong. Tell others the true
message—the only message of eternal life—through Jesus Christ who has
abolished death and brought life and immortality through the gospel.

CONSIDER: *The apostle challenges Timothy to be loyal and courageous and*
unashamed in spreading the message of eternal life through Christ.

October 25

CHARGE TO DILIGENCE

2 TIMOTHY 2:1–13

Suffer hardship with me, as a good soldier of Christ Jesus. . . .
If we endure, we will also reign with Him. (2 Timothy 2:3, 12)

One of the greatest joys I have as a seminary professor is to see my students taking the truth of God's Word and teaching it to others. Today I was fellowshiping with Chris, who is a pastor and was one of my students. He shared with me how he was teaching those entrusted to him and it excited my heart. He was passing on God's truth.

Timothy, Paul's son in the faith, was discouraged and inclined to giving up. Paul charged him to diligence in continuing to serve Christ. Is it possible? Yes! The opening words are a command, "be strong in the grace that is in Christ Jesus." It is both a command ("be strong") and yet passive ("be strengthened"). We do not strengthen ourselves; Christ strengthens us. Then Paul commands Timothy to pass it on. The truth Timothy learned from Paul he is to entrust to faithful men who will teach others. That is fourfold. That is how truth continues from one generation to another.

Just how persistent should the student be? Like a soldier, who is singularly focused on winning the battle, suffering hardship in the fight for victory, exercising discipline, entirely committed to the cause. And, like an athlete competing in a contest, having trained and now pursuing the victor's crown. Finally, like a farmer, who works to exhaustion to share in the harvest.

And what is the focus, the message? Paul reminds Timothy, "Remember Jesus Christ, risen from the dead" (v. 8). That is the focus! There is no other answer. No one else has the solution and the resolution to the dilemma of death—only Christ! Teach it, proclaim it! Suffer hardship for the gospel like Paul who was willing to be imprisoned for heralding this incredible message. We proclaim this for the sake of those who are chosen who still must hear and respond.

And what is the blessing? "If we endure, we will also reign with Him" (v. 12). The work will not be easy; there will be opposition, hardship, suffering, yet the end result is receiving the commendation of Christ and reigning with Him. Will you suffer hardship for Christ?

CONSIDER: *The believer is challenged to suffer hardship for the sake of the gospel, remembering the central message: Jesus Christ risen from the dead!*

APPROVED WORKER

2 TIMOTHY 2:14–26

---

*The Lord's bond-servant must not be quarrelsome, but be kind
to all, able to teach, patient when wronged, with gentleness
correcting those who are in opposition. (2 Timothy 2:24–25)*

A prominent evangelical scholar was debating a liberal in a public forum. The
evangelical was brilliant, and with persuasive argument clearly demolished
the liberal—but he "lost" the debate. Why? Because his arrogance and conde-
scending attitude were reflected in his argumentation. It turned the people away
from him.

The Scriptures provide important teaching on *how* a believer is to serve
the Lord—so he can win both the argument and the debate. Paul warns Timothy not to engage the false teachers in a debate about words. It is useless.
Instead, Timothy is exhorted to put his full energy in pursuing the goal of
being approved by God by accurately handling the word of truth. It pictures
a stonemason, cutting the stones to fit precisely; it means to cut a straight
line from error to truth. Negatively, the servant is charged to avoid foolish,
empty chatter, which, instead of edifying, spreads like a cancer in the assembly. Avoid it.

The Christian worker should also refrain from association with false teachers who could contaminate him or her. To illustrate his point, Paul mentions
household utensils. There are vessels of honor—gold and silver—as well as
vessels of dishonor—wood and clay. This depicts the faithful and the unfaithful in the church. As the drinking glasses are kept separate from the garbage
pail, so God's servants are warned to separate themselves from false teachers.

Serving Christ effectively calls for diligent discipline: negatively, fleeing
lust and avoiding debating false teachers, and positively, pursuing righteousness and displaying kindness and gentleness. This life can only be achieved
through being strengthened in the grace of Christ (2:1).

CONSIDER: *The Lord's servant is called to avoid quarreling and debating false
teachers but rather to faithfully handling the word of truth with grace and kindness.*

October 27

EQUIPPED FOR BATTLE

2 TIMOTHY 3:1–17

---

*All Scripture is inspired by God and profitable for teaching, for reproof,
for correction, for training in righteousness; so that the man of God may
be adequate, equipped for every good work. (2 Timothy 3:16–17)*

In the twenty-first century, America and the Western world have moved into a decidedly post-Christian era. While Christianity was respected in the past, that is no longer true. Today, Christianity is ridiculed. For example, Bill Maher, an atheist, has released a film entitled *Religulous*, a combination of "religion" and "ridiculous." Maher reveals his hostility toward all religions, saying they are forces of evil that "must die."

Paul predicted an agenda of apostasy and hatred toward Christ. He warned dangerous times would come "in the last days," referring to the broad period of the Christian era (W. E. Vine, *The Epistles to Timothy and Titus*). It would reflect a "me" generation of arrogant, ungrateful, and unloving people, who will exhibit hostility and savagery. They have a form of godliness but they deny its power—they deny the Word. Avoid them, Paul warns. These deceivers creep into houses and captivate people but their deception will ultimately become known. False teachers will be proven false. So how should we live in this environment? Follow the biblical "teaching, conduct, purpose, faith, patience, love, perseverance" (2 Tim. 3:10). And expect persecution. It will come. In a world that is hostile to Jesus Christ, we can expect nothing less than hostility.

But God has armed us for the battle. He has given us the Scriptures. "All Scripture is inspired by God," *theopneustos*, literally, "God-breathed." What is Scripture? It is the out-breath of God, the exhalation of God. That being the case, can there be errors in Scripture? No. God cannot make errors. Hence, the Scriptures are inerrant in their totality. "All Scripture" covers the Word from Genesis to Revelation—the whole and the parts—all of Scripture is inerrant and therefore entirely trustworthy and adequate for building believers to maturity.

These inerrant Scriptures are profitable for every human domain, including development in righteousness and equipping us for every good work. The question then is, how much time do you spend in the God-breathed Word? Are you being equipped for warfare in a hostile world? Are you being trained in righteousness?

CONSIDER: *In the Christian era there will be enormous degradation and hostility toward Christianity but we have the God-breathed Scriptures to equip us spiritually.*

October 28

PREACH THE WORD

2 TIMOTHY 4:1–22

Preach the word; be ready in season and out of season; reprove, rebuke, exhort, with great patience and instruction. (2 Timothy 4:2)

A father and son were both pastors of a prominent church. The father was upset because the son used the word "sin" in his preaching. The father explained that it did not portray their ministry, that he didn't want people upset or offended, that his ministry was not about sin. The son ended up leaving the church.

Paul knew that his execution was imminent. His blood would be poured out when he was decapitated. What final words would Paul have for his young disciple? With intensity, Paul charges Timothy: "preach the word." The charge is strong: "preach as your first priority" (Cleon Rogers Jr. and Cleon Rogers III, *The New Linguistic and Exegetical Key to the Greek New Testament*). As an imperial herald proclaimed in authority on behalf of the emperor, so the believer is to faithfully and courageously proclaim God's truth. When? At all times—whether it is opportune or not. We do not wait for "the right moment." We are to be "alert to seize every opportunity without paying regard to the prejudice or wishes of others" (W. E. Vine, *The Epistles to Timothy and Titus*). The verbs are strong: reprove, rebuke, exhort. Why? Because people will no longer acknowledge the truth. They want their ears tickled; they don't want to hear the harsh words of truth. Isn't that the environment today? Isn't truth regarded as "relative"? Don't they say, "well, that's your view" or "that's what it means to you"?

Amid this environment Timothy is challenged to "endure hardship, do the work of an evangelist, fulfill your ministry" (2 Tim. 4:5). Sobering words for us all. But as Paul awaited execution, he could say, "I have fought the good fight, I have finished the course, I have kept the faith" (v. 7). Throughout his ministry, amid hostility and opposition, he remained faithful. Like a boxer, he had fought the good fight; like an Olympic runner, he had finished the course; like a soldier, he had guarded the faith. Now, at the end of his life, he could look ahead for the prize: the victor's crown, the crown of righteousness. The Lord, who stood by him in all his trials, would now bring him safely to His heavenly kingdom. What a prospect! What a challenge—for you and me to run the race, to fight the battle, so that we, too, will receive the crown of righteousness.

CONSIDER: *In a depraved culture, the believer is exhorted to "preach the word" whether it is opportune or not, and thereby fulfill the ministry.*

October 29

Faithful Ministry

Titus 1:1–16

For this reason I left you in Crete, that you would set in order what remains and appoint elders in every city as I directed you. (Titus 1:5)

A prominent pastor was involved in an issue with another pastor. The pastors leveled charges at each other—publicly. The newspaper carried the controversy in great detail, informing the public. With their vitriol against each other, the pastors lost their credibility and brought shame to Christ and His church in the process.

Following Paul's release from his first Roman imprisonment, he traveled to Crete with Titus. He then left Titus in charge while he traveled on to Macedonia from where he penned this letter to his disciple Titus in Crete. Of particular importance was that Titus should appoint elders. No doubt Paul had himself begun the organization of the church in Crete but Titus was to complete the organization.

As Paul had given instructions to Timothy about the appointment of elders in the church, so Paul also specifies the qualifications for an elder (overseer) of a church to Titus. Heading the list of qualifications is "above reproach"; that is, "without indictment" (Cleon Rogers Jr. and Cleon Rogers III, *The New Linguistic and Exegetical Key to the Greek New Testament*); unlike the above story, no charge can be brought against him. He must have a good public testimony. His home life must be impeccable; he must have a good marriage with believing children. He mustn't be contentious, nor a fighter. No charges of luxurious living or squandering money should be able to be brought against him (Cleon Rogers Jr. and Cleon Rogers III, *The New Linguistic and Exegetical Key to the Greek New Testament*). He must be hospitable, committed to what is good, self-controlled, and loyal to the Lord. Above all, he must cling to the Word of God as the authority for his own life and for his ministry. He encourages and exhorts believers as well as refutes those who hold to false doctrine—all from the Scriptures, which are his foundation in ministry.

A particular purpose of Paul's message to Titus is to silence the false teachers, the legalists—in this case, the Judaizers. The opposition may come through different avenues in different ages. This is a reminder that we are in a spiritual warfare. The enemy does not let up. And our source of strength in battle comes through the Word of God. The purpose for disciplined study and teaching is to produce sound faith.

CONSIDER: *Paul instructed Titus to appoint qualified leaders in Crete who would teach believers and oppose false teachers through the Word of God.*

October 30

LIVING WISELY IN THE FELLOWSHIP

TITUS 2:1–15

> *. . . looking for the blessed hope and the appearing of the glory*
> *of our great God and Savior, Christ Jesus. (Titus 2:13)*

It is a great tragedy that young mothers have frequently failed to recognize the importance of being a mother to their children, opting instead for a career in the world while abandoning their children to a day care. The Bible exalts motherhood and the role of the mother in raising her children.

We live in two dimensions. The Bible instructs us how we should live in this world, reflecting the grace of God in our lives but we are also told to live "other worldly," looking for the imminent return of Christ. That is our ultimate hope.

Paul was concerned that Titus teach and guide the church in Crete so there would be order, with both genders and every age group functioning biblically. He was to teach sound, healthy doctrine because "correct doctrine should produce correct relationships" (Cleon Rogers Jr. and Cleon Rogers III, *The New Linguistic and Exegetical Key to the Greek New Testament*). Sound doctrine must filter into a changed life.

The Bible addresses differing age groups and how they should function spiritually. Older men should reflect a temperate dignified disposition, displaying maturity in faith, love, and patience. Their conduct should fit their stage in life. Older women are instructed to be reverent in their behavior. "They are to carry into daily life the demeanor of priestesses in a temple" (Cleon Rogers Jr. and Cleon Rogers III, *The New Linguistic and Exegetical Key to the Greek New Testament*). They are to guard themselves against gossip, teaching what is good, especially encouraging young women in their marriages. Who is better able to do this? Older women are to mentor younger women in home life, to love their husbands and their children, and to be faithful in their homes. What a large responsibility and privilege. As someone has remarked, "the hand that rocks the cradle, rules the world." Young men should be sensible, reflecting self-control, in all things an example of righteous living, with pure motives, sound in speech—not having anything bad to say. Bondslaves are instructed to subject themselves to their masters in all things.

The reason for all these instructions is that the grace of God has appeared, instructing believers to say "no" to ungodliness and worldly desires. Instead, we are to be constantly looking for the blessed hope—the any-moment return of Jesus Christ.

CONSIDER: *Believers in all categories are instructed to live faithfully with complete integrity, while looking for the any-moment return of Christ.*

October 31

LIVING WISELY IN THE WORLD

TITUS 3:1–15

He saved us, not on the basis of deeds which we have done in righteousness, but according to His mercy, by the washing of regeneration and renewing by the Holy Spirit. (Titus 3:5)

Tullian Tchividjian, the grandson of Billy Graham, is the pastor of Coral Ridge Presbyterian Church in Florida. A young man, he reflects maturity and wisdom, having written several books on how believers should live in this postmodern culture. Although he had difficulties as a teenager his life is changed. The grace of God has impacted him.

Believers are instructed to live wisely in this world. How is this possible? Something miraculous has happened to every believer. The generosity, the kindness of God in His love for mankind has appeared through Christ. In His mercy God saved us through regeneration—He gave us new life—He started our "spiritual motor" when it was dead. He renewed us when our spirit was dead in trespasses and sin and made us alive—new creatures—by giving us the indwelling of the Holy Spirit.

For this reason believers are enabled to live a life pleasing to God and respectful of other people—in the world and in the community. Guided by the Holy Spirit who has regenerated us, we are instructed to be subject to our governing authorities. Instead of an argumentative attitude, we are to reflect gentleness—reasonableness in our associations—no easy task unless the Holy Spirit has control of us. And He can, since once we were slaves to sin, but now we have been redeemed and released from sin's power. God demonstrated His kindness by sending a Savior—and our Savior saves—He rescues us from the snare of sin. Now, regenerated by the Holy Spirit we are called to "be careful to engage in good deeds" (Titus 3:8). This involves responsibility. We must be careful to busy ourselves in good deeds as if it is our profession (Cleon Rogers Jr. and Cleon Rogers III, *The New Linguistic and Exegetical Key to the Greek New Testament*). This also means we exercise caution, not to engage in meaningless disputes with legalists or heretics. These are pointless and will not resolve anything.

What an enormous blessing that we have been regenerated—given new life through the Holy Spirit, which enables us to walk in victory in every sphere of life.

CONSIDER: *Through the grace of God we have been regenerated, given life through the Holy Spirit, enabling us to walk wisely in life.*

November 1

FROM SLAVE TO BROTHER

PHILEMON 1–25

. . . that you would have him back forever, no longer as a slave,
but more than a slave, a beloved brother. (Philemon 15–16)

During the first century there were more slaves in the Roman Empire than free people. As the Romans conquered countries, they also enslaved people. Slavery was common in the Roman world. Freedom could be purchased but it was costly; some, such as Paul, were born free.

The epistle to Philemon is unique; it is a personal letter of Paul to a wealthy believer in Christ who owned slaves in Colossae. In fact, the church met in Philemon's home and Paul addresses the church as well. Paul commends Philemon for his love and faith, an indication of Philemon's spiritual maturity.

This small epistle is a story. Onesimus, a slave of Philemon, had apparently robbed his master and run away. His exploits brought him to Rome, where he met the apostle Paul. It is not known under what circumstances they happened to meet—we know, however, that it was by God's providential design. It seems they met while Paul was in prison and Onesimus was converted to faith in Christ through Paul (see verse 10). During his time in Rome, Onesimus became useful to Paul, yet Paul recognized the need for Onesimus to make restitution for his previous wrongdoing, so Paul sent Onesimus back to his master, Philemon.

The reality of Galatians 3:28, "There is neither Jew nor Greek, there is neither slave nor free man, there is neither male nor female; for you are all one in Christ Jesus" is evidenced in this epistle. Paul was writing to Philemon, appealing to him to forgive Onesimus and receive him, no longer merely as a slave but as a brother. Paul urged Philemon to receive Onesimus as he would receive Paul himself. Paul recognized the converting power of the gospel in the reformation of Onesimus. He who was formerly useless to Philemon was now useful. The gospel of Jesus Christ changes and transforms lives.

CONSIDER: *Onesimus, a runaway slave, was converted and transformed; and then Paul appealed to his master, Philemon, to accept him as a brother.*

PREEMINENCE OF CHRIST

HEBREWS 1:1–3

God, after He spoke long ago to the fathers in the prophets in many portions and in many ways, in these last days has spoken to us in His Son, whom He appointed heir of all things, through whom also He made the world. And He is the radiance of His glory and the exact representation of His nature, and upholds all things by the word of His power. When He had made purification of sins, He sat down at the right hand of the Majesty on high. (Hebrews 1:1–3)

Jesus Christ is the ultimate and final revelation. There is no other. God revealed Himself in the Old Testament "in many portions and in many ways." The Old Testament did not provide a complete revelation, it came piecemeal—Abraham, Moses, David, the prophets—they all provide some revelation. And it came in diverse ways—through dreams, visions, the tabernacle ritual, audibly—but all these were incomplete.

The culmination of revelation has come through Jesus Christ "in these last days." This is the *final* revelation; there is no other—God has spoken through His Son and He is the appointed heir of all things. He will consummate the ages; the Son who made the world and sustains it will rule over the nations of the world as His inheritance (Ps. 2:8). What a sovereign Lord we have! That should bring peace to our hearts.

The Son is the "radiance of His glory." "As the rays of light are related to the sun, and neither exists without the other, so Christ is the effulgence of the divine glory. They are essentially one; that is, both are God" (Homer Kent Jr., *Epistle to the Hebrews*). The Son displays the Father. What is God like? Look at Christ—He has "explained" God (John 1:18). Moreover, Christ is the "exact representation of His [God's] nature." As a coin reflects the mint, so Jesus reflects the Father. Jesus is the image of God. Jesus also "upholds all things." He is sovereign. "He is the One who carries all things forward on their appointed course" (Fritz Rienecker and Cleon Rogers, *Linguistic Key to the Greek New Testament*). The history of this world and universe will come to its conclusion precisely as the triune God as ordained. And the Son has resolved our greatest need by making purification for our sins.

What a great Savior and Lord we have! Do you have peace, knowing our Savior is also our sovereign Lord, fully controlling the destiny of this world? Rest in Him!

CONSIDER: *Jesus Christ is the ultimate and final revelation, the very being of God Himself, creator of the world and sovereign Lord of the world's destiny.*

November 3

SUPERIOR TO ANGELS

HEBREWS 1:4–2:4

"YOU ARE MY SON, TODAY I HAVE BEGOTTEN YOU" . . . . Of the Son He says, "YOUR THRONE, O GOD, IS FOREVER AND EVER." (Hebrews 1:5, 8)

A ngels are powerful. They struck the Sodomites with blindness (Gen. 19:11); they control governments (Dan. 10:20); they are more powerful than Satan and his demons (Rev. 12:7–9); they are divine attendants (Ezek. 1). But Christ is greater.

He is superior to angels in His person. He holds the title as Son; He is the eternally begotten Son of God. As the Father is eternal, so the Son is eternal. If there was a time when the Son was not, then the Father could not have been a Father. And, as the Son, He is the second person of the Godhead. Jesus is the *firstborn*, which emphasizes His dignity, rank, and position (Ps. 89:27); He is preeminent. Angels are subject to Jesus and they worship Him.

Christ's greatness is seen in the ascriptions given to Him. Hebrews 1:8 begins, "But of the Son He says," then, quoting Psalm 45:6, "Your throne, O God, is forever and ever." It is a clear statement of deity—Jesus is called God. He is destined to rule over His kingdom forever and ever. And in verse 10— quoting Psalm 102:25, "You, Lord, in the beginning laid the foundation of the earth"—Jesus is referred to as Lord. Twice in these verses Jesus is referred to as deity. Jesus is greater than the angels. He is God. As God, Jesus created the world. All creation is the work of His hands.

Creation will one day be changed and renovated but, since Jesus is God, He is "the same," and His "years will not come to an end" (v. 12) As God, Jesus is unchanged; He remains forever the same; He is *immutable*. Moreover, as God He is eternal. He has taken His place at the right hand of the Father, and will rule forever.

The warning to the Hebrews and to us is, "we must pay much closer attention to what we have heard, so that we do not drift away from it" (2:1). Amid discouragement, amid suffering, we must remember that Jesus is greater than any need we have and He remains forever the same. He is our compassionate Savior. It is eternally damaging to "neglect so great a salvation" (v. 3). Have you responded to the Son's offer of salvation?

CONSIDER: *Jesus is the second person of the Godhead, and as such is greater than angels in every sphere.*

November 4

Authority over Angels

Hebrews 2:5–18

"You have crowned Him with glory and honor, and have appointed Him over the works of Your hands; You have put all things in subjection under His feet." (Hebrews 2:7–8)

Christ has authority over angels. He subjected the world to Himself; angels did not. Whereas the first Adam failed to subject the earth, the last Adam, Christ, will succeed (Isa. 11:1–9). At His second coming He will be crowned with glory and honor; all creation will be subject to Him.

Christ took on humanity to resolve the human dilemma of sin, and through that, "for a little while" was made lower than the angels. The purpose was that He would suffer death, making atonement for the sins of the world. In His death, He died as a substitute, that "he might taste death 'for' [*huper* means 'on behalf of, instead of'] everyone" (v. 9). He died to redeem a fallen human race. While His death was "for everyone," an unlimited atonement, only those who appropriate His atonement receive its benefit. But through His death, Christ, as our Leader, brings many sons and daughters home to glory.

The death of Christ resulted in a new family relationship: Jesus brings us into His family as brothers and sisters. What a wonderful truth! We love our family members but now we are related to Jesus—we are His brothers and His sisters! And Christ reveals the Father to us.

It necessitated Jesus taking on humanity to secure redemption for humanity. Although Jesus was God from eternity past, He took on an additional nature, humanity, at Bethlehem, in order to redeem humanity. In that act, Jesus defeated the devil, rendering him powerless, making him "inoperative." What does this mean? The grounds of death and Satan's accusations were removed. Satan could no longer slander a believer before God. Sin's penalty was paid. The believer is released from bondage to sin that enslaved him. Satan's power over the believer has been broken (review Romans 6:1–14).

This is the glorious truth: Jesus became like us, that He would be a faithful and sympathetic high priest for us, fully making satisfaction to the Father for our sins and rendering Satan ineffectual. And He understands us. He was tempted as we are tempted, yet sinless.

CONSIDER: *Your High Brother understands you and sympathizes with you.*

SUPERIOR TO MOSES

HEBREWS 3:1–19

---

*Therefore, holy brethren, partakers of a heavenly calling, consider Jesus,
the Apostle and High Priest of our confession; . . . For He has been counted
worthy of more glory than Moses. (Hebrews 3:1, 3)*

Dwight D. Eisenhower was a great leader of this nation, both in World War II
and also as president. On June 6, 1944, he launched an armada from England to the shore of France in rescuing Europe from the Nazis. We hold men
like President Eisenhower in great esteem—and rightly so.

Yet there is but one supreme leader: Jesus Christ. When the writer contrasts Jesus with Moses, he is not denigrating Moses but he is showing us the
exalted position of Jesus. Jesus is both Apostle, representing God to men,
and High Priest, representing men to God. And Jesus was faithful in His ministry to humanity. Jesus receives more honor and glory than Moses because,
while Moses served in the house, Jesus built the house. Moses was part of the
household of Israel but Christ was the founder of the household (F. F. Bruce,
Epistle to the Hebrews).

Moses was faithful as a servant, yet Christ was more—He was faithful as
a Son. The ministry of Moses was a foreshadowing of the claims of Christ,
the good things to come. To encourage the Hebrew believers, to whom this
epistle is written, the writer shows them the necessity of faithfulness amid
suffering. They are experiencing suffering and hardship; some are thinking
of returning to Judaism to avoid persecution and suffering. The writer warns
them not to go back: "Today if you hear His voice, do not harden your hearts"
(Heb. 3:7–8). The Israelites in the wilderness repudiated Moses' leadership and
experienced God's punishment—although God continued to guide them, they
would not experience the fullness of rest that could have been theirs if they
had obeyed; so too, the writer warns these Hebrew believers not to repudiate
Jesus by hardening their hearts. The warning is severe: "Take care, brethren,
that there not be in any one of you an evil, unbelieving heart that falls away
from the living God" (v. 12). If they do not fully submit to Jesus' leadership,
they will not experience the fullness of rest that could be theirs.

They are partakers of Christ; in suffering they need to encourage one
another to continue faithfully. This is not speaking about losing one's salvation, but about not being able to enjoy all it means to rest in God. The challenge remains: living in a hostile world, filled with suffering, we must continue
strong in faith in Christ.

CONSIDER: *Christ is greater than Moses; for this reason, believers are urged to
continue strong in faith and not fall into sin.*

November 6

REST

HEBREWS 4:1–16

Since we have a great high priest who has passed through the heavens, Jesus the Son of God, let us hold fast our confession. . . . Therefore let us draw near with confidence to the throne of grace, so that we may receive mercy and find grace to help in time of need. (Hebrews 4:14, 16)

Rest. We all need rest. That is the reason we sleep every night. But more than physical rest, we need spiritual rest—the faith-rest life where we trust God implicitly.

The Israelites in the Old Testament were truly redeemed and God promised them spiritual rest in the land of Canaan—but they never entered the rest. Why? Because of the unbelief they exhibited at Kadesh (see Numbers 14).

The Hebrew Christians were being persecuted and were contemplating going back into Judaism. The writer of Hebrews encourages them to "be diligent to enter that rest" (v. 11)—God's rest. God's rest is ceasing from the legalistic works of Judaism; if they chose to return to Judaism, that was exhibiting unbelief, and they would only be able to enjoy an immature faith. God's rest is the peace that comes to the one who believes God even in difficult circumstances.

The rest of God is related to His work of creation: when the creative work was finished, He rested on the seventh day. Jesus invites us to enjoy rest in Him (Matt. 11:28–30). He invites us to enter God's rest. As the Old Testament Israelites could enter the land of rest so believers are urged to enter the life of rest (Josh. 22:4).

The exhortation is sincere: "let us be diligent to enter that rest" (v. 11). The reason why they should enter God's rest is that the Word of God is alive and active; it "brings blessing to those who receive it in faith and pronounces judgment on those who disregard it" (F. F. Bruce, *Epistle to the Hebrews*).

Our encouragement comes through our great High Priest, Jesus Christ, who has entered heaven on our behalf. Amid suffering we can draw near to Him and receive grace and mercy. He will give us the help we need. What do you need today? Come to Jesus—He will give you grace and mercy sufficient for your need.

CONSIDER: *Amid suffering believers are called to enter the faith-rest life by coming boldly to the throne of Jesus to receive mercy and grace.*

Superior to Aaron

Hebrews 5:1–10

So also Christ did not glorify Himself so as to become a high priest,
but He who said to Him, "You are My Son, today I have begotten You";
just as He says also in another passage, "You are a Priest forever
according to the order of Melchizedek." (Hebrews 5:5–6)

I understand. You have heard people say this when you have shared something with them. Sometimes they understand; sometimes they don't. We can't truly understand if we haven't walked the path. One who has not lost a spouse cannot fully understand a widow.

But Christ understands us because He took on humanity. The writer shows the humanity of the high priest and also of Christ—they had to be human to help. The high priest could understand from personal experience the problems of the people so he could encourage as well as rebuke. As human mediator, he offered sacrifices for the sins of the people as well as his own (Lev. 16:1–14). But the priest didn't take this ministry upon himself; God chose him.

God also chose Christ as our unique High Priest (Pss. 2:7; 110:4). In fact, Christ combined two offices: king and priest. Jesus is God's Son by divine appointment. He did not take this honor upon Himself but was appointed by the Father. No Old Testament priest was ever referred to this way. God also appointed Christ an eternal priest, not of the usual tribe of Levi, like Aaron, but of "the order of Melchizedek," who ruled as both priest and king (see Genesis 14:18–20; Melchizedek will be examined more closely in the November 9 devotional). Jesus combined the two offices of king and priest into one office and He rules forever as our High Priest and King.

Jesus completely identified with humanity (though He never ceased to be God), experiencing the agony of suffering on the cross, bearing the sins of humanity upon Himself. In His crying He was heard by the Father; He prayed that death would result in resurrection life. And it did. Jesus is the "source of eternal salvation" (Heb. 5:9). The efficacy of Christ's death is eternal. Can you grasp it? Has it penetrated your heart? As the Levitical priests were taken from humanity, so Christ took on humanity to be our eternally faithful High Priest.

CONSIDER: *We have eternal life because we have an eternally faithful High Priest.*

PRESS ON TO MATURITY

HEBREWS 5:11–6:20

*Therefore leaving the elementary teaching about the Christ,
let us press on to maturity. (Hebrews 6:1)*

A young man graduated from a Christian college, then studied at a prominent evangelical seminary. He left the seminary, saying he wanted to make some money. He obtained an excellent job and was on his way to achieving his goal. After a child was born to his wife, he visited her in the hospital and told her he wanted a divorce. The reason? Family responsibilities interfered with his ambition to become wealthy. So he divorced his wife and has achieved his monetary goal. But he is no longer interested in spiritual things. He is cold and indifferent to biblical truth.

The writer warns the Hebrew readers of their complacency. While they have believed in Christ, they have not progressed. They are still spiritual infants. When they should be going on to the "meat and potatoes" of the Christian life, they, like infants, need milk. However, the mature have spiritually trained (*gumnazo*) to discern good and evil. That's where these Christians should be.

So what is the lesson? "Press on to maturity." Because they were experiencing persecution, these Hebrew believers were contemplating going back into Judaism, which has similar foundational beliefs (6:1–2). But the writer is concerned for them, warning them, if they have been enlightened through the gospel, become partakers of the Holy Spirit, and then go astray, it is impossible to renew them again to repentance. Does this teach believers can lose their salvation? No. If it taught that, it would also then teach they could never again regain it (v. 6). Are these unbelievers? No. They are believers but they are spiritual infants. The writer warns them, if they go back into Judaism and do not progress, God will confirm them in spiritual atrophy—spiritual babyhood. Yet, the writer is convinced of better things for them; he expects them to go on, to be "imitators of those who through faith and patience inherit the promises."

This is a solemn reminder that we do not stand still. We either progress spiritually or we regress. The challenge is clear: "let us press on to maturity."

CONSIDER: *Believers who have never progressed spiritually are warned to go on to maturity, lest the Lord will confirm them in spiritual atrophy.*

A BETTER PRIESTHOOD

HEBREWS 7:1–28

But Jesus, on the other hand, because He continues forever, holds His priesthood permanently. Therefore He is able also to save forever those who draw near to God through Him, since He always lives to make intercession for them. (Hebrews 7:24–25)

Visiting the Lyndon B. Johnson library in Texas, we saw numerous artifacts from many nations: a jewel encrusted sword, jewelry, carvings, and many expensive and exotic items. The gifts were given to the president in recognition of his supremacy as the head of a state.

Melchizedek is a unique individual, suddenly appearing on the pages of Scripture, having no listed genealogy, no birth, no death. Furthermore, he unites the offices of king and priest into one person. And all of this is precisely the point: he stands as a type—a foreshadowing—of Christ. When Melchizedek blessed Abraham, this indicated that Abraham, representing Judaism, was subservient to Melchizedek. Abraham paid tithes to Melchizedek, substantiating this point. The Levite priests received tithes, but in this case they paid tithes (through Abraham) because Melchizedek is superior to Abram: "the lesser is blessed by the greater" (Heb. 7:7).

Since the Levitical priesthood could not bring perfection before God, it was necessary there be a change in the priesthood. Christ could not have served as priest under the Levitical priesthood because He is from the tribe of Judah, not of Levi; however, since the priesthood changed, there was a change in the Law also. Christ now serves as a permanent priest from the order of Melchizedek and His priesthood is based on the power of an indestructible life. The Levitical priests were temporary; Christ's priesthood is permanent.

Since the Levites were prevented from continuing their priesthood because of death, there was no assurance under their priesthood. But because Christ lives forever, He brings a better hope. He is a priest forever (vv. 17, 21) and therefore He is able to save forever—completely—those who trust Him. His one sacrifice forever provides atonement for those who come to Him.

We have a great Savior, who is able to save forever because He lives forever as our intercessor before the Father. Come to Him! He is the one and only Mediator.

CONSIDER: *Because Christ lives forever, He is able to save forever (completely) those who draw near to Him in faith.*

A BETTER COVENANT

HEBREWS 8:1–13

*But now He has obtained a more excellent ministry, by as much as
He is also the mediator of a better covenant, which has been
enacted on better promises. (Hebrews 8:6)*

In Orlando, Florida, a visitor is able to see The Holy Land Experience, which shows many features from ancient Jerusalem. But The Holy Land Experience is a copy, a shadow of the real. They are pictures of the reality of the tabernacle and temple in the Old Testament with some of the historic sites still visible in Jerusalem today.

Christ has inaugurated a better covenant, inasmuch as He is *seated* at the right hand of the throne in heaven. The Levitical priests stood, an implication that their work remained unfinished. Christ is seated, having completed the work of redemption. The earthly tabernacle was a tent; the tabernacle where Christ ministers is the true tabernacle, heaven itself, at the right hand of the Father. The earthly ministry of the Levitical priesthood foreshadowed the ultimate heavenly ministry.

Christ has obtained a more excellent ministry. The new covenant is based on better promises, because it is unconditional. The Mosaic covenant was conditional, dependent on Israel fulfilling certain conditions. But Christ's priesthood and ministry are superior; He is our mediator, our go-between between God and man. And He is reliable and effective in His priesthood.

Jeremiah foresaw the necessity of a new covenant when he promised a new covenant. Had the first covenant been faultless, there would have been no need for a new covenant, but the Lord promised Jeremiah, "I will effect a new covenant with the house of Israel and with the house of Judah" (Hebrews 8:8, which quotes Jeremiah 31:31). This new covenant is with Israel, the eternal covenant people of God, and it provides forgiveness of sins (Heb. 8:12; Jer. 31:34). The new covenant will ultimately be fulfilled with Israel when they repent during the tribulation (Zech. 12:10–14) but it has present application to church age believers (1 Cor. 11:25). The new covenant, then, has "a twofold application, first to Israel fulfilled in the millennium, and, second, to the church in the present age" (John Walvoord, *Millennial Kingdom*).

Christ is a great Savior and mediator of a great covenant, providing for the forgiveness of our sins. And His work is finished; it is eternally effective.

CONSIDER: *Christ has inaugurated a new covenant, rendering the old covenant, which was only a shadow of things to come, obsolete.*

A BETTER SACRIFICE (1)

HEBREWS 9:1–28

*How much more will the blood of Christ, who through the eternal
Spirit offered Himself without blemish to God, cleanse your
conscience from dead works to serve the living God? (Hebrews 9:14)*

The reading of a will is an emotional event. Why? Because it is the result of the death of someone. A last will and testament takes effect only when a person dies. Then the will of that person becomes valid and effective.

The Old Testament tabernacle was well established as an earthly sanctuary. The altar of burnt offering and the cleansing laver were in the outer court. The Holy Place hosted the table of showbread, golden candlestick, and altar of incense. The Holy of Holies held the mercy seat and the ark of the covenant. The priest entered the Holy Place only once a year, offering a blood atonement for himself and for the sins of the people.

All of this ritual prefigured a better and greater and permanent sacrifice—the sacrifice of Christ. He entered the perfect tabernacle—heaven—through His own blood and He did it "once for all, having obtained eternal redemption" (v. 12). If the Old Testament sacrifices cleansed the worshiper, "how much more will the blood of Christ" cleanse the worshiper! Christ is the Mediator of a new covenant; His atoning blood is of greater worth than the animal sacrifices. His was voluntary; the animals were involuntary. Furthermore, Jesus offered Himself "without blemish"; He was the pure, sinless Son of God (John 8:46; 1 John 3:5). His sacrifice was perfect and complete.

But the atonement required death and the "testament" was not in force until the death of the person who made it. Even in the Old Testament sacrifices it was evident that "without shedding of blood there is no forgiveness" (Heb. 9:22). But the Old Testament sacrifices were only "copies" and a shadow of the greater sacrifice, the atonement of Christ. He entered heaven itself for us and He did it only once, permanently procuring our salvation. We can rejoice that we have a perfect, completed salvation.

CONSIDER: *The Old Testament worship ritual was a copy and shadow of the greater sacrifice that Christ would provide through His atonement.*

November 12

A BETTER SACRIFICE (2)

HEBREWS 10:1–39

*For by one offering He has perfected for all time those who are
sanctified. . . . Let us hold fast the confession of our hope without
wavering, for He who promised is faithful. (Hebrews 10:14, 23)*

Persecution of Christians is at the greatest level it has been in history, with
North Korea being one of the most vicious persecutors of Christians.
Believers are imprisoned, tortured, deprived of food, and frequently left to die.
Numerous stories have recounted the communists' persecution of Christians.
What should believers do?

The Hebrew believers in Christ were being persecuted so they contemplated reverting to Judaism. The writer reminds them that it was impossible
for the animal sacrifices to take away sins. The Old Testament sacrifices were
only a shadow of the reality that would come in Christ. On the other hand,
Christ came to do the Father's will and by His one sacrifice believers have been
sanctified. His work is complete. In contrast to the Levitical priests who stood,
day after day, offering their sacrifices, Christ made one sacrifice and sat down;
redemption's work was over: "He, having offered one sacrifice for sins for all
time, sat down at the right hand of God" (Heb. 10:12).

The Holy Spirit is a witness to Christ's better sacrifice, having earlier
announced the new covenant to come (Jer. 31:33–34). The fact that there is
no further offering is a reminder that forgiveness has been provided through
the atonement of Christ.

What then does this mean for the believer? The writer gives a strong application: persevere. He bombards them with exhortations: "let us draw near . . .
let us hold fast . . . let us consider . . . not forsaking . . ." (Heb. 10:22–25). He
challenges them to continue, strong in faith, not drawing back. He urges them
to be filled with hope, holding fast to their confession of faith in Christ. And,
he challenges them to continue in love and fellowship.

With easy living, our roots may not grow deep. But suffering challenges
our faith. What shall we do? Don't go back. Draw near . . . hold fast to our hope
in Christ . . . stimulate one another to love and good deeds. Persevere because
"He who promised is faithful" (v. 23).

CONSIDER: *By His one sacrifice, Christ achieved what the Old Testament sacrifices could never accomplish, therefore we should endure and finish strong.*

November 13

TRIUMPH OF FAITH

HEBREWS 11:1–40

Now faith is the assurance of things hoped for, the conviction of things not seen. . . . And without faith it is impossible to please Him, for he who comes to God must believe that He is and that He is a rewarder of those who seek Him. (Hebrews 11:1, 6)

We were married and our first son was born when I decided to go to college. My wife and I made a commitment that she would stay home with our son so we examined the finances . . . $35 a week for my part-time job . . . house payment $110 a month . . . leaving $30 for everything else. We said, "Forget the budget. Let's just pray." So we committed our lives to the Lord and didn't tell anyone else. When I graduated from college we had no debt. How did it happen? God provided as we walked by faith.

Faith is at the core of the believer's life. In fact, it is the "title deed" to our future—the return of Christ and ultimately heaven. The writer enumerates the heroes of faith in this chapter: "by faith . . . by faith . . . by faith." Victorious through faith, they received approval by God. Ultimately, we cannot please God without faith. Faith begins by recognizing God exists and that He honors those who walk by faith. The Old Testament is replete with those who walked by faith. Noah built an ark when it had never rained! Imagine how he was ridiculed! Abraham left his home country and departed for an unknown land because God called him. What faith! Abraham was an alien, but he was "looking for the city which has foundations" (Heb. 11:10). All of these were otherworldly minded—they were "seeking a country of their own. . . . They desire a better country" (vv. 14, 16). Yet all of these died without having received the promises—but it indicates they walked by faith *to the very end.* They didn't compromise; they didn't turn back; they remained focused. And so others like Moses accepted rejection and endured suffering, but they maintained their walk of faith. Some conquered kingdoms, obtained promises, escaped the edge of the sword but others experienced severe torture, imprisonment, and death. These were "men of whom the world was not worthy" (v. 38). They walked by faith, not by sight. They trusted God amid rejection and suffering—even gave up their lives. They didn't give in. They walked by faith. How about you? Will you walk by faith—even if you suffer for it?

CONSIDER: *The life that pleases God is a life lived by faith in Him despite difficult circumstances, opposition, and suffering.*

November 14

TESTING OF FAITH

HEBREWS 12:1–29

Therefore, since we have so great a cloud of witnesses surrounding us, let us also lay aside every encumbrance and the sin which so easily entangles us; and let us run with endurance the race that is set before us, fixing our eyes on Jesus. (Hebrews 12:1–2)

Donald Grey Barnhouse once said that God would love to move us with a feather but if we don't respond, He'll use a bulldozer. While it is difficult to interpret the trials that come to us, God may well use trials to develop us spiritually. Since we are His children through faith in Christ, God disciples us to develop us in spiritual maturity.

Since the Hebrew believers were suffering so intensely, they are to consider the list of heroes (ch. 11)—individuals who suffered yet ran the race of life well, and won. But it requires laying aside weights that ensnare, like traditions of men, and the sin of unbelief. We are to run with endurance, keeping our eyes focused on Jesus who endured far greater sufferings than we will ever endure. He is the "Pioneer" who blazed the trail for us; He is the One who has completed our faith. Let us look to Him for endurance.

Discipline is also a sign that we are children in the family: "whom the Lord loves He disciplines" (Heb. 12:6). If we didn't experience discipline, it would be a sign that we are not children and are not in God's family. Furthermore, why are we disciplined? It is for our good. The end result of discipline is the "peaceful fruit of righteousness" (v. 11). That is God's goal for us—to live righteously.

The necessity, then, is to go forward, to go on in the Christian walk. Pursue sanctification. It calls for leaving the old life of immorality behind. It is ours no longer. In this new age we are privileged to approach God in a new dimension—no longer under the fear of the Mosaic Law at Mount Sinai—but under grace we have come to Mount Zion, the heavenly Jerusalem.

We have a great future. So we are challenged: don't give up; don't go back. Keep our eyes focused on Jesus—He endured and won the victory and He enables us to win the victory in life amid our trials.

CONSIDER: *To endure hardship, we are to look to Jesus who endured, also recognizing that our discipline is a sign of sonship in God's family.*

November 15

Triumph of Obedience

Hebrews 13:1–25

*Now the God of peace, who brought up from the dead the great Shepherd
of the sheep through the blood of the eternal covenant, even Jesus
our Lord, equip you in every good thing to do His will, working in
us that which is pleasing in His sight, through Jesus Christ, to whom
be the glory forever and ever. Amen. (Hebrews 13:20–21)*

Suffering undoubtedly turns the focus on self. Suffering can cause us to forget and neglect others as we focus on our hardships. The writer reminds the believers of their daily, spiritual obligations amid their sufferings. Don't discontinue loving other believers (*philadelphia*). Continue the relationships in every practical realm. Traveling believers would need hospitality—show it to them. Show love to believers who have suffered imprisonment and been mistreated. Maintain moral purity because God will ultimately judge immoral people.

While living in a materialistic society, avoid the love of money. Be content with what you have. Property had been confiscated from these Hebrew believers, yet they are instructed to be content. The reason is clear: God promised, "I will never desert you, nor will I ever forsake you" (v. 5). Because God is our Helper in time of need, we need not fear our circumstances. Jesus Christ is the same yesterday, today, and forever—just as He helped the Hebrew believers yesterday, so He will help us in our need today.

We are challenged not to digress into false teaching but rather enjoy strengthening by grace. Once more, our focus makes the difference. Our resolution will not come in this life; we are looking for the "lasting city," "the city which is to come" (v. 14). That will encourage faithfulness and endurance. Meanwhile, we link ourselves to Jesus "bearing His reproach" (v. 13); we identify with Him in suffering. Yet, we continue to offer up praise to God—this is the public acknowledgment of Christ—which some believers are afraid of doing because of ridicule and rejection. But we identify with a suffering, rejected Christ.

The challenge is evident. Amid suffering we tend to focus on self; instead, we should identify with Jesus and seek to love and serve others.

CONSIDER: *Amid suffering believers are called to attend to practical outworking of the faith, loving other believers, and bearing the reproach of Christ.*

November 16

FAITH AND TRIALS

JAMES 1:1–18

---

*Consider it all joy, my brethren, when you encounter
various trials, knowing that the testing of your faith
produces endurance. (James 1:2–3)*

The book of James, written by James, the half-brother of our Lord, reflects a similarity to the teaching of Jesus. James was writing to Jewish believers, to the "twelve tribes who are dispersed [*diaspora*] abroad" (James 1:1), who are scattered in the Roman world. They were experiencing trials and persecution from unbelieving Jews. James wrote to encourage them amid trials and also deal with carnality and divisions in the assembly. Ultimately, faith is the resolution to all their dilemmas with 2:18 being the key to the book: "show me your faith without the works, and I will show you my faith by my works." Genuine faith is seen in that it *works*—amid trials.

James begins by discussing the purpose of trials—misfortunes of various kinds that come to us—sicknesses, financial reversals, calamities . . . the list is endless. There is a divine purpose to trials, hence, we are called to exhibit joy. Trials come to us to produce spiritual maturity. The testing of our faith produces *endurance*—an important word, indicating the ability to remain strong in the circumstances.

"Why?" is not an uncommon question when trials come. James gives the answer: ask God. When we don't understand the trials—ask God. But the request for wisdom must be in faith. We cannot expect God to answer when we are unstable, reflecting faith at times and then doubt as we look at the circumstances. That is not pleasing to God. He knows what is the best thing to bring into my life to conform me to Christ. And, these testings come to both rich and poor, young and old; none are exempt.

Recognizing God's sovereignty in our trials will bring joy to the believer who will receive the crown of life. But God has no association with sin; no one can say that God solicits people to sin. He does not. Sin comes from the inner response of the old nature to an outward temptation. Instead, God gives good things, emanating from the Father of lights—and He does not change in His goodness.

Child of God, as you undergo trials today, "consider it all joy" as you recognize God's sovereign work in your life to conform you to Christ.

CONSIDER: *Trials come to believers to encourage our perseverance and maturity, so that ultimately we will receive the crown of life.*

November 17

FAITH AND PARTIALITY

JAMES 1:19–2:13

My brethren, do not hold your faith in our glorious Lord Jesus
Christ with an attitude of personal favoritism. (James 2:1)

One dear Christian couple I know spend every Monday evening taking two widows to dinner. They have been doing this for years. Why? Because they have a heart for widows. Widows are one segment of society that is frequently overlooked; yet, here is a Christian couple that doesn't show partiality—they minister to widows.

James deals with numerous issues: he describes a faith that works. Central to the mature spiritual life is caution in speech. Caution in speech and anger is essential since anger does not achieve God's righteousness. All of these issues relate to being a "doer of the word." It is inadequate to simply gather head knowledge of the Scriptures; if knowledge doesn't issue in living out the Word of God, it represents failure. Hearing brings knowledge but doing brings righteousness. It is like a man looking in a mirror and seeing he needs to shave. The mirror doesn't shave him; he must respond by shaving. Obedience to the law of God bring blessing because the man is doing what God requires of him—obedience to His Word. And that obedience is demonstrated in the act of visiting widows, a neglected group in our culture; yet, Scripture has much to say about caring for widows.

Perhaps one reason people neglect widows is that it doesn't gain them any prominence. We are warned not to hold our faith with an attitude of personal favoritism. This occurs when we nominate individuals as church officers because they are prominent in the business world, or when we befriend worldly, successful people for what that association may do for us.

James reminds us if we honor the rich we should remember that it is the rich who drag us into court and sue us; the rich blaspheme God. So what is valuable? Being rich in faith. James pointedly shows that partiality is sin. We are called to love our neighbor. That commandment fulfills the law.

CONSIDER: *Will you live your life today, tomorrow, demonstrating love to others despite their social standing?*

FAITH AND WORKS

JAMES 2:14–26

But someone may well say, "You have faith and I have works;
show me your faith without the works, and I will show you my faith
by my works." . . . Faith without works is useless. (James 2:18, 20)

Talking to a young man in an architect's office, I asked him about his relationship to Christ. "Oh, yeah," he responded. "I walked the aisle and trusted Jesus as my Savior." It wasn't long before I heard him take the name of Christ in vain. I couldn't tell the difference between his life and that of an unbeliever.

So how can we tell who is a believer? How shall we understand James' words? Does James contradict Paul who said that God justifies "the one who does not work" (Rom. 4:5)? Martin Luther had a problem with the book of James, calling it a "right strawy epistle." There is a resolution. Paul's writings show our position before God; James shows our position before other people. James explains, "*You see* that faith was working. . . . *You see* that a man is justified by works and not by faith alone" (James 2:22, 24, emphasis added). James reminds us that the only way for us to recognize whether another person is a believer is by their works. That is his point. A true faith works.

If we see a brother or sister in Christ that needs food or clothing and we don't respond, we have failed the basic command to love our neighbor. And that is a dead faith. A genuine faith will produce fruit. Actually, Paul said the same thing: "They profess to know God, but by their deeds they deny Him" (Titus 1:16).

We must be careful not to indulge in judgment. We are not God. We can't see the heart—nor do we see the individual for 168 hours a week—we don't see the totality of the lives of others.

This passage is sobering. It is a serious reminder that words are not enough. A genuine faith will ultimately produce works. This should motivate us to live out our faith by loving our neighbor.

CONSIDER: *A genuine faith will be demonstrated in works.*

FAITH AND WISDOM

JAMES 3:1–18

But the wisdom from above is first pure, then peaceable,
gentle, reasonable, full of mercy and good fruits,
unwavering, without hypocrisy. (James 3:17)

My John Wayne mug reads: "Talk low, talk slow and don't talk too much." Wise counsel. Our speech reflects our character. I recall one of my seminary professors. I talked with him often but I don't recall him ever speaking ill of anyone. If there was an issue involving personalities he remained silent. I still hold him in high esteem.

The tongue is the key to who we really are. The tongue reflects wisdom—or lack of it—and James has strong counsel. First of all he warns teachers—since teachers talk a great deal, they will be judged by what they say. Teachers are cautioned against causing their hearers to stumble. That can happen through teaching false doctrine or through harsh, ungracious words. James illustrates how a small item can have enormous control: a bit in a horse's mouth directs where the horse will run; a ship's rudder guides the path of the ship. Similarly, the tongue is a small element in the body yet it can (and will) have major effect. Like a devastating forest fire that engulfs acres of land and homes is begun by a small flame, so the tongue, a small "flame" in the body, can generate a world of wickedness, corrupting the entire person and nature of the individual. "The fire of the tongue is fed by the never-dying flames of hell" (Curtis Vaughan, *James: Bible Study Commentary*). A sobering thought.

Animals, birds, and sea creatures are tamed—but not the tongue. It is restless; it cannot keep quiet. It must speak, and frequently says the wrong thing. The same tongue that blesses God also curses men and would send them to hell. The same tongue. It is a poison.

How is this serious dilemma of the tongue resolved? Through wisdom. Wisdom from above. A wise person is one who knows the truth of God and applies it to life. He lives what he knows. He controls his tongue. We cannot generate this wisdom; it comes from God through the new birth, through the control of the Holy Spirit. Then speech will reflect gentleness, purity, peace, mercy, and other good fruits—all without hypocrisy. James's words are serious. Do your words cause a forest fire of sin or do they exhibit gentleness, mercy, and peace?

CONSIDER: *The tongue, though small, is a restless evil in our bodies that can only be tamed to reflect wisdom through control by the Holy Spirit.*

FAITH AND WORLDLINESS

JAMES 4:1–17

---

*You adulteresses, do you not know that friendship with the world
is hostility toward God? Therefore whoever wishes to be a friend
of the world makes himself an enemy of God. (James 4:4)*

I can still hear "Big Neufeld," the preacher my wife and I heard in our early years of marriage. Big Neufeld was specific—he mentioned habits and activities, warning believers to avoid them. Thankfully, we didn't carry a lot of baggage that needed to be cleaned up, but God used Big Neufeld talking about worldliness to direct us into serious commitment to Christ.

The subject of worldliness is largely avoided today; it is rarely referenced. Actually, the evangelical church is changing, attempting to become like the world in order to engage the world. Yet this philosophy runs counter to Scripture. Why does James call believers "adulteresses"? It is to remind us that when we flirt with the world we commit spiritual adultery. Being enamored with the world and desiring the things of the world will lead to quarreling and contention with others. It also affects our prayers—they don't get answered. Why? Because, being enamored with "things," we pray incorrectly and God doesn't answer.

We should see it for what it is: our love of the world is hostility—war—with God. Is that sobering? Do you want to be at war with God? No! James provides the resolution: submit to God and resist the devil. We are in a spiritual battle where there is no neutrality. To submit to God means we align ourselves under His authority. He takes control of our lives. We also take our stand in opposition to the devil. We reflect submitting to God by genuine mourning over sin, resulting in a cleansed life and a purified heart. There is a *changed* life. Humility becomes the believer's new personality. Speech is guarded and gracious. Boasting is not part of the new life. We humbly plan for tomorrow, recognizing "if the Lord wills" we will be enabled to do this or that.

James's words should penetrate our mind and heart. What is your relationship to the world? Are you in love with the world? Are you consumed with the "things" of the world? You cannot love both the world and God. A war is raging and you must take your stand.

CONSIDER: *A believer cannot love the world and also love God; we are called to submit to God and resist the devil—and the world.*

November 21

FAITH AND SUFFERING

JAMES 5:1–20

*You too be patient; strengthen your hearts, for the
coming of the Lord is near. . . . Is anyone among you
suffering? Then he must pray. (James 5:8, 13)*

Fanny Crosby is a well-known name in Christian circles, having written wonderful hymns like "He Hideth My Soul," "Saved by Grace," and many others.
But Fanny Crosby had a difficult life. When she was only weeks old, a doctor
gave a faulty procedure that left her blind throughout her ninety-five years.
Although she married, the marriage failed and they moved apart. Fanny had a
child but it died in infancy and Fanny carried the grief to her grave. Blindness
. . . failed marriage . . . death of a child. Suffering is real.

We live in a fallen world and suffering affects everyone. James has pointed
words regarding suffering. He first chastens the wealthy for their sin of exploi-
tation of their workers, failing to pay them properly. The wealthy, living in
luxury and pleasure, stand condemned since they have focused on gathering
wealth for the last days. In the process they were guilty of killing the innocent.

James encourages the suffering believers: "Be patient"—patiently endure.
Just as the farmer waits the months from seedtime until harvest, so we are
called to wait patiently and in zealous anticipation for the Lord's coming. That
focus will help us avoid complaining or groaning against others. The prime
example of patience amid suffering is Job—he persevered, remaining steadfast amid suffering.

Prayer is the important response in suffering. Pray habitually; pray continually. In sickness (*asthenei* suggests being weak spiritually and emotionally,
needing encouragement), others are to pray with the one who is suffering.
Keep relationships pure and pray energetically. The prophet Elijah is an example of devoted prayer. "The effective prayer of a righteous man can accomplish
much" (James 5:16).

Suffering is a part of life. Faith demonstrated through devoted prayer,
focusing on the Lord's return, provides the resolution for the believer.

CONSIDER: *Amid suffering, the believer is called to patience and devoted prayer.*

November 22

Suffering Encourages Hope

1 Peter 1:1–12

*And though you have not seen Him, you love Him, and though
you do not see Him now, but believe in Him, you greatly rejoice
with joy inexpressible and full of glory. (1 Peter 1:8)*

Peter was writing his letter to the *Diaspora*, the Jews who were scattered throughout the Roman Empire and who were suffering for their faith. Suffering is the theme of Peter's epistle. Peter reminded them they were "a chosen race," to proclaim the excellencies of Christ (1 Peter 2:9). They were charged with disloyalty to the state (2:13–15) and were being slandered, ridiculed (3:13–17), and maligned (4:4–5). Peter warned them of an impending "fiery ordeal" (4:12). So Peter wrote to encourage them amid their suffering, reminding them to follow Jesus Christ's example (2:21).

Peter encouraged the Jewish believers, reminding them that through the resurrection of Christ, they had been born again to a "constantly living hope"—a hope that would never diminish. This living hope is ultimately realized in heaven, an inheritance that is imperishable; it will not pass away. It is "untouched by death, unstained by evil, unimpaired by time. It is composed of immortality, purity and beauty" (Cleon Rogers Jr. and Cleon Rogers III, *The New Linguistic and Exegetical Key to the Greek New Testament*). What a prospect! Meanwhile Peter reminds them that amid their suffering and persecution, they are protected by the power of God. This is a military picture of being guarded by soldiers. Their ultimate salvation will be realized at the return of Jesus Christ.

What could this do for the persecuted believers? It would bring them joy. Peter reminds them, because of their phenomenal future, they could "greatly rejoice" (1:6). And that would constitute a testimony, a proof of their genuine faith amid their fiery testing. Their focus was to be on Christ: though they had not seen Him, yet they believed in Him and they loved Him. The result was an inexpressible joy—"This joy defies all human efforts at understanding or explanation" (Cleon Rogers Jr. and Cleon Rogers III, *The New Linguistic and Exegetical Key to the Greek New Testament*).

Where are you walking today? Are you discouraged? Suffering? Look to Jesus. Contemplate all that you have in Him: a *living* hope, an inheritance in heaven that can never be removed. Focus on this blessed hope and let it fill your heart with joy and peace.

CONSIDER: *Peter writes to Hebrew believers who are suffering, encouraging them to rejoice in Christ because of their living hope through the resurrection.*

SUFFERING ENCOURAGES GODLY LIVING
1 PETER 1:13–2:10

Knowing that you were not redeemed with perishable things
like silver or gold from your futile way of life inherited from your
forefathers, but with precious blood, as of a lamb unblemished
and spotless, the blood of Christ. (1 Peter 1:18–19)

What do you think about? That will determine who you are and, ultimately, how you will cope with life. Some Christians know too much. Their minds are absorbed with this world; they focus on Hollywood entertainment, on politics, on the financial world—their minds are filled with the world. And then they don't cope with life.

While we need to know what is happening in the world, that should not be our focus. Peter exhorts us to "fix your hope completely on the grace to be brought to you at the revelation of Jesus Christ" (1 Peter 1:13). That is the subject that should absorb our minds. As the Orientals tied up their robes to walk in a hurry, so we are to "tie up our thoughts." That will affect our lifestyle. There is a change. We have lost some of our vocabulary; drinking habits are gone, no more pornography . . . we don't live like we formerly lived. And this is in keeping with Scripture. We are commanded: "You shall be holy, for I am holy" (v. 16). Believers are to be holy in lifestyle, "set apart" from sin and for God.

The reason for our new life is the expensive price paid for our redemption: we were redeemed by the "precious blood, . . . the blood of Christ" (v. 19). It was very costly—it necessitated Christ's death—yet He Himself was "unblemished and spotless." He was innocent, without sin. Meditating on the price it cost ought to affect our motivation in living a holy life. It is only through Christ that we are believers and have a legitimate hope of heaven.

This new life is reflected in love for other believers. Hypocrisy, deceit, and envy are to be abandoned. Just like a newborn baby drinking milk grows physically, we are to grow spiritually. We live this new life in association with Christ—the One who has been rejected but has now become the cornerstone. "Believers trust in Christ much as a building rests on its cornerstone" (Roger Raymer, "1 Peter," *Bible Knowledge Commentary*).

"He who believes in Him will not be disappointed" (2:6). Once we were without hope; now we have a glorious future. Think of it—no disappointment in Christ!

CONSIDER: *Because believers have been redeemed through the precious blood of Christ we are to live a new life, holy, set apart for Christ.*

November 24

Suffering Encourages Submission

1 Peter 2:11–3:12

For you have been called for this purpose, since Christ
also suffered for you, leaving you an example for you to
follow in His steps. (1 Peter 2:21)

A young man professed faith in Christ to a devout Christian woman, enabling him to marry her. When they were married, he told her, "There, now I have you. Don't bother me with this Christian stuff anymore." She wasn't able to talk to him about Christ but she lived it—for decades. At the end of his life he openly trusted in Christ. Her quiet witness had been the effective testimony to draw him to Christ.

Peter warns the believers, living in a hostile environment, to maintain an honest and upright conduct before the godless Gentiles so there would be no valid opportunity for slander. Submission is the spiritual resolution. Believers are to submit to civil authorities in every realm. For us today, that would be civic, state, and national governments. This was significant. It would stop the slander when the pagans observed the Christians submitting to government. While believers are free, the freedom is not to be used for evil but for God, demonstrating honor and respect for those in authority.

Servants are also called to submit to their masters—even those who are unreasonable. Today that would mean the employee submits to the authority of the employer. This finds favor with God; there is no merit if the employee sins and is treated harshly, but if he patiently endures when suffering from an unreasonable employer, that finds favor with God. Our model is Christ. We are called to "follow in His steps." While He suffered unjustly, He did not respond unfavorably. In His suffering, He died a substitutionary atonement so that we could be spiritually healed.

In the home, the wife is to submit to her husband, even if he is an unbeliever. Yet he can be brought to faith in Christ as he observes her respectful behavior and her gentle and quiet spirit, not arguing or fighting back. [This does not permit husbands to be abusive.] Husbands are to live with their wives in an understanding way, having knowledge of their spiritual, physical, and emotional needs. He is to honor and respect his wife as a joint heir of the grace of life. Spiritually, they are equal; in leadership in the home, the husband is intended to be the head of the family.

Peter summarizes our life: it is to be lived in harmony, in all the venues he has stated, reflecting kindness and humility, not returning evil for evil. The Lord observes our lives and in all of these situations, He responds to our prayers.

CONSIDER: *Believers are instructed regarding submission, to the government, to employers, and in the home.*

November 25

SUBMISSION ENCOURAGES VICTORIOUS LIVING

1 PETER 3:13–4:6

*For Christ also died for sins once for all, the just for the unjust,
so that He might bring us to God, having been put to death in
the flesh, but made alive in the spirit. (1 Peter 3:18)*

A young man, involved in the occult and violent crime in Iran, came to faith in Christ but kept it a secret. When his mother found out she was extremely angry and called the police—then she threw him out of the family home. His crime of "apostasy" is punishable by death in Iran. His very life is at risk. He is suffering for the name of Jesus.

Believers are challenged not to fear when suffering because of righteousness. But how can we not fear? Peter gives the answer: "sanctify Christ as Lord in your hearts" (1 Peter 3:15). Establish Christ as unique in your heart, "venerate and adore Him, thus dispelling all fear of man" (Cleon Rogers Jr. and Cleon Rogers III, *The New Linguistic and Exegetical Key to the Greek New Testament*). If we have the right relationship with Christ, we will avert all worry and fear of man. That will be observable to others, causing them to ask about our hope—then we will have opportunity to tell them about Christ. This will result in a good conscience—whereby the believer does not deny Christ or hide his or her faith. In the end, the accuser will observe the believer's righteous life and be put to shame.

Peter makes the point: it is better "you suffer for doing what is right rather than for doing what is wrong" (v. 17). Once more, Peter gives the supreme example of suffering unjustly: Christ, the Righteous One died in place of the unrighteous. Christ died a substitutionary atonement for us so we could be reconciled to God.

Through Noah, Jesus preached "in the spirit" to the people of Noah's day. They refused to believe and they are now "in prison." Correspondingly, baptism symbolizes the break with the old life, separating believers from unbelievers who were swept away in judgment.

Peter concludes: submit to suffering, even as Christ did. We are warned not to live a pagan life as in the past, but our lives are to be conformed to the will of God. Unbelievers will be astonished, and even offended, but they will give an account to God. Meanwhile, our challenge remains to submit to suffering and remain faithful to our Lord.

CONSIDER: *Believers are called to submit to suffering, even when suffering for righteous living, recognizing our supreme example of suffering unjustly is Christ.*

SUFFERING ENCOURAGES CONFIDENCE IN CHRIST

1 PETER 4:7–19

*To the degree that you share the sufferings of Christ, keep
on rejoicing, so that also at the revelation of His glory
you may rejoice with exultation. (1 Peter 4:13)*

When California voters expressed their support for traditional marriage, intense opposition and hatred followed—especially toward believers. An Internet video, "Prop. 8: The Musical," mocked the Bible, Jesus, and Christians. The homosexual community openly vowed opposition toward supporters of traditional marriage.

Open opposition toward Christians is increasing. How do we cope? How do we live in a culture that is increasingly anti-Christian? The Bible gives us direction. Because the second coming of Christ is imminent, believers are to live wisely—especially amid persecution. These circumstances could cause even believers to become upset but Peter reminds them to keep a cool head—to think clearly so they can pray. Persecution could diminish love but Peter exhorts us to "keep fervent in your love for one another, because love covers a multitude of sins." Love will set aside differences, and will be displayed through showing hospitality to one another. Instead of thinking of self, we are challenged to serve others, using our spiritual gifts. God has gifted us, not for self but for others.

Peter warns believers concerning the "fiery ordeal" that will come upon them (1 Peter 4:12). When Nero burned Rome in A.D. 64, he blamed Christians, and intense persecution against believers took place. "Some were covered with pitch and used as living torches to light the imperial gardens at night" (Roger Raymer, "1 Peter," *Bible Knowledge Commentary*). Amid the suffering Peter says, "keep on rejoicing" (v. 13). What is the focus? Christ's return—that will determine the resolution. Meanwhile, insults and ridicule are reminders that God's Spirit rests on us as we are identified with Christ. It is a time to glorify God, not be ashamed. The sufferings are a reminder that amid difficulties—sufferings—we enter the kingdom. The conclusion: "those also who suffer according to the will of God shall entrust their souls to a faithful Creator in doing what is right" (v. 19). Through faith, we give our souls as a deposit in an act of trust to God, knowing He is sovereign, wise, and good. He does what is right.

CONSIDER: *Amid fiery persecution, believers are called to fervently love one another and entrust their souls to a sovereign God who is good.*

SUFFERING ENCOURAGES HUMILITY

1 PETER 5:1–14

*Therefore humble yourselves under the mighty hand of God,
that He may exalt you at the proper time, casting all your
anxiety on Him, because He cares for you. (1 Peter 5:6–7)*

An elder in a Bible-believing church once told me, "You have to deal rough with people. I basically don't like people." Tragically, this man did not fit the biblical qualifications to be an elder.

As a fellow elder, Peter exhorted the elders, not only because he had witnessed firsthand the sufferings of Christ through scourging and crucifixion, but also because he had seen the foreshadowing of the glory of Christ that will consume the earth at His rule (see Matthew 17:1–8). The elders function as pastors, shepherding the people. It is important that their motive is right, not motivated by obligation or greed, but willingly and eagerly. The elders are to be examples (the Greek word is *tupos* which means "type") to the people. In life, in humility, in bearing up under suffering, the leaders in the church should set the pattern by their example. All of this looks forward to the return of the Chief Shepherd—a reminder as well that they are under-shepherds of the Chief Shepherd. When Christ appears to set up His kingdom on this earth, He will reward those who have been faithful; in this case, elders will receive the unfading crown of glory.

Younger men are exhorted to submit to the elders, but all of them are to exhibit humility toward one another. Why? Because "God is opposed to the proud, but gives grace to the humble" (1 Peter 5:5). All believers, young and old, are to exhibit a humble spirit which ultimately is humility and subjection to God. Arrogance and pride against others is ultimately arrogance and pride against God. Suffering and persecution may come with humility but God invites us to bring our burdens and our worries to Him because He cares and is concerned for His own. That reminder enables the believer to be strong in faith, resisting the devil who, like a lion, looks for someone to devour. Yet at the end of it all, God Himself will "perfect, confirm, strengthen and establish you" (v. 10). We have victory in Christ. Bring your burdens to Him and stand strong in your faith!

CONSIDER: *Elders are called to shepherd God's flock with pure motives while all believers are called to walk in humility, bringing their burdens to the Lord.*

GROWING IN GRACE THROUGH THE SCRIPTURES
2 PETER 1:1–21

*Grace and peace be multiplied to you in the knowledge of
God and of Jesus our Lord; . . . For no prophecy was ever made
by an act of human will, but men moved by the
Holy Spirit spoke from God. (2 Peter 1:2, 21)*

Bookstores always carry the latest fad in books. Books promise success and victory in life, in business, in cultural pursuits. Yet these books quickly fade from the scene and ultimately prove unreliable. Only one book is reliable: the Bible. Written by men guided by the Holy Spirit, the Scriptures lead us to spiritual maturity.

Peter quickly begins by exhorting believers to grow in grace and peace in greater measure. This is not an impossible task. God has provided us with divine power so that we have everything we need to grow in life and godliness. Through the new birth we have become partakers of the divine nature; for that reason we are to be diligent to add to our faith moral excellence, knowledge, self-control, perseverance, godliness, and love for fellow believers, and through this to grow in a true knowledge of Christ.

Having challenged and exhorted his readers, Peter reminds them of the reliability of his testimony. He and the apostles did not follow subtly contrived tales of mythology about deities but about the power and coming of Jesus Christ. What is the difference? Peter and the apostles were eyewitnesses. They were on the Mount of Transfiguration when they heard the Father's voice (the "Majestic Glory" in 2 Peter 1:17), "This is My beloved son with whom I am well pleased" (see Matthew 17:5). *They saw* the glorified Christ; *they heard* the Father's voice. Their testimony is reliable. As a result, the "prophetic word"—the Scriptures—are "more sure" (v. 19). The written record of Scripture is reliable and trustworthy.

Peter reminds them that the Scriptures didn't come from the apostles' own origination. How did the Scriptures come about? Although men actively wrote the Scriptures, they were "moved by the Holy Spirit" (v. 21)—He was carrying them along to His desired end. What did they write? Precisely what the Holy Spirit guided them to write. For this reason, the Scriptures are the *inerrant* Word of God. They are totally without error in every subject they address. What is the conclusion? We "do well to pay attention" (v. 19) since the study and response to the teachings of the Scriptures is what will lead us to maturity. We must pay attention to Scripture.

CONSIDER: *The Scriptures were written by men guided by the Holy Spirit and are therefore inerrant and the sure guide to lead us to spiritual maturity.*

FACING FALSE TEACHERS

2 PETER 2:1–22

But false prophets also arose among the people, just as there will also be false teachers among you, who will secretly introduce destructive heresies, even denying the Master who bought them, bringing swift destruction upon themselves. (2 Peter 2:1)

The face of evangelicalism is changing. Some who call themselves evangelicals now deny the penal substitutionary atonement of Christ. They deny that Jesus died in the place of sinners, as a substitute for them, paying the penalty of their sins to God the Father. One of these said that if that was the case, then God the Father was guilty of divine child abuse. Open repudiation of the atoning work of Christ.

These twenty-first century false teachers are precisely what Peter prophesied. He said they were "even denying the Master who bought them." Do people really follow these men? Tragically, yes. And, as a result, the truth is distorted and blasphemed. They are adept at words—false words. But God is not asleep. He is not blind to their deception. History shows that God meted out judgment on deceivers. When the angels rebelled against God, He cast them down into the angels' hell (*tartarus*). When the people of Noah's day exhibited immorality, God sent the flood, sparing only Noah and his family. When the people of Sodom and Gomorrah openly practiced sexual immorality, God destroyed the cities, rescuing Lot (only here do we know he was "righteous"). God's act of preserving Lot is a reminder that He rescues His own from temptation but He judges the unrighteous.

These unprincipled people who "indulge the flesh" (2 Peter 2:10) are brazen, shameless—like "unreasoning animals, born as creatures of instinct to be captured and killed" (v. 12). They are shameless; they no longer hide their sin. Some of these, although having a knowledge of Christ, return to their immoral practices like a dog returning to its vomit or a pig to wallowing in its mire. They never were believers.

Peter's words are overwhelming, describing their open, brazen immorality and their rejection of Jesus Christ. This may well be a very sober reminder of where America is heading amid open, brazen sexual immorality, defiance, and rejection of Jesus Christ. These are sobering days and Peter's words have a somber message.

CONSIDER: *There were—and continue to be—false teachers who are shameless, immoral, and who deny the atonement of Christ.*

November 30

ANTICIPATING THE NEW HEAVENS AND NEW EARTH
2 PETER 3:1–18

*But grow in the grace and knowledge of our Lord and
Savior Jesus Christ. To Him be the glory, both now and to
the day of eternity. Amen. (2 Peter 3:18)*

God has created a beautiful world. The majestic beauty of Banff and Lake
Louise in Alberta, Canada, the serenity of swaying palms in Florida, the
"sound of music" hills and mountains in Austria—the beauty of this earth is
overwhelming. But what is its future? Is God going to destroy this beautiful
earth that He created?

Peter warns his readers, reminding them of what the Old Testament prophets and the New Testament apostles have prophesied. In the last days mockers
will come, ridiculing the teaching of Scripture, questioning whether Christ will
return. They deny His return by saying all things have continued as they always
have without interruption. But they forget one thing: the flood. Life hasn't always
continued the same. When flagrant sin pervaded the earth God sent the flood
and the earth was "destroyed" by water. And it will happen again—but the next
time the judgment will be by fire.

The problem with people questioning the Lord's return is that God sees
time differently. He views time in the light of eternity, hence, a thousand years
with God are like a day and a day like a thousand years. He is not restricted by
time nor is He in a hurry. He withholds His judgment to allow people to repent.

But at the end of the age—the day of the Lord when Christ will establish
His kingdom—the "heavens will pass away" (2 Peter 3:10). This means the
heavens and the earth *in their present form* will disappear; the present form
will "come to an end, lose force" (F. W. Gingrich and F. W. Danker, *A Greek-
English Lexicon of the New Testament*). This present heavens and earth "will
be destroyed with intense heat, and the earth and its works will be burned
up," meaning "be found, discovered" (F. W. Gingrich and F. W. Danker, *A Greek-
English Lexicon of the New Testament*). It will be exposed to God's judgment.
Was the earth destroyed by the flood? It was not annihilated; it was cleansed
and renovated. That is what God will do before Christ establishes His reign. At
that time the earth will be cleansed of all sin so the righteous King will reign
on a renovated, perfect earth. The result will be a "new heavens and a new
earth" (see also Isaiah 65:17 and 66:22).

In anticipation of this horrific event, believers ought to live in reverent fear
of a holy God, spotless and blameless, growing in the grace and knowledge of
our Lord and Savior Jesus Christ.

CONSIDER: *God is going to judge the earth, renovating it by fire, cleansing it
from sin—which calls believers to live righteously, growing in the grace of Christ.*

December 1

FELLOWSHIP IN LIGHT

1 JOHN 1:1–2:2

*What we have seen and heard we proclaim to you also, so that
you too may have fellowship with us; and indeed our fellowship
is with the Father, and with His Son Jesus Christ. (1 John 1:3)*

The apostle John wrote his first epistle from the city of Ephesus, perhaps
around A.D. 80. Since John had served the church at Ephesus and visited
the surrounding churches, this letter was likely directed at those believers.
John was writing with two purposes in mind: to warn believers concerning
false teachers (1:1–3; 2:19, 22–23) and to exhort believers to grow spiritually.
Apparently the believers had become careless, flirting with the world (2:15–
17). The theme of 1 John is fellowship—fellowship with Jesus Christ and with
other believers. Fellowship (*koinonia*) is sharing. It denotes a common interest, a close-knit togetherness where believers are focused on the same thing.

John writes as an eyewitness. When he tells them about Christ, it is authen-
tic because John heard Jesus, saw Jesus, and touched Jesus. John spent three
and a half years walking with the Lord—Jesus' life was revealed to John; for
that reason John is telling us about Christ. It is significant because Jesus *is the
eternal life*. He writes that we too can have fellowship with other believers but
especially with the Father and the Son.

Fellowship with Christ brings a new life—a walk in the light—living in the
truth. If someone is living in darkness—in sin—and yet professes to have fellowship with Christ, they are lying and not living the truth. But if we walk in
truth, then we experience genuine fellowship with Christ and other believers.

Does that mean believers are sinless? No. In fact, if we say we are sinless
we are deceiving ourselves. But there is a remedy. When we confess our sins
to Christ, His blood keeps on cleansing us from all sin. Furthermore, Jesus is
our "Advocate" (*Parakletos*), our defense attorney before the Father—and He
has never lost a case! That is security! His atoning blood is eternally effective,
continually cleansing us from the daily defilement of sin. Come, enjoy fellowship with Christ and other believers—made available through the shed blood
of Jesus Christ.

CONSIDER: *Through the atonement of Christ, we have fellowship with Him and
with fellow believers as the blood of Christ cleanses us from the daily defilement
of sin.*

December 2

Proof of Fellowship

1 John 2:3–14

*By this we know that we have come to know Him, if we
keep His commandments. The one who says, "I have come
to know Him," and does not keep His commandments, is
a liar, and the truth is not in him. (1 John 2:3–4)*

Erik is one of the happiest people I have ever seen. He is constantly smiling
and excited about his new life in Christ. He has not always been this way,
but he doesn't talk about his past. It is evident to all who meet Erik that he is
a new person in Christ.

How do we know if someone is a believer in Christ? John answers the
question. We know it when we obey the Word of God, keeping His commandments. Obedience to God's Word is key. If disobedience is the lifestyle, and
yet the person says, "I have come to know Him," that person is a liar. That is
the biblical statement. It is strong language. Being a believer doesn't consist in
merely saying the words. When a person has trusted in Christ, the Holy Spirit
has regenerated the person, has come to indwell and guide the person. The
believer has received a new nature, a new capacity for living righteously. If
unrighteousness persists, it is evident that the person is not a believer.

According to 1 John 2:5, the love of God is perfected in the one who keeps
and obeys God's Word. The "love of God" may be either God's love for man or
man's love for God or even "God's kind of love." This person exhibits *love*. It
is real in his life. Love is brought to completion and fulfillment in his life. It is
obvious he is a believer. John concludes that the person who says he knows
Christ will also have a walk that is consistent with his confession.

Was this something new? No. John reminds them this is an old commandment (from Leviticus 19:18; see also Galatians 5:14). Yet it is also new since
Jesus taught them to love one another (John 13:34–35). As Jesus is the light
of the world, so believers who love one another shine forth the new light of
Christ. The one who loves his brother won't cause another to stumble.

Love is proof of fellowship with God. When John addresses his readers
as "little children," "fathers," and "young men" (1 John 2:12–14), he is probably addressing three levels of maturity. At every level, they have fellowship
because love is the foundation of their new life in Christ. That is the proof of
the genuineness of the new life in Christ. Is your life reflective of your fellowship with Christ?

CONSIDER: *Love for others is the visible demonstration of the reality that a
person knows Christ.*

December 3

HINDRANCES TO FELLOWSHIP

1 JOHN 2:15–29

---

*Do not love the world nor the things in the world. If anyone loves
the world, the love of the Father is not in him. (1 John 2:15)*

It is not entirely unusual to hear professing Christians take the Lord's name
in vain. Why is that? In the workplace, in sports, in movies and television,
believers are inundated with language where the Lord's name is misused, and
they have become desensitized. Tragic. When the believer is enamored with
the world, and not constantly on guard against its influence, it will change his
or her thinking and verbiage.

Scripture is strong in its statement: "Do not love the world nor the things in
the world." But we don't "get it." A generation ago preachers proclaimed strong
messages, warning against a love of the world. Issues are far more serious
today but the warnings are now rare.

What is *the world*? The world (*kosmos*) "can signify mankind organized
in rebellion against God" (Fritz Rienecker and Cleon Rogers, *Linguistic Key to
the Greek New Testament*). The world involves both a philosophy as well as
material things. Don't love them. Don't be persuaded or guided by the world.
One who does this does not have the love of the Father in him. The world represents the threefold enticing temptation ("the lust of the flesh and lust of the
flesh and the boastful pride of life" from 1 John 2:16) that caused Adam and
Eve to sin (Gen. 3:6). This doesn't come from God; it comes from the adversary
and all that is opposed to God. And the sin-darkened world is transitory; it is
passing from existence.

So how can we tell the true from the false? We know there are "many antichrists" (v. 18) in the world—those who stand in opposition to Christ. They
demonstrate they are not believers when they depart from Christian fellowship. These are the ones who deny the uniqueness of Jesus Christ and they
have neither the Son nor the Father.

How do we know the truth? God has given us the anointing, the indwelling
Holy Spirit, whereby we know the Father and the Son. The Holy Spirit guides
us into the truth, whereby we know the Father and Son, hence, we *abide* in
Christ—we live in Him. Whoever denies the uniqueness of the Son is of Satan,
a liar and deceiver.

The lines are clearly drawn and it is imperative that we recognize this. The
world with its false message is hostile to Christ. We must take our stand, in
opposition to the world, as we live our lives in fellowship with Christ, abiding
in Him.

CONSIDER: *We are called to abide in Christ so that we will not be lured astray
by the world with its false message directed by antichrists.*

December 4

FELLOWSHIP IN LOVE (1)

1 JOHN 3:1–24

We know that we have passed out of death into life, because we love the brethren. He who does not love abides in death. (1 John 3:14)

It was Sunday evening. Only some fourteen hours before Helen's homegoing to heaven, as we were leaving church, Helen noticed John Mark, a boy with his arm in a cast. She stopped and talked to John Mark, expressing her love and concern. That was Helen. She loved people and she showed her love for others in a caring way.

Why should we love others? Because of God's love for us—that is the foundation for loving others. Can we grasp the enormity of God's love for us? He loved us so much that He sent His only Son to make atonement for our sins, satisfying the holiness of God (John 3:16; 1 John 4:10). In its unbelief, the world doesn't begin to understand this. Not only are we children of God, when Christ returns we will see Him in His resplendent glory and "we will be like Him" (1 John 3:2). We will be changed, receiving our immortal bodies. This is an enormous incentive to separating ourselves from sin and living righteous lives.

Christ came to resolve the dilemma of sin, to remove sin, to give His people victory over sin. The one who now lives in fellowship with Christ, who is born of God, no longer continues to practice sin. Christ has given the believer victory. Sin and righteousness are opposites and they designate ownership. The one living in sin is dominated by the devil; the one living in love is controlled by Christ.

This is the foundational message for believers: "love one another" (v. 11). "Love" (*agapao*) is more than a sentimental emotion; it is a reasoned-out love, loving the other person irrespective of the response. That is biblical love. It is the badge, the sign that we have passed out of death into life. If hatred persists, it is a sign of unbelief, of belonging to the adversary. We are reminded of love through the love of Christ who gave His life that we might live the new life.

The challenge for us is to continue to excel in love. We will never love enough. There will always be opportunity to love more. But this is the foundation: believe in Christ and love others. It sounds simple, but it is profound. It is the sign of who we are.

CONSIDER: *In an enormous act of love, Christ laid down His life for us so that we might have the new life, living in fellowship with Him and loving others.*

FELLOWSHIP IN LOVE (2)

1 JOHN 4:1–21

*And this commandment we have from Him, that the one
who loves God should love his brother also. (1 John 4:21)*

Is doctrine important? A prominent evangelical pastor spoke at an Islamic
convention, telling them we should partner and work together in eliminating
world problems of war, poverty, corruption, disease, and illiteracy. Can we
unite with those who have different beliefs about Christ?

Some Christians today feel we shouldn't focus on doctrine; we should simply love others, yet John combines the two thoughts: doctrine and love. He
warns us in 1 John 4: "do not believe every spirit, but test the spirits" (v. 1).
The test is concerning truth. What is it? We are to discern whether others
acknowledge the true, sinless humanity of Christ (vv. 2–3) as well as His deity
(v. 15). Both are foundational doctrines that must be acknowledged by true
believers. Only they are born of God. John's words are pointed—to believe
otherwise is antichrist. But in Christ, we are victorious; we are "overcomers"
(v. 4). We stand in the state of victory in Christ! John stalwartly reminds us of
our differences: "They are from the world. . . . We are from God" (vv. 5–6). John
contrasts the "spirit of truth and the spirit of error" (v. 6).

Genuine love can only come from those "born of God" (v. 7). It is those that
John enjoins to "love one another." Those that do not love don't, in fact, know
God. The greatest demonstration of love was God sending His Son to be the
atoning sacrifice for our sins. That is the motivation for love.

Since God loved us so magnanimously, we are exhorted, "we ought to love
one another" (v. 11). Being born of God, He lives in us to perfect love in us
and He accomplishes this through His Spirit indwelling us. As God perfects
His love in us, we have confidence in the day of judgment. Fear is eliminated.
Love removes fear.

The challenge remains: "the one who loves God should love his brother
also." Am I fulfilling this basic, foundational command? Do I know where I
should demonstrate God's love through me?

CONSIDER: *We are to hold to the truth of Jesus being fully God and fully man
and we are to exhibit our new birth through love for others.*

December 6

FELLOWSHIP IN LIFE

1 JOHN 5:1–21

---

*And the testimony is this, that God has given us eternal life, and
this life is in His Son. He who has the Son has the life; he who
does not have the Son of God does not have the life. (1 John 5:11–12)*

Life. It seems our world is filled with the opposite. Driving down the street
recently a bird darted in front of my car and was killed. I felt bad. But in
a more serious vein, we have seen several funerals recently. A young father
with two small children died suddenly. We see so much death; it is all around
us, every day.

Can we speak of life? Yes! Jesus Christ, the unique and only Son of God,
has brought us *life* and we access it through faith. Believing in Christ results in
the new birth that transforms us: it incites us to love God, love believers, and
keep God's commandments. God gives us *life* and this life enables us to live
victoriously, overcoming the world. Are you struggling in the world? Through
Christ—through faith, trusting in Him—you have the victory! The issue is
faith—your trust is in Christ, not circumstances. And your faith is anchored in
a historical event. Christ came visibly, "by water," as He was baptized, and "by
blood," when He shed His blood on the cross. *God* has given us the witness.
Can God lie? No. He is true and He has testified concerning His Son. Moreover,
the Holy Spirit bears witness to us of the reality of Christ. If anyone denies this
witness, he is a liar. God spoke in history when He sent His Son. The greatest
lie that can be perpetrated is to deny Christ's coming.

And what did Christ bring us? Life! He brought an end to tears, suffering,
and death. He brought life. Even at the casket of a loved one, we can know they
are already celebrating life. And this life is singularly in His Son. Knowing the
Son through faith is to have life; to reject and deny the Son—there is no life,
only eternal tragedy. But God enables us to have the assurance, the certainty,
of His life in us. Through believing in the Son we have life. The life in Christ
gives us a new relationship; we are in the family, we can come boldly asking
the Father and He will respond. And He gives us victory so that the adversary
cannot harm us. What a blessing from God! Life! Through Christ! Do you have
it? It is yours—through faith in Christ.

CONSIDER: *God has given us eternal, unending, qualitative life through believing in Christ.*

December 7

Walk in the Truth

2 John

If anyone comes to you and does not bring this teaching, do not receive him into your house, and do not give him a greeting. (2 John 10)

As I was waiting to have my car repaired, I sat in the waiting room, studying my Bible. Soon I was in a deep conversation with a Seventh-day Adventist who emphasized keeping the Law—particularly the Sabbath—for salvation. He was promulgating a false gospel, mixing law and grace.

John the apostle (referring to himself as "the elder") wrote three small epistles—letters—in which he emphasizes similar themes such as "truth," "walk," "new commandment," and "love." In terms of Scripture, John wrote late, perhaps around A.D. 80. This short epistle is addressed to "the chosen lady and her children." While some suggest this is a reference to a church, it is best understood as an actual lady. Her identity, however, remains unknown. She was probably a widow, known for her exemplary character and hospitality. Her house was likely the meeting place of the church in her community. Apparently she had grown children, some of whom John knew.

John wrote this epistle to warn the chosen lady against the inroads of these false teachers. The lady was hospitable and John saw the distinct danger of the lady inviting the itinerant false teachers into her home. John warns her not to receive anyone into her home that does not bring the true doctrine (v. 10). By showing hospitality to false teachers one becomes a participant in the evil deeds of the deceivers.

The solution is "walking in truth" (v. 4). John had encountered her children walking in the truth. John encourages the lady and her people to walk in love, which means "that we walk according to His commandments" (v. 6). The false teachers did not love because they were not keeping the Lord's commandments; they were deceivers. So John warns believers to be alert and not be led astray. The result will be a full reward for loving others by walking in the truth.

CONSIDER: *John exhorts the chosen lady to love by walking in the truth and not being led astray by false teachers.*

December 8

WALKING IN THE TRUTH

3 John

I have no greater joy than this, to hear of my
children walking in the truth. (3 John 4)

I remember the meeting very well. One of the leaders in the church shouted out loud, calling people to line up with him. And a number did. He had created trouble in the church, wanting to be in the forefront. Now people physically lined up beside him in the church—and they left because he couldn't assume the preeminent place.

Similar to 2 John, the apostle John wrote this letter from Ephesus near A.D. 80 to "the beloved Gaius." Gaius is unknown apart from this mention. The name was a common one, used in Roman law books in the same way we use "John Doe" today. Gaius must have been a faithful Christian since John consistently addresses him as "beloved" (vv. 1, 2, 5, 11).

John wrote to Gaius because of a problem existing in the church to which Gaius belonged. Word had come to John concerning Diotrephes, an influential member and perhaps leader of the church who loved to be first. When John sent his emissaries to deal with the problem, Diotrephes refused to receive them. In addition, Diotrephes accused John and the other believers "with wicked words" (v. 10).

John's purpose in writing was to encourage Gaius in the midst of the problem they were facing because of Diotrephes. John commends Gaius for his hospitality, reminding him of the importance of showing hospitality to the Lord's servants. John also writes to denounce the evil dealings of Diotrephes—and John himself would deal with Diotrephes when he came. Above all, John takes great joy in the fact that Gaius is "walking in truth" (v. 3). John's words indicate "the continual habitual conducting of one's life" (Fritz Rienecker and Cleon Rogers, *Linguistic Key to the Greek New Testament*).

What is the lesson? This epistle is a reminder that the adversary will constantly seek to disrupt the unity of believers. It is resolved when believers continuously live in a love relationship with each other, ministering to one another, helping and serving one another—and standing strong against error. That must be our commitment.

CONSIDER: *Gaius is commended for walking in the truth and standing against error.*

December 9

CONTEND FOR THE FAITH

JUDE

---

*Contend earnestly for the faith which was
once for all handed down to the saints. (Jude 3)*

Cultists have made inroads around the world. In America alone, there are some seventeen million cultists. They range from a rejection of the deity of Christ to the deification of man. We are in a spiritual warfare.

Jude, the half-brother of Jesus, warned his readers to "contend earnestly for"—as in an athletic contest—"the faith which was once for all handed down," entrusted and committed to believers. Jude warns his readers because ungodly people—apparently libertines—secretly slipped into the assemblies and were teaching error, discounting the grace of God, and denying the Lord Jesus Christ.

Would God overlook their evil ways? No. Jude reminds the people of God's judgment in the past: When the Israelites who were saved out of Egypt expressed unbelief, God judged the entire generation (Num. 14:22–30). When Lucifer rebelled against the Lord, leading angels with him in rebellion (Isa. 14:12–17; Ezek. 28:12–17), God judged them. When the people of Sodom and Gomorrah practiced their evil ways, God destroyed the cities with fire (Gen. 19:23–29). But these deceivers, despite knowing the history of God's judgment, continued in the same pattern of moral defilement. These false and immoral teachers are like animals without reason, and they will be judged—"the black darkness has been reserved forever" for them (v. 13).

Jude reminds his readers that all of this was already foretold by Christ and the apostles, warning believers to beware of mockers who follow ungodly lusts and cause division with their worldly mind-set. The solution for believers was to build one another up in the faith, praying together, walking in the love of God. Believers need not fall into false teaching. Jude closes with an encouraging doxology: God deserves all the glory for all eternity, as He is able to prevent believers from falling and enable them to stand secure in the day of judgment.

CONSIDER: *Christ and the apostles warned concerning the apostasy that would come through false teachers.*

December 10

THE MESSAGE FROM JESUS CHRIST

REVELATION 1:1–20

"Therefore write the things which you have seen, and the things which are, and the things which will take place after these things." (Revelation 1:19)

Many people refrain from reading Revelation because they think it is difficult to understand. Granted, there are pictures and images in this book but God nonetheless gave it to us to provide information about the future. What will this world be like prior to Christ's return? Will God judge this world? What will Christ's kingdom be like?

John writes to answer these and other questions. In fact, the book is a revelation of Jesus Christ to John about "the things which must soon take place" (Rev. 1:1). And there is a blessing to those who read these words and heed them. Why? Because "the time is near" (v. 3). John writes to seven historic churches in Asia Minor, with a message from Jesus Christ, the eternal One ("who is and who was and who is to come"; vv. 4, 8), the One who will rule over the kings of the earth. He is also the One "who loves us and released us from our sins by His blood" (v. 5). But John's message is timeless—the churches were historic but they also reflect seven types of churches that exist today.

John writes to encourage believers during the time when the Roman emperor Domitian severely persecuted the Christians for refusing to worship the emperor. John also brings the Old Testament prophesies to their consummation with the triumphant return and the establishment of Christ's earthly, eternal kingdom.

John announces, "Behold, He is coming!" (v. 7). When He comes, the tribes of the earth—Israel—will mourn in repentance. John is on the island of Patmos when he receives the message of Christ, commanding him to write, as verse 19 says, "the things which you have seen" (ch. 1), "the things which are" (chs. 2–3), and "the things which shall take place after these things" (chs. 4–22). John sees the glorified Christ, and he falls at His feet as a dead man. Christ announces, "I am the first and the last" (v. 17), which is understood to be a proclamation of His deity (see the similar phrasing in Isaiah 41:4; 44:6; and 48:12). Christ is the living One; moreover, He has the keys of death and hades, meaning Christ has the authority to judge humanity, giving them eternal life in heaven or condemning them to the lake of fire.

Revelation is both a comfort and a warning regarding what will transpire at the end of the age. It should encourage believers to zealous righteous living while joyfully anticipating Christ's return, knowing righteousness will prevail.

CONSIDER: *Christ gave John a vision of the end of the age, instructing the churches of that age and this age to live in purity and preparation.*

MESSAGE TO THE CHURCHES (1)

REVELATION 2:1–29

"He who has an ear, let him hear what the Spirit says to the churches. To him who overcomes, I will grant to eat of the tree of life which is in the Paradise of God." (Revelation 2:7)

It was an emotional moment when I visited Wittenberg, Germany, and saw the church where Martin Luther nailed his Ninety-five Theses, protesting the erroneous teaching of the Catholic Church. Luther had a message for the church of that day, especially for Johann Tetzel who began the practice of selling indulgences to those who wanted to purchase forgiveness for their upcoming sins.

Jesus Christ appeared to John with messages for seven historic churches in Asia Minor. While these were actual churches, they were also "representative of all churches at that time, as well as those of subsequent generations" (Charles Ryrie, *Revelation*). Christ "walks" among the churches—He is present and fully knowledgeable about what is happening in the churches. To the churches Christ gives a commendation for their loyalty, condemnation where they err, and a correction.

Christ first addresses Ephesus, the capital of the province of Asia, hosting the temple of Diana, one of the seven wonders of the world. Christ commends the church for its toil and perseverance in opposing evil. They put the false teachers to the test. They had worked to the point of exhaustion. Nonetheless, Christ had hard words for them: they had left their first love—they did not have a genuine love for Christ because they were not genuinely saved. The Lord warned them that He would remove their lampstand; their witness would be extinguished. But the one who "overcomes" (who is a true believer; see 1 John 5:4–5) will "eat of the tree of life" (v. 7).

The church in Smyrna, the center of Caesar worship, was severely persecuted, yet they were spiritually rich. Amid suffering, they stood strong against evil. Although living amid Satan's throne, the church at Pergamum remained steadfast and loyal to the name of Christ. But some had fallen prey to false teaching, and if they failed to repent, Christ would come to judge them with His Word. Christ commended the church at Thyatira for their love, faith, service, and perseverance, yet they tolerated immorality and false worship.

What is the message? "He who has an ear, let him hear"—it is possible to obey in one area and yet disobey in another. The solution is to repent—change our mind.

CONSIDER: *Christ observes the churches, commending them for their truth and loyalty but condemning and correcting them concerning their sin.*

December 12

MESSAGE TO THE CHURCHES (2)
REVELATION 3:1–22

*"Behold, I stand at the door and knock; if anyone hears
My voice and opens the door, I will come in to him and
will dine with him, and he with Me." (Revelation 3:20)*

When is a church "dead"? In Europe, massive church buildings stand empty, and in many of the remaining churches, the message is unbiblical. Many American congregations are straying from biblical truth as well.

Christ addresses the angel, or messenger—the pastor—of these churches in Asia Minor. He rebukes the church at Sardis: although they have a reputation as a spiritual church, they are dead. They had been absorbed by their culture. The church is warned, "Wake up!" Yet there were a few that were not contaminated. John's readers would have understood the significance of God's promise for the overcomer: "I will never blot out his name from the book of life" (v. 5). Greek and Roman cities registered all their citizens, and citizens who were degraded would have their names expunged. Conversely, these believers are promised their name will *not* be erased from the book of life.

There is no *condemnation* given to the church at Philadelphia. Christ, who has the keys (authority) "to truth and holiness as well as to opportunity, service and testimony" (John Walvoord, *Revelation of Jesus Christ*) would sustain them and empower them in ministry. Christ had opened a door of missionary activity for Philadelphia but they were being persecuted by the "synagogue of Satan" (Jewish unbelievers). Christ promises the church He will keep them from ("out of") the hour of testing. The promise extends to the church at large—the church will be raptured before the tribulation begins. Meanwhile, we must "hold fast" to the truth.

Conversely, there is no *commendation* for the church at Laodicea. They exhibited gross indifference, spiritual poverty, and self-deception, thinking they were rich when they were poor. Christ reminds them of the hot medicinal waters at Hierapolis and the cold, pure waters of Colossae. They are neither. They are lukewarm, useless; they are unbelievers whom Christ will spit out. Christ stands *outside* the church, knocking to enter.

These are somber messages. Is your church, are you, so impacted by your culture that there is no evident difference? Are you self-satisfied, falsely content spiritually?

CONSIDER: *Christ addresses the exuberant church, zealous to spread the good news, but also the self-satisfied church that He will spit out of His mouth.*

December 13

GOD IS HOLY
REVELATION 4:1–11

Immediately I was in the Spirit; and behold, a throne was standing in heaven, and One sitting on the throne. . . . "HOLY, HOLY, HOLY IS THE LORD GOD, THE ALMIGHTY, WHO WAS AND WHO IS AND WHO IS TO COME." (Revelation 4:2, 8)

I will forever remember when I was a young boy my mother heard me say, "Holy cow!" She pulled me aside and lectured me: "Listen, cows are not holy, smoke is not holy. Only God is holy." I never forgot my mother's lecture. The holiness of God is often ignored and even completely forgotten.

Yet one day every person—no exceptions—will face a holy God and give an account. Prior to the seal, trumpet, and bowl judgments, John is given a picture of the sovereign God and His Son (chs. 4–5). John is transported to heaven and he sees the glorified God enthroned. The glory of God—His majesty, purity, and justice—is reflected like expensive stones. The throne of God symbolizes His judgment (4:9; 6:10, 16–17). "The picture is that of His anger because of His holy nature reacting in response to the prevailing sinfulness of mankind, resulting in the judgment He is about to send upon the earth" (Robert Thomas, *Revelation 1–7*).

Around the throne are twenty-four crowned elders, representing the church that has been raptured and rewarded. Also around the throne are the living creatures—angels continuously giving glory to God (Ezek. 1:5; 10:14; Isa. 6:3). Their four faces reflect the most noble animal (lion), the strongest (calf/ox), the wisest (human), and the swiftest (eagle). They praise God for His holiness, His eternality, and His coming judgment (Rev. 4:8; see also Rev. 6:1, 3, 5, 7, where "come" signifies that they agree with the judgment).

The twenty-four elders prostrate themselves before God seated on His throne and cast their crowns before the throne indicating that God alone reigns (Leon Morris, *Book of Revelation*). They recognize that all things have been created for God's will.

This majestic scene is a reminder that God is holy and omnipotent—and He demands obedience. One day all will recognize His holiness. Those who scorn Him will be judged.

CONSIDER: *God is infinitely holy and for this reason He must judge the sinful world.*

December 14

Worthy Is the Lamb

Revelation 5:1–14

"Worthy is the Lamb that was slain to receive power and riches and wisdom and might and honor and glory and blessing." (Revelation 5:12)

Our culture has no concept of the sovereign lordship of Jesus Christ—the One whom they will face one day. Recently the comic strip Doonesbury had this statement about Jesus: "God's only son is this total pacifist—He wouldn't harm a flea. He's just this humble dude who's mellow to everyone—even the Romans!"

They have no understanding of Christ. Revelation 5 portrays Christ's right to judge. In the hand of God is the scroll of judgment, written on both sides and sealed with seven seals. As the seals are removed, they unfold the judgments of God (as we will see beginning in chapter 6). But who is able to "open the book" (reveal its contents) and "break its seals" (execute its judgments)? No one in heaven or on earth has the authority (the virtue) to open the seals and execute the judgments. There is loud wailing for fear that the events of the scroll will remain unopened and unfulfilled.

The Lion, revealing strength and majesty, refers to the tribe of Judah, from which Messiah will come and rule in the kingdom (Gen. 49:9–10). He is the "Root of David," springing from the stem of Jesse (Isa. 11:1; Rev. 22:16). He has overcome—He has won the victory at the cross and risen from the dead. For this reason He is worthy to open the seals.

John sees a Lamb standing, as if slain, referring to Christ (John 1:29). "Standing" refers to the resurrection. For this reason, Christ is worthy to open the seals and judge. The seven horns picture His strength while the seven eyes reveal His wisdom. The Son takes the book from the Father, indicating the authority to judge has been given to the Son (John 5:22, 27). Christ's atonement has resulted in people from every tribe and language becoming "a kingdom and priests" (Rev. 5:10). Worship surrounds the throne: innumerable angels, the four creatures, the twenty-four elders all praising Christ: "Worthy is the Lamb that was slain to receive power and riches and wisdom and might and honor and glory and blessing." Christ will be worshiped. People ridicule and blaspheme today but the day is coming when heaven and hell will acknowledge the supremacy of Jesus Christ.

CONSIDER: *Through His sacrificial death and His resurrection, Christ has both the right and the power to unleash judgment on a sinful world.*

December 15

The Seven Seals

Revelation 6:1–17

---

*And they said to the mountains and to the rocks, "Fall on us and
hide us from the presence of Him who sits on the throne, and from
the wrath of the Lamb; for the great day of their wrath has come,
and who is able to stand?" (Revelation 6:16–17)*

When I was teaching the book of Revelation at the Word of Life Bible Institute in Hungary, I asked the students, "What does a husband give his bride?" "Chocolates!" shouted a student. I was hoping they would say "love" to show that as the bride of Christ believers are not the objects of God's wrath but rather His love.

The tribulation will be the outpouring of God's wrath on a sinful, unbelieving world that has blasphemed His Son, which provides a strong case for believing that the church will be raptured prior to the outpouring of the wrath of God in the tribulation. The tribulation is also to discipline Israel and bring the Hebrew people to repentance (Jer. 30:7; Zech. 12:10–14).

The Lamb—Jesus Christ—opens the seals, initiating the tribulation. The first seal pictures the false messiah, the beast, the Antichrist riding a white horse. He will devour the whole earth through deception (Dan. 7:23–24; 8:23–25). The second seal, the red horse, represents bloodshed resulting from war. The beast will initiate the wars prophesied by Christ (see Matthew 24:1–31, especially vv. 6–7). As a result, the third seal describes the famine that follows, represented by the black horse. Food becomes scarce. The fourth horse, the ashen horse, envisions the death that follows—in catastrophic proportions, a quarter of the world's population dies. The fifth seal opens and moves the picture to heaven where the numerous martyrs who were killed for their faith are seen, calling for their blood to be avenged. The sixth seal results in cosmic convulsions: a great earthquake, the sun is darkened, the moon becomes like blood, stars fall, the sky is split, and mountains shift.

Earth's leaders recognize what is happening: the righteous Lord is pouring out His wrath on a sinful world. It is difficult to comprehend these horrors. How fortunate that we have been redeemed by the blood of Christ—that He suffered so that we need not suffer. We are the objects of God's love, not His wrath. Will you praise Him and thank Him for your future—redemption in heaven, not wrath on earth?

CONSIDER: *The seven seals are the beginning of the outpouring of God's wrath to judge people for their unbelief.*

THE 144,000

REVELATION 7:1–17

And I heard the number of those who were sealed, one hundred and forty-four thousand sealed from every tribe of the sons of Israel. . . . After these things I looked, and behold, a great multitude which no one could count, from every nation and all tribes and peoples and tongues, standing before the throne and before the Lamb, clothed in white robes, and palm branches were in their hands. (Revelation 7:4, 9)

Will people be saved during the tribulation? Will there be evangelism? Absolutely—in greater measure than this world has ever seen. Evangelism has greatly increased in the twenty-first century. Some 100,000 congregations (a third of all congregations) send teams on short-term missions trips each year. But in the tribulation it will be greater.

Revelation 7 is retrospective, looking back to the beginning of the tribulation when 144,000 Jews from every tribe are sealed (v. 4), but it also looks ahead at the great number of people that are saved in the tribulation (v. 9). Four angels are seen, holding back the judgments of the tribulation until the 144,000 are sealed. The seal was a sign of ownership and preservation; they had the name of the Lamb and the Father on their foreheads (14:1–5). The sealing was also a security and immunity from death (Robert Thomas, *Revelation 1–7*); the judgments would not begin "until" the 144,000 were sealed (7:3).

As John looks ahead, he has a vision of a scene in heaven: an innumerable number of Gentiles "from every nation and all tribes and peoples and tongues" (v. 9). Dressed in white, they are standing before the throne of God and of Christ, crying out a proclamation of salvation. They have died—probably as martyrs—in the tribulation and are now in heaven. Since only unbelievers enter the tribulation, they would have been saved during the tribulation. Their white robes indicate spiritual purity, achieved through the "blood of the Lamb" (v. 14). Although they have suffered during the tribulation, their suffering has ended; they will hunger and thirst no more, nor suffer in any way.

Perhaps you are suffering today. Perhaps all of us believers will suffer in the future as opposition to Christianity increases. But a great day is coming when suffering will end and Christ will be our eternal Shepherd, guiding us "to springs of the water of life" (v. 17). We have a glorious future. Live every day in anticipation of the future.

CONSIDER: *At the beginning of the tribulation God seals 144,000 Jews who become evangelists; as a result, a great multitude of Gentiles will be saved.*

FOUR TRUMPET JUDGMENTS

REVELATION 8:1–13

And the seven angels who had the seven trumpets prepared
themselves to sound them. The first sounded, and there came hail
and fire, mixed with blood, and they were thrown to the earth; and
a third of the earth was burned up, and a third of the trees were
burned up, and all the green grass was burned up. (Revelation 8:6–7)

There is considerable concern these days about the environment. Scientists warn that if the tropical rain forest is destroyed in the Amazon River basin the reduction in trees would cause a decline in rainfall, affecting the life of the plants and animals. Similar concerns are voiced for other parts of the world.

Whatever happens today in the world's ecology, the tribulation will see more horrific changes in the earth's environment because of God's judgments. As the seventh seal is opened, the trumpet judgments are unleashed. It is so dramatic, there is silence in heaven for half an hour—they are awestruck at what is to come. An angel with a golden censer with incense (symbolizing prayer) adds to it the prayers of the saints. Then the angel takes the censer and throws it to the earth, unleashing the seven trumpet judgments. It is a serious reminder that God answers the prayers of His people. They had prayed that God would avenge them and He answered.

With the first trumpet judgment hail and fire mixed with blood are thrown to the earth, resulting in one-third of the earth's vegetation being destroyed. At the second trumpet, a mountain is thrown into the sea and the sea becomes blood and one-third of all sea life dies. Is this literal blood? There is no reason to think otherwise. With the third trumpet, a great star falls from heaven, contaminating one-third of the rivers and waters—the water supply becomes polluted. With the fourth trumpet, a third of the sun, moon, and stars are smitten so a semi-darkness covers the earth.

As the world is being deprived of the essentials of life, people will be affected physically, lacking food and water; but with the semi-darkness covering the earth, people will also be affected emotionally. The eagle (or vulture) flying overhead depicts impending doom, as there will be an intensification of the judgments with the remaining trumpet judgments as well as the bowl judgments to follow.

CONSIDER: *God is judging the world that has ridiculed and rejected His Son.*

THREE TRUMPET JUDGMENTS

REVELATION 9:1–21

The rest of mankind, who were not killed by these plagues, did not repent of the works of their hands, so as not to worship demons, and the idols of gold and of silver and of brass and of stone and of wood, which can neither see nor hear nor walk; and they did not repent of their murders nor of their sorceries nor of their immorality nor of their thefts. (Revelation 9:20–21)

In California a murderer was brought to trial, found guilty, and sentenced to life in prison. The family of the victim was at the sentencing and heard the murderer laugh and exclaim, "Hey, life will be good in prison. I'll eat good and I'll have friends." He continued his unrepentant laughter and ridicule—evidence of his unrepentant heart.

As God continues His judgment on an immoral and hostile world, the people remain unrepentant. When the fifth angel blew his trumpet, a star—Satan—had fallen to the earth (Isa. 14:12–17; Luke 10:18), having the key to the bottomless pit. (This will eventually be the location of Satan's detention [Rev. 20:1–3].) Having the key to the pit, Satan releases the locusts (demons) from the pit who then come to ravage the people. They are prohibited from harming the vegetation and the 144,000 but for five months they torment humans. The people will seek death but it will not come. The locusts' identity as demons is evident since their king is the "angel of the abyss," whose name is Abaddon ("Destruction") and Apollyon ("Destroyer"). Satan's mission is evident: he seeks to destroy both physically and spiritually.

When the sixth trumpet sounds, four evil angels, bound at the Euphrates River, are released. Their army of 200 million horsemen invade (Israel among others) and one-third of humanity is killed through plagues, fire, and brimstone. Is this a description of modern warfare? Probably. Is this a powerful military army from the eastern continent? Quite likely. Hal Lindsey suggests the language is similar to thermonuclear warfare.

The destruction on earth is colossal. More than one-half of the earth's population has died. They know why. Have they repented? No. They are steeped in their immorality and sin. It reflects the hardness of their hearts. God's judgment is just.

CONSIDER: *The final trumpet judgments intensify the judgment on sinful humanity but mankind remains obstinate, refusing to repent.*

THE LITTLE BOOK

REVELATION 10:1–11

I took the little book out of the angel's hand and ate it, and in my mouth it was sweet as honey; and when I had eaten it, my stomach was made bitter. And they said to me, "You must prophesy again concerning many peoples and nations and tongues and kings." (Revelation 10:10–11)

John sees another angel coming down in a cloud out of heaven, his face shining like the sun, with a rainbow on his head. Pillars of fire flow from his feet, indicating he will dispense judgment on the earth. Some suggest that this angel is Christ, but it probably is not. Christ is never called an angel and this is "another" (*allon*, which means "another of the same kind") angel. Christ is not "another" angel. He is unique.

This angel has one foot on the sea, suggestive of the Gentiles, and one foot on the land, indicating Israel. The point is that judgment is coming on the entire world, with no exceptions. The angel cries out like a roaring lion, representing the impending judgment: "The Lord roars from Zion" (Joel 3:16). Seven peals of thunder sounded (like the voice of the Father to the Son in John 12:28–29), announcing the judgment. It was a reminder to a sinful world that God will bring terror in the judgments. When people reject and despise the grace of God they must face the wrath of God.

In a gesture of oath taking, the angel lifted his right hand to heaven, swearing by the eternal God who has authority over temporal creation and the Creator who has authority over creation. The message? The prophetic program will not be delayed; the mystery of God will be finished; that is, the things prophesied in the Old Testament will come to consummation with the bowl judgments and the establishment of the kingdom with the new heaven and the new earth.

Similar to Ezekiel (Ezek. 2:8; 3:2–3, 10), John is instructed to take the book and "eat it," and to take the words of the book into his heart. John was instructed to receive the revelation of God. John ate it and found it bitter because of the horror of the judgments but it was also sweet because the word of God would be performed. People may display "no fear" signs on their trucks but the day is coming when, having rejected the grace of God, unbelievers will face the wrath of God.

CONSIDER: *The little book, which announces the judgment that will come upon the entire world, is bitter because of its horror but sweet because it is right.*

December 20

The Two Witnesses

Revelation 11:1–19

"And I will grant authority to my two witnesses, and
they will prophesy for twelve hundred and sixty days,
clothed in sackcloth." (Revelation 11:3)

My wife and I were standing on the Mount of Olives with our Israeli guide as we looked at the ancient wall of Jerusalem across the valley. He explained the history of the city and the numerous invasions and destructions of Jerusalem. "It won't happen again," he stated vehemently. My wife and I exchanged sober glances, knowing the Scriptures.

The Lord opens up the future, allowing John to see the events of the last half of the tribulation. John is given a measuring rod with which he measures the temple, the Holy Place and the Holy of Holies, and the worshipers. "These worshipers are the faithful, believing Jews of the tribulation days. . . . God is giving assurance that He will take note of those who faithfully worship Him in the first half of the Tribulation" (Charles C. Ryrie, *Revelation*). But the outer court is occupied by the Gentiles who will control it for forty-two months when Antichrist seats himself in the temple of God (2 Thess. 2:4).

God raises up two unidentified witnesses who will prophesy for 1,260 days—the last half of the tribulation. Dressed in sackcloth, they warn of coming calamities as they call the nation to repentance—which will, in fact, happen (see the prophesy of their repentance in Zechariah 12:10–14). They cannot be killed, but they judge the enemies of God with fire, which consumes the enemies; they shut up the heavens from rain and send plagues as a judgment upon the enemies of God. When their witness is complete, the beast, coming out of the abyss (the haunt of demons), kills them with their bodies lying on the street in Jerusalem, called Sodom. The world rejoices over their death but after three and a half days they rise from the dead and they ascend into heaven—a personal rapture! At the same time, an earthquake hits Jerusalem, destroying one-tenth of the city and seven thousand people.

The end is near. A scene in heaven anticipates the imminent reign of Jesus Christ but the nations once more exhibit their hostility against the Lord. But that will terminate. The time has come for God to judge the dead, reward the righteous, destroy unbelievers, and establish His kingdom. John is rewarded with a glimpse into the temple in heaven. The future is certain: God *will judge* those who ridicule, who mock the name of Christ, and God *will reward* those who have remained faithful to Him.

CONSIDER: *God will raise up two witnesses at the last half of the tribulation who will bear witness for forty-two months.*

WAR WITH THE WOMAN

REVELATION 12:1–17

So the dragon was enraged with the woman, and went off to make war with the rest of her children, who keep the commandments of God and hold to the testimony of Jesus. (Revelation 12:17)

John sees a woman clothed with the sun, the moon under her feet, and a crown of twelve stars on her head. Who is the woman? While some suggest it is Mary, it is best to understand the woman as Israel, persecuted and suffering throughout the age but specifically persecuted by Satan during the tribulation. The cause of the woman's suffering "is the persecution of the nation inspired by Satan in an attempt to stop the birth and destroy the people of God" (Robert Thomas, *Revelation 8–22*).

A red dragon with seven heads and ten horns appears, identified as the devil. The seven heads are seven world powers (17:9–10) while the ten horns are ten kings (17:12; as in Dan. 7:7, 24). The ten kings represent the alliance of a final world power. The dragon swept away one-third of the stars, depicting Satan's persecution of the Jewish people. The dragon's attempt to kill the child reveals Satan's attempt to kill Christ (through Herod) as well as Satan's resolve to destroy the Jewish people throughout history. But Satan will fail. The Son that is born is Christ, whose destiny is to rule the nations in the kingdom (Isa. 11:4; Ps. 2:9; Rev. 19:15). But before that happens, the woman—Israel—is persecuted so she flees to the wilderness, the Gentile nations, where she is sustained by God for 1,260 days, the last half of the tribulation.

In heaven there is war between Michael against Satan whereupon Satan is thrown down, with no further access to God (on Satan's access to God, see Job 1), resulting in increased demonic activity during the tribulation. Since Satan has only a short time, he intensifies his persecution of the Jewish people, especially those who are believers in Christ (Rev. 12:17). Israel flees into the wilderness—the Gentile nations—seeking refuge, while Satan pursues her like a flood of water. But the nations absorb the persecution and Israel finds refuge in the nations. Satan is "enraged" with the woman because he lost his place in heaven because of her.

Who will win the battle? Christ! Heaven rejoices at the anticipated eternal kingdom reign of Christ (vv. 10–11). And His people will overcome "because of the blood of the Lamb." A war is coming. Are you on the victory side?

CONSIDER: *Satan is thrown out of heaven during the tribulation whereupon he aggressively persecutes the Jewish people.*

December 22

THE BEAST

REVELATION 13:1–18

---

*Then I saw a beast coming up out of the sea, having ten horns
and seven heads, and on his horns were ten diadems, and on his
heads were blasphemous names. (Revelation 13:1)*

The beast. The word conjures up a wild, vicious, untamed animal—correctly so. John sees a beast coming up out of the sea. The sea may represent unregenerate humanity, the "seething cauldron of national and social life" and ultimately represents "the abyss—the source—of the satanic forces" (Cleon Rogers Jr. and Cleon Rogers III, *The New Linguistic and Exegetical Key to the Greek New Testament*). The beast is the consummate world power—as the leopard represented Greece, the bear Medo-Persia, and the lion Babylon—with the dragon Satan energizing him. The head that had been slain and now healed pictures the beast's empire rising out of the ashes of the old Roman Empire.

And who is the beast? He is the ultimate anti-God ruler, the consummate rebellion against Jesus Christ. The ten horns (also seen in Dan. 7:7–8; Rev. 17:3, 7, 12) refer to the revived Roman Empire. The blasphemous names represent blasphemy against Christ, an attempt to usurp God's position (2 Thess. 2:4). The result is the ultimate abomination: people worship the dragon and they worship the beast. This was Satan's desire from the beginning (Isa. 14:14). For the final three and a half years of the tribulation, the beast receives worship as he speaks with arrogance and blasphemy.

His hatred for Christ and His people results in severe persecution against people who have come to faith in Christ during the tribulation. He wages war against them and overcomes them—he kills them. All others will worship him as the god of the ecumenical belief system.

A second beast arises out of the earth, perhaps suggesting he is Jewish. He works in alliance with the first beast, pointing people to worship the first beast. Since Satan energizes him to perform miracles, he succeeds in deceiving people. Through deception, he gives "breath to the image of the beast" (Rev. 13:15). As a result the masses worship the beast, receiving a mark, a parody of the seal of the 144,000 (described in Revelation 7). Their sign denotes loyalty to Satan and the beast, enabling them to buy and sell. And the number of the beast is 666—the epitome of evil. The conflict between good and evil is reaching its climax.

CONSIDER: *The beast, the world ruler energized by Satan, arises, persecuting believers and assuming deity whereupon the masses worship him.*

December 23

REAPING THE EARTH

REVELATION 14:1–20

So the angel swung his sickle to the earth and gathered the clusters from the vine of the earth, and threw them into the great wine press of the wrath of God. (Revelation 14:19)

We can only imagine the turmoil in John as he sees the tumult of the tribulation. The Lord allows John to see into the future: the triumph of Jesus Christ. He sees the Lamb—Jesus Christ—standing on Mount Zion, Jerusalem. It anticipates the triumphant return of Christ to Jerusalem to establish His kingdom (Ps. 2:6; Zech. 14:4). The 144,000 are the same ones who were sealed at the beginning of the tribulation (Rev. 7:4–8). The thunderous voice from heaven authenticates the Son, while a heavenly chorus around the throne in heaven is singing. The 144,000 are termed *virgins*, probably used in a figurative sense as those that have not contaminated themselves with the world. In contrast to the devil (John 8:44) and the Antichrist (2 Thess. 2:11), no lie was found in them.

An angel, flying in midheaven (in the middle of the sky in view of all) proclaims a gospel, warning the people to fear God because judgment is coming. It is a worldwide proclamation. Another angel follows, announcing the destruction of both spiritual and physical Babylon. Those who have followed the beast will experience the wrath of God, being tormented with fire and brimstone. Their punishment will be eternal—never ending and without rest (Rev. 14:11; 19:20; 20:10). But those who have become believers in the tribulation will persevere—their faith is in Jesus. And the believers who have died have entered into rest; their sufferings have ended (14:13; 6:11; 2 Thess. 1:7).

John has a vision of Christ returning to earth to judge. His golden crown is a reminder that He comes as a conqueror. The depraved earth, having worshiped the beast, is ripe for judgment. In picturesque language, Christ is shown reaping the earth with a sickle, symbolizing the judgment. The wrath of God is poured out on a sin-laden earth. A sea of blood extending 200 miles is the result. The loss of life is enormous. When people reject God and His word as revealed through Christ, there is a price to pay.

CONSIDER: *John sees Christ coming to Jerusalem as a conquering general, judging the entire earth because of the people's apostasy.*

HOLINESS NECESSITATES JUDGMENT
REVELATION 15:1–8

*And they sang the song of Moses, the bond-servant of God, and the
song of the Lamb, saying, "Great and marvelous are Your works,
O Lord God, the Almighty; Righteous and true are Your ways, King of
the nations! Who will not fear, O Lord, and glorify Your name? For You
alone are holy; For ALL THE NATIONS WILL COME AND WORSHIP BEFORE YOU,
FOR YOUR RIGHTEOUS ACTS HAVE BEEN REVEALED." (Revelation 15:3–4)*

*U*niversalism is the belief that everyone is going to heaven. The argument is
that, since God is love, He could not send anyone to hell. But universalism
is wrong. Of course, God doesn't send people to hell arbitrarily. People determine their destiny when they reject the gospel. If God is holy—and He is—then
He must judge sin. If He didn't judge sin, if He allowed those who scorn the
gospel to go to heaven, then He would not be a holy God.

But God is holy. John sees a sign in heaven—but what is it that he sees?
John sees the seven angels who are about to pour out the judgments described
in chapter 16. There is worship in heaven because God's judgment is about to
be consummated. It is termed "marvelous"—it is amazing, wondrous.

In this scene of heaven John sees a sea of glass mingled with fire, displaying the glory of God, shining and illuminating heaven. Present are the martyrs
who refused to submit to the beast or the image or the number of his name.
They remained true to Christ. They were victorious. They have a true concept
of God: He is great—supreme in all things; His works in judgment are marvelous and He is righteous and true in His judgments. If God is holy, sin must be
judged. Recognizing His holiness in judgment, who will not fear? God is unique.
He alone is holy and all the Gentile nations will come to worship Him.

John sees the temple with the Law of God in heaven while seven angels
receive the seven bowls of wrath from the four living creatures. The angels are
about to pour the seven bowls of judgment upon the earth. Smoke, depicting
the judgment of God, fills the temple. The eternal, righteous God is about to
render judgment upon the earth. These sobering words are a reminder that
God does not take sin lightly. Unbelievers may scoff but God is taking note and
His holiness demands that He must ultimately judge sin.

CONSIDER: *God is holy and His judgments on sinful humanity are righteous; the
nations will recognize this as they will come to worship Him.*

THE BOWL JUDGMENTS

REVELATION 16:1–21

*Then I heard a loud voice from the temple, saying to the seven
angels, "Go and pour out on the earth the seven bowls of
the wrath of God." (Revelation 16:1)*

Atheists are becoming more vocal and vigorous in their hatred of Christ
amid their promotion of atheism. Now they have funded a camp for children to teach them evolution and atheism. At the foundation of atheism is their
own moral code. If there is no God, then who sets the standard? They do. And
then they live as they please.

The tribulation will end with the tumult of the bowl judgments, raining
down on sinful, blaspheming humanity. Angelic messengers pour out the
judgments on humanity, immediately preceding the second coming of Christ.
Malignant boils and sores are poured out on those having the mark of the
beast while protecting those who became believers during the tribulation.

The second bowl results in the sea becoming coagulated blood, destroying all sea life. This is a reversal of Genesis 1:21 when God gave life to sea
creatures.

With the third bowl, the rivers and springs are affected, becoming blood.
They refused the water of life; now they will have no water. It is a reminder
that God is righteous and just. The evil people killed believers, now they are
reminded of their sin when the rivers become blood.

With the fourth bowl the people are scorched with fire. Do they repent? No.
They blaspheme God, revealing the hardness of the human heart.

In the fifth bowl, judgment falls on Jerusalem, the throne of the beast,
engulfing it in darkness, with pain adding horror to the event. But the people
persist in blaspheming God.

With the sixth bowl God removes His restraint, allowing the eastern
invader to cross the Euphrates River, preparing the world for Armageddon.
Satan increases his activity on the earth, as demons pour forth from the false
trinity (Satan, the beast, and the false prophet), performing signs, leading to
the Campaign of Armageddon.

The seventh bowl is climactic, bringing the judgment to completion. Babylon is split into three parts as other great cities are destroyed. Geographical
changes occur with islands and mountains disappearing; hailstones rain down
upon humanity. What is the response? Blasphemy. But God is bringing the
judgment to completion. The triumphant return of Jesus Christ is now imminent. Evil will be judged with finality.

CONSIDER: *God brings His judgment of sinful humanity to a climax with the
seven bowl judgments, bringing worldwide catastrophe.*

December 26

RELIGIOUS BABYLON'S DESTRUCTION
REVELATION 17:1–18

On her forehead a name was written, a mystery,
"BABYLON THE GREAT, THE MOTHER OF HARLOTS AND OF
THE ABOMINATIONS OF THE EARTH." (Revelation 17:5)

Time magazine carried an article entitled, "GOD: Decoding God's Changing Moods," in which the writer spoke of God vacillating "between belligerence and tolerance." He "corrected" the Bible's "errors" and then—having evaluated Christianity, Judaism, and Islam—concluded there was enough commonality in the Bible and the Qur'an to allow for tolerance and good relations between Jews, Christians, and Muslims. A world religion, uniting all faiths.

John sees the judgment of the great harlot, Babylon, who symbolizes the apostate, unified religion at the end of the age. The harlot represents a powerful union of world religions. She "sits on many waters" (Rev. 17:1), meaning she has worldwide authority. She has committed spiritual adultery; she has denied the faith. Following the Enlightenment, the 1700s saw the rise of theological liberalism, which denied the deity of Jesus Christ, His substitutionary atonement, His bodily resurrection, and many other cardinal doctrines. That false teaching has persisted into the present and will culminate in a world religion that will be accepted by political leaders. In fact, this false religion will control the beast, pictured by the harlot sitting on the beast (v. 3). As the "mother of harlots" (v. 5), she represents the apex of apostasy, unequalled in history. And she destroys believers because they stand opposed to her. Fearless, she is supported by the beast, the revived Roman Empire, the consummate Gentile power (v. 9–12). This union of world religions (the harlot) and the world political power (the beast) will persecute and kill true believers in Christ, but in the end, the beast, jealous of the world religion, will destroy the harlot—the world church—and he will establish himself as god.

But God's purpose is being worked out; He is sovereign (v. 17). His kingdom rule is now imminent. Rest in the sovereignty of God!

CONSIDER: *The great harlot, the union of world religions, will rule with the beast during the first half of the tribulation, only later to be destroyed by the beast.*

December 27

Commercial Babylon's Destruction

Revelation 18:1–24

"'Woe, woe, the great city, Babylon, the strong city! For in one hour your judgment has come.' And the merchants of the earth weep and mourn over her, because no one buys their cargoes any more." (Revelation 18:10–11)

In just three days of trading on October 24, 28, and 29 in 1929, the stock market dropped 34 percent and by July, 1932, when it bottomed out, the Dow had dropped from 381 to 41, a loss of nearly 90 percent. Wealthy people became poor overnight. Investors jumped to their death from skyscrapers. The impact was worldwide.

John saw an angel coming from heaven, announcing, "Fallen, fallen is Babylon the great!" (Rev. 18:2). Babylon is immediately identified with demons and immorality. She represents worldwide wealth and sensuality. While Revelation 17 dealt with Babylon as a religious system, chapter 18 depicts commercial Babylon, with its enormous wealth and ultimate collapse and destruction.

God commands the believers to come out of Babylon because God is about to judge her. Just as ancient Babylon attempted to build a tower to heaven, so the sins of the end-times Babylon are "piled up as high as heaven" (v. 5). God must judge. Because of her arrogance and immorality, she will be repaid double for her sins. She will be destroyed by fire. Business leaders worldwide will weep and mourn over the loss. Their wealth, their financial power will be destroyed overnight.

John receives a detailed description of the financial destruction. "Business as usual" no longer exists. The economy has collapsed. Commerce comes to a halt. People have lost their investments, their savings. The music of success has ended. It is quiet; there is no cause for rejoicing. There is worldwide impoverishment.

But heaven rejoices. This is just. These are ones who flagrantly disobeyed God's Word, indulging in greed and immorality—who murder believers in Christ. God does not overlook flagrant rejection of His Word. There is a payday someday.

CONSIDER: *God will judge commercial Babylon for her numerous sins, causing a worldwide financial collapse.*

December 28

TRIUMPHANT RETURN OF CHRIST!

REVELATION 19:1–21

And I saw heaven opened, and behold, a white horse, and
He who sat on it is called Faithful and True, and in righteousness
He judges and wages war. (Revelation 19:11)

There is excitement in heaven! Religious and commercial Babylon have been destroyed and Christ's kingdom reign is imminent. "Hallelujah"—"Praise the Lord!" is heaven's rejoicing. Christ's judgments are righteous because the corrupt, immoral harlot who killed the believers has been judged. The twenty-four elders and four living creatures join in the praise—*everyone* is called to praise the Lord. They praise Him because He is *Almighty*, having destroyed the evil forces and He *reigns!* Do you sense the excitement?

Christ is returning to earth with His bride, the church, the marriage having taken place in heaven following the rapture. The bride is clothed in white linen, reflecting the righteous acts for which she has been rewarded. The marriage supper follows, which will be the millennial kingdom on earth.

Heaven opens and John sees a rider called Faithful and True on a white horse, a symbol of victory, coming to earth to wage war (Zech. 14:3–4; Matt. 24:27–31). At His first coming Christ came quietly in obscurity; now He comes in a brilliant blaze of light for everyone to see. He comes to conquer, to rule. He is already wearing crowns, indicating He is sovereign over all the world and He will rule over the entire world. And His name is beyond description. His robe is splattered with blood, a picture of the conquest of His enemies (Isa. 63:1–3). The armies of heaven—the church and Old Testament saints—follow Him in battle. But the battle is brief. He simply speaks a word—symbolized by the sword from His mouth—and He destroys the nations (Isa. 11:4; 2 Thess. 2:8). He is King of Kings and Lord of Lords—He will rule over *all* the nations of the world. Everyone will bow to His sovereign rule (Phil. 2:9–11). Birds are invited to the "great supper," feeding on the carcasses of the defeated rebels. The factions of the world unite in a final rebellion against Christ but the beast and the false prophet are seized and thrown into the lake of fire as the remaining rebels are killed.

When you see discouraging events in the world, be reminded: a great day is coming. God is sovereign. Christ will return in triumph to rule forever in His righteous kingdom. Keep focused! Anticipate that glorious day!

CONSIDER: *Heaven rejoices as Christ returns to earth in triumph, defeating the rebellious world forces as He establishes His kingdom.*

December 29

THE MILLENNIAL KINGDOM

REVELATION 20:1–15

*Blessed and holy is the one who has a part in the first
resurrection; over these the second death has no power, but
they will be priests of God and of Christ and will reign with
Him for a thousand years. (Revelation 20:6)*

When Christ returns to establish His kingdom, all enemies will be conquered. An angel from heaven captures Satan, binds him with a chain, and throws him into the abyss. Satan is sealed in the abyss, preventing any escape or rescue and keeping Satan from deceiving people.

John sees two groups: those sitting on the thrones judging, probably representative of the church, which is given authority to judge (1 Cor. 6:2). John also sees believers martyred during the tribulation, who had not submitted to the deception of the beast. They come to life and reign with Christ for a thousand years. This is the first resurrection, the resurrection of life. Believers are blessed. The first death is physical and results in burial—but this is reversible through the gift of life and resurrection. But the second death is spiritual and eternal—and is irreversible.

At the end of the millennium, Satan is released from the abyss, and expands his deception to the ends of the earth. People who were saved during the tribulation entered the millennium in their physical bodies. They propagated children, some of whom believed, some did not. Satan deceives the unbelievers as he unites them to fight against Christ. The battle ends quickly as fire from heaven destroys the devil who is then thrown into the lake of fire where he and the beast and the false prophet are punished eternally.

All the rest of the dead—all unbelievers—are resurrected at the end of the millennium to face the Lord at the great white throne judgment. The books are opened and they are judged "according to their deeds," demonstrating they deserve eternal judgment and also to determine the degree of judgment (Luke 12:47–48). As the book of life, the register of the saved is opened and their names are missing. Justice prevails. They are thrown into the lake of fire, the eternal, unending place of judgment. It is the "second death," eternal separation of the soul from God. This is sobering. Our hearts ought to be burdened with the need to share the good news with those who do not know Christ.

CONSIDER: *At Christ's return Satan is bound for one thousand years, then released briefly and ultimately cast into the lake of fire, along with all other unbelievers.*

December 30

THE NEW HEAVEN AND NEW EARTH

REVELATION 21:1–27

Then I saw a new heaven and a new earth; for the first
heaven and the first earth passed away, and there is
no longer any sea. (Revelation 21:1)

God has set eternity in our hearts (Eccl. 3:11) and there is a longing, a yearning that will never be fulfilled in this life. No matter what we achieve financially, in fame, whatever we accomplish—we remain unfulfilled in this life.
That longing will only be fulfilled when we step on our heavenly shore. That
will be fulfillment—and home.

John sees a new heaven and a new earth, the eternal home of believers.
The first heaven and earth passed away—they are cleansed and renovated
from all stain of sin. God will not destroy what He created for fellowship with
humanity. It will return to its Edenic condition. The holy city, Jerusalem, the
capital of Messiah's world kingdom, comes down from heaven with the people
of the earth coming to the city to worship the King of Kings. Now God's original purpose will be fulfilled: He will fellowship with redeemed humanity. God
will "dwell among them" (v. 3). The preposition "among" (*meta*) means "with
someone; in someone's company; close association" (F. W. Gingrich and F. W.
Danker, *A Greek-English Lexicon of the New Testament*). God will have intimate
fellowship with His people. What a day that will be!

Tears are gone. No more sorrow, no death, no pain—they are completely
gone. Everything is new. Who can bring this about? The Lord! He is the Alpha
and Omega, the Creator and the Consummator! He created the world and He will
consummate the ages. Who can enjoy this? The one who is thirsty—come—
drink deeply; God provides this without cost. The overcomer, the believer,
will inherit this future. But the unbelieving, the cowardly, the immoral, the
idolators, will inherit the lake of fire.

John sees the New Jerusalem, the home of the bride of Christ—all believers—coming down out of heaven (relate this to John 14:2). The city is brilliant
in beauty, its wall of pure gold with the glory of God illumining the city. No
crime will touch the city since no unbeliever will enter it, "only those whose
names are written in the Lamb's book of life." As a believer, that is your future!
Are you struggling today? Worried? Troubled? Reflect on your future; find your
joy, your peace, your confidence in what is to come.

CONSIDER: *The new heaven and the new earth, renovated and cleansed, come
down to earth where God will forever fellowship with His redeemed people.*

December 31

COME!

REVELATION 22:1–21

There will no longer be any curse; and the throne
of God and of the Lamb will be in it, and His
bond-servants will serve Him. (Revelation 22:3)

We look for bargains when we go to buy something. Yet, the amazing truth is that the most valuable thing there is to be had is *free*. Yes. It's free. The Spirit and the bride say, "Come." They invite all who want to partake of *life—eternal life*—to come.

The river of the water of life is flowing from the throne of God with the tree of life on either side of the river. The tree of life that was in the garden of Eden (Gen. 2:9) bears fruit monthly. "Eating the fruit of the Tree of Life . . . is what brings immortality . . . [this] will mean a return to the original glories and privileges of God's presence with man" (Robert Thomas, *Revelation 8–22*). There will be unity among the nations; healing comes from the leaves of the tree of life. The curse—sin, suffering, death (Gen. 3:14–19)—is forever removed. The throne of God and the Lamb will be present, with believers beholding God face to face (1 Cor. 13:12), with His name on our foreheads as a sign of belonging.

There will be no darkness, no night (symbolic of evil). The Lord Himself will illuminate the city and the world with His glory. And believers will reign with the Lord *forever and ever.* This is phenomenal! Can we believe it? Yes! "These words are faithful and true" (Rev. 22:6). God has spoken. He does not lie.

John is instructed not to seal up these words—they are to be made known and read and made available. The message is critical—eternal life, eternity is the issue. "When the time is fulfilled, that is, when Christ comes, destinies will be fixed" (Charles C. Ryrie, *Revelation*). Hence, the one who is filthy will forever be filthy and the one who is righteous will forever be righteous. Happy are those who have trusted in Christ, they will live forever, having access to the tree of life; but there is a warning: those who practice sin, the immoral, the liars will not enter the heavenly paradise.

So there is a message: "I am coming quickly" (vv. 7, 12, 20). Don't delay. Respond. Come! Are you tired, weary of your old life? Come, trust in Jesus Christ as the One who atoned for your sins and be assured of *eternal* life. Come!

CONSIDER: *The clarion call of Scripture, with the view to eternity, calls and invites all who believe to the eternal celebration in God's kingdom. Come!*